California Contract Law

California Contract Law

Cases and Materials

Craig A. Smith

Adjunct Professor of Law

Santa Barbara/Ventura Colleges of Law

Member of the California Bar

CAROLINA ACADEMIC PRESS

Durham, North Carolina

ISBN 1-59460-232-8
LCCN 2006927464

CAROLINA ACADEMIC PRESS
700 Kent Street
Durham, NC 27701
Telephone (919) 489-7486
Fax (919) 493-5668
www.cap-press.com

Printed in the United States of America

Contents

California Contract Law

Introduction

California courts have long been in the vanguard of shaping the law of contracts. Cases such as *Masterson v. Sine* and *Monarco v. LoGreco* are staples of most contracts casebooks. For many years I supplemented the weekly reading assignments in the Contracts courses I taught by introducing California cases into the classroom discussions. I found that they were rich sources of factual scenarios that would capture the students' imaginations and provide an opportunity to "hammer home" some of the points that were sometimes obscurely made in other cases. Those outside California cases eventually became the inspiration for this book.

This book has two goals; first, to emphasize the principle rules of general contract law as taught in law schools which focus on the general common law of contracts and second, to compare and contrast California contract law to the general common law rules of contracts. Cases have been selected for inclusion in this book because they either highlight the differences between California law and that of other jurisdictions, or because they state general rules of contract law with more clarity than can be found in other sources, or they present interesting fact patterns which are more likely to hold the student's attention. The scope and length of this book is such that it could be used as the principle casebook in an abbreviated semester course on contracts or it can be used as I use it, a supplement to a general casebook on contract law. Besides selecting and editing cases for inclusion I have written introductions and "afterthoughts" to the topics covered in the book. I have made a very conscious effort to insure that this material is concise and sets forth in a straightforward manner the basic rules of contract law.

In offering this book to the reader I would like to thank and acknowledge the many students who encouraged me and offered suggestions. Most specially, I would like to thank my former student, Chryss Yost, who generously spent many hours of her time proofreading, editing and offering suggestions.

Readers who have questions or suggestions may contact me through my website: www.lawschoolhelp.com.

Craig A. Smith
April 2006

Chapter 1

Nature of Contract and Consideration

Definition of "Contract"

A contract is an agreement between two or more persons to do or not to do a certain thing or things. (Cal.Civ.Code § 1549)

Elements of a Contract

A valid contract requires:

(1) Parties having legal capacity to contract;

(2) Mutual consent;

(3) A lawful objective; and

(4) A sufficient consideration. (Cal.Civ.Code § 1550)

Types of Contracts

Express or Implied in Fact Contracts

A contract may be express or implied in fact, or implied in law. (Cal.Civ.Code § 1619) In an express contract, the existence and terms of the contract are stated in words or the writings of the parties. (Cal.Civ.Code § 1620) In an implied in fact contract, the existence and terms of the contract are inferred from the conduct of the parties. (Cal.Civ.Code § 1621) The distinction between an express and an implied in fact contract relates only to the manner in which the agreement is shown. Both types are based upon the express or apparent intention of the parties. (See, 1 Witkin, Summary of Cal. Law (9th ed. 1987) Contracts, §§ 11, 12.)

Implied in Law Contracts — Quasi Contracts

In an implied in law contract, or a quasi-contract as it is sometimes called, a duty or obligation is created by law for reasons of fairness or justice. For example, where one accepts or receives the benefit of another's work the law implies a promise to pay what the services are reasonably worth. (*Schaad v. Hazelton, infra*) Such duty or obligation is not based upon the express or apparent intention of the parties but rather is imposed by law in order to prevent unjust enrichment.

Schaad v. Hazelton

California Court of Appeal Third District, 1946.
72 Cal.App.2d 860, 865, 165 P.2d 517, 519.

ADAMS, P. J.

This action was brought by plaintiff, the daughter of Addie M. Hazelton, deceased, to recover from the estate of said decedent the sum of $21,178.83 claimed to be the reasonable value of services rendered by her to said decedent from July 1, 1926, to March 10, 1943, "in serving as companion, housekeeper, nurse, furnishing transportation, sewing, washing, ironing and otherwise" for said Addie M. Hazelton, "with the understanding and agreement between said Addie M. Hazelton and Plaintiff that said Addie M. Hazelton would compensate Plaintiff for said services by leaving to her ... one-half of all the estate of said Addie M. Hazelton and which estate should include all the property of said Addie M. Hazelton except the home of said Addie M. Hazelton and the home of Earl J. Hazelton." The filing of a claim against the estate of the decedent and its rejection were alleged, a copy of the claim being attached to the complaint. The action was tried before a jury and resulted in a verdict in favor of plaintiff for the sum of $4,300. Thereafter, on motion of defendant, the trial court entered a judgment in favor of defendant notwithstanding the verdict, and this appeal followed.

The only question before this court is whether there was produced before the trial court evidence which, viewed in its most favorable aspect, was sufficient to support the jury's verdict.

J. B. Hazelton and Addie M. Hazelton were husband and wife. They acquired considerable property, including a substantial home and a lumber yard in Orland. They had two children, Marjorie and Earl, both of whom were, in March, 1926, of adult age. The daughter, who was apparently unemployed, was living in the home of her parents, and the son, who was then working for his father in the lumber yard, was married and occupied a home of his own in Orland.

On July 10, 1926, plaintiff married Clarence Schaad. She brought her husband into the home of her parents where they continued to reside until May 1, 1931, when they moved to Willows, and later, to Sacramento. In July, 1934, when Mr. Schaad lost his job they returned to the Hazelton home where they continued to reside. A son was born to the Schaads in 1927, and he, too, lived in the Hazelton home with his parents. On August 5, 1941, J. B. Hazelton and Addie M. Hazelton executed a deed conveying to their daughter the family home in Orland. This deed was deposited with the attorney who had drawn same, with instructions to deliver it to the grantee upon the death of the survivor of the grantors. Prior to his death J. B. Hazelton, who was suffering from cancer, conveyed his property to his wife, and on February 23, 1942, he died.

Mrs. Hazelton died in April, 1943, leaving a will dated April 3, 1942, in which she gave the family home, variously valued at from $8,000 to $15,000, and its contents, appraised at $1,100, to her daughter, reciting that a deed to the home had already been placed in escrow. The will also stated that prior to her husband's death they had agreed between them and their children that all debts owing by their son, and by their daughter and her husband, either to them or the lumber company, were forgiven, and that it was her will that they be canceled. The will devised to plaintiff a life estate in certain other real property with remainder to her children, which property was given value of $5,000 to $8,500, gave the lumber mill and business and other real property to the son, and divided the residue between the two children equally. The whole estate was appraised by the official appraiser at $44,929.86.

Plaintiff produced no evidence whatsoever of any express contract on the part of her mother to compensate her, either by will or otherwise, for any services she might or did perform in the home shared by the two families, nor was there any testimony that either of the parties ever made any reference to any such purported agreement. Appellant does not even contend in her brief that such evidence was produced, but argues that there must have been such an agreement because (a) at the time of a family conference held just before Mr. Hazelton's death he stated to his son that the daughter had been generous in asking that the debts of the son as well as her own be forgiven, and that he wanted them to share the estate equally; (b) that the Schaad boy testified he had heard his grandmother say to his mother, more than once, that the estate was to be settled equally between the son and daughter; (c) that the Schaads paid rent, and (d) that the household expenses were apparently paid from what was called "the bank," into which Mr. Schaad and Mr. Hazelton both put money.

The statement in appellant's brief that the Schaads paid rent is a conclusion based upon the testimony of the Schaad boy that he had seen his mother give his grandmother money for the rent, and had heard his grandmother ask for the rent.

* * *

Regarding the services performed by plaintiff in the home of her parents, while there was testimony that she engaged in the general household duties, they appear to have been no different from those which she would have performed for her own family in her own home had she occupied one, except that, owing to operations which Mrs. Hazelton underwent in 1926, and in 1941, she was unable to raise her arms so as to reach the back of her head, and her daughter combed her hair for her, and during her convalescence, assisted in caring for her. It is true that after her operation in 1926 Mrs. Hazelton's health was not good, but it is undenied that except for short periods after her operations, she was able to and did assist with the housework, put up fruit, made the pies, doughnuts, etc., ironed, worked in her garden, washed dishes, did mending, and, during the infancy of the Schaad child, assisted in caring for him. Apparently during the three years that the Schaads lived elsewhere she was able to run her own home. It is undenied, also, that at the time of Mr. Hazelton's last illness a nurse was in attendance for several weeks; and that another woman came in and worked for a few hours a day when Mr. Hazelton's condition was very critical. There was also a nurse in attendance during the month preceding Mrs. Hazelton's death. While there is some testimony that plaintiff, in her own car, at times took her mother to San Francisco and elsewhere and also performed personal services for her, the evidence fails signally to show that the services performed by her in the household were other than those which would naturally be performed by a loving and dutiful daughter in the home of her parents which she and her family shared with them; and their performance is insufficient to give rise to an inference that such services were performed for her mother any more than for her father, or for her husband and her son who alike shared the benefits of same, or that there was any intention on the part of the mother that she should pay for them, or any intention on the part of plaintiff that she should be paid for them.

The statements of the parents that their two children were to share equally in this estate was but natural, and do not imply that the daughter was to be paid for her services in the home; rather the contrary. Furthermore, appellant's claim that in 1926 her mother agreed to compensate her by leaving her one-half of all her estate "except the home of said Addie M. Hazelton and the home of Earl J. Hazelton," is fictitious on its face, since at that time Mrs. Hazelton had no estate, her husband being then living; and it is not reasonable that Mrs. Hazelton could have anticipated that her husband would predecease her, or that should she survive her husband, the home would be excluded from her estate, as it was by the subsequent deed executed by both Mr. and Mrs. Hazelton.

While as a general principle of law where one performs services for another at his instance and request the law implies a promise to pay, and the request may be inferred from circumstances, and that where one accepts or receives the benefit of another's work the law implies a promise to pay what the services are reasonably worth, the rule is founded upon a mere presumption of law which may be rebutted. And where services are rendered between the members of a household or between those closely related by blood, the law will ordinarily presume that they were prompted by motives of love, friendship and kindness, rather than the desire for gain. And, as was said in Winder v. Winder, 18 Cal.2d 123, 127-128 [114 P.2d 347, 144 A.L.R. 935], "in order to support a claim for services made by a child or relation who remains with his parent or kin after majority the circumstances must show either an express contract or that compensation was in the contemplation of the parties." Also in that case the court cited and quoted from Wainwright Trust Co. v. Kinder, 69 Ind.App. 88 [120 N.E. 419], to the effect that while the intention to pay and the expectation of compensation may be inferred from conduct where equity and justice require compensation, and expectation of compensation may coexist with higher motives prompted by affection or the sense of duty, to warrant the finding of such contract, the elements of intention to pay on the one hand, and expectation of compensation on the other must be found to exist, though they may be inferred from the relation and situation of the parties, the nature and character of the services rendered, and any other facts or circumstances which may reasonably be said to throw any light upon the question at issue.

Appellant relies upon Winder v. Winder, asserting that the facts in that case and those in the case before us are parallel. We think them clearly distinguishable, for in the Winder case there was evidence that the mother, who was living alone, induced her son, the plaintiff, to live with her upon her promise to leave her property to him; also that the son paid his mother $25 a month as rent, furnished her with board and personal care, and paid all other expenses except medical, special nursing and hospitalization. There was also evidence that when, after an absence, the son resumed the care of his mother, she reaffirmed her promise to leave the home to him in return for his services. Also there the mother left all of her estate to others, with nothing to plaintiff. None of those facts appear in the present case.

In Fuller v. Everett, 100 Cal.App. 593 [280 P. 550], a daughter sought to recover from the estate of her deceased mother for the reasonable value of board and lodging, nursing and personal attendance furnished her mother, alleging that the mother had come to the home of plaintiffs at her own request, and that the services and maintenance were rendered at her special instance and upon a promise to pay therefor. There was testimony that when the mother was ill she said to her daughter that she was going home with her; that the mother thereafter repeatedly remarked that her daughter took fine care of her, and that she would never regret what she had done for the mother; that the mother often said she intended to pay her daughter and pay her well, but never said when or how she would pay her. The court said that this presented appellant's case in its strongest light, but showed no meeting of the minds upon any agreed kind or amount of compensation; that to warrant an inference that one relative became indebted to the other for such service the evidence must be such as reasonably to indicate that it was the expectation of both parties that compensation should be made; that the presumption ordinarily prevailing, that the services were to be paid for, could not be invoked in such cases, but, on the contrary, as was said in Ruble v. Richardson, 188 Cal. 150, 157, [204 P. 572], quoting from 1 Beach on Contracts, "where services are rendered by members of a family, living in one household, to each other, or necessaries are supplied by one near relation to another, the law will presume that they were gratuitous favors merely, prompted by friendship, kindness and the relationship between them. And in such case, before the person rendering the service can recover, the express promise of the party served must be shown or such facts and circumstances as will authorize the jury to find that the services were rendered in the expectation of one of receiving, and by the other of making compensation therefore."

In Ruble v. Richardson, plaintiff, who was a niece of a Mrs. Kitchen, brought suit against the executor of Mrs. Kitchen's estate claiming payment for services rendered by her to decedent in whose home she lived as a daughter performing the ordinary services of a daughter. An implied contract to pay for such services was relied upon. The court said that in the absence of evidence of an express contract plaintiff was compelled to rely upon circumstances from which the law might raise an implied promise to compensate her for services rendered; but that evidence that she had performed the ordinary services of a daughter did not raise an inference in law that there was a promise to pay for the services rendered.

In Murdock v. Murdock, 7 Cal. 511, plaintiff who was the stepmother of defendants, at the request of defendants resided in their home as mother of the family for several years. Becoming dissatisfied, she left the home, and sued for compensation for her services. The court said that there seemed to have been no mutual expectation of compensation on either side; that plaintiff did not occupy the position of a servant in the family and was not so treated; and that "where a party sustains to others a certain relation, and assumes a certain position, inconsistent with the claim set up, the proof should either show an express contract, or conclusive circumstances from which a contract might be justly implied."

* * *

We are satisfied that the evidence relied upon by appellant as giving rise to an inference that the mother intended to pay her daughter for her services in the household, or that appellant contemplated that she should receive payment for same is insufficient, and that plaintiff failed to meet the burden imposed upon her, of proving either an express contract or circumstances from which a contract could be implied. The judgment notwithstanding the verdict is, therefore, affirmed.

Peek, J., and Thompson, J., concurred.

Afterthoughts

Where the parties are not members of the same family or close relatives, the burden of proof is on the recipient of the services to show that they were rendered gratuitously or without obligation on his part to pay. (*Sowash v. Emerson* (3d Dist.1916) 32 Cal.App. 13, 161 P. 1018; *Ashley v. Martin* (1st Dist.1916) 100 Cal.App. 217, 279 P. 810.) (This latter allocation of the burden rests upon the presumption that a person rendering services to another at that person's request ordinarily will be compensated.)

Oral and Written Contracts

A contract may be oral, written, or partly oral and partly written. Unless some law provides otherwise, an oral or a partly oral and partly written contract is as valid and enforceable as a written contract.(Cal.Civ.Code § 1622)

Oral Agreement To Be Reduced To Writing

When the parties orally or in writing agree that the terms of a proposed contract are to be reduced to writing and signed by them before it is to be effective, there is no binding agreement until a written contract is signed.

This rule does not mean that a contract already reduced to writing and signed is of no binding force merely because it contemplates a subsequent and more formal instrument. If the parties have orally agreed on all the terms and conditions of a contract with the mutual intention that it shall thereupon become binding, but also agree that a formal written agreement to the same effect shall be prepared and signed, the oral agreement is binding regardless of whether it is subsequently reduced to writing.

The fact that an agreement contemplates subsequent documentation does not invalidate the agreement if the parties have agreed to its existing terms. (See, *Clarke v. Fiedler* (1941) 44 Cal.App.2d 838, 847 [113 P.2d 275] [" 'Any other rule would always permit a party who has entered into a contract like this ... to violate it, whenever the understanding was that it should be reduced to another written form, by simply suggesting other and additional terms and conditions. If this were the rule the contract would never be completed in cases where, by changes in the market, or other events occurring subsequent to the written negotiations, it became the interest of either party to adopt that course in order to escape or evade obligations incurred in the ordinary course of commercial business.' "]; *Smissaert v. Chiodo* (1958) 163 Cal.App.2d 827, 830 [330 P.2d 98].)

Whether it is the intention of the parties that the agreement should be binding at once, or when later reduced to writing or to a more formal writing, is an issue of fact and is to be determined by reference to the words the parties used, as well as upon all of the surrounding facts and circumstances.(See, 1 Witkin, Summary of Cal. Law (9th ed. 1987) Contracts, §§ 142, 143.)

Consideration

A contract is a promise that the law will enforce. However, not every promise is legally enforceable. A promise without sufficient consideration will not be enforced by a court of law.

Consideration is any act or forbearance which is of benefit to the promisor or detriment to the promisee. It may be either a benefit conferred or agreed to be conferred upon the person making the promise or some other person, or a detriment suffered or agreed to be suffered by the person to whom the promise is made or some other person. (Cal.Civ.Code § 1605) Consideration must be bargained for and given in exchange for the promise. In determining whether there was a bargained-for exchange, only the outward expression of the intention of the parties is to be considered.

Consideration Must Have Value

To be sufficient, the consideration must have some value. Something that is completely worthless cannot constitute sufficient consideration. (See 1 Witkin, Summary of California Law (9th ed. 1987) Contracts, §§ 219- 224.)

Mutual Promises Constitute Consideration

Promises by the parties bargained for and given in exchange for each other constitute consideration. In other words, mutual promises constitute consideration. (Cal.Civ.Code, § 1605; *El Rio Oils v. Pacific Coast Asphalt Co.*, 95 Cal.App. 2d 186, 193 [213 P.2d 1].) A single consideration may support several counterpromises. (*H. S. Crocker Co., Inc. v. McFaddin,* 148 Cal.App.2d 639, 645 [307 P.2d 429].)

Written Contracts Presumed to Be Supported by Consideration

Although it is not the rule in most other jurisdictions, in California, a written instrument is presumptive evidence of consideration. The burden of showing a want of consideration sufficient to support an instrument lies with the party seeking to invalidate or avoid it. (Cal.Civ.Code §§ 1614, 1615; *Rancho Santa Fe Pharmacy, Inc. v. Seyfert* (4th Dist.1990) 219 Cal.App.3d 875, 884, 268 Cal.Rptr. 505, 510)

Promise for Promise — Bilateral Contracts

Schumm v. Berg
Supreme Court of California, 1951.
37 Cal.2d 174, 31 P.2d 39, 21 A.L.R.2d 1051

CARTER, J.

Plaintiff appeals from a judgment of dismissal entered after defendants' demurrer was sustained without leave to amend in an action against a father's estate on a contract for the support and education of an illegitimate child.

Plaintiff, Johan Richard Wallace Schumm, is a minor born on February 7, 1948; he prosecutes the action by his guardian ad litem, Kay Whyner. Defendants are the executors of the estate of Wallace Beery, deceased. According to the complaint, the following facts appear: Plaintiff is the son of Beery and Gloria Schumm, neither of whom was married. He was conceived as the result of an act of sexual intercourse between Beery and Gloria on May 18, 1947. In August, 1947, Gloria's request of Beery that he marry her to legitimatize the expected child being refused, she demanded that he acknowledge his paternity of the expected child or she would institute proceedings to have him declared the father and for support of the child. Beery believed, and it was a likely result, that such a suit would be damaging to his social and professional standing as a prominent motion picture star. Under these circumstances, in August, 1947, while Gloria was pregnant with the child (and acting as the agent of the child—see discussion later herein), and for his express benefit, she entered into an oral agreement with Beery as follows: "Whereas, said Gloria Schumm conceived a child by said Wallace Beery as the result of an act of sexual intercourse between them in the County of Los Angeles, State of California, on or about May 18, 1947, and is now pregnant with said child; and

"Whereas, said Wallace Beery is a man of great wealth with very substantial income and well able to make adequate provision for the support and education of said expected child, suitable to Wallace Beery's circumstances, station in life and standard of living; and

"Whereas, said Gloria Schumm is penurious, without property or income and penniless and is unable to make any provision for the support or education of said expected child; and

"Whereas, Gloria Schumm is about to marry one, Hans Schumm; and

"Whereas, neither of the parties hereto wish to impose upon said Hans Schumm any responsibility for the maintenance and support of the said child of said Wallace Beery; and

"Whereas, said Wallace Beery deems it to be to his best interests, social and financial, that no suit be instituted against him in any Court for a public adjudication that he is the father of said expected child and for that reason desires to avoid such paternity suit and the unfavorable publicity such suit might entail.

"Now, Therefore, in consideration of the mutual covenants hereof, said Wallace Beery and Gloria Schumm agree as follows:

"(a) The said Gloria Schumm during the remainder of the period of her said pregnancy until the birth of said child shall institute no action or proceeding in any Court to establish judicially the fact that said Wallace Beery is or will be the father of said child.

"(b) Upon the marriage of said Gloria Schumm and Hans Schumm, said expected child if born alive shall be surnamed 'Schumm' and its name if a male shall include said Beery's Christian name 'Wallace,' or if a female, shall include said Beery's nickname 'Wally.'

"(c) Wallace Beery, if said child be born alive, recognizes and acknowledges the claim of Gloria Schumm in behalf of said expected child that he is morally and legally responsible for the support and education of said child in a manner suitable to said Wallace Beery's circumstances, station in life and standard of living from the date of the birth of said child until said child shall become 21 years of age, or until the death of said child, whichever shall occur sooner, and the said Wallace Beery recognizes the claim of Gloria Schumm in behalf of said expected child that he is morally responsible to afford said child a fair start in its adult life, and that considering the wealth and earning capacity of Wallace Beery the sum of $25,000 would be reasonable for such purpose and should be supplied by Wallace Beery to said child for such start.

"(d) Promptly upon the birth of said child, if born alive, said Wallace Beery shall purchase and acquire and deliver to and for said child two fully paid-up policies of a Life Insurance Company, to-wit: (1) one fully paid-up policy to be applied on account of the support and education of said child, whereby the Life Insurance Company shall have agreed to pay to said child beginning as of the date of his birth until he shall have reached the age of 21 years, or until his death, whichever occurs sooner, the sum of $100 per week; (2) a second fully paid-up policy on the Twenty Year Endowment plan, to afford said child a fair start in its adult life, whereby the Life Insurance Company on said child's twenty-first birthday, if he be then living, shall have agreed to pay to said child the sum of $25,000; the said child to have no interest in the life insurance features, if any, of said policies, which shall be exclusively matters of Wallace Beery's own concern; provided however, that said Wallace Beery in lieu of said first mentioned policy to be applied on account of support and education may promptly on the birth of said child designate a Bank in the City of Los Angeles, State of California as Trustee, and forthwith deposit with such Trustee interest or dividend bearing securities sufficient in amount to yield over and above the Trustee's charges and costs, a minimum net income of $100 per week, with provision in the Trust Agreement that the Trustee, beginning from the date of the birth of said child until the said child reaches the age of 21 years, or until said child's death, whichever occurs sooner, shall pay to said child the sum of $100 per week.

* * *

Pursuant thereto Gloria married Hans Schumm on August 21, 1947, and on the birth of plaintiff, gave him the name above mentioned including "Wallace" and the surname "Schumm"; no proceeding was instituted until after the birth. Beery refused to comply with any of the provisions of the contract, except he paid nine weekly installments of $25, beginning July 6, 1948. Damages of $104,135 are claimed. Beery died and a claim against his estate was rejected.

* * *

Defendants contend that for various reasons there was no consideration for the contract. * * * Beery was not bound because there was no mutuality of obligation. That argument is predicated upon the assumption that the contract was between plaintiff and Beery, which, as pointed out, is not the case. Plaintiff is the third party beneficiary of the contract and there is no performance required of him.

Defendants assert that Gloria's promise not to institute suit and to name plaintiff after Beery is not consideration. We cannot agree with either assertion.

On the first proposition, the argument runs to the effect that it is the illegitimate child's right under section 196a of the Civil Code to enforce the obligation of the father to support it; that the mother has no right except to bring the action in a representative capacity on the child's behalf; that, therefore, in agreeing not to sue she has suffered no detriment, for having no right, she gave up nothing; that a forbearance to sue on a void claim is not good consideration. Before dealing with that contention we note defendants' claim that there was no promise not to institute proceedings, for the promise does not say no action of any kind will be instituted by a guardian or otherwise. The promise (quoted supra) is plain enough. It clearly contemplates that Gloria will not directly or indirectly cause litigation to be instituted involving the question of Beery being the father of the child before the child is born.

The mother does have a definite interest in maintaining the action, for under section 196a the obligation to support is imposed upon both the mother and father. If the mother does not bring an action against the father and he refuses to give support, she will have to bear it. To the extent that she obtains relief against the father in such an action she is relieved of that burden. In agreeing to refrain from suing she is thereby suffering a detriment. It is not a case, therefore, where a person has no right of action and thus could not be benefited by a forbearance to prosecute an action. Gloria had the legal right to bring an action after conception and before birth. (Davis v. Stroud, 52 Cal.App.2d 308 [126 P.2d 409]; Kyne v. Kyne, 38 Cal.App.2d 122 [100 P.2d 806].

Gloria's promise to name plaintiff after Beery (given name Wallace) was adequate consideration to support the contract. It was a detriment to Gloria and a benefit to Beery. The privilege of naming a child is valid consideration for a promise. ([Case citations omitted.] Corbin on Contracts, § 127; Williston on Contracts (rev. ed.), § 115.) This is in accord with the principle that the law will not enter into an inquiry as to the adequacy of the consideration. (6 Cal.Jur 189; Williston on Contracts (rev.ed.), § 115; Rest., Contracts, § 81.) Defendants attack the foregoing authorities by asserting that they are dicta or based upon an authority not in point or did not give serious consideration to the question of the sufficiency of the "right to name" as consideration. They have cited no authority to the contrary, however, and two eminent authorities on contracts (Corbin and Williston, supra) have cited them for that proposition. Reason supports the rule, for having a child bear its father's name is commonly considered a privilege and honor, and Beery assumed it was, for he obtained such a promise running to him. Merely because in the cited cases the promise was to use the putative father's surname does not make them distinguishable. That is merely a matter of degree, and as seen, the validity of consideration does not depend on its value. Defendants refer to recitations in the contract that Beery was prominent and did not want the possible adverse publicity resulting from the instigation of a paternal suit. But that was only for the period prior to birth, and as seen, the promise to name the child after him was in his favor and presumably he considered it valuable.

* * *

Judgment reversed.

Gibson, C.J., Shenk, J., Edmonds, J., Traynor, J., and Spence, J., concurred.

SCHAUER, J., Dissented

Promise for Performance — Unilateral Contracts

Harris v. Time, Inc.

Court of Appeals of California, First Appellate District, Division Five 1987
191 Cal.App.3d 449, 237 Cal.Rptr. 584.

KING, J.

In this action where plaintiffs suffered no damage or loss other than having been enticed by the external wording of a piece of bulk rate mail to open the envelope, believing that doing so would result in the receipt of a free plastic calculator watch, we hold that the maxim "the law disregards trifles" applies and dismissal of the action was proper on this ground.

Mark Harris, Joshua Gnaizda and Richard Baker appeal from a judgment of dismissal of this class action lawsuit arising from their receipt of a direct mail advertisement from Time, Inc. They contend the court erred when it sustained Time's demurrer as to cause of action for breach of contract and granted summary judgment as to causes of action for unfair advertising. We affirm.

It all began one day when Joshua Gnaizda, the three-year-old son of a prominent Bay Area public interest attorney, received what he (or his mother) thought was a tantalizing offer in the mail from Time. The front of the envelope contained two see-through windows partially revealing the envelope's contents. One window showed Joshua's name and address. The other revealed the following statement: "JOSHUA A. GNAIZDA, I'LL GIVE YOU THIS VERSATILE NEW CALCULATOR WATCH FREE Just for, Opening this Envelope Before Feb. 15, 1985." Beneath the offer was a picture of the calculator watch itself. Joshua's mother opened the envelope and apparently realized she had been deceived by a ploy to get her to open a piece of junk mail. The see-through window had not revealed the full text of Time's offer. Printed below the picture of the calculator watch, and not viewable through the see-through window, were the following additional words: "AND MAILING THIS CERTIFICATE TODAY!" The certificate itself clearly required that Joshua purchase a subscription to Fortune magazine in order to receive the free calculator watch.

As is so often true in life situations these days, the certificate contained both good news and bad news. The good news was that Joshua could save up to 66 percent on the subscription, which might even be tax deductible.[1] Even more important to the bargain hunter, prices might never be this low again. The bad news was that Time obviously had no intention of giving Joshua the versatile new calculator watch just for opening the envelope.

Although most of us, while murmuring an appropriate expletive, would have simply thrown away the mailer, and some might have stood on principle and filed an action in small claims court to obtain the calculator watch, Joshua's father did something a little different: he launched a $15 million lawsuit in San Francisco Superior Court.

The action was prosecuted by Joshua, through his father, and by Mark Harris and Richard Baker, who had also received the same mailer. We are not informed of the ages of Harris and Baker. The complaint alleged one cause of action for breach of contract, three causes of action for statutory unfair advertising, and four causes of action for promissory estoppel and fraud.

The complaint sought the following relief: (1) a declaration that all recipients of the mailer were entitled to receive the promised item or to rescind subscriptions they had purchased, (2) an injunction against future similar mailings, (3) compensatory damages in an amount equal to the value of the item, and (4) $15 million punitive damages to be awarded to a consumer fund "to be used for education and advocacy on behalf of consumer protection and enforcement of laws against unfair business practices."

The complaint also alleged that before commencing litigation, Joshua's father demanded that Time give Joshua a calculator watch without requiring a subscription. Time not only refused to give a watch, it did not even give Joshua or his father the time of day. There was no allegation that Harris or Baker made such a demand on Time.

Time demurred to the entire complaint for failure to state facts sufficient to constitute a cause of action. The court sustained the demurrer as to the causes of action for

---

1. The record does not disclose whether Joshua could take advantage of the tax deductibility feature.

breach of contract, promissory estoppel and fraud, but overruled the demurrer as to the causes of action for unfair advertising.

However, Time subsequently obtained summary judgment on the causes of action for unfair advertising. Based on the orders sustaining the demurrer and granting summary judgment, the court rendered a judgment of dismissal.

Plaintiffs filed a notice of appeal after the court granted summary judgment, but two days before rendition of the judgment itself. We treat the notice of appeal as filed immediately after entry of judgment. (Cal. Rules of Court, rule 2(c).)

The appeal challenges the dismissal only as to the causes of action for breach of contract and unfair advertising. Plaintiffs state in their opening brief that they abandon the causes of action for promissory estoppel and fraud.

* * *

II Breach of Contract

In sustaining the demurrer as to the cause of action for breach of contract, the court stated no specific grounds for its ruling. Time had argued the complaint did not allege an offer, did not allege adequate consideration, and did not allege notice of performance by the plaintiffs. On appeal, plaintiffs challenge each of these points as a basis for dismissal.

* * *

B. Consideration

Time also argues that there was no contract because the mere act of opening the envelope was valueless and therefore did not constitute adequate consideration. Technically, this is incorrect. It is basic modern contract law that, with certain exceptions not applicable here (such as illegality or preexisting legal duty), any bargained-for act or forbearance will constitute adequate consideration for a unilateral contract. (Rest.2d, Contracts, § 71; see 1 Witkin, Summary of Cal. Law (8th ed. 1973) Contracts, §§ 162-169, pp. 153-162.) Courts will not require equivalence in the values exchanged or otherwise question the adequacy of the consideration. (Schumm v. Berg (1951) 37 Cal.2d 174, 185 [231 P.2d 39, 21 A.L.R.2d 1051]; Rest.2d, Contracts, § 79.) If a performance is bargained for, there is no further requirement of benefit to the promisor or detriment to the promisee. (Rest.2d, Contracts, § 79, coms. a & b at pp. 200-201.)

Moreover, the act at issue here—the opening of the envelope, with consequent exposure to Time's sales pitch—may have been relatively insignificant to the plaintiffs, but it was of great value to Time. At a time when our homes are bombarded daily by direct mail advertisements and solicitations, the name of the game for the advertiser or solicitor is to get the recipient to open the envelope. Some advertisers, like Time in the present case, will resort to ruse or trick to achieve this goal. From Time's perspective, the opening of the envelope was "valuable consideration" in every sense of that phrase.

Thus, assuming (as we must at this juncture) that the allegations of the complaint are true, Time made an offer proposing a unilateral contract, and plaintiffs supplied adequate consideration for that contract when they performed the act of opening the envelope and exposing themselves to the sales pitch within.

* * *

Low, P. J., and Haning, J., concurred.

Past Consideration

California does not follow the rule that past consideration is no consideration. In California, an existing legal obligation resting upon the promisor, a moral obligation originating in some benefit conferred upon the promisor, or prejudice suffered by the promisee, is also a good consideration for a promise, to an extent corresponding with the extent of the obligation, but no further or otherwise. (Cal.Civ.Code § 1606) On this point, California law is consistent with the so-called "minority" rule set forth in Restatement Second of Contracts section 86, that a promise made in recognition of a benefit previously received by the promisor is enforceable to the extent necessary to prevent injustice.

Preexisting Duty Rule

Merely doing or promising to do that which one is already legally obligated to do is not consideration. To avoid running afoul of the preexisting duty rule, modifications to contracts (unless they are contracts for the sale of goods [see, Cal.Comm.Code § 2209]) must be supported by additional consideration. However, in *Julian v. Gold*, 214 Cal. 74, 76 [3 P.2d 1009]), a landlord, without consideration, orally agreed with his tenant to take a lesser sum for monthly rental than that set up in the written lease; he accepted the reduced payments for two years and then sued to recover the difference in rent for the two years past. The court denied recovery on the ground that the oral agreement had already been executed, and stated that "[the] rule is that an executed oral agreement will serve as a modification or release of a written agreement and this [is] without regard to the presence or absence of a consideration."

Reliance As an Alternative to Consideration — Promissory Estoppel

Even in the absence of consideration, a promise may be enforced if there is detrimental reliance. That is, in response to the mere making of a promise, the person to whom the promise was made (the promisee) reasonably and foreseeably changes their position to their detriment. This is known as the doctrine of promissory estoppel.

As set forth in the Restatement Second of Contracts, section 90, three factors are necessary to invoke the doctrine of promissory estoppel.

1) Was there a promise which the promisor reasonably expected to induce action or forbearance? (Foreseeability)

2) Did the promise actually induce such action or forbearance? (Reliance)

3) Can injustice be avoided only by enforcement of the promise? (Injustice)

Earhart v. William Low Co.

Supreme Court of California, 1979
25 Cal.3d 503, 600 P.2d 1344.

TOBRINER, J.

In this case we must determine whether a party who expends funds and performs services at the request of another, under the reasonable belief that the requesting party will compensate him for such services, may recover in quantum meruit although the expenditures and services do not directly benefit property owned by the requesting party.

In the instant case, plaintiff asserts that, at defendant's request, he expended sums in commencing the construction of a mobile home park on land owned by defendant and on an adjacent parcel owned by a third party. When defendant refused to compensate plaintiff for any of the services so rendered, plaintiff sued in quantum meruit.

While permitting plaintiff to recover the sums which he expended on the parcel actually owned by defendant, the trial court denied plaintiff recovery for the expenses incurred in construction on the adjoining parcel, reasoning that under past California cases defendant received no direct "benefit" from construction on the property that he did not own. Plaintiff now appeals from the trial court's adverse judgment limiting his recovery, contending that he should be permitted to recover in quantum meruit despite the absence of defendant's ownership of the adjoining parcel.

As we shall explain, plaintiff is entitled to prove defendant's liability for the reasonable value of plaintiff's services rendered on both parcels of land. The trial court in the instant case apparently felt constrained to limit plaintiff's recovery because of this court's decision in Rotea v. Izuel (1939) 14 Cal.2d 605 [95 P.2d 927, 125 A.L.R. 1424]. In that case the court denied quasi-contractual recovery on the ground that the only "benefit" received by the defendant was the "incidental benefit" which he may have found in the satisfaction of obtaining compliance with his request.

In view of the facts of the present case, we reject such a broad limitation of the remedy of quantum meruit. Here, plaintiff claims that defendant urged him to begin work on the mobile home park for which he and defendant had long been negotiating. Plaintiff further asserts that, under defendant's supervision, he immediately commenced construction, justifiably relying on his belief that defendant would pay for the requested performance. If the trial court finds these facts to be true and, thus, that plaintiff rendered the very performance that defendant requested, we believe that principles of fairness support plaintiff's recovery for the reasonable value of his labor.

This appeal comes before us on an abbreviated record. The facts, which are sufficient for the resolution of the general legal issue presented, have been gleaned from the pleadings, the partial transcript, the trial court's findings, and the parties' briefs on appeal. (Cf. Scala v. Jerry Witt & Sons, Inc. (1970) 3 Cal.3d 359, 367 [90 Cal.Rptr. 592, 475 P.2d 864].)

Plaintiff Fayette L. Earhart is the president and owner of Earhart Construction Company. For approximately two months in early 1971, plaintiff and defendant William Low, on behalf of defendant William Low Company, engaged in negotiations for the construction of the Pana Rama Mobile Home Park. These negotiations culminated in a construction contract which was to become binding when defendant obtained the requisite financing to build the park and when plaintiff secured a labor and material or performance bond for the work. Neither condition was ever fulfilled.

The proposed park was to cover a number of acres, some of which defendant owned, and the balance of which were owned by Ervie Pillow. In May 1971 defendant and Pillow entered into an escrow agreement in which Pillow agreed to sell her tract to defendant on the condition defendant obtain financing for the mobile home park. According to plaintiff, a "special use permit" allowing the construction of a mobile home park on Pillow's land was of particular interest to defendant. Plaintiff claimed that the permit would expire on May 27, 1971, without possibility of renewal, unless work on the property were "diligently under way" by that date.

Plaintiff maintained that on May 25, 1971, defendant telephoned him to inform him that he had secured the necessary financing for the park, and, waiving all conditions to the contract, urged plaintiff to move equipment onto the property and commence work immediately in order to "save" the special use permit. Plaintiff's crew began work at once and continued to work for one week, often in the presence of defendant. On June 1, 1971, plaintiff submitted a progress bill to defendant and at that time learned that defendant had not secured the requisite financing. Defendant refused to pay plaintiff's bill, revealing that in the interim he had signed a construction contract for the park with another firm.

[Plaintiff's evidence indicated that he had performed services and furnished materials in work on the Pillow property at the urgent request of defendant. Moreover, according to plaintiff, the work was performed under circumstances in which plaintiff reasonably relied upon the belief that defendant would pay for it.]

At the conclusion of the trial, the court determined that plaintiff was entitled to recover from defendant on a theory of quantum meruit. Stating that "[g]enerally speaking, the court has a tendency to believe the testimony of Mr. Earhart and to disbelieve the testimony of Mr. Low," the trial court specifically found that plaintiff had furnished machinery, labor, and materials to defendant's property "at the special instance and request of defendant."

In assessing the amount of the damages to which plaintiff was entitled under quantum meruit, however, the court limited plaintiff's recovery to the reasonable value of the work done on defendant's tract, declining to award damages for the reasonable value of services rendered in construction on the Pillow property. Acknowledging that plaintiff's services "were furnished both to the Pillow property and to the Low property," the trial court interpreted this court's decision in Rotea v. Izuel, supra, 14 Cal.2d 605, as precluding plaintiff's recovery with respect to the work on the Pillow property. The court stated in this regard: "[I]t is an established proposition of law in California ... that you can't get recovery for services furnished to a third person, even though the services were furnished at the request of the defendant.... So the plaintiff can't recover for services furnished Mrs. Pillow.... [E]ven though the plaintiff renders services or delivers a product, if it is of no value to the defendant, then the defendant doesn't pay for it. All he pays for is the value of what he got, notwithstanding how much it cost the plaintiff to produce it. That's the proper measure in this case."

Because the court construed the governing cases as barring recovery for work on the Pillow property as a matter of law, the court made no factual findings as to whether plaintiff had actually furnished labor and materials to the Pillow property at defendant's request nor as to the value of any work that may have been done. Plaintiff now appeals from the trial judgment insofar as it denied him recovery for services allegedly rendered with regard to the adjoining Pillow parcel.

To understand the trial court's seemingly arbitrary refusal to grant complete recovery on the basis of quantum meruit, we must first examine this court's decision in Rotea v.

Izuel, supra. Briefly to summarize the facts in that case: plaintiff's wife died, leaving five minor children in plaintiff's care. Plaintiff's sister-in-law Eugenia subsequently moved into plaintiff's home to assist in taking charge of the children. Although Eugenia later became ill, she nonetheless continued to care for the children.

Antonio Izuel, Eugenia's brother, also lived in plaintiff's home. Antonio helped support the family and, over the years, along with plaintiff and plaintiff's children, took care of Eugenia during her illness. On Antonio's death, plaintiff brought suit to recover from Antonio's estate the reasonable value of services rendered by plaintiff in caring for Eugenia. In support of plaintiff's claim, plaintiff's children testified that Antonio "promised to pay [their] father out of his estate for Eugenia's care."

Preliminarily this court stated that plaintiff could not recover upon his claimed oral agreement, since it violated the statute of frauds, and that plaintiff's cause of action, "if any, was one for the reasonable value of the services performed." (14 Cal.2d at p. 608.) The court distinguished cases that admitted proof of an oral agreement to show that the parties did not intend any services to be gratuitous, on the ground that there "the services were performed with respect to and for the direct benefit of the deceased person and under such circumstances as to create an original obligation implied in law to pay the reasonable value of such services, which obligation arose independently of the terms of the invalid oral agreement." (Id., at p. 609.)

The court declined to extend the rule of those decisions to permit quasi-contractual recovery from Antonio's estate. As the court remarked, "The reason for the rule seems to be that the parties should ordinarily be required to rely upon their agreement and that in the absence of a valid agreement between the parties, the law will not imply an obligation unless the failure to imply such obligation will result in the unjust enrichment of the defendant." (Id., at pp. 610-611.) Tracing the principle of unjust enrichment in this context to the ancient action for money had and received, the court refused to assess liability without first finding receipt of a "direct benefit." (Id., at p. 611.) Since the only "benefit" received by Antonio was the "incidental benefit which he may [25 Cal.3d 510] [have found] in the satisfaction of obtaining compliance with his request," the court denied recovery. (Id.)

While the result which the court reached in Rotea is understandable in light of the mutual exchange of familial support which the record indicates, the court's statement that the satisfaction of obtaining compliance with one's request will not support quantum meruit recovery has ever since its rendition been criticized for its harshness. Commentators have attacked the requirement of a "direct benefit" to the defendant as "purely an historical one." (Comment, Quasi-Contracts (1940) 28 Cal.L.Rev. 528, 530 & See also Note, The Necessity of Conferring a Benefit for Recovery in Quasi-Contract (1968) 19 Hastings L.J. 1259, 1261-1263.)

Since the action for money had and received—the predecessor to the action for reasonable value of services rendered—originated in an equitable bill for the recovery of money tortiously retained by the defendant, the medieval courts inevitably held the action to apply in cases in which the defendant had received an actual "benefit." (See Philpott v. Superior Court (1934) 1 Cal.2d 512, 518-526 [36 P.2d 635, 95 A.L.R. 990]. See generally Goff & Jones, The Law of Restitution (1966) pp. 3-11; Ames, The History of Assumpsit (1888) 2 Harv.L.Rev. 1, 53.) Thus the courts used the action to force disgorgement from anyone who wrongfully came by money or property to which the plaintiff was entitled; the law implied an obligation to pay in order to restore sums, or "benefit," unfairly retained by the defendant.

While the unfair receipt of a tangible benefit to the defendant may have inspired the common law courts to order restitution, the court in Rotea need not have interpreted the ancient principle of unjust enrichment so literally. Even under contemporary authorities, the court could have recognized, consistent with the orthodox principle of unjust enrichment, that a defendant who receives the satisfaction of obtaining another person's compliance with the defendant's request to perform services incurs an obligation to pay for labor and materials expended in reliance on that request.

Section 1 of the Restatement of Restitution, which predates the decision in Rotea, provides that "[a] person who has been unjustly enriched at the expense of another is required to make restitution to the other." (Rest., Restitution (1937) § 1.) A person is enriched if he has "received a benefit." (Id., com. a., p. 12.) Furthermore, "[a] person confers a benefit upon another if he ... performs services beneficial to or at the request of the other...." (Id., com. b., p. 12.) [3] While the Restatement does not establish that performance of services at the request of another uniformly results in the unjust retention of "benefit," the Restatement recognizes, unlike the decision in Rotea, that performance of services at another's behest may itself constitute "benefit" such that an obligation to make restitution may arise.

To avoid the harshness of the reasoning in Rotea the Courts of Appeal have subsequently drawn frequent exceptions to the requirement of "direct benefit." In cases involving services, these courts have often implied an obligation to pay based upon the theory that performance at another's request may itself constitute a benefit. In Williams v. Dougan (1959) 175 Cal.App.2d 414 [346 P.2d 241], for example, plaintiff sought to recover in quantum meruit for the reasonable value of services he had performed in caring for animals placed in his custody by defendant. Defendant argued that since the animals did not belong to defendant, but had been left homeless by the death of their owner, plaintiff's services had conferred no "benefit" upon her.

The court held, however, that defendant's request that plaintiff accept and care for the animals sufficiently implied a promise to pay for the reasonable value of the services; as to the absence of benefit, the court concluded that "[a]lthough the question of the direct benefit flowing to the promisor is one of evidence to be considered in determining whether the law implies an agreement, it is not controlling." (Id., at p. 418.) Viewing the absence of "direct benefit" as an issue of evidentiary significance only, the court permitted plaintiff to recover the reasonable value of services he had performed in justified reliance on defendant's request.

Similarly, the court in Bodmer v. Turnage (1951) 105 Cal.App.2d 475 [233 P.2d 157] relaxed the judicial definition of "benefit" in order to grant recovery to a party who had justifiably relied on another's request for performance. The facts of that case remarkably resemble those of the instant case: defendant contracted with plaintiff, an architect, for the preparation of plans for a resort. After plaintiff complied with defendant's repeated request that plaintiff proceed with final specifications, defendant abandoned the project.

In plaintiff's action in that case for the reasonable value of his services, defendant contended that plaintiff was not entitled to relief in quantum meruit since defendant had received no benefit from plaintiff's services: as defendant argued, "the plans prepared were not such as he could use." (105 Cal.App.2d at p. 477.) The court pointed out, however, that the satisfaction of his request for performance constituted adequate "benefit" to defendant: "In addition to the contract, the evidence of the plans submitted, the changes requested and the many conferences and letters written, strongly support the conclusion that the [defendant] desired and ordered plans for the project as a whole.

While he may have intended, at times, to erect a few buildings at first and to add more later, he kept the plaintiff working on plans for the overall project. In the meantime he was unsuccessful in his attempt to borrow money on the project ... and he finally abandoned the project. He derived the benefit he had in mind, and the fact that he later decided not to use the plans he had ordered in no way indicates an absence of benefit, within the meaning of the quantum meruit rule." (Id.)

Indeed, the issue whether we should broaden the basis of quasi-contractual recovery so as to prevent any unconscionable injury to the plaintiff, is not a novel one for our court. In his dissenting opinion in Coleman Engineering Co. v. North American Aviation, Inc. (1966) 65 Cal.2d 396 [55 Cal.Rptr. 1, 420 P.2d 713], Chief Justice Traynor cogently urged that we abandon the unconscionable requirement of "benefit" to the defendant and allow recovery in quantum meruit whenever a party acts to his detriment in reliance on another's representation that he will give compensation for the detriment suffered.

In Coleman, plaintiff sued for breach of a contract for the construction of missile trailers. Plaintiff had submitted a bid for the project based on its interpretation of defendant's specifications. Defendant accepted the bid without studying it, notified plaintiff that plaintiff was the successful bidder, and sent several telegrams urging that plaintiff commence construction. After plaintiff began work, a controversy arose over the height of the trailers' center of gravity. Because of a discrepancy between the defendant's specifications and plaintiff's original interpretation, plaintiff was compelled to alter much of its completed work, thereby substantially raising its costs. While negotiations over a price adjustment ensued, plaintiff continued working at defendant's request. When the parties failed to reach an agreement, defendant awarded the construction contract to another bidder.

The majority in Coleman, affirming the trial court's determination that defendant had breached a valid contract, upheld the court's award of damages to plaintiff. (65 Cal.2d at pp. 406-407.) Writing a separate opinion, however, former Chief Justice Traynor argued that the contractual negotiations never gave rise to a binding contract because of a failure to agree on the specifications, time of performance, and price. Plaintiff's remedy should accordingly have been in quasi-contract for performance in good faith under an unenforceable contract.

The view adopted by the former Chief Justice raised the fundamental question whether a plaintiff may obtain restitution from a defendant not "benefited," since, as the Chief Justice acknowledged, defendant procured the entire performance elsewhere and enjoyed no advantage from plaintiff's partial performance. As the Chief Justice pointed out, however, "[h]ad the contemplated contract envisaged the performance of services instead of the production of trailers, there would be no doubt that Coleman could recover the reasonable value of its work whether or not it benefited North American." (65 Cal.2d at p. 419.)

The Chief Justice continued, "When one person performs services at the request of another, the law raises an obligation to pay the reasonable value of the services. (Williams v. Dougan, [supra].) ... Although this rule has usually been applied when services or work and labor were requested in their own right, rather than as incidental to the construction of a specified item to be sold to the defendant (see Williams v. Dougan, supra, ... ; Bodmer v. Turnage, [supra]), there is no basis for limiting the rule to the performance of services. If in fact the performance of services has conferred no benefit on the person requesting them, it is pure fiction to base restitution on a benefit conferred. '[I]t is submitted that allowing a recovery in these cases on a theory of benefit conferred is purely fictional, and that the real basis is a moral obligation to restore to his original position a party who has acted to his detriment in reliance on a representation, technically unenforceable, by another that he will give value for the detriment suffered.' (Note (1928) 26 Mich.L.Rev. 942, 943.)" (65 Cal.2d at p. 419.) [25 Cal.3d 514]

Thus Chief Justice Traynor would have awarded plaintiff recovery notwithstanding defendant's lack of "benefit." As the Chief Justice concluded, "The one rendering performance and incurring expenses at the request of the other should receive reasonable compensation therefore without regard to benefit conferred upon the other. Such a rule places the loss where it belongs—on the party whose requests induced performance in justifiable reliance on the belief that the requested performance would be paid for." (65 Cal.2d at p. 420.)

The determination to protect "justifiable reliance" forms not only the inspiration for Chief Justice Traynor's application of a quasi-contractual remedy in Coleman, but also provides the basis for several parallel contractual doctrines as well. The first of these doctrines rests on the theory that "part performance" of an otherwise invalid contract may satisfy the purposes of the statute of frauds. Thus a court may award damages based on an unenforceable contract if unconscionable injury would result from denying enforcement after one party has been induced to make a serious change of position. (See, e.q., Paul v. Layne & Bowler Corp. (1937) 9 Cal.2d 561, 564-565 [71 P.2d 817]; Code Civ. Proc., § 1972.) Closely allied to the doctrine of part performance is the notion that reliance by one party on an oral contract may "estop" the other from setting up a defense based upon the statute of frauds. (See Redke v. Silvertrust (1971) 6 Cal.3d 94 [98 Cal.Rptr. 293, 490 P.2d 805], cert. den., (1972) 405 U.S. 1041 [31 L.Ed.2d 583, 92 S.Ct. 1316].)

Finally, section 90 of the Restatement of Contracts—the so-called "promissory estoppel" section—provides that reasonably expected reliance may under some circumstances make binding a promise for which nothing has been given or promised in exchange. In Raedeke v. Gibraltar Savings & Loan Assn. (1974) 10 Cal.3d 665 [111 Cal.Rptr. 693, 517 P.2d 1157] we explained that a court may invoke the doctrine of promissory estoppel embodied in section 90 to bind a promisor "'when he should reasonably expect a substantial change of position, either by act or forbearance, in reliance on his promise, if injustice can be avoided only by its enforcement.'" (Id., at p. 672,.)

In view of the equitable considerations lying at the foundation of these several doctrines, and reflected in the opinion in Coleman, we conclude that compensation for a party's performance should be paid by the person whose request induced the performance. In light of this conclusion, the portion of the judgment denying plaintiff recovery with respect to the Pillow property must be reversed. As we have explained, plaintiff's evidence indicated that he had performed services and furnished materials in work on the Pillow property at the urgent request of defendant. Moreover, according to plaintiff, the work was performed under circumstances in which plaintiff reasonably relied upon the belief that defendant would pay for it.

In denying plaintiff recovery for such work, the trial court rested solely on the broad implications of our Rotea decision. Since we have disapproved those implications, we reverse the trial court's ruling. On remand, the trial court should determine, under the principles set out in this opinion, whether plaintiff is entitled to recover under quantum meruit with respect to the Pillow property and, if so, the extent of the award.

The judgment is reversed and the case is remanded to the trial court for further proceedings consistent with this opinion.

Bird, C. J., Mosk, J., and Newman, J., concurred.

Richardson, J., concurred in the result.

CLARK, J.,

Concurred and Dissented.

Manuel, J., concurred

Afterthoughts

The doctrine of promissory estoppel may be applied against public entities in appropriate circumstances. (See *Youngman v. Nevada Irrigation Dist.*, 70 Cal.2d 240, 249-251 [74 Cal.Rptr. 398, 449 P.2d 462]; *Hilltop Properties v. State of California*, 233 Cal.App.2d 349, 364-365 [43 Cal.Rptr. 605, 37 A.L.R.3d 109]; Annot. (1956) Promissory Estoppel, 48 A.L.R.2d 1069, 1086.)

Chapter 2

Mutual Assent

Mutual Consent

An essential element of any contract is the consent of the parties, or mutual assent. (Cal.Civ. Code, §§ 1550(2), 1565 (2).) To form a contract, a manifestation of mutual assent is necessary. Mutual assent may be manifested by written or spoken words, or by conduct. (*Binder v. Aetna Life Ins. Co.* (1999) 75 Cal.App.4th 832 , 89 Cal.Rptr.2d 540) One of the essential elements to the existence of a contract is the consent of the parties. This consent must be freely given, mutual, and communicated by each party to the other. (Cal.Civ.Code § 1565)

Consent is not mutual, unless the parties all agree upon the same thing in the same sense. Ordinarily, it is the outward expression of consent that is controlling. Mutual consent arises out of the reasonable meaning of the words and acts of the parties, and not from any secret or unexpressed intention or understanding. In determining if there was mutual consent, consideration is given to not only the words and conduct of the parties, but also to the circumstances under which the words are used and the conduct occurs. (Cal.Civ.Code § 1580)

Conduct alone is not effective as an expression of consent, unless that person intends to engage in the conduct and knows or has reason to know that the other party may infer consent from such conduct. (See, 1 Witkin, Summary of Cal. Law (9th ed.1987) Contracts, § 119)

Consent is not freely given if it is obtained by duress, menace, fraud, undue influence, or mistake. (Cal.Civ.Code § 1567)

Offer

An offer is an expression of willingness to enter into an agreement so made as to justify another person in understanding that his or her consent to that agreement is invited and will conclude it. An offer may request that the person to whom it is made (the offeree) manifest their acceptance by either completely performing a requested act or by promising to perform a requested act. When the offer requests that the offeree perform a requested act it is said that the offer looks towards the formation of a unilateral contract. When the offer requests that the offeree merely promise to perform the requested act, it is said that the offer looks towards the formation of a bilateral contract. Stated another way; "A unilateral contract is one in which no promisor receives a promise as consideration for his promise. A bilateral contract is one in which there are mutual promises between two parties to the contract; each party being both a promisor and a promisee." (*Davis v. Jacoby, infra.*)

Davis v. Jacoby

Supreme Court of California, 1934
1 Cal.2d 370, 34 P.2d 1026

THE COURT.

Plaintiffs appeal from a judgment refusing to grant specific performance of an alleged contract to make a will. The facts are not in dispute and are as follows:

The plaintiff Caro M. Davis was the niece of Blanche Whitehead who was married to Rupert Whitehead. Prior to her marriage in 1913 to her coplaintiff Frank M. Davis, Caro lived for a considerable time at the home of the Whiteheads, in Piedmont, California. The Whiteheads were childless and extremely fond of Caro. The record is replete with uncontradicted testimony of the close and loving relationship that existed between Caro and her aunt and uncle. During the period that Caro lived with the Whiteheads she was treated as and often referred to by the Whiteheads as their daughter. In 1913, when Caro was married to Frank Davis the marriage was arranged at the Whitehead home and a reception held there. After the marriage Mr. and Mrs. Davis went to Mr. Davis' home in Canada, where they have resided ever since. During the period 1913 to 1931 Caro made many visits to the Whiteheads, several of them being of long duration. The Whiteheads visited Mr. and Mrs. Davis in Canada on several occasions. After the marriage and continuing down to 1931 the closest and most friendly relationship at all times existed between these two families. They corresponded frequently, the record being replete with letters showing the loving relationship.

By the year 1930 Mrs. Whitehead had become seriously ill. She had suffered several strokes and her mind was failing. Early in 1931 Mr. Whitehead had her removed to a private hospital. The doctors in attendance had informed him that she might die at any time or she might linger for many months. Mr. Whitehead had suffered severe financial reverses. He had had several sieges of sickness and was in poor health. The record shows that during the early part of 1931 he was desperately in need of assistance with his wife, and in his business affairs, and that he did not trust his friends in Piedmont. On March 18, 1931, he wrote to Mrs. Davis telling her of Mrs. Whitehead's condition and added that Mrs. Whitehead was very wistful. * * * on April 12, 1931, Mr. Whitehead again wrote, addressing his letter to "Dear Frank and Caro", and in this letter made the definite offer, which offer it is claimed was accepted and is the basis of this action. In this letter he first pointed out that Blanche, his wife, was in a private hospital and that "she cannot last much longer ... my affairs are not as bad as I supposed at first. Cutting everything down I figure 150,000 can be saved from the wreck." He then enumerated the values placed upon his various properties and then continued "my trouble was caused by my friends taking advantage of my illness and my position to skin me. * * * So if you can come, Caro will inherit everything and you will make our lives happier and see Blanche is provided for to the end.

* * *

"Will you let me hear from you as soon as possible, I know it will be a sacrifice but times are still bad and likely to be, so by settling down you can help me and Blanche and gain in the end. If I had you here my mind would get better and my courage return, and we could work things out."

This letter was received by Mr. Davis at his office in Windsor, Canada, about 9:30 A. M. April 14, 1931. After reading the letter to Mrs. Davis over the telephone, and after getting her belief that they must go to California, Mr. Davis immediately wrote Mr. Whitehead a letter, which, after reading it to his wife, he sent by air mail. This letter was lost, but there is no doubt that it was sent by Davis and received by Whitehead, in fact the trial court expressly so found. Mr. Davis testified in substance as to the contents of this letter. After acknowledging receipt of the letter of April 12, 1931, Mr. Davis unequivocally stated that he and Mrs. Davis accepted the proposition of Mr. Whitehead and both would leave Windsor to go to him on April 25th. This letter of acceptance also contained the information that the reason they could not leave prior to April 25th was that Mr. Davis had to appear in court on April 22d as one of the executors of his mother's estate. The testimony is uncontradicted and ample to support the trial court's finding that this letter was sent by Davis and received by Whitehead. In fact under date of April 15, 1931, Mr. Whitehead again wrote to Mr. Davis and stated "Your letter by air mail received this a. m. Now, I am wondering if I have put you to unnecessary trouble and expense, if you are making any money don't leave it, as things are bad here.... You know your business and I don't and I am half crazy in the bargain, but I don't want to hurt you or Caro.

"Then on the other hand if I could get some one to trust and keep me straight I can save a good deal, about what I told you in my former letter."

This letter was received by Mr. Davis on April 17, 1931, and the same day Mr. Davis telegraphed to Mr. Whitehead "Cheer up—we will soon be there, we will wire you from the train."

Between April 14, 1931, the date the letter of acceptance was sent by Mr. Davis, and April 22d, Mr. Davis was engaged in closing out his business affairs, and Mrs. Davis in closing up their home and in making other arrangements to leave. On April 22, 1931, Mr. Whitehead committed suicide. Mr. and Mrs. Davis were immediately notified and they at once came to California. From almost the moment of her arrival Mrs. Davis devoted herself to the care and comfort of her aunt, and gave her aunt constant attention and care until Mrs. Whitehead's death on May 30, 1931. On this point the trial court found: "from the time of their arrival in Piedmont, Caro M. Davis administered in every way to the comforts of Blanche Whitehead and saw that she was cared for and provided for down to the time of the death of Blanche Whitehead on May 30, 1931; during said time Caro M. Davis nursed Blanche Whitehead, cared for her and administered to her wants as a natural daughter would have done toward and for her mother".

This finding is supported by uncontradicted evidence and in fact is conceded by respondents to be correct. In fact the record shows that after their arrival in California Mr. and Mrs. Davis fully performed their side of the agreement.

After the death of Mrs. Whitehead, for the first time it was discovered that the information contained in Mr. Whitehead's letter of March 30, 1931, in reference to the contents of his and Mrs. Whitehead's wills was incorrect. By a duly witnessed will dated February 28, 1931, Mr. Whitehead, after making several specific bequests, had bequeathed all of the balance of his estate to his wife for life, and upon her death to respondents Geoff Doubble and Rupert Ross Whitehead, his nephews. Neither appellant was mentioned in his will. It was also discovered that Mrs. Whitehead by a will dated December 17, 1927, had devised all of her estate to her husband. The evidence is clear and uncontradicted that the relationship existing between Whitehead and his two nephews, respondents herein, was not nearly as close and confidential as that existing between Whitehead and appellants.

After the discovery of the manner in which the property had been devised was made, this action was commenced upon the theory that Rupert Whitehead had assumed a contractual obligation to make a will whereby "Caro Davis would inherit everything"; that he had failed to do so; that plaintiffs had fully performed their part of the contract; that damages being insufficient, quasi specific performance should be granted in order to remedy the alleged wrong, upon the equitable principle that equity regards that done which ought to have been done. The requested relief is that the beneficiaries under the will of Rupert Whitehead, respondents herein, be declared to be involuntary trustees for plaintiffs of Whitehead's estate.

It should also be added that the evidence shows that as a result of Frank Davis leaving his business in Canada he forfeited not only all insurance business he might have written if he had remained, but also forfeited all renewal commissions earned on past business. According to his testimony this loss was over $8,000.

The trial court found that the relationship between Mr. and Mrs. Davis and the Whiteheads was substantially as above recounted and that the other facts above stated were true; that prior to April 12, 1931, Rupert Whitehead had suffered business reverses and was depressed in mind and ill in body; that his wife was very ill; that because of his mental condition he "was unable to properly care for or look after his property or affairs"; that on April 12, 1931, Rupert Whitehead in writing made an offer to plaintiffs that, if within a reasonable time thereafter plaintiffs would leave and abandon their said home in Windsor, and if Frank M. Davis would abandon or dispose of his said business, and if both the plaintiffs would come to Piedmont in the said county of Alameda where Rupert Whitehead then resided and thereafter reside at said place and be with or near him, and, if Frank M. Davis would thereupon and thereafter look after the business and affairs of said Rupert Whitehead until his condition improved to such an extent as to permit him so to do, and if the plaintiffs would look after and administer to the comforts of Blanche Whitehead and see that she was properly cared for until the time of her death, that, in consideration thereof, Caro M. Davis would inherit everything that Rupert Whitehead possessed at the time of his death and that by last will and testament Rupert Whitehead would devise and bequeath to Caro M. Davis all property and estate owned by him at the time of his death, other than the property constituting the community interest of Blanche Whitehead; that shortly prior to April 12, 1931, Rupert Whitehead informed plaintiffs of the supposed terms of his will and the will of Mrs. Whitehead. The court then finds that the offer of April 12th was not accepted. As already stated, the court found that plaintiffs sent a letter to Rupert Whitehead on April 14th purporting to accept the offer of April 12th, and also found that this letter was received by the Whiteheads, but finds that in fact such letter was not a legal acceptance. The court also found that the offer of April 12th was "fair and just and reasonable, and the consideration therefor, namely, the performance by plaintiffs of the terms and conditions thereof, if the same had been performed, would have been an adequate consideration for said offer and for the agreement that would have resulted from such performance; said offer was not, and said agreement would not have been, either harsh or oppressive or unjust to the heirs at law, or devisees, or legatees, of Rupert Whitehead, or to each or any of them, or otherwise".

The court also found that plaintiffs did not know that the statements made by Whitehead in reference to the wills were not correct until after Mrs. Whitehead's death, that after plaintiffs arrived in Piedmont they cared for Mrs. Whitehead until her death and "Blanche Whitehead was greatly comforted by the presence, companionship and association of Caro M. Davis, and by her administering to her wants".

The theory of the trial court and of respondents on this appeal is that the letter of April 12th was an offer to contract, but that such offer could only be accepted by performance and could not be accepted by a promise to perform, and that said offer was revoked by the death of Mr. Whitehead before performance. In other words, it is contended that the offer was an offer to enter into a unilateral contract, and that the purported acceptance of April 14th was of no legal effect.

The distinction between unilateral and bilateral contracts is well settled in the law. It is well stated in section 12 of the American Institute's Restatement of the Law of Contracts as follows:

"A unilateral contract is one in which no promisor receives a promise as consideration for his promise. A bilateral contract is one in which there are mutual promises between two parties to the contract; each party being both a promisor and a promisee."

This definition is in accord with the law of California. (Christman v. Southern Cal. Edison Co., 83 Cal.App. 249 [256 P. 618].)

In the case of unilateral contracts no notice of acceptance by performance is required. Section 1584 of the Civil Code provides, "Performance of the conditions of a proposal, ... is an acceptance of the proposal." (See Cuthill v. Peabody, 19 Cal.App. 304 [125 P. 926]; Los Angeles Traction Co. v. Wilshire, 135 Cal. 654 [67 P. 1086].)

Although the legal distinction between unilateral and bilateral contracts is thus well settled, the difficulty in any particular case is to determine whether the particular offer is one to enter into a bilateral or unilateral contract. Some cases are quite clear cut. Thus an offer to sell which is accepted is clearly a bilateral contract, while an offer of a reward is a clear-cut offer of a unilateral contract which cannot be accepted by a promise to perform, but only by performance. (Berthiaume v. Doe, 22 Cal.App. 78 [133 P. 515].) Between these two extremes is a vague field where the particular contract may be unilateral or bilateral depending upon the intent of the offerer and the facts and circumstances of each case. The offer to contract involved in this case falls within this category. By the provisions of the Restatement of the Law of Contracts it is expressly provided that there is a presumption that the offer is to enter into a bilateral contract. Section 31 provides:

"In case of doubt it is presumed that an offer invites the formation of a bilateral contract by an acceptance amounting in effect to a promise by the offeree to perform what the offer requests, rather than the formation of one or more unilateral contracts by actual performance on the part of the offeree."

Professor Williston in his Treatise on Contracts, volume 1, section 60, also takes the position that a presumption in favor of bilateral contracts exists.

In the comment following section 31 of the Restatement the reason for such presumption is stated as follows:

"It is not always easy to determine whether an offerer requests an act or a promise to do the act. As a bilateral contract immediately and fully protects both parties, the interpretation is favored that a bilateral contract is proposed."

While the California cases have never expressly held that a presumption in favor of bilateral contracts exists, the cases clearly indicate a tendency to treat offers as offers of bilateral rather than of unilateral contracts. (Roth v. Moeller, 185 Cal. 415 [197 P. 62]; Boehm v. Spreckels, 183 Cal. 239 [191 P. 5]; see, also, Wood v. Lucy, Lady Duff- Gordon, 222 N.Y. 88 [118 N.E. 214].)

Keeping these principles in mind we are of the opinion that the offer of April 12th was an offer to enter into a bilateral as distinguished from a unilateral contract. Respondents argue that Mr. Whitehead had the right as offerer to designate his offer as either unilateral or bilateral. That is undoubtedly the law. It is then argued that from all the facts and circumstances it must be implied that what Whitehead wanted was performance and not a mere promise to perform. We think this is a non sequitur, in fact the surrounding circumstances lead to just the opposite conclusion. These parties were not dealing at arm's length. Not only were they related, but a very close and intimate friendship existed between them. The record indisputably demonstrates that Mr. Whitehead had confidence in Mr. and Mrs. Davis, in fact that he had lost all confidence in everyone else. The record amply shows that by an accumulation of occurrences Mr. Whitehead had become desperate, and that what he wanted was the promise of appellants that he could look to them for assistance. He knew from his past relationship with appellants that if they gave their promise to perform he could rely upon them. The correspondence between them indicates how desperately he desired this assurance. Under these circumstances he wrote his offer of April 12th, above quoted, in which he stated, after disclosing his desperate mental and physical condition, and after setting forth the terms of his offer: "Will you let me hear from you as soon as possible—I know it will be a sacrifice but times are still bad and likely to be, so by settling down you can help me and Blanche and gain in the end." By thus specifically requesting an immediate reply Whitehead expressly indicated the nature of the acceptance desired by him—namely, appellants' promise that they would come to California and do the things requested by him. This promise was immediately sent by appellants upon receipt of the offer, and was received by Whitehead. It is elementary that when an offer has indicated the mode and means of acceptance, an acceptance in accordance with that mode or means is binding on the offerer.

Another factor which indicates that Whitehead must have contemplated a bilateral rather than a unilateral contract, is that the contract required Mr. and Mrs. Davis to perform services until the death of both Mr. and Mrs. Whitehead. It is obvious that if Mr. Whitehead died first some of these services were to be performed after his death, so that he would have to rely on the promise of appellants to perform these services. It is also of some evidentiary force that Whitehead received the letter of acceptance and acquiesced in that means of acceptance.

Shaw v. King, 63 Cal.App. 18 [218 P. 50], relied on by respondents is clearly not in point. In that case there was no written acceptance, nor was there an acceptance by partial or total performance.

For the foregoing reasons we are of the opinion that the offer of April 12, 1931, was an offer to enter into a bilateral contract which was accepted by the letter of April 14, 1931. Subsequently appellants fully performed their part of the contract. Under such circumstances it is well settled that damages are insufficient and specific performance will be granted. (Wolf v. Donahue, 206 Cal. 213 [273 P. 547].) Since the consideration has been fully rendered by appellants the question as to mutuality of remedy becomes of no importance. (6 Cal.Jur., sec. 140.)

Respondents also contend the complaint definitely binds appellants to the theory of a unilateral contract. This contention is without merit. The complaint expressly alleges the parties entered into a contract. It is true that the complaint also alleged that the contract became effective by performance. However, this is an action in equity. Respondents were not misled. No objection was made to the testimony offered to show the acceptance of April 14th. A fair reading of the record clearly indicates the case was tried by the parties on the theory that the sole question was whether there was a contract—unilateral or bilateral.

For the foregoing reasons the judgment appealed from is reversed.

Afterthought

In case of doubt as to whether an offer looks towards the formation of a bilateral contract or a unilateral contract the offeree has the choice of accepting by making a promise or by performing the requested act. (Rest.2d, Contracts § 32.)

Advertisements as Offers

Harris v. Time, Inc.

Court of Appeals of California, First Appellate District, Division Five, 1987
191 Cal.App.3d 449, 237 Cal.Rptr. 584

[Facts are set forth at page 14.]

A. Offer.

On the first point, Time argues there was no contract because the text of the unopened mailer amounted to a mere advertisement rather than an offer.

It is true that advertisements are not typically treated as offers, but merely as invitations to bargain. (1 Corbin on Contracts (1963) § 25, pp. 74-75; Rest.2d, Contracts, § 26, com, b, at p. 76.) There is, however, a fundamental exception to this rule: an advertisement can constitute an offer, and form the basis of a unilateral contract, if it calls for performance of a specific act without further communication and leaves nothing for further negotiation. (Lefkowitz v. Great Minneapolis Surplus Store (1957) 251 Minn. 188 [86 N.W.2d 689, 691]; 1 Corbin on Contracts (1963) §§ 25, 64, pp. 75-76, 264-270; Rest.2d, Contracts, § 26, com. b, at p. 76.) This is a basic rule of contract law, contained in the Restatement Second of Contracts and normally encountered within the first few weeks of law school in cases such as Lefkowitz (furs advertised for sale at specified date and time for "$1.00 First Come First Served") and Carlill v. Carbolic Smoke Ball Co. (1893) 1 Q.B. 256 (advertisement of reward to anyone who caught influenza after using seller's medicine). (See, e.g., Murphy & Speidel, Studies in Contract Law (3d ed. 1984) pp. 112, 154.)

The text of Time's unopened mailer was, technically, an offer to enter into a unilateral contract: the promisor made a promise to do something (give the recipient a calculator watch) in exchange for the performance of an act by the promise (opening the envelope). Time was not in the same position as a seller merely advertising price; the proper analogy is to a seller promising to give something to a customer in exchange for the customer's act of coming to the store at a specified time. (Lefkowitz v. Great Minneapolis Surplus Store, supra, 86 N.W.2d 689.)

Donovan v. RRL Corp.

Supreme Court of California, 2001
26 Cal.4th 261, 109 Cal.Rptr.2d 807; 27 P.3d 702

GEORGE, C.J.

Defendant RRL Corporation is an automobile dealer doing business under the name Lexus of Westminster. Because of typographical and proofreading errors made by a local newspaper, defendant's advertisement listed a price for a used automobile that was significantly less than the intended sales price. Plaintiff Brian J. Donovan read the advertisement and, after examining the vehicle, attempted to purchase it by tendering the advertised price. Defendant refused to sell the automobile to plaintiff at that price, and plaintiff brought this action against defendant for breach of contract. The municipal court entered judgment for defendant on the ground that the mistake in the advertisement precluded the existence of a contract. The appellate department of the superior court and the Court of Appeal reversed, relying in part upon Vehicle Code section 11713.1, subdivision (e), which makes it unlawful for an automobile dealer not to sell a motor vehicle at the advertised price while the vehicle remains unsold and before the advertisement expires.

We conclude that a contract satisfying the statute of frauds arose from defendant's advertisement and plaintiff's tender of the advertised price, but that defendant's unilateral mistake of fact provides a basis for rescinding the contract. Although Vehicle Code section 11713.1, subdivision (e), justifies a reasonable expectation on the part of consumers that an automobile dealer intends that such an advertisement constitute an offer, and that the offer can be accepted by paying the advertised price, this statute does not supplant governing common law principles authorizing rescission of a contract on the ground of mistake. As we shall explain, rescission is warranted here because the evidence establishes that defendant's unilateral mistake of fact was made in good faith, defendant did not bear the risk of the mistake, and enforcement of the contract with the erroneous price would be unconscionable. Accordingly, we shall reverse the judgment of the Court of Appeal.

I

While reading the April 26, 1997, edition of the Costa Mesa Daily Pilot, a local newspaper, plaintiff noticed a full-page advertisement placed by defendant. The advertisement promoted a "PRE-OWNED COUP-A-RAMA SALE!/2-DAY PRE-OWNED SALES EVENT" and listed, along with 15 other used automobiles, a 1995 Jaguar XJ6 Vanden Plas. The advertisement described the color of this automobile as sapphire blue, included a vehicle identification number, and stated a price of $25,995. The name Lexus of Westminster was displayed prominently in three separate locations in the advertisement, which included defendant's address along with a small map showing the location of the dealership. The following statements appeared in small print at the bottom of the advertisement: "All cars plus tax, lic., doc., smog & bank fees. On approved credit. Ad expires 4/27/97[.]"

Also on April 26, 1997, plaintiff visited a Jaguar dealership that offered other 1995 Jaguars for sale at $8,000 to $10,000 more than the price specified in defendant's advertisement. The following day, plaintiff and his spouse drove to Lexus of Westminster and observed a blue Jaguar displayed on an elevated ramp. After verifying that the identification number on the sticker was the same as that listed in defendant's April 26 Daily Pilot advertisement, they asked a salesperson whether they could test drive the Jaguar. Plaintiff mentioned that he had seen the advertisement and that the price "looked really good." The salesperson responded that, as a Lexus dealer, defendant might offer better prices for a Jaguar automobile than would a Jaguar dealer. At that point, however, neither plaintiff nor the salesperson mentioned the specific advertised price.

After the test drive, plaintiff and his spouse discussed several negative characteristics of the automobile, including high mileage, an apparent rust problem, and worn tires. In addition, it was not as clean as the other Jaguars they had inspected. Despite these problems, they believed that the advertised price was a very good price and decided to purchase the vehicle. Plaintiff told the salesperson, "Okay. We will take it at your price, $26,000." When the salesperson did not respond, plaintiff showed him the advertisement. The salesperson immediately stated, "That's a mistake."

After plaintiff asked to speak with an individual in charge, defendant's sales manager also told plaintiff that the price listed in the advertisement was a mistake. The sales manager apologized and offered to pay for plaintiff's fuel, time, and effort expended in traveling to the dealership to examine the automobile. Plaintiff declined this offer and expressed his belief that there had been no mistake. Plaintiff stated that he could write a check for the full purchase price as advertised. The sales manager responded that he would not sell the vehicle at the advertised price. Plaintiff then requested the sales price. After performing some calculations, and based upon defendant's $35,000 investment in the automobile, the sales manager stated that he would sell it to plaintiff for $37,016. Plaintiff responded, "No, I want to buy it at your advertised price, and I will write you a check right now." The sales manager again stated that he would not sell the vehicle at the advertised price, and plaintiff and his spouse left the dealership.

Plaintiff subsequently filed this action against defendant for breach of contract, fraud, and negligence. In addition to testimony consistent with the facts set forth above, the following evidence was presented to the municipal court, which acted as the trier of fact.

Defendant's advertising manager compiles information for placement in advertisements in several local newspapers, including the Costa Mesa Daily Pilot. Defendant's advertisement published in the Saturday, April 19, 1997, edition of the Daily Pilot listed a 1995 Jaguar XJ6 Vanden Plas but did not specify a price for that automobile; instead, the word "Save" appeared in the space where a price ordinarily would have appeared. The following Thursday afternoon, defendant's sales manager instructed the advertising manager to delete the 1995 Jaguar from all advertisements and to substitute a 1994 Jaguar XJ6 with a price of $25,995. The advertising manager conveyed the new information to a representative of the Daily Pilot that same afternoon.

Because of typographical and proofreading errors made by employees of the Daily Pilot, however, the newspaper did not replace the description of the 1995 Jaguar with the description of the 1994 Jaguar, but did replace the word "Save" with the price of $25,995. Thus, the Saturday, April 26, edition of the Daily Pilot erroneously advertised the 1995 Jaguar XJ6 Vanden Plas at a price of $25,995. The Daily Pilot acknowledged its error in a letter of retraction sent to defendant on April 28. No employee of defendant reviewed a proof sheet of the revised Daily Pilot advertisement before it was published, and defendant was unaware of the mistake until plaintiff attempted to purchase the automobile.

Except for the 1995 Jaguar XJ6 Vanden Plas, defendant intended to sell each vehicle appearing in the April 26, 1997, Daily Pilot advertisement at the advertised price. Defendant's advertisements in the April 26 editions of several other newspapers correctly listed the 1994 Jaguar XJ6 with a price of $25,995. In May 1997, defendant's advertisements in several newspapers listed the 1995 Jaguar XJ6 Vanden Plas for sale at $37,995. Defendant subsequently sold the automobile for $38,399.

The municipal court entered judgment for defendant. During the trial, the court ruled that plaintiff had not stated a cause of action for negligence, and it precluded plaintiff from presenting evidence in support of such a claim. After the close of evidence and presentation of argument, the municipal court concluded as a matter of law that a newspaper advertisement for an automobile generally constitutes a valid contractual offer that a customer may accept by tendering payment of the advertised price. The court also determined that such an advertisement satisfies the requirements of the statute of frauds when the dealer's name appears in the advertisement. Nevertheless, the municipal court held that in the present case there was no valid offer because defendant's unilateral mistake of fact vitiated or negated contractual intent. The court made factual findings that defendant's mistake regarding the advertisement was made in good faith and was not intended to deceive the public. The municipal court also found that plaintiff was unaware of the mistake before it was disclosed to him by defendant's representatives.

Plaintiff appealed from the judgment to the appellate department of the superior court (Cal. Rules of Court, rule 121), limiting his contentions to the breach of contract claim. The appellate department reversed the judgment for defendant and directed the municipal court to calculate plaintiff's damages. Relying upon the public policies underlying Vehicle Code section 11713.1, subdivision (e), the appellate department concluded that the advertisement constituted an offer capable of acceptance by tender of the advertised price. Section 11713.1, subdivision (e), provides that it is a violation of the Vehicle Code for a dealer to "[f]ail to sell a vehicle to any person at the advertised total price ... while the vehicle remains unsold, unless the advertisement states the advertised total price is good only for a specified time and the time has elapsed." The appellate department further concluded that defendant bore the risk of the mistaken transmission of its offer, because plaintiff was unaware of the mistake.

The appellate department of the superior court certified the appeal to the Court of Appeal, which ordered the case transferred to it for hearing and decision. (Cal. Rules of Court, rules 62(a), 63(a).) Like the appellate department, the Court of Appeal reversed the judgment of the municipal court and held that defendant's advertisement constituted a contractual offer that invited acceptance by the act of tendering the advertised price, which plaintiff performed. Acknowledging that the question was close, however, the Court of Appeal reasoned that Vehicle Code section 11713.1, subdivision (e), "tips the scale in favor of ... construing the advertisement as an offer...." The court disagreed with the municipal court's conclusion that defendant's unilateral mistake of fact, unknown to plaintiff at the time he tendered the purchase price, precluded the existence of a valid offer. With regard to the contention that defendant should not bear the risk of an error resulting solely from the negligence of the newspaper, the Court of Appeal made a factual finding based upon the appellate record (Code Civ. Proc., §909) that defendant's failure to review a proof sheet for the Daily Pilot advertisement constituted negligence that contributed to the placement of the erroneous advertisement.

We granted defendant's petition for review and requested that the parties include in their briefing a discussion of the effect, if any, of California Uniform Commercial Code division 2, chapter 2, sections 2201-2210, upon the present case.

II

An essential element of any contract is the consent of the parties, or mutual assent. (Civ. Code, §§1550, subd. (2), 1565, subd. (2).) Mutual assent usually is manifested by an offer communicated to the offeree and an acceptance communicated to the offeror. (1 Witkin, Summary of Cal. Law (9th ed. 1987) Contracts, §128, p. 153 (hereafter Witkin).) " ' "An offer is the manifestation of willingness to enter into a bargain, so made as to justify another person in understanding that his assent to that bargain is invited and will conclude it." ' [Citations.]" (*City of Moorpark v. Moorpark Unified School Dist.* (1991) 54 Cal.3d 921, 930 (*Moorpark*).) The determination of whether a particular communication constitutes an operative offer, rather than an inoperative step in the preliminary negotiation of a contract, depends upon all the surrounding circumstances. (1 Corbin, Contracts (rev. ed. 1993) §2.2, p. 105.) The objective manifestation of the party's assent ordinarily controls, and the pertinent inquiry is whether the individual to whom the communication was made had reason to believe that it was intended as an offer. (1 Witkin, *supra*, Contracts, §119, p. 144; 1 Farnsworth, Contracts (2d ed. 1998) §3.10, p. 237.)

In the present case, the municipal court ruled that newspaper advertisements for automobiles generally constitute offers that can be accepted by a customer's tender of the purchase price. Its conclusion that defendant's advertisement for the 1995 Jaguar did not constitute an offer was based solely upon the court's factual determination that the erroneous price in the advertisement was the result of a good faith mistake.

Because the existence of an offer depends upon an objective interpretation of defendant's assent as reflected in the advertisement, however, the mistaken price (not reasonably known to plaintiff to be a mistake) is irrelevant in determining the threshold question whether the advertisement constituted an offer. In this situation, mistake instead properly would be considered in deciding whether a contract resulted from the acceptance of an offer containing mistaken terms, or whether any such contract could be voided or rescinded. (See *Chakmak v. H. J. Lucas Masonry, Inc.* (1976) 55 Cal.App.3d 124, 129; Rest.2d Contracts, §153; 1 Corbin, Contracts, *supra*, §4.11, pp. 623-627; 2 Williston, Contracts (4th ed. 1991) §6:57, pp. 682-695.) Thus, the municipal court did not make any factual findings relevant to the issue whether defendant's advertisement constituted an offer, and we shall review the question de novo. (*Richards v. Flower* (1961) 193 Cal.App.2d 233, 235.)

Some courts have stated that an advertisement or other notice disseminated to the public at large generally does not constitute an offer, but rather is presumed to be an invitation to consider, examine, and negotiate. (E.g., *Harris v. Time, Inc.* (1987) 191 Cal.App.3d 449, 455; see Rest.2d Contracts, §26, com. b, p. 76; 1 Corbin, Contracts, *supra*, §2.4, p. 116; 1 Farnsworth, Contracts, *supra*, §3.10, p. 242; 1 Williston, Contracts (4th ed. 1990) §4:7, pp. 285-287, 294.) Nevertheless, certain advertisements have been held to constitute offers where they invite the performance of a specific act without further communication and leave nothing for negotiation. Advertisements for rewards typically fall within this category, because performing the requested act (e.g., returning a lost article or supplying particular information) generally is all that is necessary to accept the offer and conclude the bargain. (1 Witkin, *supra*, Contracts, §188, p. 200; Rest.2d Contracts, §29, com. b, illus. 1, p. 84; 1 Corbin, Contracts, *supra*, §2.4, p. 119.)

Various advertisements involving transactions in goods also have been held to constitute offers where they invite particular action. For example, a merchant's advertisement that listed particular goods at a specific price and included the phrase "First Come First Served" was deemed to be an offer, because it constituted a promise to sell to a customer at that price in exchange for the customer's act of arriving at the store at a particular time. (*Lefkowitz v. Great Minneapolis Surplus Store* (1957) 251 Minn. 188 [86 N.W. 2d 689, 691]; Rest.2d Contracts, §26, com. b, illus. 1, p. 76.) Similarly, external wording on the envelope of an item of bulk rate mail promising to give the recipient a watch "just for opening the envelope" before a certain date was held to constitute an operative offer accepted by performance of the act of opening the envelope. (*Harris v. Time, Inc., supra*, 191 Cal.App.3d 449, 455-456.) In addition, an advertisement stating that anyone who purchased a 1954 automobile from a dealer could exchange it for a 1955 model at no additional cost constituted an offer that was accepted when the plaintiff purchased the 1954 vehicle. (*Johnson v. Capital City Ford Co.* (La.Ct.App. 1955) 85 So.2d 75, 79-80; see also *Cobaugh v. Klick-Lewis* (Pa.Super.Ct. 1989) 561 A.2d 1248, 1249-1250 [sign at golf course stated "hole-in-one wins" an automobile at a specified price].) In such cases, courts have considered whether the advertiser, in clear and positive terms, promised to render performance in exchange for something requested by the advertiser, and whether the recipient of the advertisement reasonably might have concluded that by acting in accordance with the request a contract would be formed. (1 Williston, Contracts, *supra*, § 4:7, pp. 296-297; 1 Corbin, Contracts, *supra*, § 2:4, pp. 116-117; see, e.g., *Chang v. First Colonial Sav. Bank* (1991) 242 Va. 388 [410 S.E.2d 928, 929-930] [bank's newspaper advertisement stating "Deposit $14,000 and receive … $20,136.12 upon maturity in 3 1/2 years" constituted an offer that was accepted by the plaintiffs' deposit of that sum for the specified period].)

Relying upon these decisions, defendant contends that its advertisement for the 1995 Jaguar XJ6 Vanden Plas did not constitute an offer, because the advertisement did not request the performance of a specific act that would conclude the bargain. According to defendant, plaintiff's assertion that the advertisement was an offer conflicts with the generally accepted "black-letter" rule that an advertisement that simply identifies goods and specifies a price is an invitation to negotiate.

This court has not previously applied the common law rules upon which defendant relies, including the rule that advertisements generally constitute invitations to negotiate rather than offers. Plaintiff observes that such rules governing the construction of advertisements have been criticized on the ground that they are inconsistent with the reasonable expectations of consumers and lead to haphazard results. (See Eisenberg, *Expression Rules in Contract Law and Problems of Offer and Acceptance* (1994) 82 Cal. L.Rev. 1127, 1166-1172.) Plaintiff urges this court to reject the black-letter advertising rule.

In the present case, however, we need not consider the viability of the black-letter rule regarding the interpretation of advertisements *in general*. Like the Court of Appeal, we conclude that a licensed automobile dealer's advertisement for the sale of a particular vehicle at a specific price—when construed in light of Vehicle Code section 11713.1, subdivision (e)—reasonably justifies a consumer's understanding that the dealer intends the advertisement to constitute an offer and that the consumer's assent to the bargain is invited and will conclude it.

Vehicle Code section 11713.1 sets forth comprehensive requirements governing a licensed automobile dealer's advertisements for motor vehicles. This statute requires, among other things, that an advertisement for a specific automobile identify the vehicle by its identification number or license number (*id.*, subd. (a)), disclose the type of charges that will be added to the advertised price at the time of sale (*id.*, subd. (b)), and refrain from containing various types of misleading information (*id.*, subds. (i), (l), (o), (p), (r)).

In addition, Vehicle Code section 11713.1, subdivision (e) (hereafter section 11713.1(e)), states that it is a violation of the Vehicle Code for the holder of any dealer's license to "[f]ail to sell a vehicle to any person at the advertised total price, exclusive of [specified charges such as taxes and registration fees], while the vehicle remains unsold, unless the advertisement states the advertised total price is good only for a specified time and the time has elapsed."

The administrative regulation implementing section 11713.1(e) states in relevant part: "A specific vehicle advertised by a dealer … shall be willingly shown and sold at the advertised price and terms while such vehicle remains unsold…, unless the advertisement states that the advertised price and terms are good only for a specific time and such time has elapsed. Advertised vehicles must be sold at or below the advertised price irrespective of whether or not the advertised price has been communicated to the purchaser." (Cal. Code Regs., tit. 13, § 260.04, subd. (b).)

Plaintiff asserts that because a dealer is prohibited by section 11713.1(e) from failing to sell a particular vehicle at the advertised price, an advertisement for such a vehicle cannot be a mere request for offers from consumers or an invitation to negotiate, but instead must be deemed an operative offer that is accepted when a consumer tenders the full advertised price. We agree that, in light of the foregoing regulatory scheme, a licensed automobile dealer's advertisement for a particular vehicle at a specific price constitutes an offer.

As one commentator has observed, legislation can affect consumer expectations and cause reasonable individuals to regard certain retail advertisements for the sale of goods as offers to complete a bargain. (1 Corbin, Contracts, *supra*, § 2.4, p. 118.) By authorizing disciplinary action against a licensed automobile dealer that fails to sell a vehicle at the advertised price, section 11713.1(e) creates a reasonable expectation on the part of consumers that the dealer intends to make an offer to sell at that price, and that the consumer can accept the offer by paying the price specified in the advertisement. Interpreted in light of the regulatory obligations imposed upon dealers, an advertisement for a particular automobile at a specific price constitutes an objective manifestation of the dealer's willingness to enter into a bargain on the stated terms, and justifies the consumer's understanding that his or her assent to the bargain is invited and will conclude it. Such an advertisement therefore constitutes an offer that is accepted when a consumer tenders the advertised price.

Defendant and its supporting amici curiae contend that section 11713.1(e) was not intended to modify the common law of contracts, and that therefore the statute should not be considered in determining whether a contract arose from defendant's advertisement and plaintiff's tender of the advertised price. As we shall explain (pt. IV, *post*), we agree that section 11713.1(e) does not reflect a legislative intent to supplant the common law governing contracts for the sale of motor vehicles by licensed dealers. Nevertheless, the statute does govern the conduct of dealers and thus creates an objective expectation that dealers intend to sell vehicles at the advertised price. Therefore, even though section 11713.1(e) does not alter the applicable common law regarding contractual offers, consumer expectations arising from the statute are relevant in determining whether defendant's advertisement constituted an offer pursuant to governing principles of contract law.

Amicus curiae California Motor Car Dealers Association further asserts that an advertisement for the sale of a vehicle does not constitute an offer because consumers have reason to believe that an automobile dealer does not intend to conclude the bargain until agreement is reached with regard to numerous terms other than price and until the contract is reduced to writing. (See Rest.2d Contracts, §§ 26, 27; 1 Witkin, *supra*, Contracts, § 142, pp. 166-167.) For example, a written contract for the sale of an automobile by a dealer typically includes terms such as the form of payment, warranties, insurance, title, registration, delivery, taxes, documentation fees, and, if applicable, financing. (See *Twaite v. Allstate Ins. Co.* (1989) 216 Cal.App.3d 239, 243; *O'-Keefe v. Lee Calan Imports, Inc.* (1970) 128 Ill.App.2d 410 [262 N.E.2d 758, 760]; see also Civ. Code, § 2981 et seq. [requirements for conditional contracts for the sale of motor vehicles].) In addition, specific written disclosures, required by statute, must appear in the contract. (E.g., Veh. Code, § 11713.1, subd. (v) [retail automobile sales contract clearly and conspicuously must disclose whether the vehicle is being sold as used or new], subd. (x) [dealer must disclose on the face of the contract whether the transaction is or is not subject to a fee received by an "autobroker" as defined in the Vehicle Code].)

Plaintiff, on the other hand, contends that the existence of a contract is not defeated by the circumstance that he and defendant might have included additional terms in their ultimate written agreement, or that acceptance of defendant's offer might have been communicated by means other than tender of the purchase price, for example by signing a written contract. Plaintiff relies upon the following principle: "Manifestations of assent that are in themselves sufficient to conclude a contract will not be prevented from so operating by the fact that the parties also manifest an intention to prepare and adopt a written memorial thereof; but the circumstances may show that the agreements are preliminary negotiations." (Rest.2d Contracts, § 27.) Plaintiff also observes that "[a]n offer to make a contract shall be construed as inviting acceptance in any manner and by any medium reasonable in the circumstances," unless otherwise indicated. (Cal. U. Com. Code, § 2206, subd. (1)(a).)

Although dealers are required by statute to prepare a written contract when selling an automobile, and such a contract contains terms other than the price of the vehicle, we agree with plaintiff that a dealer's advertisement specifying a price for a particular vehicle constitutes a sufficient manifestation of the dealer's assent to give rise to a contract. As we have explained, in light of section 11713.1(e) such an advertisement objectively reflects the dealer's intention to sell the vehicle to a member of the public who tenders the full advertised price while the vehicle remains unsold and before the advertisement expires. The price almost always is the most important term of the bargain, and the dealer's intention to include other terms in a written contract does not preclude the existence of mutual assent sufficient to conclude a contract.

In sum, because section 11713.1(e) makes it unlawful for a dealer not to sell a particular vehicle at the advertised price while the vehicle remains unsold and before the advertisement expires, plaintiff reasonably could believe that defendant intended the advertisement to be an offer. Therefore, we conclude that defendant's advertisement constituted an offer that was accepted by plaintiff's tender of the advertised price.

Afterthoughts

An offer must be sufficiently definite, or must call for such definite terms in the acceptance, that the performance promised is reasonably certain of definition.

Parties may engage in preliminary negotiations, oral or written, before reaching an agreement. These negotiations only result in a binding contract when all of the essential terms are definitely understood and agreed upon even though the parties intend that a formal writing including all of these terms shall be signed later, unless the law requires that the contract be in writing, or unless the apparent agreement is void or voidable. (See, 1 Witkin, Summary of Cal. Law (9th ed. 1987) Contracts, §§ 128, 133, 136, 145)

Liberalized Rules Apply to Formation of Contracts for the Sale of Goods Pursuant to the Uniform Commercial Code

Scope of Article 2 of the Uniform Commercial Code

The thrust of the Uniform Commercial Code is to facilitate commerce by making it easier to do business. To that end, the Code relaxes the rules of contract formation. However, the Code and its liberalized rules of contract formation do not apply to every type of contract. Division 2 of the California Uniform Commercial Code applies only to the sale of goods (Cal.Comm. Code, §§ 2102, 2105, subd. (1); *English v. Ralph Williams Ford* (1971) 17 Cal.App.3d 1038, 1046 [motor vehicles]). Also notable, is that while California's version of the code retains the same numbering system as the Uniform Act, the hyphen between the article number and section is dropped in the California Commercial Code. Hence, UCC section 2-102 would be referred to as California Commercial Code section 2102.

Kazerouni v. De Satnick

California Court of Appeal, Second District Division Five, 1991.
228 Cal.App.3d 871, 279 Cal.Rptr. 74

ASHBY, J.

In this action on a promissory note, the court by nonjury trial gave judgment for plaintiff and respondent Akbar Kazerouni against defendants and appellants Steve and Mary De Satnick. The judgment further provides that appellants take nothing by their cross-complaint for breach of warranty.

Respondent sold his business (Photo Run Inc., a photo-developing store) to appellants for $310,000, taking back a promissory note for $101,000 payable at $1,500 per month. After four payments appellants defaulted on the note. The issue at trial was whether appellants' performance was excused, or appellants were entitled to damages, for a misrepresentation in the sale documents as to the approximate monthly receipts and approximate monthly net profits of the business. The trial court found against appellants because, although the listing agreement misstated the monthly receipts and net profits, appellants did not rely upon such misstatement; prior to the close of escrow appellants received accurate financial records from respondent including corporate tax returns for two years and three financial statements, and personally observed the operation of the business for a two-week period.

Appellants do not dispute the court's factual finding that appellants did not rely upon the misstatement. They contend on appeal that as a matter of law reliance was not required. They contend that the representation in the sale documents was an "express warranty" and that under a provision of the California Uniform Commercial Code involving express warranties by a seller of goods, reliance by the buyer is not required. (Cal. U. Com. Code, § 2313; Keith v. Buchanan (1985), 22-24 [220 Cal.Rptr. 392].fn. 3)

Appellants' contention lacks merit because section 2313 relates to warranties in the sale of goods, and the dispute here does not involve goods. California Uniform Commercial Code section 2102 provides, "Unless the context otherwise requires, this division applies to transactions in goods." Section 2105 defines "goods" as "all things (including specially manufactured goods) which are movable at the time of identification to the contract for sale...."

The pattern of monthly receipts or profits of respondent's business, as to which appellants claim an express warranty, does not involve goods or movables. This is not a dispute over a warranty of the equipment or inventory which were included in the sale of the business. Nor is this a case where it would be impossible or unreasonable to segregate the nongoods aspects of the sale in determining the proper law to be applied. Appellants cite no authority applying section 2313 to representations of the monthly receipts or profits of a going business. Appellants have not shown that section 2313 has any application to this case. Thus, appellants fail to sustain their contention that the trial court misapplied the law by requiring appellants to prove reliance. The judgment is affirmed.

Turner, P. J., and Boren, J., concurred.

Acceptance

Acceptance is a manifestation of willingness to be bound by the terms of the offer made in the manner invited or required by the offer. An acceptance of an offer must be absolute and unconditional. All of the terms of the offer must be accepted without change or condition. (Cal.Civ.Code § 1585) Acceptance results in the formation of a contract, both parties are bound and neither party can withdraw from the bargain without incurring liability to the other.

To be effective, an acceptance of an offer that looks to formation of a bilateral contract must be communicated to the person who made the offer. If the offer prescribes any conditions concerning the communication of its acceptance, the conditions must be conformed to, but in the absence of such conditions, any reasonable and usual mode of communication may be adopted.

Performance of the conditions of an offer, or the acceptance of the consideration offered with a proposal, is an acceptance even though a notice of acceptance is not transmitted. (See, Cal.Civ.Code § 1584; See also, 1 Witkin, Summary of Cal. Law (9th ed. 1987) Contracts, §§ 189, 190, 193-196, 200.)

Option Contracts

An option contract is a promise not to withdraw or revoke an offer for a stated period of time. However, unless separate consideration is given in exchange for the promise not to revoke or withdraw the offer, the promise is merely a gratuitous promise and unenforceable. Under the California rule, the holder of a formal option loses the right to exercise it once it has communicated a formal rejection, and this is so even though the purported exercise occurs within the time specified in the option agreement. (*Landberg v. Landberg* (1972) 24 Cal.App.3d 742, 757 [101 Cal.Rptr. 335].)

Marsh v. Lott
Court of Appeals of California, Second District, 1908
8 Cal.App. 384, 97 P. 163

SHAW, J.

Action for specific performance of a contract, whereby plaintiff asserts that in consideration of 25 cents he was given an option to purchase, for the sum of $100,000, certain real estate owned by defendant. Judgment was rendered for defendant. Plaintiff appeals from the judgment, and from an order denying his motion for a new trial.

The contract, specific performance of which is sought, is as follows: "For and in consideration of the sum of twenty-five cents to me in hand paid, I hereby give Robt. Marsh & Co. an option to purchase, at any time up to and including June 1st, 1905, with privilege of 30 days extension, from date hereof, the following described property, to wit: South 1/2 of lot 9 & all of lot 8, block 101, Bellevue Terrace tract, and all of the property owned by myself in above block, for the sum of one hundred thousand dollars, payable thirty thousand cash, balance on or before 4 years, 4 1/2 % net. I agree to furnish an unlimited certificate of title showing said property to be free from all incumbrance, and to convey the same in such condition by deed of grant, bargain and sale, & pay regular commission. M.A. Lott. [Seal.] Date: Feby. 25th, 1905. Property: 90x165. Building: 6 flats—2 cottages. Rents: $260.00." On June 1, 1905, plaintiff notified defendant in writing that he exercised the right accorded by said contract regarding the extension of time therein specified, and elected to extend the same for a period of 30 days. On June 2, 1905, defendant, by a written instrument served upon plaintiff, revoked said option, and notified him that she withdrew said property from sale.

On June 29, 1905, within the extended time, plaintiff left at the residence of defendant an instrument, of which the following is a copy: "June 29, 1905. Mrs. M.A. Lott, 507 South Olive Street, City. Dear Madame: Referring to your agreement with me dated February 25, 1905, by which you gave me the privilege of purchasing the south half of lot nine and the whole of lot eight, in block one hundred and one, Bellevue Terrace tract, in this city, I again tender you in gold coin of the United States the sum of $30,000 as provided in said agreement, and demand of you performance on your part as in said agreement provided. This tender will also be made to your attorney, J. Wiseman MacDonald, Esq., as per request this morning when I tendered you $30,000 in gold coin at your residence on said property. Yours truly, Robert Marsh & Company."

The contention of appellant is that certain findings are not supported by the evidence. The findings material to a consideration of the case are as follows: The court found that the sum of 25 cents paid for the option was an inadequate and insufficient consideration for the same, and that the said option contract was not just and reasonable to defendant and no adequate consideration was paid to her for it. By finding 9 it appears that "after such revocation and withdrawal of said option, plaintiff, under the name of Robert Marsh & Co., on the 29th day of June, 1905, in an instrument left at the defendant's house, offered to pay to the defendant the sum of $30,000, and under the said name demanded from defendant a conveyance of the said property, but plaintiff did not at any time actually tender $30,000, or any sum at all in cash, to the defendant, nor did he, in his, or any other name, at any time, tender or offer to defendant any note or mortgage, or other evidence of indebtedness in the amount of $70,000, or any sum at all, either carrying interest at 4 1/2 per cent. net, or at any rate at all, nor did he, in his own name, or any other name, at any time, offer to pay defendant the balance of $70,000, on or before four years from the date of said option, or at any time, with interest at 4 1/2 per cent. net, or with or without interest." And by finding 10 it appears that "plaintiff has not duly or at all performed all and every provision and thing on his part in said option agreement contained. He has made no tender or offer to defendant, save as is set forth in finding No. 9 hereof. Plaintiff is willing to perform the matters on the part of Robert Marsh & Co. to be performed according to the terms of the said option, and is able to pay the sum of thirty thousand dollars."

If there was no sufficient consideration for the option, then it was a mere *nudum pactum*, and defendant's revocation thereof, notwithstanding her promise to the contrary, was effectual in terminating any right of plaintiff to consummate the purchase. Page on Contracts, § 35; Wristen v. Bowles, 82 Cal. 84, 22 Pac. 1136; Brown v. San Francisco Savings Union, 134 Cal. 448, 66 Pac. 592. If, on the other hand, the offer was to remain open a fixed time and was made upon a valuable consideration, equity will ignore the attempted revocation, and treat a subsequent acceptance, made within the time defined in the option, exactly as if no attempted revocation had been made. Page on Contracts, § 35; Ross v. Parks, 93 Ala. 153, 8 South. 368, 11 L.R.A. 148, 30 Am.St.Rep. 47; Black v. Maddox, 104 Ga. 157, 30 S.E. 723; Mueller v. Nortmann, 116 Wis. 468, 93 N.W. 538, 96 Am.St.Rep. 997; Guyer v. Warren, 175 Ill. 328, 51 N.E. 580.

Subdivision 1 of section 3391, of the Civil Code makes an adequate consideration for the contract one of the conditions for the specific enforcement thereof. The provision, however, has reference to the consideration to be paid for the property, the right to purchase which at a stipulated price within a given time is the subject of the option. It has no application to the sufficiency of the consideration paid for the executed contract, whereby defendant transferred to plaintiff the right to elect to purchase at the stipulated price. It is not the option which it is sought to enforce, but that which, by plaintiff's acceptance of defendant's offer, has ripened into an executory contract, whereby, for an adequate consideration, the one agrees to buy and the other agrees to sell. "The sale of an option is an executed contract; that is to say, the lands are not sold, the contract is not executed as to them, but the option is as completely sold and transferred in praesenti as a piece of personal property instantly delivered on payment of the price." Ide v. Leiser, 10 Mont. 5, 24 Pac. 695, 24 Am.St.Rep. 17. From the very nature of the case no standard exists whereby to determine the adequate value of an option to purchase specific real estate. The land has a market value susceptible of ascertainment, but the value of an option upon a piece of real estate might, and oftentimes does, depend upon proposed or possible improvements in the particular vicinity. To illustrate: If A., having information that the erection of a gigantic department store is contemplated in a certain locality, wishes an option for a specified time to purchase property owned by B. in the vicinity of such proposed improvement, and takes the option on B.'s property at the full market price at the time, must he pay a greater sum therefor because of his knowledge and the fact of B.'s ignorance of the proposed improvement? It is not possible that B., upon learning of the proposed improvement, can, in the absence of facts constituting fraud, etc., revoke or rescind the option upon the claim that he sold and transferred the right specified therein for an inadequate consideration. In our judgment any money consideration, however small, paid and received for an option to purchase property at its adequate value is binding upon the seller thereof for the time specified therein, and is irrevocable for want of its adequacy.

The provisions of section 3391, Civ.Code, are but a codification of equitable principles that have existed from time immemorial, and the sufficiency of the price paid for an option has never been measured by its adequacy. In Warvelle on Vendors (2d Ed.) § 125, it is said: "If the option is given for a valuable consideration, whether adequate or not, it cannot be withdrawn or revoked within the time fixed, and it will be binding and obligatory upon the owner, or his assigns with notice, until it expires by its own limitation." In Mathews Slate Co. v. New Empire Slate Co. (C.C.) 122 Fed. 972, it is said: "This court is of the opinion that if two persons enter into a contract in writing under seal, by which the one party, in consideration of $1, the payment of which is acknowledged, agrees to sell and convey to the other party within a specified time certain lands and premises, on payment by the other party of a specified consideration, such contract is valid and binding, and ought to be and may be specifically enforced. The seller has the right to fix his price, and covenant and agree that, on receiving that price within a certain time, he will convey the premises, and, if within that time the purchaser of the option tenders the money and demands a conveyance, he is entitled to it. To hold otherwise is to destroy the efficacy of such contracts and agreements." Mr. Freeman in his note to the case of Mueller v. Nortmann, 96 Am.St.Rep. 997, says: "An option given by the owner of land for a valuable consideration, whether adequate or not, agreeing to sell it to another at a fixed price if accepted within a specified time, is binding upon the owner and all his successors in interest with knowledge thereof." See, also, Tibbs v. Zirkle, 55 W.Va. 49, 46 S.E. 701, 104 Am.St.Rep. 977; Cummins v. Beavers, 103 Va. 230, 48 S.E. 891, 106 Am.St.Rep. 881; Mueller v. Nortmann, supra; Johnston v. Trippe

(C.C.) 33 Fed. 530. It therefore follows that the purported revocation made by defendant on June 2, 1905, was ineffectual for the purpose of terminating plaintiff's right to exercise the privilege of electing to accept the offer prior to the time designated therein for its expiration.

* * *

The finding that the consideration paid for the option was inadequate, while not supported by the evidence, is nevertheless harmless error, for the reason that had the court found in accordance with appellant's contention it could not, according to the view we take of the case, have changed the result.

There are other points ably presented by the learned counsel for appellant, but, as a consideration of such points discloses no reason for reversing either the judgment or order, it seems unnecessary to discuss them.

The judgment and order are affirmed.

When Is Acceptance Effective?

Acceptance Effective on Dispatch — The "Mailbox Rule"

A written notice of acceptance is effective when placed into the course of transmission by an authorized or reasonable means to the person who made the offer. If the accepting party uses an unauthorized or unreasonable means of transmittal, the acceptance is not effective until actually received by the person who made the offer within any time limit set forth or implied in the offer. (Cal.Civ.Code § 1583)

Gibbs v. American Savings & Loan Assn.

Court of Appeals of California, Second Appellate District, Division Five, 1990
217 Cal.App.3d 1372, 266 Cal.Rptr. 517

LUCAS, P. J.

James and Barbara Gibbs appeal from judgment against them and in favor of American Savings & Loan Association (American Savings) in their action to enforce a purported contract for the sale of real property. We affirm.

Facts

In August 1984, James and Barbara Gibbs (the Gibbses) submitted an offer for $180,000 to American Savings to purchase a house in Woodland Hills which American Savings had taken back through foreclosure. American Savings, through its employee, Dorothy Folkman, agreed that the Gibbs could move into the subject property and rent it until the close of escrow. No action was taken on this offer.

On March 27, 1985, pursuant to a request by Ms. Folkman, the Gibbs submitted a new offer because American Savings could not find their original offer. The purchase price was again $180,000. On the morning of June 6, 1985, the Gibbses received a counteroffer from American Savings containing several additional terms and conditions, but with no mention of purchase price. According to Barbara Gibbs, she immediately drove to her husband's jobsite where she and her husband signed this counteroffer. She drove to her office, typed an envelope with a certified mail tag, placed the counter-offer in the envelope, and before 10 o'clock that morning, she handed it to the mail clerk at her office, instructing him to mail it for her.

At approximately 11 a.m. that same morning, Barbara Gibbs had a telephone conversation with Dorothy Folkman in which Folkman said the counteroffer was in error, since American Savings had intended to increase the sales price to $198,000. Folkman also advised the Gibbses that because of this error, the counteroffer was revoked.

American Savings took the position that no contract had been formed. The Gibbses insisted that they had accepted the counteroffer before it was revoked and that a contract thus existed. The Gibbses brought the within action for damages, specific performance, breach of contract and declaratory relief. After trial, the court found that Barbara Gibbs did not place the acceptance of the counteroffer in the course of transmission when she gave it to the mail clerk in her office on June 6, 1985; thus there was no acceptance on that date. The postmark on the envelope was June 7, 1985. Dorothy Folkman's oral revocation of the counteroffer on June 6, 1985, preceded the Gibbses' acceptance of that counteroffer on June 7 and therefore no contract for sale of the property was ever formed. The Gibbses appeal from the judgment thereafter entered.

Discussion

* * *

[W]e find substantial evidence supports the trial court's judgment. Barbara Gibbs testified that she received the counteroffer from American Savings at about 8:45 or 9 a.m. on June 6, 1985. She and her husband signed the counteroffer at 9:39 a.m. that day. She then drove about one mile to her office, prepared an envelope and certified mail receipt, and gave the ready-to-mail, signed counteroffer to the mail clerk in her office for mailing. This purportedly occurred before 10 a.m. on June 6.

Barbara Gibbs further testified that the clerk brought the mail to the Woodland Hills Post Office and returned with her receipt by 10:15 a.m. on June 6. However, the certified mail receipt was not produced at trial, and the envelope in which the signed counteroffer was mailed to American Savings was postmarked June 7, 1985, not June 6. According to the Domestic Mail Manual of the United States Postal Service, section 144.471, the date shown in the meter postmark of any type of mail must be the actual date of deposit. Section 144.534 of the manual provides that metered mail bearing the wrong date of mailing shall be run through a canceling machine or otherwise postmarked to show the proper date. The postmarked envelope constitutes substantial evidence that the acceptance was mailed on June 7, not June 6.

Civil Code section 1583 provides: "Consent is deemed to be fully communicated between the parties as soon as the party accepting a proposal has put his acceptance in the course of transmission to the proposer, ..." This rule has long been interpreted to require that the acceptance be placed out of the control of the accepting party in order to be considered "in the course of transmission." (Ivey v. Kern County Land Co. (1896) 115 Cal. 196, 201 [46 P. 926].) Typically, this is found when the acceptance is delivered to the post office. (Morello v. Growers Grape Prod. Assn. (1947) 82 Cal.App.2d 365, 370-371 [186 P.2d 463].) California's "'effective upon posting'" rule, as codified in section 1583, thus holds that an acceptance of an offer is effective and deemed communicated upon its deposit in the mail. (Palo Alto Town & Country Village, Inc. v. BBTC Company (1974) 11 Cal.3d 494, 500-501 [113 Cal.Rptr. 705, 521 P.2d 1097].)

The postmark on the counteroffer in the case before us shows such deposit occurred on June 7, 1985, not on June 6. The counteroffer was not placed in the course of transmission beyond the control of the offeree when Barbara Gibbs gave it to the mail clerk in her office with instructions to deliver it to the post office. It was placed in the course of transmission within the meaning of Civil Code section 1583 when it was deposited with the United States Postal Service on June 7, 1985.

It is basic contract law that an offer may be revoked any time prior to acceptance. (Civ. Code, § 1586.) Both Barbara Gibbs and Dorothy Folkman from American Savings testified that they spoke together on the telephone on the morning of June 6, 1985. During that call, Folkman became aware of American Savings' error in failing to include the $198,000 purchase price in the counteroffer, advised Barbara Gibbs of the error and stated that American Savings was revoking the counteroffer. Inasmuch as the counteroffer was revoked on June 6, prior to the Gibbses' acceptance, no contract was formed.

A similar result was reached in the Florida case of Kendel v. Pontius (Fla. 1971) 244 So.2d 543, 544. In Kendel, the buyers delivered their signed acceptance to their attorney who was to mail it to the seller. Before the attorney mailed the signed acceptance to the seller, the seller revoked the offer. The court held delivery to the buyers' attorney did not constitute posting. No contract was formed because the seller's revocation preceded the mailing of the acceptance.

We find no reason to depart from this well-reasoned law.

Disposition

The judgment is affirmed.

Ashby, J., and Turner, J., concurred.

Afterthoughts

The Restatement Second of Contracts, section 63(a) provides, among other things, that if an acceptor entrusts a notice of acceptance or acceptance to his or her agent for transmittal, the acceptance is not effective until the agent puts this notice or acceptance out of his or her possession. The possession of the agent is the possession of the principal.

Termination of the Power of Acceptance

Revocation of Offers

An offer may be revoked any time prior to acceptance. (Cal.Civ.Code § 1586) This is so even though the offer is stated to be good or irrevocable for a specified period. An offer is revoked when notice of the revocation is communicated to the offeree before the offeree's acceptance is communicated to the offeror. (Cal.Civ.Code, § 1587, subd. 1.) Both revocation and acceptance can be communicated by any usual and reasonable mode and notice of revocation or acceptance is complete when placed in the course of transmission to the recipient. (*Bellasi v. Shackelford* (1962) 201 Cal.App.2d 265, 267-268 [19 Cal.Rptr. 925]; Civ. Code, §§ 1582, 1583.) Note that with respect to revocation and rejection of offers, the "majority" rule is that revocation and rejection of an offer are effective when received. However, in California, revocation and rejection are effective upon dispatch. (Cal.Civ.Code §§ 1587 and 1583.)

An offer is revoked by,

1. *Express revocation.* By the person who made the offer, giving notice of revocation to the person to whom the offer has been made, in the same manner required to communicate the acceptance; or

2. *Implied revocation.* By the person who made the offer, taking some action inconsistent with keeping the offer open, and the person to whom the offer is made receiving reliable information of that fact; or

3. *Lapse.* By the lapse of the time set forth in the offer for the acceptance, or if no time is set forth, the lapse of a reasonable time without communication of the acceptance; or by the failure of the person accepting the offer to fulfill a condition precedent to acceptance; or

4. *Rejection.* Manifestation on the part of the person to whom the offer is made, that they are not accepting the offer; or

5. *Counteroffer.* A counter-proposal made by the person to whom the offer is made; or

6. *Death or Incapacity of the Offeror.* By the death or insanity of the person making the offer. (Cal.Civ.Code § 1587)

Acceptance Varying Offer — Mirror Image Rule

An acceptance must be absolute and unqualified. A qualified acceptance is a new proposal. (Cal.Civ.Code § 1585) In other words, an acceptance, which adds qualifications or conditions or which in any way varies from the terms of the original offer, is treated as a rejection and counter offer. This is true no matter how trivial the qualification or condition. This is known as the "Mirror Image Rule." Under traditional common law, no contract was reached if the terms of the offer and the acceptance varied. A change in the terms set forth in the offer, or a conditional acceptance, is a rejection of the offer. Once an offer has been rejected, it cannot be accepted, unless the person who made the offer remakes the offer following the rejection. A change in terms, or a conditional or qualified acceptance communicated to the person who made the original offer, is a counter offer. (Cal.Civ.Code § 1585) A counter offer may be accepted, rejected totally, or rejected by a further counter offer. A contract results only when an offer or a counter offer is absolutely and unconditionally accepted. As the following case demonstrates, this rigid rule of the common law has been relaxed with respect to contracts for the sale of goods.

Contracts for the Sale of Goods — Abandonment of the Mirror Image Rule

Steiner v. Mobil Oil Corp.

Supreme Court of California, 1977
20 Cal.3d 90, 569 P.2d 751, 141 Cal.Rptr. 157

TOBRINER, J.

In this case, over one year after apparently accepting plaintiff's offer, the Mobil Oil Corporation sought to impose upon plaintiff the very contractual terms which plaintiff expressly rejected in his offer. As justification for its conduct, Mobil asserted that the crucial provision of plaintiff's offer was lost in the labyrinth of the Mobil bureaucracy, and thus that Mobil decisionmakers had no opportunity to pass on plaintiff's offer as such. [1a] As we shall see, however, the trial court correctly concluded that section 2207 of the California Uniform Commercial Code bars Mobil from in this way converting its own error into plaintiff's misfortune.

Section 2207, subdivision (1), provides that parties may form an agreement, even if the terms of offer and acceptance do not entirely converge, if the offeree gives a definite expression of acceptance, and if the terms of acceptance do not explicitly condition agreement upon the offeror's consent to the offeree's new proposed terms. In this case, as the trial court found, defendant Mobil did not condition its acceptance of plaintiff's offer upon plaintiff's agreement to Mobil's alteration of plaintiff's offer and thus a contract was formed. Section 2207, subdivision (2), provides in turn that, if the terms of the offer and acceptance differ, the terms of the offer become part of a contract between merchants if the offer expressly limits acceptance to its own terms, or if the varying terms of the acceptance materially alter the terms of the offer. As the trial court found, under either of these clauses, the terms of Steiner's offer must prevail, because Steiner's offer was expressly conditional upon Mobil's agreement to provide a guaranteed discount, and Mobil's substitution of a discount terminable at its discretion materially affected Steiner's interests.

Accordingly, the trial court did not err in granting judgment for plaintiff, and we shall thus affirm its judgment.

1. The facts in this case

Defendant Mobil Oil Corporation, in appealing from a judgment for plaintiff Steiner, does not challenge the facts as found by the trial court, but rather confines itself to an attack on the trial court's conclusions of law. The facts in this case, thus, are not in dispute.

Joseph R. Steiner is an independent service station operator. He purchases the gasoline which he sells from Mobil, but, except for any incidental rights which the gasoline contract confers, Mobil owns no interest in Steiner's property.

In 1971, the third party who leased the service station property to Steiner informed him that the property was for sale. Steiner contacted Mobil sales representative Tony Montemarano. Montemarano informed Steiner that Mobil would not purchase the property, but that Mobil was interested in assisting Steiner in making the purchase.

Thereafter, Steiner entered into extended negotiations with J. S. Chenen, Mobil's area manager and Montemarano's superior. Steiner and Chenen agreed that Mobil would supply the down payment on the property, amounting to $30,000. In return, Steiner would enter into a 10-year contract with Mobil. The contract would treat the cash advance as a prepaid competitive allowance, to be amortized over the 10-year period through Steiner's purchase of 5.8 million gallons of gasoline.

The negotiations did not terminate with the agreement concerning the down payment. Steiner had concluded that he would not be able to do business successfully if he were compelled to purchase gasoline from Mobil at the standard tank wagon price. As the trial court found, Steiner told Chenen that he, Steiner, "needed a firm competitive allowance for the length of his distributor's agreement to make his cash flow adequate to meet the payments on the property." Steiner and Chenen agreed that a satisfactory arrangement with Mobil would include not only the $30,000 prepaid competitive allowance, but also a further competitive allowance reducing Mobil's tank wagon price by 1.4 cents per gallon. Mobil would also supply Steiner with $3,000 worth of improvements.

As Chenen made clear to Steiner, neither Chenen nor his immediate supervisor, district manager D. L. Dalbec, possessed the authority to accept the negotiated terms on

Mobil's behalf. The negotiations therefore did not culminate in an agreement as such but rather in a proposal to be submitted to R. D. Pfaff, the division general manager, who did possess authority to agree to the proposal on Mobil's behalf.

Moreover, the proposal did not take the form of a documented single contract. Chenen and Steiner utilized a series of standard Mobil forms in putting together the proposal, modifying the forms where necessary. Steiner signed those of the forms, such as the basic retail dealer contract, which required his signature. The package of documents which comprised the proposal, therefore, needed only Pfaff's approval to become effective.

Near the close of the process of negotiating and assembling the proposal, Steiner obtained a copy of the standard Mobil form which would embody the 1.4 cents per gallon competitive allowance. This form, which did not require Steiner's signature, stated: "This allowance may be changed or discontinued by us at any time upon notice to you in writing...." Upon receipt of the form Steiner immediately contacted Chenen by telephone, told Chenen that he would not go ahead with the deal if Mobil could revoke the competitive allowance at any time, and demanded assurances that no such revocation would occur.

In order to placate Steiner, Chenen, after consultation and authorization from Dalbec, sent Steiner a letter, dated December 2, 1971, which declared "[¶] The ten year Retail Dealer Contract dated December 15, 1971, effective January 1, 1972, is signed by you on the basis that Mobil grant a $30,000 Prepaid Competitive Allowance, and a $.014 Competitive Allowance at time of delivery. [¶] If Mobil management does not accept in full the above conditions outlined in your competitive offer, the above mentioned contract will be void."

The trial court found that "Chenen was authorized by Mobil to write the letter" to Steiner. Moreover, as the trial court also found, because of the letter, "through ... Chenen and Dalbec Mobil had both knowledge and notice" of Steiner's demand for a guaranteed competitive allowance. "Mobil had reason to know that the transaction and agreement would be materially affected and that plaintiff would not enter therein if [the guaranteed discount] term was not part of the 'package.'" The trial court further concluded that, for Chenen and Dalbec, the transmission of Steiner's offer to division general manager Pfaff "was part of their regular duties" and thus that Chenen and Dalbec "were obligated, in the exercise of good faith and ordinary care and diligence, to communicate the substance of plaintiff's [offer] to Pfaff."

In fact, however, Chenen and Dalbec did not transmit to Pfaff the letter which Chenen had sent to Steiner; Mobil's copy of that letter remained in the district office files. In preparing the proposal for submission to Pfaff, Chenen and Dalbec assembled a package which included the various documents that Steiner had executed, the standard form providing the revocable 1.4 cents per gallon competitive allowance, and various memoranda explaining the advantages of the deal for Mobil. Early in 1972, several months after Chenen and Dalbec had transmitted the proposal to him, Pfaff approved it as submitted.

Chenen informed Steiner of Pfaff's approval by telephone. Steiner had called Chenen to find out what was happening with the proposal which they had negotiated. Chenen told Steiner that Mobil had a check for him, and that the next thing for Steiner to do was to open an escrow account and proceed with the purchase of the property.

Subsequently, Montemarano delivered to Steiner at his service station a manila folder containing the documents approved by Pfaff. These documents, the trial court found, were "numerous and complex in nature." Nonetheless, there was no cover letter describing the contents of the folder. Although the folder included Mobil's standard competitive allowance form, with its clause providing for revocation at will, Montemarano did not call this fact to Steiner's attention.

Thus, as the trial court found, at no time after Chenen sent Steiner the December 2 letter "did Mobil advise [Steiner] that a non-cancellable allowance would not be part of the agreement." Moreover, Steiner "did not at any time reread all of the documents delivered to him by Mobil, particularly the form letter ... setting forth the provision regarding the 1.4 cents per gallon competitive allowance being cancellable." Mobil did not "specifically bring" to Steiner's attention "the statements made in the form letter ... concerning the cancellable condition of the competitive allowance."

By April 1972, Steiner had completed the process of acquiring the service station property. Beginning in March, Mobil afforded Steiner the benefit of the 1.4 cents per gallon competitive allowance in billing him for gasoline and continued to do so until the summer of 1973. On July 16, 1973, Chenen informed Steiner by letter that, in accordance with the provisions of Mobil's notice of competitive allowance, Mobil would reduce Steiner's discount to 0.5 cents per gallon as of August 1, 1973.

Steiner brought this suit in the Los Angeles County Superior Court, seeking declaratory and monetary relief. The trial court, sitting without a jury, found that Mobil "had reason to know" that Steiner would not enter into an agreement unless Mobil agreed that he "was to have a non-cancellable ... competitive allowance ... to run as long as the distributor agreement was in force." Moreover, the trial court found, in returning the package of documents to Steiner, "Mobil intended to make a contract, not to make a counter offer." The trial court concluded that "in the exercise of good faith and reasonable care and diligence Mobil was required to specifically bring to the attention of plaintiff the statements made in the form letter sent by Dalbec concerning the cancellable condition of the competitive allowance."

The trial court ruled that, under California Uniform Commercial Code section 2207, Mobil had entered into a contract with Steiner which guaranteed Steiner a 1.4 cents per gallon discount for 10 years. "Mobil made a definite and seasonable expression of acceptance of plaintiff's offer, although its reply contained a material term different from that offer." Moreover, "[i]n accepting plaintiff's offer Mobil did not either orally or in writing expressly condition its acceptance upon plaintiff's assent to the different terms as to the competitive allowance in Mobil's acceptance." The trial court granted Steiner a declaratory judgment to that effect, and awarded Steiner damages of $4,953.63. Mobil appeals the trial court's judgment.

2. Under California Uniform Commercial Code section 2207, Steiner's contract with Mobil grants Steiner a 1.4 cents per gallon discount for the duration of the contract.

Neither Mobil nor Steiner disputes the trial court's conclusion that the sales provisions of the California Uniform Commercial Code apply in this case. Moreover, Mobil and Steiner do not challenge the trial court's conclusion that the outcome of this case turns on the applicability of section 2207. As we shall see, the relevant provisions of that statute confirm the trial court's conclusion that Mobil breached its agreement with Steiner when it unilaterally reduced Steiner's competitive discount. Initially, we shall identify the considerations which underlie section 2207 and thus structure our interpretation of the statute. Thereafter, we shall proceed to the application of section 2207 itself.

Under traditional common law, no contract was reached if the terms of the offer and the acceptance varied. "In order to make a bargain it is necessary that the acceptor shall give in return for the offeror's promise exactly the consideration which the offeror requests." (1 Williston, The Law of Contracts (1st ed. 1920) § 73, p. 128.) This "mirror image" rule of offer and acceptance was plainly both unfair and unrealistic in the commercial context. "The fact that the parties did intend a contract to be formed and both had a reasonable commercial understanding that the deal was closed, is ignored." (Murray, Intention Over Terms: An Exploration of UCC 2-207 and New Section 60, Restatement of Contracts (1969) 37 Fordham L.Rev. 317, 319.)

Section 2207 rejects the "mirror image" rule. (See e.g., Roto-Lith, Ltd. v. F. P. Bartlett & Co. (1st Cir. 1962) 297 F.2d 497, 500.) "This section of the Code recognizes that in current commercial transactions, the terms of the offer and those of the acceptance will seldom be identical." (Dorton v. Collins & Aikman Corp. (6th Cir. 1972) 453 F.2d 1161, 1166.)

Under section 2207, for example, the parties may conclude a contract despite the fact that, after reaching accord, they exchanged forms which purport to memorialize the agreement, but which differ because each party has drafted his form "to give him advantage." (White & Summers, Uniform Commercial Code (1972) p. 23; see, e.g., Rite Fabrics, Inc. v. Stafford-Higgins Co., Inc. (S.D.N.Y. 1973) 366 F.Supp. 1.) Similarly, the parties may form a contract even if the terms of offer and acceptance differ because one or the other party, in stating its initial position, relies upon "forms drafted to cover the majority of [its] transactions in a uniform, standard manner" (Duesenberg & King, Sales and Bulk Transfers under the Uniform Commercial Code (1976) § 3.02, p. 3-9), and subsequently fails to amend its form to reflect the deal which the other party claims was actually negotiated. (See, e.g., Ebasco Services Inc. v. Pennsylvania Power & L. Co. (E.D.Pa. 1975) 402 F. Supp. 421, 434-435.)

In place of the "mirror image" rule, section 2207 inquires as to whether the parties intended to complete an agreement: "Under this Article a proposed deal which in commercial understanding has in fact been closed is recognized as a contract." (§ 2207, Cal. U. Com. Code, com. 2.) If the parties intend to contract, but the terms of their offer and acceptance differ, section 2207 authorizes a court to determine which terms are part of the contract, either by reference to the parties' own dealings (see § 2207, subds. (1), (2)), or by reference to other provisions of the code. (See § 2207, subd. (3).)

Section 2207 is thus of a piece with other recent developments in contract law. Instead of fastening upon abstract doctrinal concepts like offer and acceptance, section 2207 looks to the actual dealings of the parties and gives legal effect to that conduct. Much as adhesion contract analysis teaches us not to enforce contracts until we look behind the facade of the formalistic standardized agreement in order to determine whether any inequality of bargaining power between the parties renders contractual terms unconscionable, or causes the contract to be interpreted against the more powerful party, section 2207 instructs us not to refuse to enforce contracts until we look below the surface of the parties' disagreement as to contract terms and determine whether the parties undertook to close their deal. Section 2207 requires courts to put aside the formal and academic stereotypes of traditional doctrine of offer and acceptance and to analyze instead what really happens. In this spirit, we turn to the application of section 2207 in this case.

Section 2207, subdivision (1), provides: "A definite and seasonable expression of acceptance or a written confirmation which is sent within a reasonable time operates as an acceptance even though it states terms additional or different from those offered or agreed upon, unless acceptance is expressly made conditional on assent to the additional or different terms."

In this case, as the trial court found, Mobil provided "[a] definite and seasonable expression of acceptance." Steiner offered to enter into a 10-year dealer contract with Mobil only if Mobil, among other things, agreed to advance Steiner $30,000, and to give Steiner a 1.4 cents per gallon competitive discount on the price of Mobil gasoline for the duration of the contract. When Steiner telephoned Chenen, Mobil's employee, to inquire as to the fate of Steiner's offer, Chenen told Steiner that Mobil had a check for him, that he should open an escrow account, and that he should go ahead with the purchase of the service station property—in context a clear statement that Mobil had approved the deal.

Moreover, through Montemarano, another Mobil employee, Mobil returned to Steiner various executed documents in an envelope unaccompanied by any cover. The documents provided written confirmation of the deal. The fact that Mobil returned the documents without in any way calling Steiner's attention to them is further evidence that Mobil regarded the process of negotiation as over and the deal as complete.

As the trial court also found, Mobil did not in any way make its acceptance "expressly ... conditional" on Steiner's "assent to the additional or different terms." Chenen, in telling Steiner to go ahead with the purchase, did not suggest that Mobil had conditioned its acceptance. In returning the executed documents, Mobil enclosed no cover letter; again, it did not use the occasion in any way to condition expressly its acceptance.

Thus, neither of the restrictions which limit section 2207, subdivision (1)'s application are relevant in this case. Despite the fact that the terms of Mobil's acceptance departed partially from the terms of Steiner's offer, Mobil and Steiner did form a contract. To determine the terms of this contract, we turn to section 2207, subdivision (2).

Section 2207, subdivision (2), provides: " ... additional terms are to be construed as proposals for addition to the contract. Between merchants such terms become part of the contract unless: [¶] (a) The offer expressly limits acceptance to the terms of the offer; [¶] (b) They materially alter it; or [¶] (c) Notification of objection to them has already been given or is given within a reasonable time after notice of them is received."

Under section 2207, subdivision (2), Mobil's revocable discount provision does not become part of the agreement between Steiner and Mobil. In order to become part of the agreement, Mobil's provision must not fall within any of the categories defined by section 2207, subdivision (2), subsections (a), (b), and (c). Mobil's term, however, clearly comes within subsections (a) and (b).

Subsection (a) provides that no additional term can become part of the agreement if Steiner's offer "expressly limit[ed] acceptance to the terms of the offer." (§ 2207, subd. (2)(a).) Mobil concedes that Steiner's offer provided that the competitive allowance of 1.4 cents per gallon would run for the full length of the 10-year dealer contract. Chenen's December 2 letter to Steiner explicitly acknowledges Mobil's awareness that "[i]f Mobil management does not accept in full the above conditions outlined in your competitive offer, the above mentioned contract is void."

Moreover, Mobil's acceptance falls within subsection (b) since without question the acceptance "materially alter[ed]" the terms of Steiner's offer. (See § 2207, subd. (2)(b).) The Uniform Commercial Code comment notes that a variation is material if it would "result in surprise or hardship if incorporated without express awareness by the other party...." (§ 2-207, U. Com. Code, com. 4.) Here, Steiner clearly indicated to Mobil in the course of the negotiations that, without the 1.4 cents per gallon discount, he could not economically operate the service station. Mobil's alteration, therefore, amended the terms of the offer to Steiner's significant detriment; accordingly, the alteration was necessarily "material."

To reiterate, subsections (a), (b), and (c) of section 2207, subdivision (2), operate in the alternative. If any one of the three subsections applies, the variant terms of an acceptance do not become part of an agreement. Here, as we have seen, the provisions of both subsections (a) and (b) are met. Mobil's declaration that the 1.4 cents per gallon discount was terminable at Mobil's discretion did not become part of the contract. Instead, Steiner and Mobil formed a contract incorporating the terms of Steiner's offer: Under this contract, Steiner was guaranteed a 1.4 cents per gallon discount throughout the 10-year period of the dealer contract.

Thus, on their face, subdivisions (1) and (2) of section 2207 confirm the trial court's conclusion that Mobil breached its agreement with Steiner. We now turn to Mobil's opposing argument that we should adopt an interpretation of section 2207 which conflicts with the trial court's conclusion.

3. Contrary to Mobil's argument, California Uniform Commercial Code sections 2204 and 2207 do not incorporate the traditional rule that parties to a contract must mutually assent to all essential terms.

We set forth Mobil's contentions, which, although elaborately developed, can be simply stated. Section 2207 does not apply if the general contract formation rules of section 2204 are not met. Section 2204 does not change the traditional rule that, in order to create an enforceable contract, the parties must mutually assent to all essential terms of the supposed agreement. In order to square section 2207 with section 2204, Mobil argues, we must construe section 2207, subdivision (1), to provide that there is no "definite" acceptance unless the parties agree to all essential terms. Moreover, Mobil contends, we must also hold that, under the same section, an acceptance which alters an essential term of an offer is an acceptance "expressly made conditional on assent" to the variant term. Finally, Mobil concludes that, since its acceptance, in changing the duration of the discount, modified an essential term of Steiner's offer, i.e., price, we must find that Steiner cannot claim a continued discount.

As we shall explain, Mobil's arguments do not survive scrutiny. The official comments accompanying section 2204, other provisions of the code, and the case law interpreting section 2204, all support the conclusion that section 2204 does not require mutual assent to all essential terms. Mobil's interpretations of the definite agreement and conditional acceptance provisions of section 2207, subdivision (1), likewise conflict with other subdivisions of section 2207.

a. California Uniform Commercial Code section 2204 does not incorporate the traditional requirement of mutual assent to all essential terms.

Section 2204 incorporates three subdivisions. The third of these subdivisions directly refutes Mobil's claims. "Even though one or more terms are left open a contract for sale does not fail for indefiniteness if the parties have intended to make a contract and there is a reasonably certain basis for giving an appropriate remedy." (§ 2204, subd. (3).)

Section 2204, subdivision (3), does not, by its terms, require parties to a contract to assent to all essential terms. Instead, this provision states that a court, if it is to enforce a contract, must first make two findings. Initially, the court must find some basis for concluding that the parties engaged in a process of offer and acceptance, rather than inconclusive negotiations. Second, the court must find that it possesses sufficient information about the parties' incomplete transaction to apply the provisions of the California Uniform Commercial Code which fill in the gaps in parties' contracts. As we have already seen, both of these minimal requirements are met in this case: the parties did not engage in inconclusive negotiations, and section 2207 readily fills in the terms of their contract.

To overcome the literal language of section 2204, subdivision (2), Mobil argues that the traditional requirement of "a meeting of the minds upon the essential features of the agreement" (Ellis v. Klaff (1950) 96 Cal.App.2d 471, 478 [216 P.2d 15]; see Roffinella v. Roffinella (1923) 191 Cal. 753, 758 [218 P. 397]) is so fundamental that the code could not conceivably have rejected it. The California code comment, however, explicitly states: "'[A] meeting of the minds on the essential features of the agreement' is not required...." (§ 2204, com. 2.)

Other code provisions sustain the comment's view. As we have already pointed out, section 2207, subdivision (2)(b), expressly acknowledges the possibility that parties may reach a contract without agreeing to all "material" terms. Mobil does not attempt to distinguish "material" from "essential" terms; in any event, we do not think that it could successfully do so. Section 2305, subdivision (1), provides an even more dramatic refutation of Mobil's argument. As we have noted, Mobil treats price as an "essential" term. Nonetheless, this section states: "The parties if they so intend can conclude a contract for sale even though the price is not settled." (§ 2305, subd. (1).)

The case law interpreting section 2204 reinforces the interpretation offered by the code comment and the implication of other code provisions: the rules of contract formation under the California Uniform Commercial Code do not include the principle that the parties must agree to all essential terms in order to form a contract. Courts have held that, under section 2204, subdivision (3), parties may form a contract even though they do not agree as to the terms of payment (Southwest Engineering Co. v. Martin Tractor Co. (1970) 205 Kan. 684 [473 P.2d 18, 23-24]), the time or place for performance (Taunton v. Allenberg Cotton Company, Inc. (M.D.Ga. 1973) 378 F.Supp. 34, 39), or the quantity of the goods sold (City of Louisville v. Rockwell Manufacturing Co. (6th Cir. 1973) 482 F.2d 159, 164)—all terms which might appear to be "essential" to an agreement.

More significantly, in view of Mobil's emphasis on the essential character of price terms, a number of courts have held that, under section 2204, subdivision (3), the parties may frame a contract without fully agreeing as to price. (See, e.g., Alter & Sons, Inc. v. United Engineers & Constructors, Inc. (S.D.Ill. 1973) 366 F.Supp. 959, 965; J. W. Knapp Co. v. Sinas (1969) 19 Mich.App. 427 [172 N.W.2d 867, 869]; see also Oskey Gasoline and Oil Company, Inc. v. OKC Refining Inc., supra, 364 F.Supp. 1137, 1144.) Concededly, one court has suggested in dictum that section 2204, subdivision (3), incorporates the requirement of assent to essential terms. (See Blackhawk Heat. & P. Co., Inc. v. Data Lease Fin. Corp. (Fla. 1974) 302 So.2d 404, 408.) We think, however, that the Delaware Supreme Court stated the prevailing view: "[T]he omission of even an important term does not prevent the finding under [section 2204, subdivision (3)] that the parties intended to make a contract." (Pennsylvania Co. v. Wilmington Trust Co. (1960) 39 Del.Ch. 453, 463 [166 A.2d 726].)

b. California Uniform Commercial Code section 2207, subdivision (1), should not be narrowly read to conform to the principle of mutual assent to all essential terms.

As we have seen, section 2204 quite clearly does not incorporate the rule that parties must mutually assent to all essential terms. Mobil has thus failed to establish the premise that it would postulate as justifying a narrow reading of section 2207, subdivision (1). We shall, however, briefly consider Mobil's other and further arguments concerning the construction of section 2207, and show that these arguments, taken in isolation, are consistent neither with the language of section 2207, subdivision (1), nor with the logic of section 2207 as a whole.

Initially, Mobil focuses on section 2207, subdivision (1)'s requirement of a "definite ... expression of acceptance." Mobil would define "definite" by reference to the extent of the difference between offer and acceptance: the more significant the divergence, the less definitely a response is an acceptance. This construction suffers from two flaws. First, in section 2207, subdivision (1), "definite" modifies "expression" and not "acceptance," and thus refers to the process of offer and acceptance and not to the terms of the acceptance itself. Second, in any event, section 2207 as a whole bars any interpretation of "definite" which, as Mobil urges, would exclude from the ranks of acceptances all but collateral variations on the terms of offers. Section 2207, subdivision (2)(b)'s concern with material variations necessarily implies that acceptances incorporating such variations can satisfy the requirements of subdivision (1).

Mobil would also construe the final clause of section 2207, subdivision (1), which provides that, if acceptance "is expressly made conditional on assent to ... additional or different terms," the "acceptance" does not operate as an acceptance but as a counteroffer. Specifically Mobil argues that we should read this provision broadly, by adopting the interpretation advanced in Roto-Lith, Ltd. v. F. P. Bartlett & Co., supra, 297 F.2d at page 500: "a response which states a condition materially altering the obligation solely to the disadvantage of the offeror is an 'acceptance ... expressly ... conditional on assent to the additional ... terms.'"

Again, however, Mobil's construction does not accord with the language of the section. Such an interpretation of the conditional acceptance clause would transform acceptances into counteroffers without regard to whether the acceptance is in fact, as section 2207, subdivision (1), requires, "expressly made conditional on assent to ... additional or different terms." Moreover, under Mobil's reading, the conditional acceptance clause of section 2207, subdivision (1), would largely duplicate the function of the material variation clause of section 2207, subdivision (2)(b).

As Mobil concedes, courts and commentators alike have repeatedly criticized the Roto-Lith interpretation of section 2207, subdivision (1). (See, e.g., Dorton v. Collins & Aikman Corp., supra, 453 F.2d at p. 1168 & fn. 5; Duesenberg & King, supra, § 3.04 [1], pp. 3-40 to 3-49; 76 Harv.L.Rev. (1963) 1481.) Most courts have rejected Roto-Lith, and have instead interpreted the conditional acceptance clause literally, as we did earlier. (See Ebasco Services Inc. v. Pennsylvania Power & L. Co., supra, 402 F.Supp. at pp. 437-438.) Recognizing the superiority of the majority view, we reject Mobil's attempt to advance the Roto-Lith interpretation of section 2207, subdivision (1).

4. Conclusion.

In this case, as we have seen, the trial court correctly concluded that under section 2207 the guaranteed discount included in the terms of Steiner's offer, and not Mobil's standard revocable discount provision, became part of the agreement between Mobil and Steiner. Mobil cannot assert as a defense the failure of its own bureaucracy to respond to, or even fully recognize, Steiner's efforts to modify the standard Mobil dealer contract.

The judgment is affirmed.

Bird, C. J., Mosk, J., Clark, J., Richardson, J., Manuel, J., and Jefferson, J., concurred.

Afterthoughts

An exception to the common law mirror image rule exists in the context of contracts for the sale of goods. (See Calif. Commercial Code §§ 2204-2207 [UCC §§ 2-204-2-207])

The question of the relevance of the distinction between "additional" and "different" terms has become a matter of some controversy among courts and commentators. Section 2207, subdivision (1), refers to acceptances in which terms are either "additional to or different from" the terms of an offer. Section 2207, subdivision (2), however, expressly concerns itself with only "additional terms." Noting this difference, several courts and commentators have concluded that section 2207, subdivision (2), applies if an acceptance adds terms to an offer, but does not apply if an acceptance alters the terms of an offer. (See, e.g., *American Parts Co., Inc. v. American Arbitration Ass'n* (1967) 8 Mich.App. 156 [154 N.W.2d 5, 11].) Other courts and commentators, however, suggest that section 2207, subdivision (2), applies without regard to whether the varying terms of an acceptance differ from or add to an offer. (See, e.g., *Ebasco Services Inc. v. Pennsylvania Power & L. Co.*, 402 F.Supp. 421, 440 & fn. 27; Comment, Section 2-207 of the Uniform Commercial Code—New Rules for the "Battle of the Forms" (1971) 32 U.Pitt.L.Rev. 209, 211.)

In *Steiner, supra,* The Supreme Court concluded that the applicability of section 2207, subdivision (2), should not turn upon a characterization of the varying terms of an acceptance as "additional" or "different." First, Uniform Commercial Code comment 3 specifically states that "[w]hether or not additional or different terms will become part of the agreement depends upon the provisions of subsection (2)."; see also UCC com. 2.) Second, the distinction between "additional" and "different" terms is ambiguous. Since an offer's silence with respect to a particular issue may indicate an intention to adopt the code's gap-filling provisions, even an acceptance of a term which at first glance appears to be plainly "additional" is at least arguably "different." (See Air Products & Chem., Inc. v. Fairbanks Morse, Inc. (1973) 58 Wis.2d 193 [206 N.W.2d 414, 424].) Third, the distinction between additional and different terms serves no clear purpose. If additional and different terms are treated alike for purposes of section 2207, subdivision (2), an offeror does not, as some contend, lose "the ability to retain control over the terms of his offer." (Duesenberg & King, supra, at p. 3-37.) Under section 2207, subdivision (2), if the offeror wishes to retain such control, he may do so by framing his offer so that it "expressly limits acceptance to the terms of the offer...." (§ 2207, subd. (2)(a).) (Footnote 5 of *Steiner* opinion.)

Contract Must Be Certain as to Its Essential Terms

A contract will be enforced if it is sufficiently definite for the court to ascertain the parties' obligations and to determine whether those obligations have been performed or breached. (*Boyd v. Bevilacqua* (1966) 247 Cal.App.2d 272, 287 [55 Cal.Rptr. 610]; *Hennefer v. Butcher* (1986) 182 Cal.App.3d 492, 500- 501 [227 Cal.Rptr. 318]; *Robinson & Wilson, Inc. v. Stone* (1973) 35 Cal.App.3d 396, 407 [110 Cal.Rptr. 675].) Stated otherwise, the contract will be enforced if it is possible to reach a fair and just result even if, in the process, the court is required to fill in some gaps. (*Okun v. Morton* (1988) 203 Cal.App.3d 805, 817 [250 Cal.Rptr. 220].)

Where any of the essential terms of an apparent agreement are left for future determination, and it is understood by the parties that the agreement is not complete until they are settled, or where it is understood that the agreement is incomplete until reduced to writing and signed by the parties, no contract results until this is done.

An agreement definite in its essential terms is not rendered unenforceable by reason of uncertainty in some minor, nonessential detail. Such details may be left to the further agreement of the parties.

When a consideration is executory, (yet to be performed) it is not indispensable that the contract should specify its amount or the means of ascertaining it. It may be left to the decision of a third person, or regulated by any specified standard. (Cal.Civ.Code § 1610.) Though an essential term is uncertain or not agreed upon, if the contract provides a means or formula by which that essential term can be determined, the contract is enforceable. Performance by the parties may also render clear what was uncertain, and the contract becomes enforceable.(See, 1 Witkin, Summary of Cal. Law (9th ed. 1987) Contracts, §§ 147, 155, 156.)

"Where the matters left for future agreement are unessential, each party will be forced to accept a reasonable determination of the unsettled point, or if possible the unsettled point may be left unperformed and the remainder of the contract be enforced." (*City of Los Angeles v. Superior Court* (1959) 51 Cal.2d 423, 433, 333 P.2d 745, 750.)

Chapter 3

The Statute of Frauds

Oral contracts are legal and valid. Unless some law provides otherwise, an oral, or a partly oral and partly written contract, is as valid and enforceable as a written contract. (Cal.Civil Code § 1622) However, an important exception to the above general rule is found in the Statute of Frauds. The Statute of Frauds provides that certain types of contracts are invalid unless evidenced by a written note or memorandum thereof, signed by the party to be charged. California's basic Statute of Frauds, which is based on the original English Statute of Frauds enacted in 1677, is set forth, in part, below.

California Civil Code Section 1624.

(a) The following contracts are invalid, unless they, or some note or memorandum thereof, are in writing and subscribed by the party to be charged or by the party's agent:

(1) An agreement that by its terms is not to be performed within a year from the making thereof.

(2) A special promise to answer for the debt, default, or miscarriage of another, except in the cases provided for in Section 2794.

(3) An agreement for the leasing for a longer period than one year, or for the sale of real property, or of an interest therein; such an agreement, if made by an agent of the party sought to be charged, is invalid, unless the authority of the agent is in writing, subscribed by the party sought to be charged.

(4) An agreement authorizing or employing an agent, broker, or any other person to purchase or sell real estate, or to lease real estate for a longer period than one year, or to procure, introduce, or find a purchaser or seller of real estate or a lessee or lessor of real estate where the lease is for a longer period than one year, for compensation or a commission.

(5) An agreement that by its terms is not to be performed during the lifetime of the promisor.

(6) An agreement by a purchaser of real property to pay an indebtedness secured by a mortgage or deed of trust upon the property purchased, unless assumption of the indebtedness by the purchaser is specifically provided for in the conveyance of the property.

Other California Statutes That Require Written Contracts

"Statute of Frauds" is a collective term describing the various statutory provisions which render unenforceable certain types of contracts unless they are evidenced by a writing. In addition to the "basic" Statute of Frauds contained in Civil Code section 1624, various other California statutes require that certain types of contracts be put in writing. (Home improvement contracts in excess of $500; (Bus. & Prof. Code, §7159); mobilehome sales (Health & Saf. Code, §18035.1); prepaid rental listing services (Bus. & Prof. Code, §10167.9); home solicitation contracts (Cal.Civ.Code, §1689.7); automotive repairs (Bus. & Prof. Code, §9884.9,); dance studio lessons (Cal.Civ.Code, §1812.52); health studio services (Cal.Civ.Code, §1812.82); discount buying services (Cal.Civ.Code, §1812.107); funeral services (Bus. & Prof. Code, §7685.2); attorney fee contracts (Bus. & Prof. Code, §6147, and §6148); and contracts for the sale of goods for a price of $500 or more. (Cal.Comm.Code §2201.) [Partial list.])

Equal Dignities Rule

Authority granted to an agent to enter into a contract that is within the statute of frauds (i.e., its operation and enforceability depend upon compliance with the writing requirements of the statute) can only be given by an instrument in writing. (Cal.Civ.Code §2309.) This is known as the "equal dignities rule."

Contracts That Are within the Statute of Frauds

Contracts Not To Be Performed within One Year

A contract that by its terms is not to be performed within a year from the making thereof is within the Statute of Frauds. (Cal.Civ.Code §1624(a)(1).)

White Lighting Co. v. Wolfson
Supreme Court of California, 1968.
68 Cal.2d 336, 438 P.2d 345, 66 Cal.Rptr. 697

TOBRINER, J.

Although it discusses other matters, this opinion sets forth three principal rulings: first, that the statute of frauds does not apply to an oral employment contract, even though it provides in part for the measurement of the employee's compensation by annual receipts of the employer, unless its terms foreclose the employee's completion of the performance of the contract within one year; second, that the statute of frauds does not apply to an oral contract in its entirety if the court by reference to the terms of the agreement can separate those promises of performance not falling within the statute from those that do so; third, that a claim based on excessive attachment constitutes a cause of action for abuse of process rather than for malicious prosecution and such a claim may be brought in the action in which the attachment issued.

Plaintiff White Lighting Company, hereinafter "White," sued defendant Wolfson to recover $850 for money due and owing. Wolfson denied the indebtedness and filed his first cross-complaint against White, Shaft (the president, controlling owner, and a director of White), Beber (an officer and director of White), and Basin (a corporation) on November 9, 1964. The cross-complaint alleged in substance that Wolfson and cross-defendants entered into an oral employment contract which obligated White to employ Wolfson on a "permanent" basis; that in connection with it Wolfson had been fraudulently induced to buy 5,000 shares of White stock from cross-defendant Basin; that the sale of the White shares violated section 5 of the 1933 Securities Act; and that White and cross-defendants Shaft and Beber had breached an oral termination of employment agreement. The trial court sustained general and special demurrers to the cross-complaint with leave to amend.

* * *

We shall explain why we have concluded that the trial court erred in sustaining general demurrers without leave to amend to the first, second, fourth, and fifth counts of the second amended cross-complaint. The causes of action alleged in the first two counts are not barred by the statute of frauds;

* * *

1. The statute of frauds does not apply to an oral employment contract, even though it provides in part for the measurement of the employee's compensation by annual receipts of the employer, unless its terms foreclose the employee's completion of the performance of the contract within one year.

Wolfson alleged as the first count of the second amended cross-complaint that during October 1963 cross-defendants promised him that if he would continue with White as vice president and sales manager he would receive a salary of $300 per week, automobile and other business expenses, and one percent of the annual gross sales of White exceeding one million dollars per year, payable quarterly commencing November 1, 1963. Although Wolfson relied to his detriment on these oral representations and performed all the conditions, cross-defendants refused not only to comply with the promise as to the percentage of gross receipts but also to give Wolfson any information by which he could determine if any amount was owing to him. Although Wolfson's employment was to be on a "permanent" basis, it was not to continue for any specified period. To this count the trial court sustained a general demurrer without leave to amend on the ground that the alleged oral employment contract violated the statute of frauds. (Civ. Code, § 1624, subd. 1.)

Even though part of an employee's compensation is to be measured by annual receipts of the employer, the statute of frauds does not apply to an employment contract unless its terms provide that the employee cannot completely perform it within one year from the making of the contract. Civil Code section 1624, subdivision 1, invalidates "an agreement that by its terms is not to be performed within a year from the making thereof" unless the contract "or some note or memorandum thereof, is in writing and subscribed by the party to be charged or by his agent." The cases hold that section 1624, subdivision 1, applies only to those contracts which, by their terms, cannot possibly be performed within one year (E.g., Hollywood Motion Picture Equipment Co. v. Furer (1940) 16 Cal.2d 184, 187 [105 P.2d 299]; Keller v. Pacific Turf Club (1961) 192 Cal.App.2d 189, 195-196 [13 Cal.Rptr. 346].)

The contractual provision that Wolfson would receive one percent of the annual gross sales of White exceeding one million dollars per year does not in itself convert the oral employment contract into one which by its terms cannot be performed within a year. Decisions involving other oral employment contracts with similar terms as to compensation support this conclusion. Thus the statute of frauds does not apply to employment contracts for an indefinite period merely because the contract provides that payment will be forthcoming on termination of the employment relationship. (Lloyd v. Kleefisch (1941) 48 Cal.App.2d 408, 414 [120 P.2d 97].) Nor does the statute of frauds apply to employment contracts because the compensation for the services is to be measured by their value to the employer over a period of more than one year. (Reed Oil Co. v. Cain (1925) 169 Ark. 309 [275 S.W. 333].) Moreover, in Pecarovich v. Becker (1952) 113 Cal.App.2d 309, 315-316 [248 P.2d 123], the court held that the statute of frauds does not apply to an oral contract relating to the services and annual salary of a football coach for a three-year period; the court explained that the contract authorized the employer to terminate the employment relationship at the end of each year by payment of a named sum.

Our conclusion coincides with the position unanimously taken by the few courts that have dealt with oral employment contracts involving bonus or profit-sharing provisions. Thus in Dennis v. Thermoid Co. (1942) 128 N.J.L. 303, 305 [25 A.2d 886], the court held that a provision for a bonus payable at the end of the year did not render an oral employment contract not performable within that year.

Since in the instant case the alleged oral contract may be terminated at will of either party, it can, under its terms, be performed within one year. When Wolfson's employment relationship with White was terminated, Wolfson had completely performed; White's performance consisted of nothing more than compensating Wolfson. (See Roberts v. Wachter (1951) 104 Cal.App.2d 271, 280-281 [231 P.2d 534].) Moreover, as we have explained, the inclusion of the provision for a bonus ascertainable only after one year does not invalidate the oral agreement under the statute of frauds.

2. The statute of frauds does not apply to an oral contract in its entirety if the court by reference to the terms of the agreement can separate those promises of performance not falling within the statute from those that do so.

Wolfson cross-complained that during the month of June 1964 Beber requested his resignation as vice president of White, and that consequently he entered into an oral settlement agreement with Beber and Shaft acting as agents of White. Pursuant to this oral contract, Beber, Shaft, and other undisclosed associates were to purchase from Wolfson the 5,000 White shares for a total sum of $15,000, and White was to pay Wolfson $1,200 for moving expenses to Chicago, one month's severance pay in the sum of $1,200, and the share of the gross receipts due him for the period of employment from October 1, 1963, to July 15, 1964. Yet White has paid Wolfson only $600 representing two weeks' severance pay.

The trial court sustained a general demurrer without leave to amend to this count on the ground that the alleged oral termination of employment contract violated the "sale of goods" section of the statute of frauds. (Former Civ. Code, §§ 1624a, subd. (1), 1724, subd. (1).) The trial court properly concluded that the alleged "repurchase" agreement falls under the applicable "sale of goods" section of the statute of frauds because it constitutes "a contract to sell and deliver stock in a corporation of the value of $500 or upwards...." (Berkey v. Halm (1950) 101 Cal.App.2d 62, 67 [234 P.2d 885].)

The trial court erred, however, in relying upon the statute of frauds to sustain a general demurrer to the entire second count. [6] If a claimant alleges two or more promises of performance "that can easily be distinguished and separated by the court by reference to the agreement itself" (2 Corbin on Contracts, § 313, at pp. 127-128), only that promise of performance which falls clearly within the statute of frauds cannot be enforced. (2 Corbin, op. cit. supra, at pp. 124-127; Pollyanna Homes, Inc. v. Berney (1961) 56 Cal.2d 676, 678 [16 Cal.Rptr. 345, 365 P.2d 401].)

Here, by reference to the alleged agreement itself, the "repurchase" promise can be clearly distinguished and separated from the promises to pay one month's salary, traveling expenses, and Wolfson's share of the gross receipts accrued during his period of employment as vice president. Any other construction of the alleged oral termination of employment contract would transgress the policy of restricting the application of the statute of frauds exclusively to those situations which are precisely covered by its language. (Sunset-Sternau Food Co. v. Bonzi (1964) 60 Cal.2d 834, 838 [36 Cal.Rptr. 741, 389 P.2d 133].)

3. The court erred in sustaining a general demurrer to Wolfson's common count in quantum meruit on the asserted ground that Wolfson sought the same compensation as that alleged in the two counts on the express contracts.

Wolfson alleged that between October 1, 1963, and July 15, 1964, he rendered services to White as a vice president and sales manager at the request of Shaft and Beber acting as agents of White. Wolfson further alleged that the reasonable value of his services was $25,000, and that White had paid him only $11,400.

In sustaining a general demurrer without leave to amend to this count on the ground that Wolfson sought the same compensation alleged in the two express contract counts, the trial court erred. As a general rule, a demurrer will lie to a common count based on the same facts as a specific count alleging an express contract if the specific count does not state a cause of action. This rule does not apply, however, to the case in which a general demurrer lies to the specific count on the ground of the statute of frauds. (Parker v. Solomon (1959) 171 Cal.App.2d 125, 136 [340 P.2d 353].) "In this respect there is a distinction between a count which fails to state facts sufficient to establish the existence of a contract and one which pleads a contract which is unenforceable because it is not in writing." (Leoni v. Delany (1948) 83 Cal.App.2d 303, 306-307 [188 P.2d 765, 189 P.2d 517].)

Moreover, the trial court sustained a demurrer to the common count only because of its relationship to the first two counts in which Wolfson, pursuant to alleged express oral contracts, sought compensation for his services. Since the trial court erred in sustaining a general demurrer to the first count and the entire second count, the demurrer to the common count cannot stand.

* * *

Traynor, C. J., Peters, J., Mosk, J., Burke, J., and Sullivan, J., concurred.

McCOMB, J. dissented.

Foley v. Interactive Data Corp.

Supreme Court of California, 1988
47 Cal.3d 654, 765 P.2d 373; 254 Cal.Rptr. 211

LUCAS, C. J.

After Interactive Data Corporation (defendant) fired plaintiff Daniel D. Foley, an executive employee, he filed this action seeking compensatory and punitive damages for wrongful discharge. In his second amended complaint, plaintiff asserted three distinct theories: (1) a tort cause of action alleging a discharge in violation of public policy (Tameny v. Atlantic Richfield Co. (1980) 27 Cal.3d 167 [164 Cal.Rptr. 839, 610 P.2d 1330, 9 A.L.R.4th 314]), (2) a contract cause of action for breach of an implied-in-fact promise to discharge for good cause only (e.g., Pugh v. See's Candies, Inc. (1981) 116 Cal.App.3d 311 [171 Cal.Rptr. 917] [all references are to this case rather than the 1988 posttrial decision appearing at 203 Cal.App.3d 743]), and (3) a cause of action alleging a tortious breach of the implied covenant of good faith and fair dealing (e.g., Cleary v. American Airlines, Inc. (1980) 111 Cal.App.3d 443 [168 Cal.Rptr. 722]). The trial court sustained a demurrer without leave to amend, and entered judgment for defendant.

* * *

We will also conclude, however, that plaintiff has sufficiently alleged a breach of an "oral" or "implied-in-fact" contract, and that the statute of frauds does not bar his claim so that he may pursue his action in this regard. Finally, we will hold that the covenant of good faith and fair dealing applies to employment contracts and that breach of the covenant may give rise to contract but not tort damages.

Facts

Because this appeal arose from a judgment entered after the trial court sustained defendant's demurrer, "we must, under established principles, assume the truth of all properly pleaded material allegations of the complaint in evaluating the validity" of the decision below. (Tameny v. Atlantic Richfield Co., supra, 27 Cal.3d 167, 170; Alcorn v. Anbro Engineering, Inc. (1970) 2 Cal.3d 493, 496 [86 Cal.Rptr. 88, 468 P.2d 216].)

According to the complaint, plaintiff is a former employee of defendant, a wholly owned subsidiary of Chase Manhattan Bank that markets computer-based decision-support services. Defendant hired plaintiff in June 1976 as an assistant product manager at a starting salary of $18,500. As a condition of employment defendant required plaintiff to sign a "Confidential and Proprietary Information Agreement" whereby he promised not to engage in certain competition with defendant for one year after the termination of his employment for any reason. The agreement also contained a "Disclosure and Assignment of Information" provision that obliged plaintiff to disclose to defendant all computer-related information known to him, including any innovations, inventions or developments pertaining to the computer field for a period of one year following his termination. Finally, the agreement imposed on plaintiff a continuing obligation to assign to defendant all rights to his computer-related inventions or innovations for one year following termination. It did not state any limitation on the grounds for which plaintiff's employment could be terminated.

Over the next six years and nine months, plaintiff received a steady series of salary increases, promotions, bonuses, awards and superior performance evaluations. In 1979 defendant named him consultant manager of the year and in 1981 promoted him to branch manager of its Los Angeles office. His annual salary rose to $56,164 and he received an additional $6,762 merit bonus two days before his discharge in March 1983. He alleges defendant's officers made repeated oral assurances of job security so long as his performance remained adequate.

Plaintiff also alleged that during his employment, defendant maintained written "Termination Guidelines" that set forth express grounds for discharge and a mandatory seven-step pretermination procedure. Plaintiff understood that these guidelines applied not only to employees under plaintiff's supervision, but to him as well. On the basis of these representations, plaintiff alleged that he reasonably believed defendant would not discharge him except for good cause, and therefore he refrained from accepting or pursuing other job opportunities.

The event that led to plaintiff's discharge was a private conversation in January 1983 with his former supervisor, Vice President Richard Earnest. During the previous year defendant had hired Robert Kuhne and subsequently named Kuhne to replace Earnest as plaintiff's immediate supervisor. Plaintiff learned that Kuhne was currently under investigation by the Federal Bureau of Investigation for embezzlement from his former employer, Bank of America. Plaintiff reported what he knew about Kuhne to Earnest, because he was "worried about working for Kuhne and having him in a supervisory position..., in view of Kuhne's suspected criminal conduct." Plaintiff asserted he "made this disclosure in the interest and for the benefit of his employer," allegedly because he believed that because defendant and its parent do business with the financial community on a confidential basis, the company would have a legitimate interest in knowing about a high executive's alleged prior criminal conduct.

In response, Earnest allegedly told plaintiff not to discuss "rumors" and to "forget what he heard" about Kuhne's past. In early March, Kuhne informed plaintiff that defendant had decided to replace him for "performance reasons" and that he could transfer to a position in another division in Waltham, Massachusetts. Plaintiff was told that if he did not accept a transfer, he might be demoted but not fired. One week later, in Waltham, Earnest informed plaintiff he was not doing a good job, and six days later, he notified plaintiff he could continue as branch manager if he "agreed to go on a 'performance plan.' Plaintiff asserts he agreed to consider such an arrangement." The next day, when Kuhne met with plaintiff, purportedly to present him with a written "performance plan" proposal, Kuhne instead informed plaintiff he had the choice of resigning or being fired. Kuhne offered neither a performance plan nor an option to transfer to another position.

Defendant demurred to all three causes of action. After plaintiff filed two amended pleadings, the trial court sustained defendant's demurrer without leave to amend and dismissed all three causes of action. The Court of Appeal affirmed the dismissal as to all three counts. We will explore each claim in turn.

* * *

II. Breach of Employment Contract

Plaintiff's second cause of action alleged that over the course of his nearly seven years of employment with defendant, the company's own conduct and personnel policies gave rise to an "oral contract" not to fire him without good cause. The trial court sustained a demurrer without leave to amend on two grounds: that the complaint did not state facts sufficient to give rise to such contract, and that enforcement of any such contract would be barred by the statute of frauds. The Court of Appeal affirmed, relying on the latter ground alone. We consider both grounds, discussing the statute of frauds issue first.

A. Statute of Frauds Defense

Civil Code section 1624, subdivision (a), invalidates "[a]n agreement that by its terms is not to be performed within a year from the making thereof" unless the contract "or some note or memorandum thereof, [is] in writing and subscribed by the party to be charged or by the party's agent." [8a] In White Lighting Co. v. Wolfson (1968) 68 Cal.2d

336 [66 Cal.Rptr. 697, 438 P.2d 345], we held that this portion of the statute of frauds "applies only to those contracts which, by their terms, cannot possibly be performed within one year." (Id., at p. 343.) In that case the employee alleged the breach of an express oral agreement whereby the defendant promised to employ him on a "permanent" basis and pay him a fixed commission on an "annual basis." We concluded that the trial court erroneously sustained the defendant's demurrer because, although the agreement contemplated employment on a "permanent" basis, the statute does not apply to an employment contract of indefinite duration "unless its terms foreclose the employee's completion of the performance of the contract within one year...." (Id., at p. 341.)

Relying exclusively on its own decision in Newfield v. Insurance Co. of the West (1984) 156 Cal.App.3d 440 [203 Cal.Rptr. 9], the Court of Appeal here nevertheless held that plaintiff's alleged employment contract, if modified to include a promise to discharge him for cause only, is barred by the statute of frauds. Neither Newfield nor the opinion below distinguishes, or even cites, the rule in White Lighting, supra, 68 Cal.2d 336. The rationale of both opinions is summed up in the following passage from Newfield: "[A]llegedly only [employee] had the right to terminate the contract. [9] Equality or justice between the parties would no longer exist in this alleged kind of oral contract. [¶] Appellant cannot have it both ways. Either his employment relationship was a contract in which both parties had equal rights to terminate at will (in which case it was not in violation of the statute of frauds), or it was a contract where the employer did not have the right to terminate at will, and there was a reasonable expectation of employment for more than one year (in which case the statute of frauds does apply, barring this action)." (156 Cal.App.3d at p. 446.)

Newfield is irreconcilable with the rule in White Lighting. Even if the original oral agreement had expressly promised plaintiff "permanent" employment terminable only on the condition of his subsequent poor performance or other good cause, such an agreement, if for no specified term, could possibly be completed within one year. (See White Lighting, supra, 68 Cal.2d at pp. 343-344.) Because the employee can quit or the employer can discharge for cause, even an agreement that strictly defines appropriate grounds for discharge can be completely performed within one year—or within one day for that matter.

Our courts have consistently held that such contracts are not within the statute of frauds. (See, e.g., Plumlee v. Poag (1984) 150 Cal.App.3d 541 [198 Cal.Rptr. 66]; Bondi v. Jewels by Edwar, Ltd. (1968) 267 Cal.App.2d 672 [73 Cal.Rptr. 494]; Wescoatt v. Meeker (1944) 63 Cal.App.2d 618 [147 P.2d 41]; Lloyd v. Kleefisch (1941) 48 Cal.App.2d 408 [120 P.2d 97].) Decisions from other states uniformly hold that a good-cause termination clause does not render an employment agreement unenforceable under the statute of frauds. (E.g., Weiner v. McGraw-Hill, Inc. (1982) 57 N.Y.2d 458 [457 N.Y.S.2d 193, 443 N.E.2d 441, 33 A.L.R.4th 1101]; Toussaint v. Blue Cross & Blue Shield of Mich. (1980) 408 Mich. 579 [292 N.W.2d 880]; Hardison v. A.H. Belo Corp. (Tex.Civ.App. 1952) 247 S.W.2d 167.) [10] These authorities support the general rule that if a condition terminating a contract may occur within one year of its making, then the contract is performable within a year and does not fall within the scope of the statute of frauds. This is true even though performance of the contract may extend for longer than one year if the condition does not occur. (See generally,1 Witkin, Summary of Cal. Law (9th ed. 1987) Contracts, § 282, p. 274.)

Other courts have pointed out that within a year an employee such as plaintiff could have (1) been discharged for cause (see, e.g., Rowe v. Noren Pattern and Foundry Co. (1979) 91 Mich.App. 254 [283 N.W.2d 713]); (2) retired, died or voluntarily left employment (see, e.g., Martin v. Federal Life Ins. Co. (1982) 109 Ill.App.3d 596 [440

N.E.2d 998]); or (3) been terminated if declining profitability compelled a general layoff or cessation of business altogether (see, e.g., Stauter v. Walnut Grove Products (Iowa 1971) 188 N.W.2d 305). "Interpreting the allegations of the complaint liberally, as we must, we cannot say as a matter of law that the contract ... could not be performed within a year." (Plumlee v. Poag, supra, 150 Cal.App.3d 541, 549.)

Defendant attacks these precedents as performing "legalistic gymnastics," and calls instead for enforcement of Civil Code section 1624 according to the fair import of its language. That proclamation ignores a considerable piece of history. More than 60 years ago a British court declared that "[i]t is now two centuries too late to ascertain the meaning of [the statute of frauds] by applying one's own mind independently to the interpretation of its language. Our task is a much more humble one; it is to see how that section has been expounded in decisions and how the decisions apply to the present case." (Hanau v. Ehrlich (1911) 2 K.B. 1056, 1069.)

The decision in White Lighting, supra, 68 Cal.2d 336, follows a long line of precedent. In 1897, the Supreme Judicial Court of Massachusetts rejected an employer's contention that the statute of frauds invalidated an oral agreement for "permanent employment" so long as the plaintiff, an enameler, performed his work satisfactorily. The majority, including Chief Justice Field and Justice Holmes, rejected the employer's defense. "It has been repeatedly held that, if an agreement whose performance would otherwise extend beyond a year may be completely performed within a year on the happening of some contingency, it is not within the statute of frauds. [Citations.] In this case, we say nothing of other contingencies. The contract would have been completely performed if the defendant had ceased to carry on business within a year." (Carnig v. Carr (1897) 167 Mass. 544 [46 N.E. 117, 118].)

The Legislature, which in 1872 enacted Civil Code section 1624, was aware of precedent limiting the reach of the one-year provision of the statute of frauds. The Code Commissioners' notes specifically advised that "in a similar statute in New York these words have been construed as applying only to contracts which cannot possibly be executed within a year, under any contingency.... To bring a contract within the statute relating to parol agreements, not to be performed within one year, it must appear to be necessarily incapable of performance within that time." [11] When the Legislature enacts language that has received definitive judicial construction, we presume that the Legislature was aware of the relevant judicial decisions and intended to adopt that construction. (See Buchwald v. Katz (1972) 8 Cal.3d 493, 502 [105 Cal.Rptr. 368, 503 P.2d 1376].) This presumption gains further strength when, as in this case, it is clear that the Legislature was explicitly informed of the prior construction.

In sum, the contract between plaintiff and defendant could have been performed within one year of its making; plaintiff could have terminated his employment within that period, or defendant could have discharged plaintiff for cause. Thus, the contract does not fall within the statute of frauds and the fact that it was an implied or oral agreement is not fatal to its enforcement.

Afterthoughts

"In its actual application, however, the courts have been perhaps even less friendly to this provision [the 'one year' section] than to the other provisions of the statute [of frauds]. They have observed the exact words of this provision and have interpreted them literally and very narrowly.... To fall within the words of the provision, therefore, the agreement must be one of which it can truly be said at the very moment it is made, 'This agreement is not to be performed within one year'; in general, the cases indicate that there must not be the slightest possibility that it can be fully performed within one year." (Corbin on Contracts, [One Volume Edition] § 444, at p. 446.)

Sufficiency of the Note or Memorandum

The California Statute of Frauds does not require that the contract itself be in writing, it only requires that the contract be evidenced in writing by "some note or memorandum thereof." That is an important distinction to keep in mind.

Brewer v. Horst-Lachmund Co.

Supreme Court of California, 1900
127 Cal. 643, 60 P. 418

GRAY, C.

This is an action for a breach of contract of sale and purchase brought by the vendor against the vendee. The complaint sets out an agreement whereby plaintiff agreed to sell, and defendant agreed to buy, of plaintiff fifty-seven thousand one hundred and ten pounds of hops at eleven and five-eighths cents per pound; that plaintiff tendered the hops and defendant refused to take or pay for them, and that thereupon plaintiff sold said hops to a third person for the best obtainable price, which was eight hundred and thirty dollars and ninety-three cents less than defendant had agreed to pay therefor. Plaintiff obtained judgment for said eight hundred and thirty dollars and ninety-three cents, and defendant appeals. The case comes here on the judgment-roll.

The answer sets up the statute of frauds, alleging that the agreement sued on "was an agreement for the sale of goods and chattels at a price exceeding two hundred dollars; and defendant did not accept or receive any part of said goods and chattels, and did not pay any part of the purchase money therefor; and said sale was not made at auction; and said agreement was not, nor was any sufficient, proper, or adequate memorandum or note thereof, in writing, subscribed by defendant, or by any agent of defendant."

The court found as to the contract that Fred E. Alter was the general agent in the state of California and was empowered to make contracts therein for defendant. That C. A. Wagner was defendant's agent in the county of Sacramento, empowered to solicit samples in that and adjoining counties from hopgrowers and transmit the same to defendant's said general agent at Santa Rosa, California, "and to contract with such growers for the purchase from them in behalf of defendant corporation of such of said hops as might by the latter be desired, subject to the approval of the defendant corporation, through its general agent said Alter." That plaintiff was a hopgrower, having a farm near Ben Ali, Sacramento county, and in September, 1897, said Wagner, as agent for defendant, obtained samples of a certain lot of hops, consisting of two hundred and ninety-six bales, weighing fifty-seven thousand one hundred and ten pounds, belonging to said plaintiff, and transmitted said samples to Alter at Santa Rosa, at the same time informing said Alter of the fact that said samples were from the lot aforesaid comprising two hundred and ninety-six bales of the last pickings of hops grown by plaintiff during the year 1897 upon his said farm; that at the same time said Wagner designated said samples by the trade number or symbol "13"; that it was and is the custom which prevails generally among dealers in hops to mark and designate by number the different samples furnished them by growers, and such custom was followed by defendant in the transaction herein set forth. That hops are sold, according to the custom of trade and usage in California, by the pound. That on October 11, 1897, plaintiff and defendant's agent, Wagner, entered into an oral contract, subject to the approval of Alter, whereby plaintiff sold and defendant bought the aforesaid lot of hops, provided the same were in quality equal to the samples marked "13," and it was agreed that defendant should inspect the hops on or before October 16th. On the same day, October 11th, Wagner telegraphed to Santa Rosa as follows:

October 11, 1897.
Horst & Lachmund Co., Santa Rosa, Cal.

Bought thirteen at eleven five-eighths net you; confirm purchase by wire to Brewer, nineteen sixteen M street, inspection on or before Saturday. Do you want fifteen at eleven quarter?

"C. A. WAGNER."

Alter received this message the same day, and thereupon sent to plaintiff, and plaintiff received, the following telegram:

Santa Rosa, Cala., Oct. 11-97.
Geo. Brewer, 1916 M street, Sacramento, Cala.

We confirm purchase Wagner eleven five-eight cents. like sample.
"(Signed) HORST AND LACHMUND CO."

That these telegrams are the only written evidence of the contract between the parties. That the said Alter knew that the number or symbol designated "13," used in the telegram first set out above, referred to and meant the hops belonging to plaintiff, as aforesaid, comprising said two hundred and ninety-six bales or thereabouts, and were the last pickings of plaintiff's hops grown upon his said farm in 1897, and also knew the situation of the hops and the other facts hereinbefore mentioned. And that defendant subsequently inspected the hops, and, without any lawful or just cause, rejected them and refused to receive them when tendered by plaintiff.

The only question presented for decision is, did these telegrams constitute a sufficient note or memorandum of the contract to satisfy the requirements of the statute of frauds? The trial court, by its judgment, answered this question in the affirmative. And, in view of all the facts found, we think the court reached the proper conclusion. If there were nothing to look to but the telegrams, the court might find it difficult, if not impossible, to determine the nature of the contract, or that any contract was entered into between the parties. But the court is permitted to interpret the memorandum (consisting of the two telegrams) by the light of all the circumstances under which it was made; and if, when the court is put into possession of all the knowledge which the parties to the transaction had at the time, it can be plainly seen from the memorandum who the parties to the contract were, what the subject of the contract was, and what were its terms, then the court should not hesitate to hold the memorandum sufficient. Oral evidence may be received to show in what sense figures or abbreviations were used; and their meaning may be explained as it was understood between the parties. (*Mann v. Higgins*, 83 Cal. 66; *Berry v. Kowalsky*, 95 Cal. 134; 29 Am. St. Rep. 101; *Callahan v. Stanley*, 57 Cal. 476.) Also: "Parol evidence is always admissible to explain the surrounding circumstances, and situation and relations of the parties, at and immediately before the execution of the contract, in order to connect the description with the only thing intended, and thereby to identify the subject matter, and to explain all terms and phrases used in a local or special sense." (*Preble v. Abrahams*, 88 Cal. 245; *Towle v. Carmelo etc. Co.*, 99 Cal. 397.) Interpreting the telegrams by the foregoing rules, it is not difficult to see that the parties to the contract are George Brewer, of 1916 M street, Sacramento, California, vendor, and Horst and Lachmund Company, of Santa Rosa, California, vendee; that the contract was one of purchase and sale, and the subject of it was the property represented in the first telegram by "thirteen" and well known by the parties to consist of two hundred and ninety-six bales of hops, and to be the last pickings of hops grown by plaintiff upon his farm in Sacramento county during the year 1897, and that the price to be paid for said hops was eleven and five-eighths cents per pound.

The two telegrams bear the same date; on their face the last one was sent to plaintiff in response to the first; and it is clear that they should be read together to determine whether they constitute the note or memorandum required by the statute of frauds. (*Elbert v. Los Angeles Gas Co.*, 97 Cal. 244; *Breckinridge v. Crocker*, 78 Cal. 529.) We are satisfied that the telegrams, thus read by the light of the circumstances surrounding the parties, are sufficient to take the contract out of the statute of frauds. Any other conclusion than the one here reached would certainly impair the usefulness of modern appliances to modern business, tend to hamper trade, and increase the expense thereof.

* * *

Haynes, C., and Chipman, C., concurred.

For the reasons given in the foregoing opinion the judgment is affirmed. Garoutte, J., Van Dyke, J., Harrison, J.

Franklin v. Hansen

California Supreme Court, 1963.
59 Cal.2d 570, 381 P.2d 386, 30 Cal.Rptr. 530

PEEK, J.

In this appeal the defendant Charles P. Hansen seeks a reversal of a judgment in the amount of $5,000 in favor of plaintiff Donald V. Franklin, a licensed real estate broker, for claimed commissions in procuring a buyer for defendant's real property.

Defendant owned residential property in Newport Beach. Plaintiff had acted as an agent for defendant in the rental of the property and had informed defendant that he would like to represent defendant in selling the property. A sale price of $115,000 was agreed upon and although plaintiff obtained several offers for the property over a period of several months, all were for less than the agreed price. Defendant eventually agreed that he would accept an offer for $100,000. None of the transactions between the parties up to this point were in writing, defendant having assured plaintiff that a signed listing would be unnecessary as his word was good.

On January 15, 1960, plaintiff obtained an offer for $100,000 and telephoned defendant, requesting an authorization by telegram to sell the property. In response, defendant sent the following telegram: "Los Angeles, California ... D. V. Franklin, 208 Marine Balboa Island California. This is confirm that I will sell 608 South Bay Front Balboa Island for 100,000 cash this offer good until noon 1-19-60. Chas. P. Hansen."

On January 19, 1960, plaintiff again telephoned defendant and advised that he had sold the property and had accepted a check for $5,000 as a down payment. Defendant stated that he was pleasantly surprised, that delivery could take place when the present lease terminated in a few months, and consented to the suggested escrow agent. But when a standard form deposit receipt providing for payment of a 5 per cent commission to plaintiff was presented to defendant, he refused to sign, and indicated that he wished "to get out of the deal." On January 22 defendant and the prospective buyers appeared at plaintiff's office. When the buyers refused to waive their rights under the agreement defendant admitted that he was "stuck" with the sale and that plaintiff would receive his commission. Subsequently, however, he refused to sign any of the documents necessary to complete the sale of the property, and also refused to pay the agreed commission.

Plaintiff's complaint alleges breach of a commission contract, reciting defendant's promise to abide by the verbal listing of the property, the telegram in "confirmation thereof," the arrangements for the sale of the property, the defendant's refusal to proceed with the sale and his promise to pay the 5 per cent commission notwithstanding.

Relying on the statute of frauds defendant demurred to the complaint for commissions, which demurrer was overruled. The trial court heard, over defendant's objections, parol evidence as to all transactions between the parties and awarded judgment as prayed by plaintiff. Defendant contends on this appeal that neither the telegram nor any other writing constituted a sufficient memorandum or ratification of a contract of employment to satisfy the statute of frauds.

Section 1624 of the Civil Code provides in part: "The following contracts are invalid, unless the same, or some note or memorandum thereof, is in writing and subscribed by the party to be charged or by his agent: ... 5. An agreement authorizing or employing an agent or broker to purchase or sell real estate for compensation or a commission." (See also Code Civ. Proc., § 1973, subd. 5; Civ. Code, § 2310.)

We have before considered the nature of a memorandum sufficient to satisfy subdivision 5 of section 1624. (See Pacific Southwest Dev. Corp. v. Western Pac. R. R. Co., 47 Cal.2d 62 [301 P.2d 815].) There a broker sued to recover compensation for services rendered to a buyer in procuring an option to purchase real property. The broker's offer of proof demonstrated substantial services rendered to the buyer, but the only writing subscribed by the buyer was a letter to the broker as follows: " 'I am in a position to take an option on the Lenfest property at $3,000.00 per acre. We would not wish to pay more than $1,500.00 for the option and would want it for 90 days, with a contingent extension of time long enough to have the property rezoned.... If you think this proposal is worth your trip, let me know perhaps by telephone tomorrow and I will arrange to meet you at San Jose—maybe we can get the deal signed up.... ' " (47 Cal.2d 62, 68.)

At page 69 in the foregoing case the court stated: "The only writing with which defendant can be charged here is the letter of August 29, 1950..., and as above quoted, it made no reference to the fact of employment by defendant of plaintiff or to any compensation. True, the latter reference is not essential if there is a contract of employment, for a reasonable amount as a commission will be inferred. [Citations.] But where there is a failure to mention the fact of employment, the further fact that there is no mention of a commission is significant. The authorities require that a writing 'subscribed by the party to be charged, or his agent' must unequivocally show the fact of employment of the broker seeking to recover a real estate commission [citations]. It must therefore be concluded that the writings here are insufficient under the statute of frauds to sustain plaintiff's claim."

Here, too, as to the content thereof, the writing in the instant case is similar to that in the cited case since it also fails to expressly recite or make reference to the existence of any employment contract or to any compensation. In both cases parol evidence demonstrated that the real nature of the agreement between the parties was one of employment; that the broker in each instance rendered substantial, bargained-for-services which culminated in the achievement of the objective for which employed; and that neither broker was guilty of overreaching or improper and unethical practices. It does not appear that we can give full effect to the Pacific Southwest Dev. Corp. case and at the same time sustain the instant award.

The sufficiency of a writing to satisfy the statute of frauds cannot be established by evidence which is extrinsic to the writing itself. (Code Civ. Proc., § 1973.) While a telegram, sufficient in content, may satisfy the statute (Niles v. Hancock, 140 Cal. 157 [73 P. 840]; Gibson v. De La Salle Institute, 66 Cal.App.2d 609 [152 P.2d 774]), still it must contain the essential elements of a specific, consummated agreement. (Zellner v. Wassman, 184 Cal. 80 [193 P. 84]; Fritz v. Mills, 170 Cal. 449 [150 P. 375].) Where it discloses no promise or agreement and cannot be made clear as to its significance without resort to parol evidence, it is inadequate. (Ellis v. Klaff, 96 Cal.App.2d 471 [216 P.2d 15]; Sherwood v. Lowell, 34 Cal.App. 365 [167 P. 554].) But where it imports the essentials of a contractual obligation although it fails to do so in an explicit, definite or complete manner, it is always permissible to show the circumstances which attended its making. Thus in Gibson v. De La Salle Institute, supra, 66 Cal.App.2d 609, parol evidence was resorted to in explanation of certain trade terms contained in a telegram offer. Likewise in Brewer v. Horst & Lachmund Co., 127 Cal. 643 [60 P. 418, 50 L.R.A. 240], an agent, using certain code words, wired his principal that he had purchased goods, and the principal sent a confirming telegram to the seller, also utilizing code words. Extrinsic evidence was held admissible in explanation of the two telegrams and they together were deemed to satisfy the statute of frauds. Such evidence is also admissible to resolve ambiguities on the face of the memorandum (Balfour v. Fresno Canal & Irr. Co., 109 Cal. 221, 225-226 [41 P. 876]), or to ascertain a term of the agreement by resort to another document referred to in the memorandum. (Searles v. Gonzales, 191 Cal. 426 [216 P. 1003, 28 A.L.R. 78].) But in each of the foregoing instances the memorandum itself demonstrated the existence of a contractual intent on the part of the one to be charged, and extrinsic evidence was necessary only to define the limits thereof.

The telegram in the instant case fails to use any words in recognition of a contractual obligation for a commission. While it may be a sufficient memorandum of an agreement to sell the property, it is the alleged commission agreement which is sought to be enforced. There are no ambiguities to be resolved or references to extrinsic materials which would aid in ascertaining a meaning not made definite on the face of the document. True, the writer purports to "confirm," but he also states in definite and certain language that which he confirms. The meaning of the telegram is clear and definite—it requires no aid in its interpretation, and it does not imply, infer or suggest a commission agreement. It is only by resort to extrinsic matters not suggested by the writing that it is possible to determine with any justification that defendant had agreed to compensate plaintiff for his services. This is not sufficient under the established law.

It is suggested in a number of cases, and urged in the instant case, that a more liberal construction of the statute of frauds should be employed to protect a broker from being defrauded by a landowner. (See Note 80 A.L.R. 1457.) The statute, of course, does not purport to afford a greater degree of protection to an agent or broker, as distinguished from a principal. Real estate brokers are licensed as such only after they have demonstrated a knowledge of the laws relating to real estate transactions (Bus. & Prof. Code, §§ 10150, 10153), and it would seem that they would thus require less protection against pitfalls encountered in transactions regulated by those laws. In Pacific Southwest

Dev. Corp. v. Western Pac. R. R. Co., supra, 47 Cal.2d 62, the court stated at page 70: "Plaintiff is a licensed real estate broker and, as such, is presumed to know that contracted for real estate commissions are invalid and unenforceable unless put in writing and subscribed by the person to be charged. [Citations.] Nevertheless, plaintiff failed to secure proper written authorization to protect itself in the transaction. Rather it assumed the risk of relying upon claimed oral promises of defendant, and it has no cause for complaint if its efforts go unrewarded."

Moreover, the cases on which plaintiff relies as giving more favorable treatment to an agent or broker are distinguishable. Thus in Kennedy v. Merickel, 8 Cal.App. 378 [97 P. 81], a writing which expressly provided for the payment of commissions, although the amount was left uncertain, was held at page 381 to be "a sufficient compliance with the statute." As authority for the foregoing statement the court relied on Imperato v. Wasboe, 47 Misc. 150 [93 N.Y.S. 489], wherein the following memorandum was held sufficient under the New York statute: "Mr. P. Imperato, Real Estate Broker—Dear Sir: ... There will be no need of my meeting you if you haven't a party who desires to purchase my house No. 416 East 124th Street at $15,000, as I am not very anxious to dispose of my property, and I do not intend to sell for any less. Very truly yours, O. Wasboe." Significantly the memorandum addresses the agent as a "Real Estate Broker" and recognizes that the agent is acting in such capacity (i.e., " ... if you haven't a party who desires to purchase my house ..."). Authorization to sell at $15,000 was held by the New York court to have been sufficiently established by the writing.

Again, in Toomy v. Dunphy, 86 Cal. 639, 640 [25 P. 130], a note which recited: " 'Henry Toomy can arrange for the sale of my ranch in Nevada, as per within memorandum,' " was held to sufficiently establish the employment of Toomy as an agent, and the fact of consideration for such services was implied therefrom.

Of the cases to which we are referred, the foregoing lends plaintiff most support. But in each case the writing evidenced at least the employment relationship, whereas the memorandum in the case before us is silent as to the existence of such a relationship.

Written evidence of the employment relationship has always been deemed an essential requirement of the statute of frauds. In addition to the Pacific Southwest Dev. Corp. case, supra, other decisions have held that the failure to expressly provide for employment is fatal to the sufficiency of any memorandum. Thus, in Morrill v. Barneson, 30 Cal.App.2d 598 [86 P.2d 924], a letter which fully described the property, the sale price and terms thereof, and provided for the payment of the "regular 5% commission," was held insufficient because it failed to expressly create an employment relationship with anyone. In Herzog v. Blatt, 80 Cal.App.2d 340 [180 P.2d 30], a memorandum in the form of an offer to accept "8400 net" for designated property was also held insufficient because it too failed to authorize anyone to act for the owner. And in Kleinsorge & Heilbron v. Liness, 17 Cal.App. 534 [120 P. 444], a writing setting forth the price, terms and description of property offered for sale by the signer thereof, which writing was delivered to the plaintiff real estate brokers although not expressly addressed to them, was held insufficient as not bearing written evidence of a contract of employment or authorization. For the proposition that a sufficient writing "must unequivocally show on its face the fact of employment of the broker" see also Blanchard v. Pauley, 92 Cal.App.2d 244, 247 [206 P.2d 864]; Sanstrum v. Gonser, 140 Cal.App.2d 732 [295 P.2d 532]; Edens v. Stoddard, 126 Cal.App.2d 56, 60 [271 P.2d 610]; Hooper v. Mayfield, 114 Cal.App.2d 801, 807 [251 P.2d 330].

Plaintiff herein has neither alleged nor urged the application of an equitable estoppel, pursuant to which doctrine a party to an oral agreement might be estopped to rely on the statute of frauds in instances where the elements of the doctrine can be established. (See Monarco v. Lo Greco, 35 Cal.2d 621, 626 [220 P.2d 737].)

In view of the foregoing we are compelled to the conclusion that the memorandum in the case now before us is obviously insufficient to satisfy the requirements of the statute of frauds under the prevailing standards. Accordingly, the judgment is reversed.

Gibson, C. J., Traynor, J., Schauer, J., McComb, J., Peters, J., and Tobriner, J., concurred.

Donovan v. RRL Corp.

California Supreme Court, 2001
26 Cal.4th 261, 109 Cal.Rptr.2d 807; 27 P.3d 702

GEORGE, C.J.

[Facts appear at p. 31 of text.]

Defendant contends that even if its advertisement constituted an offer that was accepted by plaintiff's tender of the purchase price, plaintiff is not authorized by law to enforce the resulting contract, because there was no signed writing that satisfied the requirements of the statute of frauds for the sale of goods. Plaintiff, on the other hand, maintains that defendant's name, as it appeared in the newspaper advertisement for the sale of the vehicle, constituted a signature within the meaning of the statute.

The applicable statute of frauds states in relevant part: "Except as otherwise provided in this section a contract for the sale of goods for the price of five hundred dollars ($500) or more is not enforceable by way of action or defense unless there is some writing sufficient to indicate that a contract for sale has been made between the parties and *signed by the party against whom enforcement is sought or by his or her authorized agent or broker.* A writing is not insufficient because it omits or incorrectly states a term agreed upon[,] but the contract is not enforceable under this paragraph beyond the quantity of goods shown in the writing." (Cal. U. Com. Code, § 2201, subd. (1),.)

The California Uniform Commercial Code defines the term "signed" as including "any symbol executed or adopted by a party with present intention to authenticate a writing." (Cal. U. Com. Code, § 1201, subd. (38).) The comment regarding the corresponding provision of the Uniform Commercial Code states: "The inclusion of authentication in the definition of 'signed' is to make clear that as the term is used in [the code] a complete signature is not necessary. Authentication may be printed, stamped, or written; it may be by initials or by thumbprint. It may be on any part of the document and in appropriate cases may be found in a billhead or letterhead. No catalog of possible authentications can be complete and the court must use common sense and commercial experience in passing upon these matters. The question always is whether the symbol was executed or adopted by the party with present intention to authenticate the writing." (U. Com. Code com., reprinted at 23A West's Ann. Cal. U. Com. Code (1964 ed.) foll. § 1201, p. 65; see 1 Witkin, *supra*, Contracts, § 281, p. 273 [citing California decisions generally consistent with this comment]; Rest.2d Contracts, § 134.)

Some decisions have relaxed the signature requirement considerably to accommodate various forms of electronic communication. For example, a party's printed or typewritten name in a telegram has been held to satisfy the statute of frauds. (E.g., *Hessenthaler v. Farzin* (Pa.Super.Ct. 1989) 564 A.2d 990, 993-994; *Hillstrom v. Gosnay*

(1980) 188 Mont. 388 [614 P.2d 466, 470].) Even a tape recording identifying the parties has been determined to meet the signature requirement of the Uniform Commercial Code. (*Ellis Canning Company v. Bernstein* (D.Colo. 1972) 348 F.Supp. 1212, 1228.)

When an advertisement constitutes an offer, the printed name of the merchant is intended to authenticate the advertisement as that of the merchant. (See Rest.2d Contracts, § 131, com. d, illus. 2, p. 335 [newspaper advertisement constituting an offer to purchase certain goods, with offeror's name printed therein, satisfies the requirements of the statute of frauds].) In other words, where the advertisement reasonably justifies the recipient's understanding that the communication was intended as an offer, the offeror's intent to authenticate his or her name as a signature can be established from the face of the advertisement.

In the present case, the parties presented no evidence with regard to whether defendant intended that its name in the advertisement constitute a signature. Therefore, the issue whether the appearance of defendant's name supports a determination that the writing was "signed" is closely related to the question whether the advertisement constituted an offer. Those characteristics of the advertisement justifying plaintiff's belief that defendant intended it to be an offer also support a finding that defendant intended that its name serve as an authentication.

As established above, defendant's advertisement reflected an objective manifestation of its intention to make an offer for the sale of the vehicle at the stated price. Defendant's printed name in the advertisement similarly evidenced an intention to authenticate the advertisement as an offer and therefore constituted a signature satisfying the statute of frauds.

Excusing the Writing Requirement

Phillippe v. Shapell Industries

Supreme Court of California, 1987
43 Cal.3d 1247, 743 P.2d 1279; 241 Cal.Rptr. 22

EAGLESON, J.

A jury found in favor of plaintiff, a licensed real estate broker, in his action to recover a broker's commission from defendant, a real property buyer. Defendant appeals. The primary issue before us is whether a licensed real estate broker may assert equitable estoppel against a statute of frauds defense in an action by the broker to recover a real estate commission.

We conclude that a licensed real estate broker cannot invoke equitable estoppel to avoid the statute of frauds unless the broker shows actual fraud. To decide otherwise would be contrary to nearly unanimous precedent spanning several decades and to the purpose of the statute of frauds. The trial court's judgment in favor of plaintiff is reversed with directions to enter judgment in favor of defendant.

Facts

[Plaintiff David E. Phillippe (hereafter Phillippe) is a real estate broker. Defendant Shapell Industries, Inc. (hereafter Shapell) is a corporation engaged in the construction of residential housing tracts and periodically purchases land for such construction. Without the benefit of any written agreement, Phillippe undertook to represent Shapell in negotiations for the acquisition of a particular parcel known as the "Great Lakes Property." Those negotiations did not produce a bargain. Following the breakdown of initial discussions, direct negotiations between Shapell and the owner followed, and in March 1976 Shapell signed a purchase and sale agreement for 63 acres. The sale closed on August 27, 1976. The sale price was $2,718,750. Shapell's written purchase offer did not provide for any commission to Phillippe.]

When Phillippe learned that Shapell had agreed to buy the Great Lakes property, he wrote to Aaron on June 9, 1976, and requested a commission on the purchase. Phillippe reminded Aaron that Phillippe had agreed to work for Shapell "on the condition and with the understanding that our firm was working for and represented Shapell, the buyer, as brokers and would be paid a brokerage commission from buyer of 6% of the total consideration paid for the acquired property." Phillippe also reviewed his efforts regarding the Great Lakes property.

On June 16, 1976, Aaron responded by letter informing Phillippe that Shapell would not pay him a commission. Aaron claimed that there had been no mutual agreement of representation and that Shapell had been negotiating for the Great Lakes property "prior to and independent of any representations" by Phillippe.

In April 1977, Phillippe filed suit against Shapell to recover a 6 percent broker's commission for the sale of the Great Lakes property and other alleged damages. The case was tried in February 1982 and went to the jury on three theories of recovery. First, Phillippe sought recovery of a 6 percent broker's commission on the basis of either a written agreement of employment, a memorandum of employment sufficient to satisfy the statute of frauds, or an equitable estoppel to preclude Shapell from asserting the statute of frauds as a defense. Second, Phillippe sought a 6 percent finder's fee based on an alleged agreement with Shapell. Third, he sought a 6 percent commission based on an alleged agreement between himself and Shapell as brokers to share a commission.

The jury found by special verdict that Phillippe was the procuring cause of the purchase of the Great Lakes property by Shapell and awarded Phillippe $125,000 on his first theory of recovery but rejected his other two theories of recovery. The trial court denied Shapell's motion for a new trial and entered judgment in favor of Phillippe.

Shapell appeals on the grounds, inter alia, that Phillippe's claim is barred by Civil Code section 1624, subdivision (d), the subdivision of California's statute of frauds dealing with real estate brokerage commissions, and that Shapell is not estopped from asserting the statute of frauds as a defense. Phillippe cross-appeals on the ground that the jury failed to award him all the damages to which he is entitled.

Discussion

The Agreement between Phillippe and Shapell Is Subject to the Statute of Frauds.

Civil Code section 1624, subdivision (d) provides that an agreement authorizing or employing an agent, broker, or any other person to purchase or sell real estate is invalid unless the agreement or some note or memorandum of the agreement is in writing and subscribed by the party to be charged or by his agent. Phillippe contends Civil Code section 1624(d) does not apply to the agreement between him and Shapell. We disagree.

Phillippe argues that the statute is inapplicable because he was not acting as a broker for the Great Lakes property purchased by Shapell, but only as a "professional consultant in the field of subdivision land acquisition." A licensed broker may be able under appropriate circumstances to recover under an oral agreement or in quantum meruit for certain services other than the purchase, sale, or leasing of real property. (Owen v. National Container Corp. of Cal. (1952) 115 Cal.App.2d 21, 25-26 [251 P.2d 765]; Carey v. Cusak (1966) 245 Cal.App.2d 57, 69 [54 Cal.Rptr. 244].) Phillippe fails to cite, and we are unable to find in the record, any evidence of professional services rendered to Shapell other than those a broker would reasonably be expected to perform in trying to consummate a sale, for example, furnishing Shapell with descriptions of the property. Phillippe's pretrial pleadings contradict his claim that he was a professional consultant. In his first amended complaint, he alleged that, after he located and presented the Great Lakes property to Shapell, it "took over all activities leading to the eventual purchase of the property by Shapell," and that, when a broker was employed by Shapell, the broker "served only as a flunky and assistant to Shapell's employees." Phillippe's services were merely incidental to his efforts to bring about a sale of the property to Shapell. Any agreement to perform those Services is thus subject to section 1624(d). (Owen v. National Container Corp. of Cal., supra, 115 Cal.App.2d 21, 28; see generally 1 Miller & Starr, Current Law of Cal. Real Estate (1975) § 1.55, pp. 74-75.)

Phillippe's own evidence makes clear that he was acting as a broker. In his April 5, 1973, letter to Prince, Phillippe stated that he was "waiting for a price quote on the property." When Phillippe wrote to Aaron on June 9, 1976, requesting a commission, Phillippe described his relationship with Shapell and the nature of his services as follows: "Early in 1973 our firm was asked by Ron Prince of Shapell to do an extensive survey of properties available for sale on the Palos Verdes Peninsula. We agreed to do so on the condition and with the understanding that our firm was working for and represented Shapell, the buyer, as brokers and would be paid a brokerage commission from buyer of 6% of the total consideration paid for the acquired property." Phillippe viewed himself as a broker. The nature of his claimed compensation was that of a broker's fee—it was contingent on a sale, and it was in the customary amount charged by brokers. We agree with the observation that, "if an object looks like a duck, walks like a duck and quacks like a duck, it is likely to be a duck." (In re Deborah C. (1981) 30 Cal.3d 125, 141 [177 Cal.Rptr. 852, 635 P.2d 446] [conc. opn. of Mosk, J.].) It is clear that Phillippe was acting as a broker.

We view Phillippe's characterization of himself as other than a broker as semantic sleight-of-hand. Phillippe tried this case on the primary theory that he is entitled to a broker's commission. The jury found in Phillippe's favor only on his claim for a broker's commission. He now says he was never acting as a broker. Even if that were so, the general rule is that a party may not for the first time on appeal change his theory of recovery. (Bogacki v. Board of Supervisors (1971) 5 Cal.3d 771, 780 [97 Cal.Rptr. 657, 489 P.2d 537].)

Phillippe also contends section 1624(d) is not applicable to his agreement with Shapell because it is an agreement between brokers. Phillippe's argument on this point is less than clear, but he appears to contend that the statute of frauds does not apply because either: (1) one of the principals to the transaction, Shapell, is a licensed broker, or (2) the agreement was between brokers to share a commission. Neither point has merit.

First, the primary purpose of section 1624(d) is to protect real estate sellers and purchasers from the assertion of false claims by brokers for commissions. (Pac. etc. Dev. Corp. v. Western Pac. R. R. Co. (1956) 47 Cal.2d 62, 67 [301 P.2d 825].) We perceive no logical reason why a licensed broker or agent who is acting as a seller or purchaser of real property should not be entitled to this protection. Licensees are as subject to false claims as are unlicensed members of the public. Phillippe's argument appears to be that licensed brokers know the requirements of the statute of frauds and thus do not need its protection. His argument is too broad because, if it were accepted, judges, lawyers, and any other group who might reasonably be presumed to know the law, including the statute of frauds, would be stripped of its protection. The fact that Shapell is a licensed broker acting as a principal in the transaction does not render the statute of frauds inapplicable to the agreement with Phillippe. (Marks v. Walter G. McCarty Corp. (1949) 33 Cal.2d 814, 823 [205 P.2d 1025].)

Second, if Phillippe means the statute does not apply because there was an agreement with Shapell to share a broker's commission, we reject that argument as well. Shapell was acting as a principal, not as a broker. The jury found by special verdict that there was no valid agreement between Phillippe and Shapell to share a broker's commission. Substantial evidence supports that finding. It must not be disturbed on appeal. (Jessup Farms v. Baldwin (1983) 33 Cal.3d 639, 660 [190 Cal.Rptr. 355, 660 P.2d 813].) Thus, we need not decide whether such commission-sharing agreements are within the ambit of section 1624(d), but we note that the Courts of Appeal have found that such agreements are not subject to the statute. (See, e.g., Iusi v. Chase (1959) 169 Cal.App.2d 83, 86 [337 P.2d 79]; Holland v. Morgan & Peacock Properties (1959) 168 Cal.App.2d 206, 210 [335 P.2d 769].)

In light of the foregoing, we hold that the agreement between Shapell and Phillippe is subject to the requirements of section 1624(d).

The Agreement between Shapell and Phillippe Does Not Meet the Requirements of Section 1624.

A broker's real estate commission agreement is invalid under section 1624(d) unless the agreement "or some note or memorandum thereof, is in writing and subscribed by the party to be charged or by the party's agent." The writing must unequivocally show on its face the fact of employment of the broker seeking to recover a real estate commission. (Franklin v. Hansen (1963) 59 Cal.2d 570, 573 [30 Cal.Rptr. 530. 381 P.2d 386]; Pac. etc. Dev. Corp. v. Western Pac. R. R. Co., supra, 47 Cal.2d 62, 68.) To satisfy this requirement, Phillippe relies on the considerable correspondence between Shapell and himself. "It is for the court to determine whether letters which have passed between parties constitute an agreement between them." (Wristen v. Bowles (1889) 82 Cal. 84, 87 [22 P. 1136]; Niles v. Hancock (1903) 140 Cal. 157, 163 [73 P. 840].) We have carefully reviewed the record. We find no written agreement or memorandum sufficient to comply with section 1624(d).

The only writings that relate to a commission on the Great Lakes property are from Phillippe to Shapell. There is no evidence of a writing signed by Shapell showing the fact of Phillippe's employment to act as a broker for Shapell as to the Great Lakes property. There is only one letter in the exchange of correspondence referring to Phillippe's employment that is signed by Shapell. That is the letter of May 4, 1973, from Prince, Shapell's director of land acquisition, to Phillippe in which Shapell offered to buy the Filiorum property. Prince stated: "Buyer [Shapell] agrees to pay the Management Trend Company [Phillippe's firm] a commission [which] when added to the net price of the land will equal 6% of the total consideration. This commission should be paid at the close of escrow." As noted earlier, this sale was never consummated due to geology problems.

Where a broker's only agreement with his principal relates solely to specifically described property, the principal is not liable to the broker for a commission on the purchase of different property unless the broker's written employment agreement covers the other property. (Frederick v. Curtright (1955) 137 Cal.App.2d 610, 614 [290 P.2d 875].) The only writing signed by Shapell referred to the Filiorum property, not to the Great Lakes property, and is not sufficient under section 1624(d) to cover the Great Lakes property.

A writing signed by Shapell is not all that is lacking. The alleged oral commission agreement entered into in January 1973 was devoid of specifics. For example, there was no agreement as to the price range of properties that Phillippe would present to Shapell. There was no agreement as to geographic location other than the possible limitation to the Palos Verdes Peninsula, an area so large and loosely defined as to be almost meaningless. Nor was there any time specified within which Phillippe was to present the properties. We need not decide whether the absence of one or more such specifics would be fatal to the alleged agreement. The total lack of meaningful terms and conditions is the problem. Under the oral agreement, Shapell could have been charged with a commission for any property presented at any time by Phillippe. Such open-ended liability is unacceptable.

We hold there was no writing sufficient under the statute of frauds.

The Doctrine of Equitable Estoppel Does Not Prohibit Shapell from Asserting the Statute of Frauds As a Defense.

Phillippe argues that Shapell should be estopped from asserting the statute of frauds as a defense even if the agreement between them was oral and thus invalid under the statute. Phillippe contends estoppel is proper because he changed his position by performing services in reliance on Shapell's oral promise to pay a commission on the Great Lakes property. Phillippe correctly cites Monarco v. Lo Greco (1950) 35 Cal.2d 621 [220 P.2d 737] for the proposition that estoppel is proper to avoid unconscionable injury or unjust enrichment that would result from refusal to enforce an oral promise. The principle set forth in Monarco does not, however, support the application of equitable estoppel in the present case.

The Courts of Appeal have consistently held, with two narrow exceptions not present here, that a licensed broker may not assert estoppel against a statute of frauds defense in an action to recover a commission under an oral employment agreement. (See, e.g., Deeter v. Angus (1986) 179 Cal.App.3d 241, 248 [224 Cal.Rptr. 801]; Augustine v. Trucco (1954) 124 Cal.App.2d 229, 237-238 [268 P.2d 780].) This court has also repeatedly denied the availability of estoppel and other equitable remedies to licensed brokers in such actions. In Tenzer v. Superscope, Inc., supra, 39 Cal.3d 18, which did not involve a licensed broker, we noted that the rules withholding traditional equitable remedies, including the doctrine of estoppel, from licensed real estate brokers have been vigorously criticized, but we reserved for later decision the question whether licensed brokers may invoke equitable remedies to avoid the sometimes harsh results of the statute of frauds. We now answer that question.

We held in Tenzer that an unlicensed real estate finder was entitled to invoke the doctrine of equitable estoppel against a statute of frauds defense in his action to recover a commission under an oral finder's fee agreement. Because real estate brokers must be licensed to conduct business (Bus. & Prof. Code, § 10130), almost all actions to recover commissions will be by licensed brokers, not by unlicensed finders. Thus, Tenzer stated a very narrow exception to section 1624(d) that will not significantly thwart the purpose of that section. To extend the Tenzer exception to licensed brokers would significantly undermine section 1624(d).

In allowing equitable estoppel in Tenzer, we carefully distinguished between unlicensed finders and licensed brokers. "The rationale for the rigorous application of the statute of frauds to bar claims by licensed real estate brokers is related to the statutory licensing requirements. 'Real estate brokers are licensed as such only after they have demonstrated a knowledge of the laws relating to real estate transactions (Bus. & Prof. Code, §§ 10150, 10153), and it would seem that they would thus require less protection against pitfalls encountered in transactions regulated by those laws. In Pacific Southwest Dev. Corp. v. Western Pac. R. R. Co. [1956] 47 Cal.2d 62 [301 P.2d 825], the court stated at page 70: "Plaintiff is a licensed real estate broker and, as such, is presumed to know that contracted for real estate commissions are invalid and unenforceable unless put in writing and subscribed by the person to be charged. [Citations.] Nevertheless, plaintiff failed to secure proper written authorization to protect itself in the transaction. Rather it assumed the risk of relying upon claimed oral promises of defendant, and it has no cause for complaint if its efforts go unrewarded."'" (39 Cal.3d at pp. 27-28, quoting Franklin v. Hansen (1963) 59 Cal.2d 570, 575 [30 Cal.Rptr. 530, 381 P.2d 386].)

The courts have long had little sympathy for the broker who fails to adhere to the statute of frauds. In Marks v. Walter G. McCarty Corp., supra, 33 Cal.2d 814, the plaintiff broker had dealt for several months with the owner of a hotel without obtaining a signed employment agreement. The hotel was eventually sold as a result of the broker's efforts, but he was not paid a commission. This court accepted the trial court's findings that the defendant had promised to pay the broker a commission and that the broker was the procuring cause of the sale, but decided that the broker was not entitled to recover a commission because his agreement did not comply with the statute of frauds. "The plaintiff, a man of experience in this line of business, knew how to protect himself in the transaction but failed to do so." (Id., at p. 823.)

We believe the distinction between licensed brokers and unlicensed finders remains valid. We are not alone. Many "courts distinguish between persons in the traditional categories [of the statute of frauds] and brokers, who are assumed to be familiar with the laws governing their occupation." (Rest.2d Contracts (1981) § 126, reporter's note, p. 317.) An applicant for a broker's license must demonstrate by written examination that he or she has an understanding of "the general purposes and general legal effect of agency contracts." (Bus. & Prof. Code, § 10153.) To obtain an original broker's license, an applicant must have been a licensed and actively employed real estate salesperson for at least two years. (Bus. & Prof. Code, § 10150.6.) The Legislature has recently increased the educational requirements to obtain a broker's license to include mandatory successful completion at an accredited institution of a course in the legal aspects of real estate. (Bus. & Prof. Code, § 10153.2, subd. (a).) To renew their licenses, brokers must now successfully complete continuing professional education courses including legal study. (Bus. & Prof. Code, § 10170.5.) The requirements that licensed brokers know the law is stronger than ever before. Licensed brokers are conclusively presumed to know the requirements of section 1624(d).

What is the effect of this presumed knowledge? In Monarco v. Lo Greco, supra, 35 Cal.2d 621, 623, the court observed that estoppel can be applied "to prevent fraud." The court explained that it was not speaking of actual fraud but of the "fraud" that inheres in situations where there is an unconscionable injury to the promisee under an invalid oral contract or unjust enrichment to the promisor. (Ibid.; see generally1 Witkin, Summary of Cal. Law (9th ed. 1987) Contracts, § 325, p. 305.)

In Pacific Southwest, supra, 47 Cal.2d 62, decided after Monarco, the court held that a licensed real estate broker seeking to recover a commission under an oral agreement could not assert equitable estoppel to avoid the statute of frauds. The court addressed both factors set forth in Monarco—unconscionable injury and unjust enrichment. The court determined that the mere fact that the broker had rendered services under an oral agreement did not constitute a change of position to his detriment. (Id., at p. 70.) He suffered no unconscionable injury. Stated another way, the broker's reliance on the oral contract was not reasonable in light of the broker's presumed knowledge of the requirements of the statute of frauds. To give rise to equitable estoppel, the promisee's reliance must be reasonable. (See Bigelow, Law of Estoppel (6th ed. 1913) p. 682; Note, Part Performance, Estoppel and the California Statute of Frauds (1951) 3 Stan.L.Rev. 281, 289.) We agree with the statement in Pacific Southwest that the broker "assumed the risk of relying upon claimed oral promises of defendant, and it [the broker] has no cause for complaint if its efforts go unrewarded." (47 Cal.2d at p. 70; Marks v. Walter G. McCray Corp., supra, 33 Cal.2d 814, 823.) Phillippe did nothing more than perform services pursuant to an invalid agreement. Phillippe's reliance on the oral contract was not reasonable, and he therefore suffered no unconscionable injury. (Colburn v. Sessin (1949) 94 Cal.App.2d 4, 6 [209 P.2d 989].)

In accord with our analysis that a licensed broker cannot reasonsbly rely on an unenforceable oral promise of compensation, we disapprove of Le Blond v. Wolfe, supra, 83 Cal.App.2d 282, to the extent that the court allowed a licensed broker to assert equitable estoppel. The broker contended that he had suffered an unconscionable injury by cancelling an otherwise valid contract with a real estate seller in reliance on the buyer's oral promise that he would pay the broker's commission. A broker cannot create an unconscionable injury by taking extreme action. If it is unreasonable to perform services in reliance on an oral promise the broker knows to be invalid under the statute of frauds, it is even more unreasonable to cancel an enforceable written contract in reliance on an oral promise that the broker knows to be unenforceable.

Phillippe's reliance was especially unreasonable in light of his knowledge that Shapell is also a licensed broker. Phillippe had to have known that Shapell was aware that commission agreements must be in writing. That Shapell never confirmed in writing any agreement regarding the Great Lakes property should have indicated to Phillippe that Shapell believed either there was no such agreement or that it would not be enforceable. (We do not suggest that Shapell secretly intended to rely on section 1624(d) to avoid what Shapell itself believed was an agreement with Phillippe. There is no such evidence in the record.)

The alternate basis for estoppel is unjust enrichment. Phillippe has not shown any unjust enrichment of Shapell. The most Phillippe has shown is that Shapell did not pay for his services. The fact that a broker's principal does not pay for the broker's services under an unenforceable oral contract does not constitute unjust enrichment sufficient to support equitable estoppel. In Marks v. Walter G. McCarty, supra, 33 Cal.2d 814, the court denied recovery to a broker under an oral contract despite having accepted the trial court's finding that the broker was the procuring cause of the sale. Likewise here, the jury's finding that Phillippe was the procuring cause of the sale to Shapell does not by itself establish unjust enrichment sufficient to give rise to equitable estoppel.

To determine that mere nonpayment constitutes unjust enrichment sufficient for estoppel would also conflict with consistent holdings that licensed brokers, who cannot recover under oral agreements invalid under the statute of frauds, are also prohibited from recovery in quantum meruit for the reasonable value of their services. (Beazell v.

Schrader (1963) 59 Cal.2d 577, 582 [30 Cal.Rptr. 534, 381 P.2d 390]; Jamison v. Hyde (1903) 141 Cal. 109, 113 [74 P.695]; Augustine v. Trucco, supra, 124 Cal.App.2d 229, 237-238.) "[T]he purpose of the statute would be largely defeated if the broker should be allowed to recover in quantum meruit for his services…, either on the oral contract itself or in quasi-contract for reasonable compensation. This is made obvious by the fact that reasonable compensation would be determined by the commission that is customarily paid in the community, and the oral contract that the broker alleges to have been made is practically always a contract to pay this customary commission." (2 Corbin on Contracts (1950) §416, p. 438.) The quantum meruit theory of recovery in these circumstances "has been so roundly rejected by the [C]alifornia courts that many recent attempts by brokers to recover commissions do not event raise it." (Cal. Real Property Sales Transactions (Cont.Ed.Bar 1981) §2.55, p. 110.) The authors of the Restatement Second of Contracts reached the same conclusion. Section 375 states: "A party who would otherwise have a claim in restitution under a contract is not barred from restitution for the reason that the contract is unenforceable by him because of the Statute of Frauds unless the statute provides otherwise or its purpose would be frustrated by allowing restitution." Comment a, illustration 3 of section 375 expressly states that recovery in restitution by a real estate broker would frustrate the purpose of the statute. The overwhelming majority of other jurisdictions has adopted the Restatement view. (See, Annot. (1955) 41 A.L.R.2d 905, 908; 7 Powell, The Law of Real Property (Rohan ed. 1987) ¶938.16[3], pp. 84C-56 to 84C-63.) If nonpayment is insufficient to allow recovery in quantum meruit, nonpayment is equally insufficient to support equitable estoppel on the ground of unjust enrichment.

There would be no point in deciding, as we have, that a licensed broker cannot show an unconscionable injury sufficient to assert estoppel based only on the fact that the broker performed services without payment, but then to conclude that the nonpayment constitutes unjust enrichment sufficient to allow estoppel. A dissatisfied broker could prevail by merely labeling his theory of recovery as unjust enrichment rather than unconscionable injury.

We hold that a licensed real estate broker or salesperson cannot assert equitable estoppel against a statute of frauds defense to an oral commission agreement that is subject to Civil Code section 1624(d) unless there is a showing of actual fraud by the party to be charged under the invalid oral agreement. Because licensed brokers are involved in almost every real estate sale, to decide otherwise would be to eviscerate if not abrogate section 1624(d).

Sound Policy Reasons Support the Denial of Equitable Estoppel to a Licensed Broker.

The original statute of frauds was enacted in England more than 300 years ago. (An Act for the Prevention of Frauds and Perjuries, 1677, 29 Car. 2, ch. 3.) Variations of the original English statute have been widely enacted in the United States. The State of California first enacted its version in 1872. The Legislature expanded the statute in 1878 to include real estate commission agreements. Despite much criticism, section 1624(d) remains effective more than a century after its passage. Whatever else it may be, section 1624(d) is durable.

The statute of frauds is also indisputably significant. It has been characterized as, "the most important statute ever enacted in either country [England and the United States], relating to civil affairs." (Bishop, Law of Contracts (1878) §498, p. 177.) By acknowledging the statute's importance, we do not express our opinion as to its worth. Whether this court likes section 1624(d) is not relevant to our decision. We have no prerogative to create an exception that would effectively render this durable and important statute a nullity. "Courts may not read into a statute an exception not incorporated therein by the Legislature [citation omitted], unless such an exception must reasonably and necessarily be implied...." (Pacific Motor Transport Co. v. State Bd. of Equalization (1972) 28 Cal.App.3d 230, 235 [104 Cal.Rptr. 558]; cf. Estate of Banerjee (1978) 21 Cal.3d 527, 540 [147 Cal.Rptr. 157, 580 P.2d 657] [exceptions to a general provision of a statute are strictly construed].) If section 1624(d) should be modified, the Legislature can do so.

We believe the legislative preference for written contracts is stronger than ever before. The Legislature has demonstrated with increasing frequency its desire to provide consumers with the security and certainty of written contracts in a wide variety of transactions. This legislative trend is not new. More than 20 years ago, a commentator noted that, "[n]otwithstanding what appears to be a disfavorable attitude of the courts towards the Statute [of Frauds], the legislative trend has been in the direction of expanding rather than restricting the scope of the writing requirement." (Comment, Equitable Estoppel and the Statute of Frauds in California, supra, 53 Cal.L.Rev. 590, 592.)

* * *

Section 1624(d) can equally be characterized as a consumer protection statute, perhaps this state's first. The essential purpose of the statute is reflected in the very title of its English precursor, "An Act for Prevention of Frauds and Perjuries." The purchase or sale of real estate, especially a home, is always a significant event. For most people, such purchase or sale is probably the single most important financial transaction in their lives. Commercial real property transactions are of similar importance to the parties involved. Section 1624(d) manifests a valid legislative intent to protect real estate buyers and sellers from unfounded claims for brokers' commissions. The statute of frauds also serves a cautionary purpose. By requiring a writing, the statute serves to emphasize to contracting parties the significance of their agreement. The importance of real estate transactions makes this aspect of the statute especially salutary.

Faced with a clear legislative desire for written contracts in a wide variety of contexts and the special significance of real estate transactions, we cannot conclude that section 1624(d) is a legislative anachronism that should be judicially swept away. In Buckaloo v. Johnson, supra, 14 Cal.3d 815, which also involved a licensed broker's commission, the court made clear that, "[t]he statute of frauds conclusively establishes that brokerage contracts with either the vendor or the vendee must be in writing. We have neither the authority nor the inclination to circumvent that declared policy...." (Id., at p. 827.) Our view has not changed.

It is not unfair to require licensed brokers to comply with the statute of frauds. Only those persons licensed by the California Department of Real Estate may lawfully act as real estate brokers in this state. (Bus. & Prof. Code, § 10130.) To bring an action to recover a real estate commission, a broker must plead and prove that he was duly licensed at the time his cause of action arose. (Bus. & Prof. Code, § 10136.) The effect of these laws is obvious—only a person duly licensed may earn and recover compensation as a real estate broker. It is not too much to ask in return for that valuable privilege that a licensed broker comply with the statute of frauds.

Section 1624(d) is perhaps more fairly applied now against brokers than when first enacted. Brokers were not then required to be licensed, and they may have had little or no legal knowledge. Application of section 1624(d) might have come as a surprise a century ago. In view of the current educational requirements, a broker cannot be surprised by section 1624(d).

Phillippe, the California Association of Realtors as amicus curiae, and various commentators contend that brokers are often not in sufficiently strong bargaining positions to obtain written employment contracts from their principals and suggest that this disparity of bargaining power is most common in the commercial real estate market. Phillippe urges that section 1624(d) should not bar recovery on an oral contract in that situation because the statute is contrary to industry custom and practice. We reject that contention for several reasons.

Section 1624(d) does not include an exception based on the relative bargaining strength of the parties to a contract. Any such exception must be created by the Legislature, not by this court. If the Legislature believes that section 1624(d) is not workable in the real estate marketplace, the Legislature can act accordingly. Even if we had the prerogative and inclination to create judicially such an exception, we have been provided with no factual basis for doing so. Phillippe did not introduce any evidence that there was an inequitable disparity between himself and Shapell. Amicus curiae and the legal commentators also cite no facts, and we are unaware of any, that support their criticism that the marketplace and the statute are in conflict. We decline to create a major exception to section 1624(d), and in so doing set aside decades of precedent, based on the unsupported assertions of the statute's critics.

The lack of evidence aside, we are not persuaded that section 1624(d) is inappropriate merely because there may be a disparity of bargaining power between a broker and his principal. The resolution of disputes would be complicated. Even defining bargaining power would be troublesome. Would it include legal knowledge and commercial sophistication? If so, how would a court measure those factors? Would it include financial strength? If so, to determine whether there was a disparity, a court would likely have to conduct a detailed examination of the parties' respective financial conditions thus creating a need for considerable pretrial discovery and protracted litigation.

Those engaged in real property transactions ordinarily desire certainty in their financial dealings. If bargaining power were relevant, the parties would not know (and could not know) at the time of entering into an oral agreement whether it would be an enforceable contract. Each party would have to speculate as to whether he posssessed some quality, e.g., finances, knowledge, or even better negotiating skills, that created an imbalance in bargaining power. Whenever a dispute arose, a court would then have to determine whether there was a disparity of power. To hold that the validity of a commission agreement depends on relative bargaining power would lead to great uncertainty. We believe a distinction based on disparity of bargaining power would lead to unnecessary complexities.

We are also not persuaded that section 1624(d) should be disregarded in a commercial setting. That suggestion is premised on the unsupported allegation that written commission agreements are often not used in commercial real estate transactions. No evidence is before us regarding industry custom. We decline to speculate as to what the custom, if any, may be.

We are inclined to believe that the business community in general may favor written contracts. They provide certainty and predictability. In the only empirical study we have been able to locate, more than half of the businesses (manufacturers) surveyed favored enforcement of only those agreements that comply with the statute of frauds, and almost two-fifths favored a change in the law to make even fewer agreements enforceable. (Comment, The Statute of Frauds and the Business Community: A Re-appraisal in Light of Prevailing Practices (1957) 66 Yale L.J. 1038, 1058.) More than 50 years ago, one of the leading commentators on contracts observed that the statute of frauds was even then becoming more useful due to the increasing volume and complexity of commercial transactions. (Llewellyn, What Price Contract? — An Essay in Perspective (1931) 40 Yale L.J. 704, 747.) The commercial world is now even more complex, and Llewellyn's observation appears to remain sound, perhaps more so than when he made it. The business community's preference for written contracts was stated most colorfully in the memorable malaprop attributed to motion picture producer Samuel Goldwyn: "An oral contract isn't worth the paper it's written on." (Shavelson, Hollywood Signs: Movie Moguls Who Gave the Golden Era Its Shine, L. A. Times (July 27, 1986) Calendar Section, p. 24.) Written contracts appear to have diverse, substantial support.

Last and most important, there is no exception for commercial transactions stated in the statute. An unequivocal statute must take precedence over mere custom. Indeed, the widespread custom of not using written contracts in real estate transactions was apparently a reason why section 1624(d) was enacted in the first instance.

Our Decision Does Not Leave Licensed Brokers Unprotected.

In Tenzer v. Superscope, supra, 39 Cal.3d 18, the court held that the statute of frauds does not preclude an action for actual fraud. (Id, at pp. 28-31.) Although the plaintiff in Tenzer was an unlicensed real estate finder, the Tenzer court did not distinguish in its discussion of actual fraud between unlicensed finders and licensed brokers and did not suggest that its holding regarding actual fraud should be limited to unlicensed finders. (This lack of distinction between unlicensed finders and licensed brokers is in marked contrast to the Tenzer court's careful distinction between the two groups in its discussion of equitable estoppel.)

Phillippe did not plead a cause of action for actual fraud. We believe it necessary, however, to explain how our present holding necessarily would affect an action by a licensed broker for actual fraud. To recover for fraud in any case the plaintiff must show that he reasonably relied on the defendant's misrepresentations. The plaintiff cannot recover if his reliance was not justified or reasonable. (Wagner v. Benson (1980) 101 Cal.App.3d 27, 36 [161 Cal.Rptr. 516]; see generally 4 Witkin, Summary of Cal. Law (8th ed. 1974) Torts, §475, p. 2734; 3 Pomeroy, Equity Jurisprudence (5th ed. 1941) §891, pp. 505-510.) As discussed above, a broker's presumed knowledge of the statute of frauds precludes him from showing the reasonable reliance on an oral agreement that is necessary to assert equitable estoppel. (Pac. etc. Dev. Corp. v. Western Pac. R. R. Co., supra, 47 Cal.2d 62, 70; Marks v. Walter G. McCarty Corp., supra, 33 Cal.2d 814, 823; Osborne v. Huntington Beach etc. School Dist. (1970) 5 Cal.App.3d 510, 515 [85 Cal.Rptr. 793].) Likewise, an oral promise by a broker's principal to execute the required writing at a later date will not give rise to estoppel. (Colburn v. Sessin, supra, 94 Cal.App.2d 4, 5.) By parity of reasoning, a broker's reliance on an oral promise to pay a commission or an oral promise to execute the required writing at a later date cannot be sufficiently reasonable to support an action for fraud. A broker's reliance, however, on a representation that the necessary contract has in fact been executed may be reasonable and thus support an action for fraud or the assertion of equitable estoppel. (§1623; Owens v. Foundation for Ocean Research, supra, 107 Cal.App.3d 179, 183-184.)

There may be other types of promises on which a broker could reasonably rely. We do not purport in this opinion to identify every such promise. We believe, however, that a licensed broker's reliance can be reasonable only in rather limited circumstances. Whether a broker's reliance is reasonable must be determined on the facts of each case.

Conclusion

We hold that Phillippe's alleged oral commission agreement is invalid under section 1624(d). Phillippe cannot avoid the requirements of section 1624(d) by asserting equitable estoppel. We reverse the judgment in all respects and remand with directions to enter judgment including costs on appeal in favor of Shapell. In light of our decision, we need not address the issues raised by Phillippe in his cross-appeal.

Redke v. Silvertrust

Supreme Court of California, 1971
6 Cal.3d 94, 90 P.2d 805, 98 Cal.Rptr. 293

BURKE, J.

Plaintiff Mitzi Lee Redke brought an action in Los Angeles Superior Court to enforce the terms of an oral agreement allegedly made for her benefit between her mother Ann Hayden, and her stepfather, Samuel Hayden, both of whom are now deceased, whereupon Sam agreed to bequeath certain of Ann's separate property to Mitzi. Defendants, who are the executors of Sam's estate, co-trustees of a trust created by him, and testamentary trustees under Ann's will, appeal from a judgment in Mitzi's favor. We have concluded that, except for one minor modification, the judgment should be affirmed.

The pertinent facts underlying the dispute are as follows: In 1955, Sam, a widower with three adult children, married Ann, mother of Mitzi and Warren. By 1963, Ann's separate property had grown from approximately $20,000-$40,000 to over a million dollars, largely a result of Sam's assistance in managing her investments. Ann executed a will and an inter vivos trust which provided that half of her separate property would be placed in a marital deduction trust for Sam, giving him a general power of appointment over that property; the remaining half was to be placed in trust for her children, Mitzi and Warren. Sam executed a similar will and trust leaving half of his property to Ann, and half in trust for Mitzi and Warren.

On February 22, 1963, Warren died unexpectedly from a heart attack. Ann, who was suffering from terminal cancer, was informed of her son's death the following day. That news was a shock to Ann, and she immediately became concerned about providing for Mitzi, whose husband was also ill. Consequently, she informed Sam, in the presence of her nurse, Mitzi and another person, that she wanted to call her lawyers to change her will and trust to leave all of her separate property to Mitzi. Sam assured her that no such changes were necessary, and promised that if Ann died, Sam would leave his share of Ann's property to Mitzi upon his own death and would see that Mitzi received all of Ann's property. Ann agreed. Thereafter, the only substantial changes made in Ann or Sam's estate plans prior to Ann's death were amendments to their trusts to give Warren's share of their trust estates to Mitzi; Ann also executed a document transferring to her trust most of her remaining property.

Ann died on April 5, 1963. On the following day, Sam offered to give to Mitzi Ann's jewelry and furs, a matter discussed separately below. Sam also reaffirmed to various persons, including Mitzi, his promise to leave Mitzi his share of Ann's property. Nevertheless, within a few months following Ann's death, Sam met and married Ruth Allender and shortly thereafter amended his trust and will eliminating all provision for Mitzi and naming as beneficiaries his new wife and his natural children. Sam died in 1965, and Mitzi filed creditor's claims against his estate based upon the oral agreement and the separate gift of furs and jewelry.

At trial, defendants denied the existence of the alleged oral agreement and contended, among other things, that such an agreement would be unenforceable under the statute of frauds and void as contrary to public policy, being an illegal evasion of federal and state death taxes. The trial court made extensive findings which, in effect, recognized the existence of the oral agreement and upheld its validity and enforceability. The court held that upon Ann's death Sam became constructive trustee for the benefit of Mitzi of all of Ann's separate property, furs and jewelry received by Sam from and after Ann's death, together with all income, interest and profits derived therefrom. The court's judgment ordered defendants to deliver to Mitzi certain designated stock valued at $392,186.48, with dividends and increments thereto, plus 7 percent interest from the date of judgment. In addition to this stock, Mitzi was awarded $457,916.06, plus 7 percent interest from the date of judgment. Mitzi also obtained judgment for all damages which she or Ann's estate may incur by reason of Sam's negligence or misconduct.

1. The Oral Agreement

In general, a contract to make a particular testamentary disposition of property is valid and enforceable. As in every contract, "there is an implied covenant of good faith and fair dealing that neither party will do anything which injures the right of the other to receive the benefits of the agreement. [Citations.] Where the parties contract to make a particular disposition of property by will, the agreement necessarily includes a promise not to breach the contract by revoking the will and failing to dispose of the property as agreed." (Brown v. Superior Court, 34 Cal.2d 559, 564-565 [212 P.2d 878]; Brewer v. Simpson, 53 Cal.2d 567, 588-589 [2 Cal.Rptr. 609, 349 P.2d 289].) If the contract is executed between spouses, a failure to perform it constitutes a violation of their confidential relationship and is constructive fraud which justifies the imposition of a constructive trust. (Day v. Greene, 59 Cal.2d 404, 411 [29 Cal.Rptr. 785, 380 P.2d 385, 94 A.L.R.2d 802].)

The trial court correctly determined that the statute of frauds did not render the agreement unenforceable. "Although the statute requires that an agreement to make a provision by will be in writing (Civ. Code, § 1624, subd. 6; Code Civ. Proc., § 1973, subd. 6), a party will be estopped from relying on the statute where fraud would result from refusal to enforce an oral contract [citation]. The doctrine of estoppel has been applied where an unconscionable injury would result from denying enforcement after one party has been induced to make a serious change of position in reliance on the contract or where unjust enrichment would result if a party who has received the benefits of the other's performance were allowed to invoke the statute. [Citation.]" (Day v. Greene, supra, 59 Cal.2d 404, 409-410; see Monarco v. Lo Greco, 35 Cal.2d 621, 623 [220 P.2d 737]; Notten v. Mensing, 3 Cal.2d 469, 474 [45 P.2d 198]; Mintz v. Rowitz, 13 Cal.App.3d 216, 223-225 [91 Cal.Rptr. 435].)

The trial court found that Ann, by reason of her trust and confidence in Sam, and in reliance upon his oral promise, changed her position to her detriment, and to Mitzi's detriment, by not changing her will and trust to make Mitzi her sole beneficiary; she changed her position by maintaining the status quo despite her concern over her daughter's welfare. Defendants do not question the evidentiary support for this finding, nor do they dispute the applicable law set forth above. They do, however, contend that Sam and Ann subsequently abandoned the agreement, a factual question which the trial court resolved in plaintiff's favor. There was ample evidence to support the court's finding that the agreement was not abandoned, including the fact that after Ann's death, Sam affirmed to five witnesses, including Mitzi, his agreement to leave his share of Ann's property to Mitzi. We conclude that the trial court correctly held that defendants are estopped to rely upon the statute of frauds.

* * *

The judgment is modified by striking therefrom the award of post-judgment interest upon any stocks found to have been delivered by defendants to plaintiff in compliance with the terms of the judgment. As so modified, the judgment is affirmed and the cause is remanded to the Los Angeles County Superior Court for further proceedings not inconsistent with this opinion. Plaintiff shall receive her costs on appeal.

Wright, C. J., McComb, J., Peters, J., Tobriner, J., Mosk, J., and Sullivan, J., concurred.

Afterthoughts

A defendant is precluded from asserting the statute of frauds where the plaintiff would be unconscionably injured or the defendant unjustly enriched and plaintiff in reliance on the oral promise has changed his position. (*Monarco v. Lo Greco* (1950) 35 Cal.2d 621 [220 P.2d 737].) In other words, reliance by one party on an oral contract may "estop" the other from setting up a defense based upon the statute of frauds. Where a contract, which is required by law to be in writing, is prevented from being put into writing by the fraud of a party thereto, any other party who is by such fraud led to believe that it is in writing, and acts upon such belief to his prejudice, may enforce it against the fraudulent party. (Cal.Civ.Code § 1623)

Chapter 4

Policing the Bargain

Capacity to Contract — Minors and Persons of Unsound Mind

Minors

In California, a minor may make a contract in the same manner as an adult, subject to the power of disaffirmance. (Cal.Fam.Code §6700) A contract of a minor may be disaffirmed by the minor before majority (reaching the age of 18) or within a reasonable time afterwards. (Cal.Fam.Code §6710) A minor cannot make a contract relating to real property or any interest therein, or make a contract relating to any personal property not in the immediate possession or control of the minor. (Cal.Fam.Code §6701(b)(c).)

A contract, otherwise valid, entered into during minority, may not be disaffirmed on that ground either during the actual minority of the person entering into the contract, or at any time thereafter, if all of the following requirements are satisfied:

(a) The contract is to pay the reasonable value of things necessary for the support of the minor or the minor's family.

(b) These things have been actually furnished to the minor or to the minor's family.

(c) The contract is entered into by the minor when not under the care of a parent or guardian able to provide for the minor or the minor's family. (Cal.Fam.Code §6712)

Persons of Unsound Mind

A person entirely without understanding has no power to make a contract of any kind, but the person is liable for the reasonable value of things furnished to the person necessary for the support of the person or the person's family. (Cal.Civ.Code §38) A person is rebuttably presumed to be of unsound mind if the person is substantially unable to manage his or her own financial resources or resist fraud or undue influence. (Cal.Civ.Code §39(b).)

Duress

Duress consists of:

(1) Unlawful confinement of the person of the party, or of a close relative;

(2) Unlawful detention of the property of any such person; or,

(3) Confinement of such person, lawful in form, but fraudulently obtained, or fraudulently made unjustly harrassing or oppressive. (Cal.Civ.Code § 1569)

Duress is not limited to threats against the person. It may also consist of threats to business or property interests. (*Sistrom v. Anderson*, 51 Cal.App.2d 213, 220-221 [124 P.2d 372]) In general, the taking of legal action or the threat to take such action cannot constitute duress. (*Hanford Gas etc. Co. v. Hanford*, 163 Cal. 108, 112 [124 P. 727]; *Burke v. Gould*, 105 Cal. 277, 283 [38 P. 733]; *Sistrom v. Anderson*, 51 Cal.App.2d 213, 221 [124 P.2d 372].)

Accord and Satisfaction in California

Traditionally, the common law has sanctioned a subtle form of duress or coercion known as "accord and satisfaction." An accord and satisfaction is the offering of some performance different from that originally called for and the acceptance of the different performance as a full and complete performance. Take the following example: You've agreed with a cabinetmaker to perform some work at your home. The agreed price is $1,000.00 but you feel that she has botched the job and that the cost of remedying the defect would be $150.00. You send her a check for $850.00 explaining why you feel that is a fair amount and state that the check is being offered in "full payment" of the amount owed under the agreement. A "payment in full "check operates as an accord and satisfaction where the creditor negotiates the check with full awareness of the terms on which it was offered. Traditionally, a creditor could write all manner of disclaimer on the check to no avail. If she accepted the check with awareness of the basis on which it was offered she entered into a valid accord and satisfaction. This was true irrespective of whether the creditor's "acceptance" took the form of simply cashing the check, holding the check uncashed for an unreasonable period of time, protesting the condition orally or on the check before cashing it or striking the "payment in full" language before negotiating the check, and without regard to whether it represents only the amount that the debtor admits owing.

California law is no longer in accord (no pun intended) with the above stated common law rule. California Civil Code section 1526 provides that a payment in full check does not operate as an accord and satisfaction if the creditor strikes out the restrictive words or can prove that she cashed the check without knowledge of the restriction. In order to show that the creditor should have known of the restriction the debtor must give notice in writing to the creditor "not less than 15 days nor more than 90 days prior to receipt of the check or draft ... that a check or draft will be tendered with a restrictive endorsement and that acceptance and cashing of the check or draft will constitute an accord and satisfaction." Then and only then will an accord and satisfaction have been entered into upon the creditor's cashing of the check. (Cal.Civ.Code § 1526(b)(2).)

Fraud and Deceit

Conduct may be fraudulent because of an intentional misrepresentation, concealment, a false promise or a negligent misrepresentation.

Intentional Misrepresentation

The essential elements of a claim of fraud by an intentional misrepresentation are:

1. The defendant must have made a representation as to a past or existing material fact.

2. The representation must have been false.

3. The defendant must have known that the representation was false when made or must have made the representation recklessly without knowing whether it was true or false;

4. The defendant must have made the representation with an intent to defraud the plaintiff, that is, he or she must have made the representation for the purpose of inducing the plaintiff to rely upon it and to act or to refrain from acting in reliance thereon.

5. The plaintiff must have been unaware of the falsity of the representation; must have acted in reliance upon the truth of the representation and must have been justified in relying upon the representation.

6. And, finally, as a result of the reliance upon the truth of the representation, the plaintiff must have sustained damage. (See, Cal.Civ.Code § 1572)

Expression of Opinion

Ordinarily, expressions of opinion are not treated as representations of fact upon which to base actionable fraud. However, when one party possesses or holds himself or herself out as possessing superior knowledge or special information regarding the subject of a representation, and the other party is so situated that he or she may reasonably rely upon such supposed superior knowledge or special information, a representation made by the party possessing or holding himself herself out as possessing such knowledge or information will be treated as a representation of fact. This is so, even though the representation, if made by any other person, might be regarded as an expression of opinion. When a party states an opinion as a fact, in such a manner that it is reasonable to rely and act upon it as a fact, it may be treated as a representation of fact. (See, 5 Witkin, Summary of Cal. Law (9th ed. 1988) Torts, §§ 678-681.)

Nondisclosure of Known Facts

Reed v. King

Court of Appeals of California, Third Appellate District, 1983
145 Cal.App.3d 261, 193 Cal.Rptr. 130

BLEASE, J.

In the sale of a house, must the seller disclose it was the site of a multiple murder?

Dorris Reed purchased a house from Robert King. Neither King nor his real estate agents (the other named defendants) told Reed that a woman and her four children were murdered there 10 years earlier. However, it seems "truth will come to light; murder cannot be hid long." (Shakespeare, Merchant of Venice, act II, scene II.) Reed learned of the gruesome episode from a neighbor after the sale. She sues seeking rescission and damages. King and the real estate agent defendants successfully demurred to her first amended complaint for failure to state a cause of action. Reed appeals the ensuing judgment of dismissal. We will reverse the judgment.

Facts

We take all issuable facts pled in Reed's complaint as true. King and his real estate agent knew about the murders and knew the event materially affected the market value of the house when they listed it for sale. They represented to Reed the premises were in good condition and fit for an "elderly lady" living alone. They did not disclose the fact of the murders. At some point King asked a neighbor not to inform Reed of that event. Nonetheless, after Reed moved in neighbors informed her no one was interested in purchasing the house because of the stigma. Reed paid $76,000, but the house is only worth $65,000 because of its past.

The trial court sustained the demurrers to the complaint on the ground it did not state a cause of action. The court concluded a cause of action could only be stated "if the subject property, by reason of the prior circumstances, were presently the object of community notoriety...." Reed declined the offer of leave to amend.

Discussion

Does Reed's pleading state a cause of action? Concealed within this question is the nettlesome problem of the duty of disclosure of blemishes on real property which are not physical defects or legal impairments to use.

Reed seeks to state a cause of action sounding in contract, i.e. rescission, or in tort, i.e., deceit. In either event her allegations must reveal a fraud. (See Civ. Code, §§ 1571-1573, 1689, 1709-1710.) "The elements of actual fraud, whether as the basis of the remedy in contract or tort, may be stated as follows: There must be (1) a false representation or concealment of a material fact (or, in some cases, an opinion) susceptible of knowledge, (2) made with knowledge of its falsity or without sufficient knowledge on the subject to warrant a representation, (3) with the intent to induce the person to whom it is made to act upon it; and such person must (4) act in reliance upon the representation (5) to his damage." (1 Witkin, Summary of Cal. Law (8th ed. 1973) Contracts, § 315.)

The trial court perceived the defect in Reed's complaint to be a failure to allege concealment of a material fact. "Concealment" and "material" are legal conclusions concerning the effect of the issuable facts pled. As appears, the analytic pathways to these conclusions are intertwined.

Concealment is a term of art which includes mere nondisclosure when a party has a duty to disclose. (See, e.g., Lingsch v. Savage (1963) 213 Cal.App.2d 729, 738 [29 Cal.Rptr. 201, 8 A.L.R.3d 537]; Rest.2d Contracts, § 161; Rest.2d Torts, § 551; Rest., Restitution, § 8, esp. com. b.) Reed's complaint reveals only nondisclosure despite the allegation King asked a neighbor to hold his peace. There is no allegation the attempt at suppression was a cause in fact of Reed's ignorance. (See Rest.2d Contracts, §§ 160, 162-164; Rest.2d Torts, § 550; Rest., Restitution, § 9.) Accordingly, the critical question is: does the seller have a duty to disclose here? Resolution of this question depends on the materiality of the fact of the murders.

In general, a seller of real property has a duty to disclose: "where the seller knows of facts materially affecting the value or desirability of the property which are known or accessible only to him and also knows that such facts are not known to, or within the reach of the diligent attention and observation of the buyer, the seller is under a duty to disclose them to the buyer. [Citations omitted.]" (Lingsch v. Savage, supra, 213 Cal.App.2d at p. 735.) This broad statement of duty has led one commentator to conclude: "The ancient maxim caveat emptor ('let the buyer beware.') has little or no application to California real estate transactions." (1 Miller & Starr, Current Law of Cal. Real Estate (rev.ed. 1975) § 1:80.)

Whether information "is of sufficient materiality to affect the value or desirability of the property ... depends on the facts of the particular case." (Lingsch, supra, 213 Cal.App.2d at p. 737.) Materiality "is a question of law, and is part of the concept of right to rely or justifiable reliance." (3 Witkin, Cal. Procedure (2d ed. 1971) Pleading, § 578, p. 2217.) Accordingly, the term is essentially a label affixed to a normative conclusion. Three considerations bear on this legal conclusion: the gravity of the harm inflicted by nondisclosure; the fairness of imposing a duty of discovery on the buyer as an alternative to compelling disclosure, and the impact on the stability of contracts if rescission is permitted.

Numerous cases have found nondisclosure of physical defects and legal impediments to use of real property are material. (See 1 Miller & Starr, supra, § 181.) However, to our knowledge, no prior real estate sale case has faced an issue of nondisclosure of the kind presented here. (Compare Earl v. Saks & Co., supra, 36 Cal.2d 602; Kuhn v. Gottfried (1951) 103 Cal.App.2d 80, 85-86 [229 P.2d 137].) Should this variety of ill-repute be required to be disclosed? Is this a circumstance where "non-disclosure of the fact amounts to a failure to act in good faith and in accordance with reasonable standards of fair dealing[?]" (Rest.2d Contracts, § 161, subd. (b).)

The paramount argument against an affirmative conclusion is it permits the camel's nose of unrestrained irrationality admission to the tent. If such an "irrational" consideration is permitted as a basis of rescission the stability of all conveyances will be seriously undermined. Any fact that might disquiet the enjoyment of some segment of the buying public may be seized upon by a disgruntled purchaser to void a bargain. In our view, keeping this genie in the bottle is not as difficult a task as these arguments assume. We do not view a decision allowing Reed to survive a demurrer in these unusual circumstances as indorsing the materiality of facts predicating peripheral, insubstantial, or fancied harms.

The murder of innocents is highly unusual in its potential for so disturbing buyers they may be unable to reside in a home where it has occurred. This fact may foreseeably deprive a buyer of the intended use of the purchase. Murder is not such a common occurrence that buyers should be charged with anticipating and discovering this disquieting possibility. Accordingly, the fact is not one for which a duty of inquiry and discovery can sensibly be imposed upon the buyer.

Reed alleges the fact of the murders has a quantifiable effect on the market value of the premises. We cannot say this allegation is inherently wrong and, in the pleading posture of the case, we assume it to be true. If information known or accessible only to the seller has a significant and measurable effect on market value and, as is alleged here, the seller is aware of this effect, we see no principled basis for making the duty to disclose turn upon the character of the information. Physical usefulness is not and never has been the sole criterion of valuation. Stamp collections and gold speculation would be insane activities if utilitarian considerations were the sole measure of value. (See also Civ. Code, § 3355 [deprivation of property of peculiar value to owner]; Annot. (1950)

12 A.L.R.2d 902 [Measure of Damages for Conversion or Loss of, or Damage to, Personal Property Having No Market Value].)

Reputation and history can have a significant effect on the value of realty. "George Washington slept here" is worth something, however physically inconsequential that consideration may be. Ill-repute or "bad will" conversely may depress the value of property. Failure to disclose such a negative fact where it will have a foreseeably depressing effect on income expected to be generated by a business is tortious. (See Rest.2d Torts, § 551, illus. 11.) Some cases have held that unreasonable fears of the potential buying public that a gas or oil pipeline may rupture may depress the market value of land and entitle the owner to incremental compensation in eminent domain. (See Annot., Eminent Domain: Elements and Measure of Compensation for Oil or Gas Pipeline Through Private Property (1954) 38 A.L.R.2d 788, 801-804.)

Whether Reed will be able to prove her allegation the decade-old multiple murder has a significant effect on market value we cannot determine. If she is able to do so by competent evidence she is entitled to a favorable ruling on the issues of materiality and duty to disclose. Her demonstration of objective tangible harm would still the concern that permitting her to go forward will open the floodgates to rescission on subjective and idiosyncratic grounds.

A more troublesome question would arise if a buyer in similar circumstances were unable to plead or establish a significant and quantifiable effect on market value. However, this question is not presented in the posture of this case. Reed has not alleged the fact of the murders has rendered the premises useless to her as a residence. As currently pled, the gravamen of her case is pecuniary harm. We decline to speculate on the abstract alternative.

The judgment is reversed.

Evans, Acting P. J., and Carr, J., concurred.

Afterthoughts

The following have been held to be of sufficient materiality to require disclosure: the home sold was constructed on filled land (*Burkett v. J.A. Thompson & Son* (1957) 150 Cal.App.2d 523, 526 [310 P.2d 56]); improvements were added without a building permit and in violation of zoning regulations (*Barder v. McClung* (1949) 93 Cal.App.2d 692, 697 [209 P.2d 808]) or in violation of building codes (*Curran v. Heslop* (1953) 115 Cal.App.2d 476, 480-481 [252 P.2d 378]); the structure was condemned (*Katz v. Department of Real Estate* (1979) 96 Cal.App.3d 895, 900 [158 Cal.Rptr. 766]); the structure was termite-infested (*Godfrey v. Steinpress* (1982) 128 Cal.App.3d 154 [180 Cal.Rptr. 95]); there was water infiltration in the soil (*Barnhouse v. City of Pinole* (1982) 133 Cal.App.3d 171, 187-188 [183 Cal.Rptr. 881]); the amount of net income a piece of property would yield was overstated. (*Ford v. Cournale* (1973) 36 Cal.App.3d 172, 179-180 [111 Cal.Rptr. 334, 81 A.L.R.3d 704].) (Footnote 5, *Reed v. King, supra.*)

Is there a duty to disclose the presence of noisy neighbors? See, *Shapiro v. Sutherland* (1998) 64 Cal.App.4th 1534, 76 Cal.Rptr.2d 101.

Generally where material facts are known to one party and not to the other, failure to disclose them is not actionable fraud unless there is some relationship between the parties which gives rise to a duty to disclose such known facts. A duty to disclose known facts arises where the party having knowledge of the facts is in a fiduciary or a confidential relationship. A fiduciary or a confidential relationship exists whenever under the circumstances trust and confidence reasonably may be and is reposed by one person in the integrity and fidelity of another. A duty to disclose known facts arises in the absence of a fiduciary or a confidential relationship where one party knows of material facts and also knows that such facts are neither known nor readily accessible to the other party. (See, 5 Witkin, Summary of Cal. Law (9th ed. 1988) Torts §§ 697-701.)

Active Concealment of Known Facts

Intentional concealment exists where a party:

(1) Knows of defects in a property and intentionally conceals them; or

(2) Actively prevents investigation and discovery of material facts by the other party; or

(3) While under no duty to speak, nevertheless does so, but does not speak honestly or makes misleading statements or suppresses facts that materially qualify those stated. (See, 5 Witkin, Summary of Cal. Law (9th ed. 1988) Torts, §§ 702-703.)

Promise without Intention to Perform

If in order to induce one to enter into an agreement, "a party makes an independent promise without intention of performing it, this separate false promise constitutes fraud which may be proven to nullify the main agreement; but if the false promise relates to the matter covered by the main agreement and contradicts or varies the terms thereof, any evidence of the false promise directly violates the parole evidence rule and is inadmissible." (*Bank of America v. Lamb Finance Co.* (2d Dist.1960) 179 Cal.App.2d 498, 3 Cal.Rptr. 877; *Bank of America etc. Ass'n. v. Pendergrass* (1935) 4 Cal.2d 258, 48 P.2d 659)

The essential elements of a claim of fraud by a false promise are:

(1) The defendant must have made a promise as to a material matter and, at the time it was made, he or she must have intended not to perform it;

(2) The defendant must have made the promise with an intent to defraud the plaintiff; that is, he or she must have made the promise for the purpose of inducing plaintiff to rely upon it and to act or refrain from acting in reliance upon it;

(3) The plaintiff must have been unaware of the defendant's intention not to perform the promise; he or she must have acted in reliance upon the promise and must have been justified in relying upon the promise made by the defendant;

(4) And, finally, as a result of reliance upon defendant's promise, the plaintiff must have sustained damage. (See, Cal.Civ.Code § 1572)

Perry v. Atkinson

California Court of Appeal Fourth Appellate District, Division One, 1987
195 Cal.App.3d 14, 240 Cal.Rptr. 402

HUFFMAN, J.

Plaintiff Lee Perry appeals a judgment favoring defendant Richard Atkinson after the court granted summary adjudication of issues and sustained Atkinson's demurrer to Perry's second amended complaint for fraud and deceit.

Factual and Procedural Background

Perry and Atkinson met in July 1976. Although Atkinson was married, he and Perry began having an intimate relationship which continued for more than a year. During that year, Perry and Atkinson developed a relationship of trust and confidence. In August 1977 Perry learned she was pregnant with Atkinson's child. When Perry told Atkinson, he became upset and urged her to have an abortion. Perry did not want to have an abortion, but Atkinson persisted. He told Perry that although he would like her to have his child, he wanted to postpone doing so for a year. He promised Perry that even if they were not together in a year, he would conceive a child with her by artificial insemination.

Based on Atkinson's promise, Perry terminated her pregnancy by an abortion, causing her physical and mental pain. After the abortion, Perry discovered Atkinson had never intended to keep his promise of another baby. As a result, Perry became depressed, requiring psychiatric treatment, incurring extensive medical bills and losing six months of earnings.

Perry sued Atkinson for fraud and deceit and intentional infliction of emotional distress. In essence, Perry alleged she terminated her pregnancy by an abortion based on Atkinson's promise he would impregnate her the following year either through sexual intercourse or artificial insemination. Perry alleged Atkinson's representation was false; he had no intention of impregnating her again; and he made these statements to deceive her in order to have her abort the pregnancy. As to Perry's first amended complaint, Atkinson moved for summary judgment or alternatively summary adjudication of issues. Before the hearing on Atkinson's motions, Perry filed a second amended complaint, adding allegations of physical harm and further facts regarding her confidential relationship with Atkinson. Atkinson demurred to Perry's second amended complaint.

After hearing, the court rendered its written decision, denying Atkinson's motion for summary judgment as to Perry's cause of action for intentional infliction of emotional distress, and granting Atkinson's motion for summary adjudication as to the fraud and deceit cause of action. The court reasoned public policy prohibits a cause of action for fraud and deceit concerning intimate matters involving procreation. The court concluded that to control the promises of the parties by legal action would constitute an unwarranted governmental intrusion into matters affecting the individual's right to privacy. The court also sustained without leave to amend Atkinson's demurrer to Perry's fraud and deceit cause of action in her second amended complaint, reasoning such cause of action would violate public policy and constitute an unwarranted governmental intrusion into matters affecting an individual's right to privacy. The court entered judgment in favor of Atkinson on the cause of action for fraud and deceit. We conclude on the facts here no cause of action exists for fraud and deceit and accordingly affirm the judgment.

Discussion

* * *

II

Perry contends her second amended complaint states a cause of action for fraud and deceit which is factually and legally sufficient to withstand Atkinson's demurrer. The gravamen of Perry's complaint is that Atkinson defrauded her by promising to impregnate her if she had an abortion—a promise he did not intend to keep—on which he intended her to rely and on which she did rely to her detriment. Such misrepresentation, she asserts, is actionable as a tort.

In deciding whether Perry can state a cause of action for fraud and deceit, our inquiry must be directed to the specific conduct giving rise to such a claim. Although Perry's cause of action is couched in terms of a tort, the behavior of which she complains is Atkinson's breach of a promise to impregnate her after she had an "unwanted" abortion. Thus, the issue before us is whether Perry has a cause of action for fraudulent breach of a promise to impregnate.

In Stephen K. v. Roni L. (1980) 105 Cal.App.3d 640 [164 Cal.Rptr. 618, 31 A.L.R.4th 383], the defendant father (Stephen) in a paternity action cross-complained against his child's mother (Roni), alleging Roni had falsely represented she was taking birth control pills and in reliance on that representation, Stephen had sexual relations with her resulting in the birth of a child he did not want. The court held Roni's conduct towards Stephen was not actionable, reasoning "although Roni may have lied and betrayed the personal confidence reposed in her by Stephen, the circumstances and the highly intimate nature of the relationship wherein the false representations may have occurred, are such that a court should not define any standard of conduct therefor." (Id. at p. 643.) The court further stated that Stephen's claim of tortious misrepresentation was "nothing more than asking the court to supervise the promises made between two consenting adults as to the circumstances of their private sexual conduct. To do so would encourage unwarranted governmental intrusion into matters affecting the individual's right to privacy." (Id. at pp. 644-645.)

We find the court's reasoning in Stephen K. persuasive as applied to the facts here. Although Atkinson may have deliberately misrepresented his intentions to Perry in order to persuade her to have the abortion, their procreative decisions were so intensely private that we decline to intervene. Tort liability cannot apply to the choice, however motivated, of whether to conceive or bear a child.

Further, the California Legislature recognizes that certain sexual conduct and interpersonal decisions are, on public policy grounds, outside the realm of tort liability. For example, Civil Code section 43.5 provides in part that no cause of action exists for alienation of affection, seduction of a person over the age of legal consent, or breach of promise of marriage. Also, Civil Code section 43.4 precludes a cause of action for a fraudulent promise to marry or cohabit after marriage, entailing not only the marriage ritual but fulfillment of all "matrimonial obligations and expectations." (Boyd v. Boyd (1964) 228 Cal.App.2d 374, 377 [39 Cal.Rptr. 400].) If no cause of action can exist in tort for a fraudulent promise to fulfill the rights, duties and obligations of a marriage relationship, then logically no cause of action can exist for a fraudulent promise by a married man to impregnate a woman not his wife. (See Langley v. Schumacker (1956) 46 Cal.2d 601, 604-607 [297 P.2d 977] (Spence, J., dis.) [superseded by Civ. Code, §43.4 as stated in Boyd v. Boyd, supra, 228 Cal.App.2d at p. 376].)

Perry contends Atkinson's right to privacy in fraudulently inducing her to have an abortion must give way to Perry's right to protection from and compensation for physical harm and to the government's interest in protecting the health and welfare of its citizens. In support of her argument, Perry cites Barbara A. v. John G. (1983) 145 Cal.App.3d 369 [193 Cal.Rptr. 422] and Kathleen K. v. Robert B. (1984) 150 Cal.App.3d 992 [198 Cal.Rptr. 273, 40 A.L.R.4th 1083].

In Barbara A., the court was confronted with the issue of whether a woman who had suffered injuries from an ectopic pregnancy has a cause of action in tort against the responsible man for his misrepresentations of infertility. The court held the plaintiff could state a cause of action for battery and deceit because the right to privacy does not insulate sexual relations from judicial scrutiny when that right is used as a shield from liability at the expense of the other party. (Barbara A. v. John G., supra, 145 Cal.App.3d at p. 381.) The court attempted to distinguish Stephen K. on both factual and public policy grounds: "In essence, Stephen was seeking damages for the 'wrongful birth' of his child [fn. omitted] resulting in support obligations and alleged damages for mental suffering. Here, no child is involved; appellant is seeking damages for severe injury to her own body. [¶] Although the Stephen K. court alluded to Stephen's claim as separate and apart from the issue of either parent's obligation to raise and support the child, it reached its decision without attempting to resolve the problem of the mother's reduced financial ability to support the child if she were required to pay damages to the father. We think this concern over the child, and not governmental intrusion into private sexual matters, ... is the central issue in Stephen K. and compels different public policy considerations." (Id. at pp. 378-379.)

We see no significant distinction between Stephen K. and Barbara A. In both, the complaining parties alleged they engaged in sexual relations induced by a false representation regarding their partners' procreative ability. Both cases fall squarely within Civil Code section 43.5, subdivision (c) precluding a cause of action for seduction. (See Barbara A. v. John G., supra, 145 Cal.App.3d at p. 386 (Scott, J., dis.).)

The Barbara A. court attempts to distinguish its holding from that of Stephen K. on the ground no child is involved and the public policy considerations regarding parental obligations are absent in Barbara A. However, the court in Stephen K. specifically refused to address the issues of child support and parental obligations. (Stephen K. v. Roni L., supra, 105 Cal.App.3d at p. 643.) Instead, it based its holding on the public policy consideration that "the practice of birth control, if any, engaged in by two partners in a consensual sexual relationship is best left to the individuals involved, free from any governmental interference." (Id. at p. 645.) Because Stephen K. and Barbara A. cannot readily be reconciled, we choose here to follow the sound reasoning of Stephen K.

Moreover, Perry's reliance on Kathleen K. is misplaced. In that case, a woman brought an action against a man because she had contracted genital herpes through sexual intercourse with him. Citing Barbara A., the court held the constitutional right of privacy did not protect the defendant from his tortious conduct in failing to inform the plaintiff he was infected with venereal disease. "The right of privacy is not absolute, and in some cases is subordinate to the state's fundamental right to enact laws which promote public health, welfare and safety, even though such laws may invade the offender's right of privacy. (Barbara A. v. John G., supra, 145 Cal.App.3d at p. 380.)" (Kathleen K. v. Robert B., supra, 150 Cal.App.3d at p. 996.) The court further reasoned that "as in Barbara A., there is no child involved, and the public policy considerations with respect to parental obligations are absent." (Ibid.)

Kathleen K. is distinguishable from the present case. The tortious transmission of a contagious disease implicates policy considerations beyond the sexual conduct and procreative decisions of two consenting adults. The state's interest "in the prevention and control of contagious and dangerous diseases" (id. at p. 996), is sufficient to allow a cause of action for fraudulent concealment of the risk of infection with venereal disease. The absence of such policy considerations here compels a different result.

In essence, Perry seeks judicial enforcement, by way of damages, of a promise to impregnate. The courts should not undertake the adjudication of promises and representations made by consenting adults regarding their sexual relationships. Once we attempt to determine in court, by means of tort law, the bona fides of promises such as are alleged here, we will of necessity be required to set standards for the making and performing of such promises. The court in Stephen K. and the Legislature by its actions in passing statutes such as Civil Code sections 43.4 and 43.5 have given wise counsel against such folly.

Public policy compels our holding no cause of action exists for Atkinson's fraud and deceit in misrepresenting his intentions to provide Perry with the means to have a child.

Disposition

Judgment affirmed.

Reliance

A party claiming to have been defrauded by a false representation or promise must have relied upon the representation or promise; that is, the representation or promise must have been a cause of plaintiff's conduct in entering into the transaction and without such representation or promise plaintiff would not have entered into such transaction. The fraud, if any, need not be the sole cause if it appears that reliance upon the representation or promise substantially influenced such party's action, even though other influences operated as well. (See, 5 Witkin, Summary of Cal. Law (9th ed. 1988) Torts, § 711)

Effect of Independent Investigation

If a party claiming to have been defrauded makes an independent investigation of the subject matter of the alleged false representation or promise and the decision to engage in the transaction is the result of his or her independent investigation and not his or her reliance upon the representation or promise, he or she is not entitled to recover. (See, 5 Witkin, Summary of Cal. Law (9th ed. 1988) Torts, § 712-713; *Carpenter v. Hamilton* (1936) 18 Cal.App.2d 69, 75, 62 P.2d 1397, 1401.)

Unconscionability

The general rule is that a court can refuse to enforce an unconscionable provision in a contract or may limit the application of a particular clause to prevent an unconscionable result.

American Software, Inc. v. Ali

California Court of Appeal, First District, Division Five, 199
46 Cal.App.4th 1386, 54 Cal.Rptr.2d 477

KING, J.

The appellant, American Software, Inc., appeals from a decision of the trial court granting a former employee, respondent Melane Ali, unpaid commissions based upon

software sales she generated while in American Software's employ but which were re-
mitted by customers after she voluntarily severed her employment. The key issue in this
appeal is whether a provision of Ali's employment contract which, generally speaking,
terminates her right to receive commissions on payments received on her accounts 30
days after severance of her employment is unconscionable, and therefore, unenforceable. The trial court found that Ali was entitled to recover the disputed commissions because this contractual provision was unconscionable. We disagree and reverse.

Facts

Ali was an account executive for American Software from September 5, 1991, to
March 2, 1994. The employment relationship commenced after Ali was approached by
a professional recruiter on behalf of American Software and was terminated when Ali
voluntarily resigned because she had a job offer from one of American Software's com-
petitors. Ali was hired to sell and market licensing agreements for software products to
large companies. These products are designed to the customer's specifications for the
purpose of integrating the customer's accounting, manufacturing, sales and distribution processes.

In exchange for her services, American Software agreed to pay Ali a base monthly
salary plus a draw. If products were sold during the month, any commissions paid were
reduced by the amount of the draw. However, the draw portion of the salary was paid
regardless of whether or not the salesperson earned commissions to cover the draw. Any
negative amount would be carried over from month-to-month until such time as the
commissions were large enough to cover the previous draws, or until such time as the
employment relationship was severed. If the amount of draws exceeded commissions at
the time of termination, American Software would suffer the loss. At the time of her
resignation, Ali's annual guaranteed salary, exclusive of commissions, was $75,000. Her
base monthly salary was $3,333 per month and her nonrefundable draw was $2,917.

The terms and conditions of Ali's employment were set out in a written contract
which was prepared by American Software. Ali reviewed the contract, and had an attorney, who she described as a "buddy," review it prior to employment. Of pertinence to
the instant controversy, the contract included the specific circumstances under which
Ali was to receive commissions after termination of employment with American Software. The employment agreement first states that "[c]ommissions are considered
earned when the payment is received by the Company." It goes on to provide: "In the
event of termination, the right of all commissions which would normally be due and
payable are forfeited 30 days following the date of termination in the case of voluntary
termination and 90 days in the case of involuntary termination."

Based on her testimony at trial, there is no question that Ali was aware of this provision prior to her execution of the agreement and commencement of work at American
Software. She testified she reviewed the two-and-one-half-page contract for one-half
hour and caused certain handwritten deletions and revisions to be made to it, most notably deleting a provision requiring her to reimburse American Software $5,000 for the
recruiter's fee in the event that she terminated her employment within a year. Ali testified that she signed the employment contract even though she believed certain provisions were unenforceable in California.

After Ali left American Software's employment, she sought additional commissions in
connection with transactions with IBM and Kaiser Foundation Health Plan. American
Software received payment from both companies more than 30 days after Ali's resignation.

After Ali's claim for unpaid commissions was denied by the Labor Commissioner, she sought de novo review in the superior court. (Lab. Code, § 98.2.) The trial court awarded Ali approximately $30,000 in unpaid commissions after finding that the contract provision regarding postemployment commissions was unconscionable and thus, unenforceable. The trial court found the evidence "overwhelming that the forfeiture provision inures to the benefit of the party with superior bargaining power without any indication of a reason for tying such benefit to the timing of a payment, rather than to the service actually provided in completing the sale." American Software timely appealed.

Discussion

In 1979, our Legislature enacted Civil Code section 1670.5, which codified the established doctrine that a court can refuse to enforce an unconscionable provision in a contract. (For a review of the legislative history of Civ. Code, § 1670.5, see IMO Development Corp. v. Dow Corning Corp. (1982) 135 Cal.App.3d 451, 459-460 [185 Cal.Rptr. 341].) While the term "unconscionability" is not defined by statute, the official comment explains the term as follows: "The basic test is whether, in the light of the general background and the needs of the particular case, the clauses involved are so one-sided as to be unconscionable under the circumstances existing at the time of the making of the contract.... The principle is one of the prevention of oppression and unfair surprise [citation] and not of disturbance of allocation of risks because of superior bargaining power." (Legis. committee com., Deering's Ann. Civ. Code (1994 ed.) § 1670.5, pp. 328-329.)

Most California cases analyze unconscionability as having two separate elements-procedural and substantive. (See, e.g., Shaffer v. Superior Court (1995) 33 Cal.App.4th 993, 1000 [39 Cal.Rptr.2d 506]; Vance v. Villa Park Mobilehome Estates (1995) 36 Cal.App.4th 698, 709 [42 Cal.Rptr.2d 723].) Substantive unconscionability focuses on the actual terms of the agreement, while procedural unconscionability focuses on the manner in which the contract was negotiated and the circumstances of the parties. California courts generally require a showing of both procedural and substantive unconscionability at the time the contract was made. (See A & M [46 Cal.App.4th 1391] Produce Co. v. FMC Corp. (1982) 135 Cal.App.3d 473, 487 [186 Cal.Rptr. 114, 38 A.L.R.4th 1].) Some courts have indicated that a sliding scale applies-for example, a contract with extraordinarily oppressive substantive terms will require less in the way of procedural unconscionability. (Ilkhchooyi v. Best (1995) 37 Cal.App.4th 395, 410 [45 Cal.Rptr.2d 766]; Carboni v. Arrospide (1991) 2 Cal.App.4th 76, 83 [2 Cal.Rptr.2d 845]; Dean Witter Reynolds, Inc. v. Superior Court (1989) 211 Cal.App.3d 758, 768 [259 Cal.Rptr. 789].)

Indicia of procedural unconscionability include "oppression, arising from inequality of bargaining power and the absence of real negotiation or a meaningful choice" and "surprise, resulting from hiding the disputed term in a prolix document." (Vance v. Villa Park Mobilehome Estates, supra, 36 Cal.App.4th at p. 709.) Substantive unconscionability is indicated by contract terms so one-sided as to "shock the conscience." (California Grocers Assn. v. Bank of America (1994) 22 Cal.App.4th 205, 214 [27 Cal.Rptr.2d 396], italics in original.) A less stringent standard of "reasonableness" was applied in A & M Produce Co. v. FMC Corp., supra, 135 Cal.App.3d at pages 486-487. This standard was expressly rejected by Division Two of this court in California Grocers Assn. as being inherently subjective. (California Grocers Assn., supra, at p. 214.) We agree. With a concept as nebulous as "unconscionability" it is important that courts not be thrust in the paternalistic role of intervening to change contractual terms that the parties have agreed to merely because the court believes the terms are unreasonable. The terms must shock the conscience.

The critical juncture for determining whether a contract is unconscionable is the moment when it is entered into by both parties-not whether it is unconscionable in light of subsequent events. (Civ. Code, § 1670.5.) Unconscionability is ultimately a question of law for the court. (Ilkhchooyi v. Best, supra, 37 Cal.App.4th at p. 411; Vance v. Villa Park Mobilehome Estates, supra, 36 Cal.App.4th at p. 709; Patterson v. ITT Consumer Financial Corp. (1993) 14 Cal.App.4th 1659, 1663 [18 Cal.Rptr.2d 563].)

In assessing procedural unconscionability, the evidence indicates that Ali was aware of her obligations under the contract and that she voluntarily agreed to assume them. In her business as a salesperson it is reasonable to assume she had become familiar with contracts and their importance. In fact, in Ali's testimony, she indicated that as part of her responsibilities for American Software, she helped negotiate the terms of a contract with IBM representing over a million dollars in sales. The salient provisions of the employment contract are straightforward, and the terms used are easily comprehensible to the layman. She had the benefit of counsel. Nor is this a situation in which one party to the contract is confronted by an absence of meaningful choice. The very fact that Ali had enough bargaining "clout" to successfully negotiate for more favorable terms on other provisions evidences the contrary. She admits that she was aware of the postemployment commissions clause, but did not attempt to negotiate for less onerous terms. In short, this case is a far cry from those cases where fine print, complex terminology, and presentation of a contract on a take-it-or-leave-it basis constitutes the groundwork for a finding of unconscionability.

Nor do we find substantive unconscionability. Ali's arguments of substantive unconscionability rest largely on events that occurred several years after the contract was entered into-her loss of sizable commissions on sales she had solicited during her employment but where payment was delayed for various reasons so that it was not received within 30 days after her departure. However, as indicated by the very wording of California's unconscionability statute, we must analyze the circumstances as they existed "at the time [the contract] was made" to determine if gross unfairness was apparent at that time. (Civ. Code, § 1670.5, subd. (a).)

When viewed in light of the circumstances as they existed on August 23, 1991, when the instant contract was executed, we cannot say the contract provision with respect to compensation after termination was so unfair or oppressive in its mutual obligations as to "shock the conscience." (California Grocers Assn. v. Bank of America, supra, 22 Cal.App.4th at p. 214.) If the official notes accompanying Uniform Commercial Code section 2-302, upon which Civil Code section 1670.5 is based, is to be relied upon as a guide, the contract terms are to be evaluated "in the light of the general commercial background and the commercial needs of the particular trade or case, ..." (U. Com. Code, ß 2-302, com. 1). Corbin suggests that the test is whether the terms are "so extreme as to appear unconscionable according to the mores and business practices of the time and place." (1 Corbin, Contracts (1963) § 128, p. 551.)

Our survey of case law indicates that the contract provision challenged here is commonplace in employment contracts with sales representatives, such as Ali, who have ongoing responsibilities to "service" the account once the sale is made. (See, e.g., Chretian v. Donald L. Bren Co. (1984) 151 Cal.App.3d 385, 389 [198 Cal.Rptr. 523]; J.S. De-Weese Co. v. Hughes-Treitler Mfg. (Mo.App. 1994) 881 S.W.2d 638, 644-646; see also Entis v. Atlantic Wire & Cable Corporation (2d Cir. 1964) 335 F.2d 759, 762.) In briefing below, the rationale for deferring commissions until payment is actually received by the customer was explained by American Software: "[I]f the entire commission were to be deemed earned by merely obtaining buyers, the burden of servicing those buyers pending receipt of revenues would fall on American Software's other salespersons unfamiliar with the earlier transaction who would receive nothing for their efforts." In Watson v. Wood Dimension, Inc. (1989) 209 Cal.App.3d 1359, 1363-1365 [257 Cal.Rptr. 816], the court upheld an award of posttermination commissions for a reasonable period of time based on quantum meruit in the total absence of contractual provisions governing the situation. If a court can impose these terms on parties in the absence of an agreement, then it is difficult to see how such terms can be considered "unconscionable" when the parties agree to them.

Nor do we find that the terms of this contract represent "an overly harsh allocation of risks ... which is not justified by the circumstances under which the contract was made." (Carboni v. Arrospide, supra, 2 Cal.App.4th at p. 83.) The contract terms with regard to Ali's compensation involved certain risks to both parties to the bargain. The contract in the instant case placed a risk on Ali that she would lose commissions from her customers if payment was not received by American Software within 30 days after her resignation. American Software took the risk that at the time of Ali's termination, she would not have earned sufficient commissions to cover the substantial draws "credited" to her. This is part of the bargaining process-it does not necessarily make a contract unconscionable. The contract simply does not appear to be "overly harsh or one-sided, with no justification for it at the time of the agreement." (Vance v. Villa Park Mobilehome Estates, supra, 36 Cal.App.4th at p. 709.)

Much of the parties' arguments in this case revolve around Ellis v. McKinnon Broadcasting Co. (1993) 18 Cal.App.4th 1796 [23 Cal.Rptr.2d 80]. In Ellis the court examined a provision in an employment contract denying the plaintiff, an advertising salesperson, commissions on advertising if the employer had not yet received payment for the advertising prior to termination of the salesperson's employment. The employer collected nearly $100,000 in advertising fees from the plaintiff's sales after he voluntarily left his employment two years later, which meant that the plaintiff would have been entitled to approximately $20,000 in commissions had he continued his employment. The court described the pivotal inquiry as assessing "the substantive reasonableness of the challenged provision" and proceeded to find elements of procedural unconscionability, unfair surprise, and oppression, as well as substantive unconscionability. (Id. at pp. 1805-1806, italics added.)

Despite the many analogous facts and issues, we reach a different conclusion than Ellis. In this instance, the conflicting result can most easily be explained by the fact that the Ellis court closely followed the A&M Produce analytical structure in considering whether the commissions provision was "reasonable"-an approach we have specifically rejected in favor of the more rigorous "shock the conscience" standard enunciated in California Grocers Assn. v. Bank of America supra, 22 Cal.App.4th at page 214. We also find the result in Ellis hard to reconcile with other California appellate decisions which have shown considerable restraint in second-guessing provisions in employment contracts governing payment of sales commissions upon termination of employment. (See, e.g., Chretian v. Donald L. Bren, Co., supra, 151 Cal.App.3d at pp. 389-390; Neal v. State Farm Ins. Cos. (1961) 188 Cal.App.2d 690 [10 Cal.Rptr. 781].) A critical review of Ellis in the legal literature observes, "[T]he test on unconscionability is not whether the parties could have written a better or more reasonable contract. The proper test in these cases is whether the bargain is so one-sided as to shock the conscience and whether there was some bargaining impropriety resulting from surprise or oppression. The Neal and Chretian courts, unlike the court in Ellis, displayed the proper restraint and deference to agreements that were not egregiously one-sided in the allocation of risks." (Prince, Unconscionability in California: A Need for Restraint and Consistency (1995) 46 Hastings L.J. 459, 545.)

In the present case, there are no unclear or hidden terms in the employment agreement and no unusual terms that would shock the conscience, all leading to the conclusion that the contract accurately reflects the reasonable expectations of the parties. Overall, the evidence establishes that this employment contract was the result of an arm's-length negotiation between two sophisticated and experienced parties of comparable bargaining power and is fairly reflective of prevailing practices in employing commissioned sales representatives. Therefore, the contract fails to qualify as unconscionable. The judgment is reversed. Costs are awarded to American Software, Inc.

Peterson, P. J., and Haning, J., concurred.

Bolter v. Superior Court (Harris Research, Inc.)
California Court of Appeal, Fourth Dist., Div. Three, 2001
87 Cal.App.4th 900, 104 Cal.Rptr.2d 888

O'LEARY, J.

Franchise owners, Florence Bolter (doing business as Bolter's Chem-Dry), Sandra Valdez (doing business as Canyon Chem-Dry), and Stephen R. Knight (doing business as Knight's Chem-Dry) filed the underlying writ petition challenging the court's ruling their breach of contract action against Harris Research, Inc., must be arbitrated in Utah. The franchisees acknowledge their franchise agreements mandate that all disputes be arbitrated in Utah, but claim the provision is unconscionable and violates Business and Professions Code section 20040.5. Finding their first contention has merit, we grant the writ relief requested.

I

Harris is the franchisor of a carpet cleaning operation known as "Chem-Dry" businesses. In the early 1980's, petitioners first purchased their Chem-Dry franchises, operating their small businesses in Orange County. Over the years, when their franchise agreements lapsed, petitioners executed renewals and sometimes new franchise agreements.

In April 1998, petitioners filed a complaint seeking damages and declaratory relief, alleging Harris breached the franchise contracts and the covenants of good faith and fair dealing. Petitioners claimed Harris continually modified the franchise agreements at every opportunity to "liberalize the obligations of [Harris]" and "constrict the rights of the franchisees." They said Harris threatened to terminate their franchises if they refused to execute the newer agreements.

Petitioners have many complaints about franchise agreements signed within the past four years. For example, the new agreements provide that if petitioners terminate their franchises, they will be forced to surrender their customer lists and clients' telephone numbers. Petitioners say they must make their income tax returns available upon request and claim Harris enforces strict advertising restrictions contained in the agreement against petitioners but not other franchisees. Additionally, petitioners assert Harris has saturated their franchise territories, diminishing the value of their franchises. Finally, petitioners are outraged by Harris's new requirement they purchase from Harris an overpriced water extraction system called the Velda, and its expensive fixtures and attachments. When petitioners originally bought their franchises, they utilized a "carbonated method of carpet cleaning," which did not involve the bulky, heavy equipment used by carpet steam or water extraction systems.

In their complaint, petitioners claimed that "at the time [Harris] commenced the wrongful conduct upon which this action is based, all [petitioners] had extant written agreements with [Harris] providing that jurisdiction would be in, and the governing law would be of, the State of California" but "some of the more recent agreements provide that the franchisee shall submit to the jurisdiction of the State of Utah in any litigation involving the contract...."

In response to the suit, Harris commenced separate arbitration proceedings against each petitioner in Utah and sought removal of petitioners' lawsuit to federal court. Within a few weeks, the district court issued an order to show cause (OSC) why the claims of one petitioner, Sandra Valdez, should not be severed and dismissed to allow her the opportunity to file her claim "in the proper forum—the American Arbitration Association office in Salt Lake City, Utah." The court also asked Harris to advise the court if the other franchisees were bound by similar arbitration agreements. Harris filed a motion, asking the federal court to stay the proceedings pending arbitration.

Meanwhile, petitioners' counsel wrote to the American Arbitration Association (AAA), stating arbitration could not proceed in Utah because California's Business and Professions Code section 20040.5 declares franchise agreements restricting venue to a forum outside the State of California void. He suggested that the arbitrations be stayed pending the outcome of the OSC in federal court. However, 10 days later, petitioners decided to dismiss their federal action and file an identical lawsuit in state court, including an additional defendant, A.Y.S., Inc.

At the end of May 1998, an AAA officer held a telephone conference hearing to discuss petitioners' objections to the hearing locale. A few weeks later, the hearing officer sent a letter to the parties confirming the arrangements made during the conference call to select an arbitrator. He included a list of 20 arbitrators from whom the parties could choose. Petitioners' counsel immediately replied with a letter, stating his clients were "not in a position to either strike or accept any of the submitted arbitrators." He repeated his objection under Business and Professions Code section 20040.5 and reminded the hearing officer of the officer's statement "it was the practice of the AAA to have an arbitrator appointed to determine the issue of arbitrability." He noted, "While I cannot at this time prevent AAA [from] what it might do, it seems that the entire exercise would be futile: [I]f the arbitrator determines the dispute is arbitrable, I would have to file an action to enjoin any attempt at arbitration ... [and] [i]f the arbitrator determines the matter is not arbitrable in Utah, such a finding would only serve to confirm the mandate of rather clear law from a sister state [i.e., Business and Professions Code section 20040.5]." Finally, he wrote, "I want to be *absolutely* certain that nothing is done by me or my clients which could even remotely be interpreted as some sort of consent to arbitration, or waiver of the right to invoke the above-referenced law."

The following month, petitioners' counsel voiced his objections again in a letter, asserting arbitrability should be decided by the courts rather than the AAA. The AAA decided a second hearing on the matter would be held in each of the three pending arbitrations before three different appointed arbitrators. Petitioners' counsel declined to participate in the hearings. The arbitrators proceeded to hold telephone conference hearings and each issued a ruling concluding the disputes were arbitrable.

Petitioners applied for a temporary restraining order and OSC in the trial court, seeking to stay the arbitration proceedings. Harris filed a motion to stay the lawsuit pending resolution of the arbitration. Judge Francisco F. Firmat considered both motions on the same day and issued an order on March 2, 1999, denying Harris's request for a stay and granting petitioners' motion to temporarily stop the arbitrations until a hearing could be held to address the following questions: (1) Are the issues of arbitrability to be decided by the court or the AAA? (2) Have any issues been resolved by a prior decision of the AAA, and if so, are plaintiffs bound by those decisions? (3) Are the arbitration agreements contained in contracts of adhesion, and if so, then are the provisions unconscionable or do they create undue hardship? (4) If they are unconscionable, should the court refuse to enforce the arbitration agreement?

Three months later, Judge John M. Watson granted petitioners' motion to vacate the dismissal of A.Y.S., Inc., from the action. The court also vacated the trial date and the hearing on the arbitrability issues outlined by Judge Firmat. This prompted Harris to file a motion to "(1) confirm arbitration awards re: the issue of arbitrability; (2) compel completion of arbitration; and (3) stay proceedings pending arbitration." Harris argued that the issues raised in the complaint were subject to arbitration and claimed arbitrability had been decided by the AAA arbitrators. It maintained the arbitrators' orders were subject to res judicata and that "unless a petition to correct or vacate an [arbitrator's] award has been timely filed (and that time has expired) the court must render judgment confirming the ... arbitration orders." It further asserted that "[t]he orders of the arbitrator[s] as confirmed by the judgment of [the trial] court should put to rest all of the issues ... raised concerning the validity or enforceability of the arbitration agreements. An arbitration award bars relitigation of matters heard or that could have been heard in the arbitration proceeding." Judge Watson decided to confirm the arbitration awards, grant the motion to compel completion of the arbitrations, and stay the trial. He set a review hearing for May 22, 2000.

Petitioners filed a writ petition seeking relief from the ruling. We issued an alternative writ of mandate directing the trial court to "hold a hearing and make an independent legal determination on the issues of arbitrability." In response, the trial court vacated the prior order confirming the arbitration rulings and set a hearing for February 2, 2000. Accordingly, we dismissed the alternative writ as moot.

At the hearing, the parties had an opportunity to briefly address the matter. The court accepted more declarations and documents but refused petitioners' request for an evidentiary hearing. The court took the matter under submission, advising the parties they would be notified if further information was needed.

On April 18, 2000, the court issued an order granting Harris's motion to compel arbitration in Utah and dismissing the case. On May 1, 2000, the court signed a document prepared by Harris containing the "findings of fact and conclusions of law" in support of the order. It included the statement, inter alia, "The arbitration provisions in the franchise agreements, even if adhesive, are not unconscionable and do not impose an unreasonable burden on [petitioners]." Petitioners filed the underlying writ petition, and we issued an order to show cause and temporarily stayed the arbitration proceedings.

II

We begin by noting both parties have spent a great deal of time and effort discussing the application of Business and Professions Code section 20040.5 and dispute whether it is preempted by the Federal Arbitration Act (FAA). While we recognize the preemption issue has not been resolved in California, we find the answer to this case lies in general contract law principles. Keeping in mind the values of judicial economy, we confine our analysis accordingly.

"A written provision in a contract to submit to arbitration a dispute arising out of the contract is valid, irrevocable and enforceable except on 'such grounds as exist at law or in equity for the revocation of any contract.' (9 U.S.C. § 2 [contracts subject to the FAA]; Code Civ. Proc., § 1281 [contracts governed by state arbitration law].) Accordingly, the existence of a valid agreement to arbitrate is determined by reference to state law principles regarding the formation, revocation and enforceability of contracts generally. [Citations.]" (*Kinney v. United HealthCare Services, Inc.* (1999) 70 Cal.App.4th 1322, 1327-1328 [83 Cal.Rptr.2d 348].)

Contrary to Harris's belief, arbitration agreements are not subject to a different standard than other contracts. As recently noted by the Supreme Court, "[U]nder both federal and California law, arbitration agreements are valid, irrevocable, and enforceable, save upon such grounds as exist at law or in equity for the revocation of *any* contact." (*Armendariz v. Foundation Health Psychcare Services, Inc.* (2000) 24 Cal.4th 83, 98 [99 Cal.Rptr.2d 745, 6 P.3d 669], fn. omitted,.) It further explained, "[A]lthough we have spoken of a 'strong public policy of this state in favor of resolving disputes by arbitration' [citation], Code of Civil Procedure section 1281 makes clear that an arbitration agreement is to be rescinded on the same ground as other contracts or contract terms. In this respect, arbitration agreements are neither favored nor disfavored, but simply placed on an equal footing with other contracts." (*Id.* at pp. 126-127.)

Turning to the case at hand, we first address petitioners' argument the mandatory arbitration provisions contained in their franchise agreements were unconscionable and therefore unenforceable. The doctrine of unconscionability is a judicially created doctrine which was codified in 1979 when the Legislature enacted Civil Code section 1670.5. (*Armendariz v.* Foundation Health Psychcare Services, Inc, supra, 24 Cal.4th at pp. 113-114.) That section provides in relevant part, "If the court as a matter of law finds the contract or any clause of the contract to have been unconscionable at the time it was made the court may refuse to enforce the contract...." (Civ. Code, § 1670.5, subd. (a).) While the statute does not attempt to precisely define "unconscionable," there is a large body of case law recognizing the term has "both a procedural and a substantive element, both of which must be present to render a contract unenforceable. [Citation.] The procedural element focuses on the unequal bargaining positions and hidden terms common in the context of adhesion contracts. [Citation.] While courts have defined the substantive element in various ways, it traditionally involves contract terms that are so one-sided as to 'shock the conscience,' or that impose harsh or oppressive terms. [Citation.]" (*24 Hour Fitness, Inc. v. Superior Court* (1998) 66 Cal.App.4th 1199, 1212-1213 [78 Cal.Rptr.2d 533].)

Both elements need not be present to the same degree. "[T]he more substantively oppressive the contract term, the less evidence of procedural unconscionability is required to come to the conclusion that the term is unenforceable, and vice versa." (*Armendariz v. Foundation Health Psychcare Services, Inc., supra,* 24 Cal.4th at p. 114.) Additionally, a "claim of unconscionability often cannot be determined merely by examining the face of a contract, but will require inquiry into its [commercial] setting, purpose, and effect." (*Perdue v. Crocker National Bank* (1985) 38 Cal.3d 913, 926 [216 Cal.Rptr. 345, 702 P.2d 503].)

Thus, "[u]nconscionability analysis begins with an inquiry into whether the contract is one of adhesion. [Citation.] 'The term [contract of adhesion] signifies a standardized contract, which, imposed and drafted by the party of superior bargaining strength, relegates to the subscribing party only the opportunity to adhere to the contract or reject it.' [Citation.]" (*Armendariz v. Foundation Health Psychcare Services, Inc., supra,* 24 Cal.4th at p. 113.) [2b] Such was the case here: Harris made no attempt to refute petitioners' characterization of it as a "large wealthy international franchiser." And it is undisputed petitioners have limited financial means, owning small "one-man operated" Dry-Chem franchises. Petitioners were told they must agree to the new franchise terms in order to *continue* running their franchises. Only a person contemplating whether to purchase a franchise for the first time would have been in the position to reject Harris's "take it or leave it" attitude. Harris was certainly aware established franchise owners simply could not afford to dispute, much less attempt to negotiate, the place and manner arbitration was to occur. Perhaps this is why Harris did not focus on this issue below or on appeal.

When a contract is adhesive, "the court must then determine whether 'other factors are present which, ... operate to render it [unenforceable].' [Citation.]" (*Armendariz v. Foundation Health Psychcare Services, Inc., supra,* 24 Cal.4th at p. 113.) Harris maintains the court correctly determined the arbitration provisions in the franchise agreements, even if adhesive, do not impose an unreasonable burden on petitioners. Citing to *Lagatree v. Luce, Forward, Hamilton & Scripps* (1999) 74 Cal.App.4th 1105, 1124 [88 Cal.Rptr.2d 664], Harris argues adhesive arbitration agreements are valid and enforceable because " ' "[t]here is nothing inherently unfair or oppressive about arbitration clauses." ... In fact, ... the FAA shows a strong federal policy in favor of arbitration.... ' [Citations.]"

We acknowledge there is much authority, including the cases Harris relies upon, holding adhesive arbitration provisions are not per se unconscionable. (*Izzi v. Mesquite Country Club* (1986) 186 Cal.App.3d 1309, 1318 [231 Cal.Rptr. 315].) However, it is also generally recognized that "there may be arbitration provisions which do give an advantage to one party.... In those cases, ... it is not the requirement of arbitration alone which makes the provision unfair but rather the place or manner in which the arbitration is to occur." (*Strotz v. Dean Witter Reynolds, Inc.* (1990) 223 Cal.App.3d 208, 216, fn. 7 [272 Cal.Rptr. 680], overruled on other grounds in *Rosenthal v. Great Western Fin. Securities Corp.* (1996) 14 Cal.4th 394, 407 [58 Cal.Rptr.2d 875, 926 P.2d 1061].) It is those provisions, regarding "place and manner," which we take issue with here.

The agreement provides, in relevant part, as follows: All disputes regarding the franchise agreement "[s]hall be submitted for arbitration to the Salt Lake City, Utah office of the [AAA] on demand of either party. Notwithstanding the foregoing, any controversies, disputes or claims related to or based on the marks may, at [Harris's] sole election, be brought and maintained in any court of competent jurisdiction. Such arbitration proceedings shall be conducted in Salt Lake City, Utah and, except as otherwise provided in this Agreement, shall be heard by one arbitrator in accordance with the then current commercial arbitration rules of the [AAA].... [¶] The arbitrator shall have the right to award or include in his or her award any relief which he or she deems proper in the circumstances, ... [except] exemplary or punitive damages.... [¶] [Harris] and [franchisee] agree that all arbitration shall be conducted on an individual, not class-wide, basis and that an arbitration proceeding between [Harris] and [franchisee] shall not be consolidated with any other arbitration proceeding involving [Harris] and any other natural person, association, corporation, partnership or other entity." In addition, the agreement provided, "All matters relating to arbitration shall be governed by the [FAA] ... [and] this Agreement and the franchise shall be governed by the laws of the State of Utah."

In order to assess the reasonableness of Harris's "place and manner" restrictions, the respective circumstances of the parties become relevant. As explained above, Harris is a large international corporation and petitioners are small "Mom and Pop" franchisees located in California. When petitioners first purchased their Chem-Dry franchises in the early 1980's, Harris was headquartered in California, and the franchise agreement did not contain an arbitration provision. Thus, they never anticipated Harris would relocate its headquarters to Utah and mandate that all disputes be litigated there.

Under the circumstances, the "place and manner" terms are unduly oppressive: The agreement requires franchisees wishing to resolve any dispute to close down their shops, pay for airfare and accommodations in Utah, and absorb the increased costs associated in having counsel familiar with Utah law. To rub salt in the wound, the agreement provides franchisees are precluded from consolidating arbitrations to share these increased costs among themselves. And the potential to recoup expenses with a favorable verdict is limited by the restriction against exemplary or punitive damages.

Because Dry-Chem franchises are by nature small businesses, it is simply not a reasonable or affordable option for franchisees to abandon their offices for any length of time to litigate a dispute several thousand miles away. As Sandra Valdez explained, "I labor hard and daily to make a living from my franchise, and I have complete responsibility, myself, for running the franchise out of my home. I attend to all the advertising, administrative and selling efforts. It is necessary for me to be home daily in order to receive calls from potential customers, schedule cleanings, and do all that must ordinarily be done in connection with such a family-run business."

Likewise, Stephen Knight, who owns three Chem-Dry franchises, stated he is "basically a one-man operation." He has several employees who do the cleaning, but he personally attends to all the administrative duties such as taking phone calls from customers and scheduling cleaning jobs. He claimed he would lose much of his business if forced to litigate the matter outside California. Florence Bolter declared she is 66 years old and solely responsible for running her franchises. She also cares for her husband who is "severely ill" and "could not get by in [her] absence."

Moreover, petitioners declared they are all suffering from severe financial hardships and could not afford to maintain their claims if forced to litigate the matter out of state. Knight attested he is "barely able to afford [the] costs [of the suit] as it is" in California. Valdez echoed these sentiments, explaining it has "become more and more difficult to make a living" due to Harris's misconduct, which is the basis of the lawsuit. She said the franchise was purchased for $32,500, but she would "be fortunate now if we could sell it for $10,000 to $15,000." Similarly, Florence Bolter said she recently had to declare bankruptcy.

Harris's prohibition against consolidation, limitation on damages and forum selection provisions have no justification other than as a means of maximizing an advantage over the petitioners. Arguably, Harris understood those terms would effectively preclude its franchisees from ever raising any claims against it, knowing the increased costs and burden on their small businesses would be prohibitive. As aptly stated in *Armendariz*, "Arbitration was not intended for this purpose." (*Armendariz v. Foundation Health Psychcare Services, Inc., supra,* 24 Cal.4th at p. 118.)

Petitioners assert the presence of unconscionable "place and manner" provisions leads to the conclusion the arbitration agreement as a whole is unenforceable. They submit Harris's "position has always been that the parties entered into an agreement to arbitrate in the State of Utah, as opposed to an agreement to arbitrate, and a separate agreement as to venue." We disagree. It is not necessary to throw the baby out with the bath water, i.e., the unconscionable provisions can be severed and the rest of the agreement enforced.

This is a remedy contemplated by the Legislature. Civil Code section 1670.5, subdivision (a) provides that, "If the court ... finds the contract or any clause of the contract to have been unconscionable ... the court may refuse to enforce the contract, or it may enforce the remainder of the contract without the unconscionable clause, or it may so limit the application of any unconscionable clause as to avoid any unconscionable result." The Legislative Committee comment explains, "Under this section the court, in its discretion, may refuse to enforce the contract as a whole if it is permeated by the unconscionability, or it may strike any single clause or group of clauses which are so tainted or which are contrary to the essential purpose of the agreement, or it may simply limit unconscionable clauses so as to avoid unconscionable results." (Legis. Com. com., 9 West's Ann. Civ. Code, foll. § 1670.5 (1985 ed.) p. 494.)

We find no legal ground to grant petitioners' request to strike the entire arbitration agreement. "[P]ermeation is indicated by the fact that there is no single provision a court can strike or restrict in order to remove the unconscionable taint from the agreement." (*Armendariz v. Foundation Health* Psychcare Services, Inc., supra, 24 Cal.4th at pp. 124-125.) As explained, we did not find the requirement of arbitration alone to be unduly unfair but rather the "place and manner" in which the arbitration was to occur. The unconscionable provisions contained in the agreement relating to the arbitration of all controversies, disputes or claims in Salt Lake City, Utah, are clearly severable from the remainder of the arbitration agreement. (Cf. *id.* at pp. 123-127 [court found arbitration agreement permeated by an unlawful purpose due to number of defects].) Unconscionability can be cured by striking those provisions, leaving an otherwise valid and complete agreement to submit disputes to arbitration.

Let a writ of mandate issue directing the superior court to vacate its judgment and enter a new and different order striking the provisions of the agreement mandating that all arbitrations take place in the State of Utah. This court's previously issued stay order is dissolved. Petitioners shall recover their costs on appeal.

Crosby, Acting P. J., and Bedsworth, J., concurred.

Donovan v. RRL Corp.

California Supreme Court, 2001
26 Cal.4th 261, 109 Cal.Rptr.2d 807; 27 P.3d 702

[Facts appear at p. 31.]

The final factor defendant must establish before obtaining rescission based upon mistake is that enforcement of the contract for the sale of the 1995 Jaguar XJ6 Vanden Plas at $25,995 would be unconscionable. Although the standards of unconscionability warranting rescission for mistake are similar to those for unconscionability justifying a court's refusal to enforce a contract or term, the general rule governing the latter situation (Civ. Code, § 1670.5) is inapplicable here, because unconscionability resulting from mistake does not appear at the time the contract is made. (Rest.2d Contracts, § 153, com. c, p. 395; 1 Witkin, *supra*, Contracts, § 370, pp. 337-338.)

An unconscionable contract ordinarily involves both a procedural and a substantive element: (1) oppression or surprise due to unequal bargaining power, and (2) overly harsh or one-sided results. (*Armendariz v. Foundation Health Psychcare Services, Inc.* (2000) 24 Cal.4th 83, 114.) Nevertheless, " 'a sliding scale is invoked which disregards the regularity of the procedural process of the contract formation, that creates the terms, in proportion to the greater harshness or unreasonableness of the substantive terms themselves.' [Citations.]" (*Ibid.*) For example, the Restatement Second of Contracts states that "[i]nadequacy of consideration does not of itself invalidate a bargain, but gross disparity in the values exchanged may be an important factor in a determination that a contract is unconscionable and may be sufficient ground, without more, for denying specific performance." (Rest.2d Contracts, § 208, com. c, p. 108.) In ascertaining whether rescission is warranted for a unilateral mistake of fact, substantive unconscionability often will constitute the determinative factor, because the oppression and surprise ordinarily results from the mistake—not from inequality in bargaining power. Accordingly, even though defendant is not the weaker party to the contract and its mistake did not result from unequal bargaining power, defendant was surprised by the mistake, and in these circumstances overly harsh or one-sided results are sufficient to establish unconscionability entitling defendant to rescission.

Our previous cases support this approach. In *Kemper, supra,* we held that enforcement of the city's option to accept a construction company's bid, which was 28 percent less than the intended bid, would be unconscionable. Our decision reasoned that (1) the plaintiff gave prompt notice upon discovering the facts entitling it to rescind, (2) the city therefore was aware of the clerical error before it exercised the option, (3) the city already had awarded the contract to the next lowest bidder, (4) the company had received nothing of value it was required to restore to the city, and (5) "the city will not be heard to complain that it cannot be placed in statu quo because it will not have the benefit of an inequitable bargain." (*Id.* at p. 703.) Therefore, "under all the circumstances, it appears that it would be unjust and unfair to permit the city to take advantage of the company's mistake." (*Id.* at pp. 702-703.) Nothing in our decision in *Kemper* suggested that the mistake resulted from surprise related to inequality in the bargaining process. (Accord, *Farmers Sav. Bank, Joice v. Gerhart* (Iowa 1985) 372 N.W.2d 238, 243-245 [holding unconscionable the enforcement of sheriff's sale against bank that overbid because of a mistake caused by negligence of its own attorney].) Similarly, in *Elsinore, supra,* 54 Cal.2d 380, we authorized rescission of a bid based upon a clerical error, without suggesting any procedural unconscionability, even where the other party afforded the contractor an opportunity to verify the accuracy of the bid before it was accepted.

In the present case, enforcing the contract with the mistaken price of $25,995 would require defendant to sell the vehicle to plaintiff for $12,000 less than the intended advertised price of $37,995—an error amounting to 32 percent of the price defendant intended. Defendant subsequently sold the automobile for slightly more than the intended advertised price, suggesting that that price reflected its actual market value. Defendant had paid $35,000 for the 1995 Jaguar and incurred costs in advertising, preparing, displaying, and attempting to sell the vehicle. Therefore, defendant would lose more than $9,000 of its original investment in the automobile. Plaintiff, on the other hand, would obtain a $12,000 windfall if the contract were enforced, simply because he traveled to the dealership and stated that he was prepared to pay the advertised price.

These circumstances are comparable to those in our prior decisions authorizing rescission on the ground that enforcing a contract with a mistaken price term would be unconscionable. Defendant's 32 percent error in the price exceeds the amount of the errors in cases such as *Kemper* and *Elsinore*. For example, in *Elsinore, supra,* "54 Cal.2d at page 389, we authorized rescission for a $6,500 error in a bid that was intended to be $96,494—a mistake of approximately 7 percent in the intended contract price. As in the foregoing cases, plaintiff was informed of the mistake as soon as defendant discovered it. Defendant's sales manager, when he first learned of the mistake in the advertisement, explained the error to plaintiff, apologized, and offered to pay for plaintiff's fuel, time, and effort expended in traveling to the dealership to examine the automobile. Plaintiff refused this offer to be restored to the status quo and did not seek in this action to recover damages for the incidental costs he incurred because of the erroneous advertisement. Like the public agencies in *Kemper* and *Elsinore*, plaintiff should not be permitted to take advantage of defendant's honest mistake that resulted in an unfair, one-sided contract. (Cf. *Drennan v. Star Paving Co.* (1958) 51 Cal.2d 409, 415-416 [no rescission of mistaken bid where other party detrimentally altered his position in reasonable reliance upon the bid and could not be restored to the status quo].)

The circumstance that section 11713.1(e) makes it unlawful for a dealer not to sell a vehicle at the advertised price does not preclude a finding that enforcing an automobile sales contract containing a mistaken price would be unconscionable. Just as the statute does not eliminate the defense of mistake, as established above, the statute also does not dictate that enforcing a contract with an erroneous advertised price necessarily must be considered equitable and fair for purposes of deciding whether the dealer is entitled to rescission on the ground of mistake. In *Kemper, supra,* 37 Cal.2d 696, we concluded that it would be unconscionable to bar rescission of a bid pursuant to a city charter provision prohibiting the withdrawal of bids, where "it appear[ed] that it would be unjust and unfair to permit the city to take advantage of the company's mistake." (*Id.* at p. 703.) Thus, notwithstanding the public interest underlying the charter provision, our decision in *Kemper* precluded the city from relying upon that provision to impose absolute contractual liability upon the contractor. (*Id.* at p. 704.)

Accordingly, section 11713.1(e) does not undermine our determination that, under the circumstances, enforcement of the contract for the sale of the 1995 Jaguar XJ6 Vanden Plas at the $25,995 mistaken price would be unconscionable. The other requirements for rescission on the ground of unilateral mistake have been established. Defendant entered into the contract because of its mistake regarding a basic assumption, the price. The $12,000 loss that would result from enforcement of the contract has a material effect upon the agreed exchange of performances that is adverse to defendant. Furthermore, defendant did not neglect any legal duty within the meaning of Civil Code section 1577 or breach any duty of good faith and fair dealing in the steps leading to the formation of the contract. Plaintiff refused defendant's offer to compensate him for his actual losses in responding to the advertisement. "The law does not penalize for negligence beyond requiring compensation for the loss it has caused." (3 Corbin, Contracts, *supra,* § 609, p. 684.) In this situation, it would not be reasonable for this court to allocate the risk of the mistake to defendant.

Afterthoughts

Although California has not adopted UCC 2-302, it has enacted a nearly identical statute dealing with unconscionability which is found at California Civil Code section 1670.5. The applicability of section 1670.5 is not limited to transactions in goods but applies to all types of contracts.

Illegality

Illegal contracts are those which are:

(1) contrary to an express provision of law;

(2) contrary to the policy of express law, though not expressly prohibited; or,

(3) otherwise contrary to good morals. (Cal.Civ.Code § 1667.)

All contracts which have for their object, directly or indirectly, to exempt any one from responsibility for his own fraud, or willful injury to the person or property of another, or violation of law, whether willful or negligent, are against the policy of the law. (Cal.Civ.Code § 1668)

As a general rule, if a contract can be performed legally, a court will presume that the parties intended a lawful mode of performance. (*West Covina Enterprises, Inc. v. Chalmers*, 49 Cal.2d 754, 759 [322 P.2d 13].)

Drafting Tip — Illegality

Even if part of a contract is determined to be unenforceable because it is illegal, against public policy or unconscionable, that does not necessarily mean that the remainder of the contractual terms cannot be enforced. The careful drafter who wants to ensure that the valid portions of a contract remain enforceable might use language such as:

> *If any provision of this Contract is held unenforceable, then such provision will be modified to reflect the parties' intention. All remaining provisions of this Contract shall remain in full force and effect.*

Chapter 5

Damages

General Damages

"General damages" are those that flow naturally and typically as a consequence of the breach. The measure of general damages for the breach of a contract is that amount which will compensate the injured party for all the detriment or loss caused by the breach, or which in the ordinary course of things, would be likely to result therefrom. The injured party should receive those damages naturally arising from the breach, or those damages which might have been reasonably contemplated or foreseen by both parties, at the time they made the contract, as the probable result of the breach. As nearly as possible, the injured party should receive the equivalent of the benefits of performance,(Cal.Civ.Code § 3300) provided the damages are "clearly ascertainable in both their nature and origin" (Cal.Civ.Code, § 3301) As a corollary to this rule, no person can recover a greater amount in damages for the breach of an obligation than he or she could have gained had all parties fully performed. (Cal.Civ.Code § 3358.) In other words, a plaintiff in a breach of contract action is entitled to the benefits he or she would have obtained if both parties had fully performed, but no more.

The general rule in California is that one who has been injured by a breach of contract has an election to pursue any of three remedies, to wit: "He may treat the contract as rescinded and may recover upon a quantum meruit so far as he has performed; or he may keep the contract alive, for the benefit of both parties, being at all times ready and able to perform; or, third, he may treat the repudiation as putting an end to the contract for all purposes of performance, and sue for the profits he would have realized if he had not been prevented from performing." (*Oliver v. Campbell*, 43 Cal.2d 298, 302 [273 P.2d 15]; *Alder v. Drudis*, 30 Cal.2d 372, 381 [182 P.2d 195].) Affirmation of the contract, on the one hand, and rescission and restitution on the other, are alternative remedies. Election to pursue one is a bar to invoking the other. (*Alder v. Drudis*, (1947) 30 Cal.2d 372, 383; *Lenard v. Edmonds*, 151 Cal.App.2d 764, 768 [312 P.2d 308]

Special Damages

"Special damages" are those that result as a direct consequence of the breach but are peculiar or unique to the injured party's particular situation or circumstances. Special damages are recoverable when special circumstances exist which cause some unusual injury to the non-breaching party. The plaintiff can only recover special damages if defendant knew or should have known of the special circumstances at the time defendant entered into the contract. Any award for special damages must be reasonable. (See, 1 Witkin, Summary of Cal. Law (9th ed. 1987) Contracts, §§ 815-818)

Loss of Profits

Loss of profits, present or future, as an element of special damages, may be recovered for a breach of contract if:

(1) The loss is the direct and natural consequence of the breach,

(2) It is reasonably probable that the profits would have been earned except for the breach, and

(3) The amount of loss can be shown with reasonable certainty.

If future loss of profits is reasonably certain, any reasonable basis for determining the amount of the probable profits lost is acceptable. (See, Cal.Civ.Code § 3301; 1 Witkin, Summary of Cal. Law (9th ed. 1987) Contracts, §§ 823-827.)

Limitations on Damages

(1) Damages may not be punitive or exemplary and may not be imposed as a form of chastisement. (Cal.Civ.Code, § 3294; *Foley v. Interactive Data Corp.* (1988) 47 Cal.3d 654, 254 Cal.Rptr. 211, 765 P.2d 373.)

(2) Damages are limited to losses that might reasonably be contemplated or foreseen by the parties. (Cal.Civ.Code, §§ 3300, 3358)

(3) Damages must be clearly ascertainable and reasonably certain, both in their nature and origin. (Cal.Civ.Code, § 3301)

(4) Damages for mental suffering and emotional distress are generally not recoverable in an action for breach of an ordinary contract. (*Kwan v. Mercedes-Benz of North America, Inc.* (1994) 23 Cal.App.4th 174, 188 [28 Cal.Rptr.2d 371]

Foreseeability

Contract damages are generally limited to those within the contemplation of the parties when the contract was entered into or at least reasonably foreseeable by them at that time; consequential damages beyond the expectation of the parties are not recoverable.

Emotional Distress

As a general rule, damages will not be awarded to compensate for the mental distress or emotional trauma that may be caused by a breach of contract. The next two cases demonstrate the general rule and an exception.

Erlich v. Menezes

Supreme Court of California, 1999
21 Cal.4th 543, 87 Cal.Rptr.2d 886, 981 P.2d 978.

BROWN, J.

We granted review in this case to determine whether emotional distress damages are recoverable for the negligent breach of a contract to construct a house. A jury awarded the homeowners the full cost necessary to repair their home as well as damages for emotional distress caused by the contractor's negligent performance. Since the contractor's negligence directly caused only economic injury and property damage, and breached no duty independent of the contract, we conclude the homeowners may not recover damages for emotional distress based upon breach of a contract to build a house.

I. Factual and Procedural Background

Both parties agree with the facts as ascertained by the Court of Appeal. Barry and Sandra Erlich contracted with John Menezes, a licensed general contractor, to build a "dream house" on their ocean-view lot. The Erlichs moved into their house in December 1990. In February 1991, the rains came. "[T]he house leaked from every conceivable location. Walls were saturated in [an upstairs bedroom], two bedrooms downstairs, and the pool room. Nearly every window in the house leaked. The living room filled with three inches of standing water. In several locations water 'poured in in streams' from the ceilings and walls. The ceiling in the garage became so saturated ... the plaster liquefied and fell in chunks to the floor."

Menezes's attempts to stop the leaks proved ineffectual. Caulking placed around the windows melted, " 'ran down [the] windows and stained them and ran across the driveway and ran down the house [until it] ... looked like someone threw balloons with paint in them at the house.' " Despite several repair efforts, which included using sledgehammers and jackhammers to cut holes in the exterior walls and ceilings, application of new waterproofing materials on portions of the roof and exterior walls, and more caulk, the house continued to leak-from the windows, from the roofs, and water seeped between the floors. Fluorescent light fixtures in the garage filled with water and had to be removed.

"The Erlichs eventually had their home inspected by another general contractor and a structural engineer. In addition to confirming defects in the roof, exterior stucco, windows and waterproofing, the inspection revealed serious errors in the construction of the home's structural components. None of the 20 shear, or load-bearing walls specified in the plans were properly installed. The three turrets on the roof were inadequately connected to the roof beams and, as a result, had begun to collapse. Other connections in the roof framing were also improperly constructed. Three decks were in danger of 'catastrophic collapse' because they had been finished with mortar and ceramic tile, rather than with the light-weight roofing material originally specified. Finally, the foundation of the main beam for the two-story living room was poured by digging a shallow hole, dumping in 'two sacks of dry concrete mix, putting some water in the hole and mixing it up with a shovel.' " This foundation, required to carry a load of 12,000 pounds, could only support about 2,000. The beam is settling and the surrounding concrete is cracking.

According to the Erlichs' expert, problems were major and pervasive, concerning everything "related to a window or waterproofing, everywhere that there was something related to framing," stucco, or the walking deck.

Both of the Erlichs testified that they suffered emotional distress as a result of the defective condition of the house and Menezes's invasive and unsuccessful repair attempts. Barry Erlich testified he felt "absolutely sick" and had to be "carted away in an ambulance" when he learned the full extent of the structural problems. He has a permanent heart condition, known as superventricular tachyarrhythmia, attributable, in part, to excessive stress. Although the condition can be controlled with medication, it has forced him to resign his positions as athletic director, department head and track coach.

Sandra Erlich feared the house would collapse in an earthquake and feared for her daughter's safety. Stickers were placed on her bedroom windows, and alarms and emergency lights installed so rescue crews would find her room first in an emergency.

Plaintiffs sought recovery on several theories, including breach of contract, fraud, negligent misrepresentation, and negligent construction. Both the breach of contract claim and the negligence claim alleged numerous construction defects.

Menezes prevailed on the fraud and negligent misrepresentation claims. The jury found he breached his contract with the Erlichs by negligently constructing their home and awarded $406,700 as the cost of repairs. Each spouse was awarded $50,000 for emotional distress, and Barry Erlich received an additional $50,000 for physical pain and suffering and $15,000 for lost earnings.

By a two-to-one majority, the Court of Appeal affirmed the judgment, including the emotional distress award. The majority noted the breach of a contractual duty may support an action in tort. The jury found Menezes was negligent. Since his negligence exposed the Erlichs to "intolerable living conditions and a constant, justifiable fear about the safety of their home," the majority decided the Erlichs were properly compensated for their emotional distress.

The dissent pointed out that no reported California case has upheld an award of emotional distress damages based upon simple breach of a contract to build a house. Since Menezes's negligence directly caused only economic injury and property damage, the Erlichs were not entitled to recover damages for their emotional distress.

We granted review to resolve the question.

II. Discussion

A.

In an action for breach of contract, the measure of damages is "the amount which will compensate the party aggrieved for all the detriment proximately caused thereby, or which, in the ordinary course of things, would be likely to result therefrom" (Civ. Code, § 3300), provided the damages are "clearly ascertainable in both their nature and origin" (Civ. Code, § 3301). In an action not arising from contract, the measure of damages is "the amount which will compensate for all the detriment proximately caused thereby, whether it could have been anticipated or not" (Civ. Code, § 3333).

"Contract damages are generally limited to those within the contemplation of the parties when the contract was entered into or at least reasonably foreseeable by them at that time; consequential damages beyond the expectation of the parties are not recoverable. [Citations.] This limitation on available damages serves to encourage contractual relations and commercial activity by enabling parties to estimate in advance the financial risks of their enterprise." (*Applied Equipment Corp. v. Litton Saudi Arabia Ltd.* (1994) 7 Cal.4th 503, 515 [28 Cal.Rptr.2d 475, 869 P.2d 454] (*Applied Equipment*).) "In contrast, tort damages are awarded to [fully] compensate the victim for [all] injury suffered. [Citation.]" (*Id.* at p. 516.)

" '[T]he distinction between tort and contract is well grounded in common law, and divergent objectives underlie the remedies created in the two areas. Whereas contract actions are created to enforce the intentions of the parties to the agreement, tort law is primarily designed to vindicate "social policy." [Citation.]' " (*Hunter v. Up-right, Inc.* (1993) 6 Cal.4th 1174, 1180 [26 Cal.Rptr.2d 8, 864 P.2d 88], quoting *Foley v. Interactive Data Corp.* (1988) 47 Cal.3d 654, 683 [254 Cal.Rptr. 211, 765 P.2d 373] (*Foley*).) While the purposes behind contract and tort law are distinct, the boundary line between them is not (*Freeman & Mills, Inc. v. Belcher Oil Co.* (1995) 11 Cal.4th 85, 106 [44 Cal.Rptr.2d 420, 900 P.2d 669] (conc. and dis. opn. of Mosk, J.) (*Freeman & Mills*)) and the distinction between the remedies for each is not " 'found ready made.' " (*Ibid.,* quoting Holmes, The Common Law (1881) p. 13.) These uncertain boundaries and the apparent breadth of the recovery available for tort actions create pressure to obliterate the distinction between contracts and torts-an expansion of tort law at the expense of contract principles which Grant Gilmore aptly dubbed "con*torts.*" In this case we consider whether a negligent breach of a contract will support an award of damages for emotional distress-either as tort damages for negligence or as consequential or special contract damages.

B.

In concluding emotional distress damages were properly awarded, the Court of Appeal correctly observed that "the same wrongful act may constitute both a breach of contract and an invasion of an interest protected by the law of torts." (*North American Chemical Co. v. Superior Court* (1997) 59 Cal.App.4th 764, 774 [69 Cal.Rptr.2d 466], citing 3 Witkin, Cal. Procedure (4th ed. 1996) Actions, § 139, pp. 203-204.) Here, the court permitted plaintiffs to recover both full repair costs as normal contract damages and emotional distress damages as a tort remedy.

* * *

D.

Having concluded tort damages are not available, we finally consider whether damages for emotional distress should be included as consequential or special damages in a contract claim. "Contract damages are generally limited to those within the contemplation of the parties when the contract was entered into or at least reasonably foreseeable by them at the time; consequential damages beyond the expectations of the parties are not recoverable. [Citations.] This limitation on available damages serves to encourage contractual relations and commercial activity by enabling parties to estimate in advance the financial risks of their enterprise." (*Applied Equipment, supra,* 7 Cal.4th at p. 515.)

" '[W]hen two parties make a contract, they agree upon the rules and regulations which will govern their relationship; the risks inherent in the agreement and the likelihood of its breach. The parties to the contract in essence create a mini-universe for themselves, in which each voluntarily chooses his contracting partner, each trusts the other's willingness to keep his word and honor his commitments, and in which they define their respective obligations, rewards and risks. Under such a scenario, it is appropriate to enforce only such obligations as each party voluntarily assumed, and to give him only such benefits as he expected to receive; this is the function of contract law.' " (*Applied Equipment, supra,* 7 Cal.4th at p. 517.)

Accordingly, damages for mental suffering and emotional distress are generally not recoverable in an action for breach of an ordinary commercial contract in California. (*Kwan v. Mercedes-Benz of North America, Inc.* (1994) 23 Cal.App.4th 174, 188 [28 Cal.Rptr.2d 371] (*Kwan*); *Sawyer v. Bank of America* (1978) 83 Cal.App.3d 135, 139 [145 Cal.Rptr. 623].) "Recovery for emotional disturbance will be excluded unless the breach also caused bodily harm or the contract or the breach is of such a kind that serious emotional disturbance was a particularly likely result." (Rest.2d Contracts, § 353.) The Restatement specifically notes the breach of a contract to build a home is not "particularly likely" to result in "serious emotional disturbance." (*Ibid.*)

Cases permitting recovery for emotional distress typically involve mental anguish stemming from more personal undertakings the traumatic results of which were unavoidable. (See, e.g., *Burgess v. Superior Court, supra,* 2 Cal.4th 1064 [infant injured during childbirth]; *Molien v. Kaiser Foundation Hospitals* (1980) 27 Cal.3d 916 [167 Cal.Rptr. 831, 616 P.2d 813, 16 A.L.R.4th 518] [misdiagnosed venereal disease and subsequent failure of marriage]; *Kately v. Wilkinson* (1983) 148 Cal.App.3d 576 [195 Cal.Rptr. 902] [fatal waterskiing accident]; *Chelini v. Nieri* (1948) 32 Cal.2d 480 [196 P.2d 915] [failure to adequately preserve a corpse].) Thus, when the express object of the contract is the mental and emotional well-being of one of the contracting parties, the breach of the contract may give rise to damages for mental suffering or emotional distress. (See *Wynn v. Monterey Club* (1980) 111 Cal.App.3d 789, 799-801 [168 Cal.Rptr. 878] [agreement of two gambling clubs to exclude husband's gambling-addicted wife from clubs and not to cash her checks]; *Ross v. Forest Lawn Memorial Park* (1984) 153 Cal.App.3d 988, 992-996 [203 Cal.Rptr. 468, 42 A.L.R.4th 1049] [cemetery's agreement to keep burial service private and to protect grave from vandalism]; *Windeler v. Scheers Jewelers* (1970) 8 Cal.App.3d 844, 851-852 [88 Cal.Rptr. 39] [bailment for heirloom jewelry where jewelry's great sentimental value was made known to bailee].)

Cases from other jurisdictions have formulated a similar rule, barring recovery of emotional distress damages for breach of contract except in cases involving contracts in which emotional concerns are the essence of the contract. (See, e.g., *Hancock v. Northcutt* (Alaska 1991) 808 P.2d 251, 258 ["contracts pertaining to one's dwelling are not among those contracts which, if breached, are particularly likely to result in serious emotional disturbance"; typical damages for breach of house construction contracts can appropriately be calculated in terms of monetary loss]; *McMeakin v. Roofing & Sheet Metal Supply* (1990) 1990 Okla.Civ.App. 101 [807 P.2d 288] [affirming order granting summary judgment in favor of defendant roofing company after it negligently stacked too many brick tiles on roof, causing roof to collapse and completely destroy home, leading to plaintiff's heart attack one month later]; *Day v. Montana Power Co.* (1990) 242 Mont. 195 [789 P.2d 1224] [owner of restaurant that was destroyed in gas explosion allegedly caused by negligence of utility company employee not entitled to recover damages for emotional distress]; *Creger v. Robertson* (La.Ct.App. 1989) 542 So.2d 1090 [reversing award for emotional distress damages caused by foul odor emanating from a faulty foundation, preventing plaintiff from entertaining guests in her residence]; *Groh v. Broadland Builders, Inc.* (1982) 120 Mich.App. 214 [327 N.W.2d 443] [reversing order denying motion to strike allegations of mental anguish in case involving malfunctioning septic tank system, and noting adequacy of monetary damages to compensate for pecuniary loss of "having to do the job over," as distinguished from cases allowing recovery because situation could never be adequately corrected].)

Plaintiffs argue strenuously that a broader notion of damages is appropriate when the contract is for the construction of a home. Amici curiae urge us to permit emotional distress damages in cases of negligent construction of a personal residence when the negligent construction causes gross interference with the normal use and habitability of the residence.

Such a rule would make the financial risks of construction agreements difficult to predict. Contract damages must be clearly ascertainable in both nature and origin. (Civ. Code, §3301.) A contracting party cannot be required to assume limitless responsibility for all consequences of a breach and must be advised of any special harm that might result in order to determine whether or not to accept the risk of contracting. (1 Witkin, Summary of Cal. Law (9th ed. 1987) Contracts, §815, p. 733.)

Moreover, adding an emotional distress component to recovery for construction defects could increase the already prohibitively high cost of housing in California, affect the availability of insurance for builders, and greatly diminish the supply of affordable housing. The potential for such broad-ranging economic consequences-costs likely to be paid by the public generally-means the task of fashioning appropriate limits on the availability of emotional distress claims should be left to the Legislature. (See Tex. Prop. Code Ann. §27.001 et seq. (1999); Haw. Rev. Stat. §663-8.9 (1998).)

Permitting damages for emotional distress on the theory that certain contracts carry a lot of emotional freight provides no useful guidance. Courts have carved out a narrow range of exceptions to the general rule of exclusion where emotional tranquility is the contract's essence. Refusal to broaden the bases for recovery reflects a fundamental policy choice. A rule which focuses not on the risks contracting parties voluntarily assume but on one party's reaction to inadequate performance, cannot provide any principled limit on liability.

The discussion in *Kwan*, a case dealing with the breach of a sales contract for the purchase of a car, is instructive. "[A] contract for [the] sale of an automobile is not essentially tied to the buyer's mental or emotional well-being. Personal as the choice of a car may be, the central reason for buying one is usually transportation.... [¶] In spite of America's much-discussed 'love affair with the automobile,' disruption of an owner's relationship with his or her car is not, in the normal case, comparable to the loss or mistreatment of a family member's remains [citation], an invasion of one's privacy [citation], or the loss of one's spouse to a gambling addiction [citation]. In the latter situations, the contract exists primarily to further or protect emotional interests; the direct and foreseeable injuries resulting from a breach are also primarily emotional. In contrast, the undeniable aggravation, irritation and anxiety that may result from [the] breach of an automobile warranty are secondary effects deriving from the decreased usefulness of the car and the frequently frustrating process of having an automobile repaired. While [the] purchase of an automobile may sometimes lead to severe emotional distress, such a result is not ordinarily foreseeable from the nature of the contract." (*Kwan, supra,* 23 Cal.App.4th at p. 190.)

Most other jurisdictions have reached the same conclusion. (See *Sanders v. Zeagler* (La. 1997) 686 So.2d 819, 822-823 [principal object of a contract for the construction of a house was to obtain a place to live and emotional distress damages were not recoverable]; *Hancock v. Northcutt, supra,* 808 P.2d at pp. 258-259 [no recovery for emotional distress as a result of defective construction; typical damages for breach of house construction contracts can appropriately be calculated in terms of monetary loss]; *City of Tyler v. Likes* (Tex. 1997) 962 S.W.2d 489, 497 [mental anguish based solely on property damage is not compensable as a matter of law].)

We agree. The available damages for defective construction are limited to the cost of repairing the home, including lost use or relocation expenses, or the diminution in value. (*Orndorff v. Christiana Community Builders* (1990) 217 Cal.App.3d 683 [266 Cal.Rptr. 193].) The Erlichs received more than $400,000 in traditional contract damages to correct the defects in their home. While their distress was undoubtedly real and serious, we conclude the balance of policy considerations-the potential for significant increases in liability in amounts disproportionate to culpability, the court's inability to formulate appropriate limits on the availability of claims, and the magnitude of the impact on stability and predictability in commercial affairs-counsel against expanding contract damages to include mental distress claims in negligent construction cases.

Disposition

The judgment of the Court of Appeal is reversed and the matter is remanded for further proceedings consistent with this opinion.

George, C. J., Kennard, J., Baxter, J., and Chin, J., concurred.

WERDEGAR, J.,- Concurred and Dissented

Mosk, J., concurred.

Saari v. Jongordon Corp.

California Court of Appeal First District, 1992
5 Cal.App.4th 797, 7 Cal.Rptr.2d 82

REARDON, J.

A jury found in favor of respondents Tyme Saari, Peggy Dowling and Patrick Hinrichsen on their action for damages against appellant Jongordon Corporation for breach of a contract to cremate the remains of Robert Saari. The complaint had also alleged causes of action for negligent and intentional emotional distress. Motions for judgment notwithstanding the verdict and for new trial were denied.

Jongordon appeals from the judgment and the order denying judgment notwithstanding the verdict, contending that (1) Hinrichsen is not entitled to recover damages for emotional distress because he was not closely related to Robert Saari; (2) the $175,000 award of damages to Hinrichsen was excessive; (3) judgment notwithstanding the verdict should have been granted on the claims of Saari and Dowling; and (4) the $62,500 award of damages for emotional distress to Saari was based on inadmissible evidence and/or was excessive. We affirm the judgment and the order denying judgment notwithstanding the verdict.

I. Facts

Respondent Patrick Hinrichsen was the close friend and longtime companion of Robert Saari. The two men lived together in a home they owned in joint tenancy. In December 1984, Robert Saari and Hinrichsen entered into a written agreement with appellant Jongordon Corporation, doing business as the Neptune Society. Jongordon agreed that, on Robert's death, it would cremate his body and release his ashes to Hinrichsen. No religious service was to be performed.

In January 1985, Robert Saari died. His mother, respondent Tyme Saari, released her son's remains to Hinrichsen, who turned the body over to Jongordon. In violation of the terms of the contract, Jongordon scattered Robert's ashes at sea, performed a Christian religious service on his remains, and failed to release the ashes to Hinrichsen.

Richard Jongordon-the president and owner of Jongordon Corporation-agreed not to contact any of Robert's family about the mishandling of his ashes until Hinrichsen instructed him to do so. However, he telephoned Tyme Saari and respondent Peggy Dowling, Robert's sister, and informed them that although Hinrichsen had wanted to hold a party rather than a service for the deceased, Jongordon had performed a religious service and scattered the ashes at sea. He also told the two women that Hinrichsen was unable to attend the service as a result of illness.

In July 1985, Tyme Saari, Dowling and Hinrichsen filed a complaint against Jongordon and others, each alleging causes of action for breach of contract, breach of covenant of good faith and fair dealing, negligence, intentional and negligent infliction of emotional distress, mishandling of dead bodies and breach of fiduciary duty. They sought compensatory damages, attorney fees, costs and $500,000 in punitive damages.

Jongordon demurred to the complaint. The demurrer was sustained on the breach of contract and breach of covenant causes of action alleged by Saari and Dowling. In all other respects, the demurrer was overruled. Jongordon also moved for judgment on the pleadings on some causes of action alleged by Dowling and Hinrichsen. The motion was granted on Dowling's causes of action for negligence, mishandling of dead bodies and breach of fiduciary duty, but was otherwise denied. A motion for reconsideration was granted and these three causes of action were reinstated.

A first trial ended in a mistrial. At the second trial, Saari, Dowling and Hinrichsen withdrew the causes of action for negligent and intentional infliction of emotional distress on the basis that the underlying acts would be actionable as negligent mishandling. Ultimately, the jury found in their favor. Saari was awarded $62,500; Dowling, $5,000; and Hinrichsen, $175,000. The jury found that Jongordon acted with malice, oppression or fraud, but awarded Saari, Dowling and Hinrichsen only token punitive damages of $1 each. Judgment was entered accordingly. Both sides filed motions for judgment notwithstanding the verdict and for new trial, without success.

II. Emotional Distress

Jongordon first contends that Patrick Hinrichsen is not entitled to recover damages for emotional distress because he was not closely related to Robert Saari. This argument assumes that Hinrichsen's right to recover sounded in tort, thus ignoring the obvious—that he also sought recovery based on the contract he and Robert Saari formed with Jongordon. (See Health & Saf. Code, § 7100.) The duty Jongordon owed Hinrichsen flowed from the contract and the statutory scheme, not from any tort duty based on a special relationship.

After briefing was completed, the California Supreme Court announced a new decision affecting cases such as the one before us. (See Christensen v. Superior Court, supra, 54 Cal.3d 868.) The parties submitted letters explaining their views of the impact of this decision on our case. In its letter, Jongordon argued that Christensen implies that only family members are entitled to recover for emotional distress in mortuary remains cases.

Having read this decision carefully, we have a different view of it. As Jongordon concedes, Christensen did not directly address the issue of the standing of persons such as Hinrichsen to recover. The specific issue before the court was whether persons other than statutory right holders or contracting parties could recover for emotional distress. The court framed this issue by stating that the defendants sought "to limit liability to the statutory right holders or those who contract for funeral-related services...." (Christensen v. Superior Court, supra, 54 Cal.3d at p. 896.) The court ultimately held that "the class of persons who may recover for emotional distress negligently caused by [a mortuary or crematorium] is not limited to those who have the statutory right to control disposition of the remains and those who contract for disposition." (Id., at p. 876,.) This language is instructive to us, as it suggests that the court assumed the right of recovery of statutory right holders and contracting parties existed, determining only the extent to which other persons were entitled to recover.

Another factor reinforces our conclusion that the court did not intend Christensen to preclude contracting parties from recovering for emotional distress. In the typical contract case, it is not foreseeable that breach will cause emotional distress. Thus, a rule has evolved that damages for emotional distress are generally not recoverable in an action for breach of contract. However, some contracts-including mortuary and crematorium contracts-so affect the vital concerns of the contracting parties that severe emotional distress is a foreseeable result of a breach. (Allen v. Jones (1980) 104 Cal.App.3d 207, 211 [163 Cal.Rptr. 445].) The right to recover damages for emotional distress for breach of mortuary and crematorium contracts has been well established in California for many years. (See, e.g., Chelini v. Nieri (1948) 32 Cal.2d 480, 481-482 [196 P.2d 915].) If the California Supreme Court intended to disapprove this firmly entrenched principle of contract law, it would have done so expressly. If anything, Christensen suggests in dicta that this legal principle is still valid. In that decision, the court noted that "[e]ven in the context of an action for breach of contract, where recovery of damages solely for emotional distress resulting from a breach is not normally allowed, the provision of services related to the disposition of human remains has been distinguished because of the unique nature of the services." (Christensen v. Superior Court, supra, 54 Cal.3d at pp. 894-895.) Jongordon's interpretation of Christensen is too slim a basis on which to ignore an accepted principle of existing law. (See Luck v. Southern Pacific Transportation Co. (1990) 218 Cal.App.3d 1, 19 [267 Cal.Rptr. 618], cert. den. 498 U.S. 939 [112 L.Ed.2d 309, 111 S.Ct. 344].) Hinrichsen was entitled to seek damages for emotional distress as part of his damages for breach of the crematorium contract.

* * *

The judgment and the order denying judgment notwithstanding the verdict are affirmed.

Anderson, P. J., and Perley, J., concurred.

Afterthoughts

The general rule in California is that damages for mental suffering may not be recovered in an action for breach of an ordinary commercial contract. (*Quigley v. Pet, Inc.* (1984) 162 Cal.App.3d 877, 887-888 [208 Cal.Rptr. 394]; *Wynn v. Monterey Club* (1980) 111 Cal.App.3d 789, 799 [168 Cal.Rptr. 878]; *Sawyer v. Bank of America* (1978) 83 Cal.App.3d 135, 139 [145 Cal.Rptr. 623]; *O'Neil v. Spillane* (1975) 45 Cal.App.3d 147, 159 [119 Cal.Rptr. 245].)

California courts have recognized, on the other hand, the existence of extraordinary contracts, ones "which so affect the vital concerns of the individual that severe mental distress is a foreseeable result of breach. For many years, our courts have recognized that damages for mental distress may be recovered for breach of a contract of this nature. [Citations.]" (*Allen v. Jones* (1980) 104 Cal.App.3d 207, 211 [163 Cal.Rptr. 445].) Stated another way, the exceptional contracts are those whose terms " 'relate to matters which concern directly the comfort, happiness, or personal welfare of one of the parties, or the subject matter of which is such as directly to affect or move the affection, self-esteem, or tender feelings of that party.... ' " (*Wynn v. Monterey Club, supra,* 111 Cal.App.3d at p. 800, quoting *Westervelt v. McCullough* (1924) 68 Cal.App. 198, 208-209 [228 P. 734].)

The rule against emotional distress damages for breach of contract has been applied in California to bar such damages, for example, for breach of a choral singer's employment contract (*Westwater v. Grace Church* (1903) 140 Cal. 339, 341-343 [73 P. 1055]), in an action for rescission of a real estate gift on the ground of undue influence (*O'Neil v. Spillane, supra,* 45 Cal.App.3d at pp. 159-160), and for a bank's breach of its contractual obligation to buy automobile insurance for a borrower (*Sawyer v. Bank of America, supra,* 83 Cal.App.3d at pp. 138-139).

The exceptional contracts for whose breach distress damages have been allowed include the agreement of two gambling clubs with a husband to exclude his wife from the clubs and not to cash her checks (*Wynn v. Monterey Club, supra,* 111 Cal.App.3d at pp. 799-801), a mortician's contract to preserve a dead body (*Chelini v. Nieri* (1948) 32 Cal.2d 480, 481-482 [196 P.2d 915]) and to ship cremated remains (*Allen v. Jones, supra,* 104 Cal.App.3d at pp. 210-213), a cemetery's agreement to keep a burial service private and protect the gravesite from vandalism (*Ross v. Forest Lawn Memorial Park* (1984) 153 Cal.App.3d 988, 992-996 [203 Cal.Rptr. 468, 42 A.L.R.4th 1049]), and a bailment for jewelry of great sentimental value where that value was made known to the bailee (*Windeler v. Scheers Jewelers* (1970) 8 Cal.App.3d 844, 851-852 [88 Cal.Rptr. 39]).

In this area, California law appears substantially in accord with the Restatement Second of Contracts, which provides: "Recovery for emotional disturbance will be excluded unless the breach also caused bodily harm or the contract or the breach is of such a kind that serious emotional disturbance was a particularly likely result." (Rest.2d Contracts, § 353; cited and followed in *Quigley v. Pet, Inc., supra,* 162 Cal.App.3d at p. 888.)

Certainty

Damages which are speculative, remote, imaginary, contingent, or merely possible cannot serve as a legal basis for recovery. (Cal.Civ.Code § 3301; *Earp v. Nobmann* (1981) 122 Cal.App.3d 270, 294 [175 Cal.Rptr. 767].)

McDonald v. John P. Scripps Newspaper

California Court of Appeal, Second District, Division Six, 1989
210 Cal.App.3d 100, 257 Cal.Rptr. 473

GILBERT, J.

* * *

Facts

Gavin [L. McDonald] was a contestant in the 1987 Scripps Howard National Spelling Bee, sponsored in Ventura County by the newspaper, the Ventura County Star-Free Press. The contest is open to all students through the eighth grade who are under the age of 16. Gavin won competitions at the classroom and school-wide levels. This earned him the chance to compete against other skilled spellers in the county-wide spelling bee. The best speller in the county wins a trip to Washington D.C. and a place in the national finals. The winner of the national finals is declared the national champion speller.

Gavin came in second in the county spelling bee. Being adjudged the second best orthographer in Ventura County is an impressive accomplishment, but pique overcame self-esteem. The spelling contest became a legal contest.

We search in vain through the complaint to find a legal theory to support this metamorphosis. Gavin alleges that two other boys, Stephen Chen and Victor Wang, both of whom attended a different school, also competed in the spelling contest. Stephen had originally lost his school-wide competition to Victor. Stephen was asked to spell the word "horsy." He spelled it "h-o-r-s-e-y." The spelling was ruled incorrect. Victor spelled the same word "h-o-r-s-y." He then spelled another word correctly, and was declared the winner.

Contest officials, who we trust were not copy editors for the newspaper sponsoring the contest, later discovered that there are two proper spellings of the word "horsy," and that Stephen's spelling was correct after all.

Contest officials asked Stephen and Victor to again compete between themselves in order to declare one winner. Victor, having everything to lose by agreeing to this plan, refused. Contest officials decided to allow both Victor and Stephen to advance to the county-wide spelling bee, where Gavin lost to Stephen.

Taking Vince Lombardi's aphorism to heart, "Winning isn't everything, it's the only thing," Gavin filed suit against the Ventura County Star-Free Press and the Scripps Howard National Spelling Bee alleging breach of contract, breach of implied covenant of good faith and fair dealing, and intentional and negligent infliction of emotional distress.

In his complaint, Gavin asserts that contest officials violated spelling bee rules by allowing Stephen Chen to compete at the county level. He suggests that had Stephen not progressed to the county-wide competition, he, Gavin, would have won. For this leap of faith he seeks compensatory and punitive damages.

The trial court sustained Scripps's demurrer without leave to amend because the complaint fails to state a cause of action. The action was dismissed, and Gavin appeals.

Discussion

Gavin asserts that he has set forth the necessary elements of a cause of action for breach of contract, and that these elements are: "(1) The contract; (2) Plaintiff's performance; (3) Defendant's breach; (4) Damage to plaintiff. 4 Witkin, California Procedure, Pleading, § 464 (3rd Ed. 1985)."

Gavin's recitation of the law is correct, but his complaint wins no prize. He omitted a single word in the fourth element of an action for breach of contract, which should read "damage to plaintiff therefrom." (4 Witkin, Cal. Procedure (3d ed. 1985) Pleading, § 464, p. 504.) Not surprisingly, the outcome of this case depends on that word. A fundamental rule of law is that "whether the action be in tort or contract compensatory damages cannot be recovered unless there is a causal connection between the act or omission complained of and the injury sustained." (Capell Associates, Inc. v. Central Valley Security Co. (1968) 260 Cal.App.2d 773, 779 [67 Cal.Rptr. 463]; State Farm Mut. Auto. Ins. Co. v. Allstate Ins. Co. (1970) 9 Cal.App.3d 508, 528 [88 Cal.Rptr. 246]; Civ. Code, §§ 3300, 3333.)

The erudite trial judge stated Gavin's shortcoming incisively. "I see a gigantic causation problem....." Relying on the most important resource a judge has, he said, "common sense tells me that this lawsuit is nonsense."

Even if Gavin and Scripps had formed a contract which Scripps breached by allowing Stephen Chen to compete at the county level in violation of contest rules, nothing would change. Gavin cannot show that he was injured by the breach. Gavin lost the spelling bee because he misspelled a word, and it is irrelevant that he was defeated by a contestant who "had no right to advance in the contest."

Gavin argues that had the officials "not violated the rules of the contest, Chen would not have advanced, and would not have had the opportunity to defeat" Gavin. Of course, it is impossible for Gavin to show that he would have spelled the word correctly if Stephen were not his competitor. Gavin concedes as much when he argues that he would not have been damaged if defeated by someone who had properly advanced in the contest. That is precisely the point.

Gavin cannot show that anything would have been different had Stephen not competed against him. Nor can he show that another competitor would have also misspelled that or another word, thus allowing Gavin another opportunity to win. "It is fundamental that damages which are speculative, remote, imaginary, contingent, or merely possible cannot serve as a legal basis for recovery." (Earp v. Nobmann (1981) 122 Cal.App.3d 270, 294 [175 Cal.Rptr. 767].)

Gavin offers to amend the complaint by incorporating certain rules of the spelling bee which purportedly show that the decision to allow Stephen to advance in the competition was procedurally irregular. This offer to amend reflects a misunderstanding of the trial court's ruling. The fatal defect in the complaint is that Gavin cannot show that but for Stephen Chen's presence in the spelling bee, Gavin would have won.

* * *

In Shapiro v. Queens County Jockey Club (1945) 184 Misc. 295 [53 N.Y.S.2d 135], plaintiff's horse was the only horse to run the full six furlongs in the sixth race at Aqueduct Race Track after racing officials declared a false start. A half hour later the sixth race was run again, and plaintiff's horse came in fifth out of a total of six.

The Shapiro court held that plaintiff had no cause of action against the race track. Plaintiff could not support the theory that his horse would have won the second time around if all the other horses had also run the six furlongs after the false start. Plaintiff was not content to merely chalk up his loss to a bad break caused by the vicissitudes of life. The lesson to be learned is that all of us, like high-strung horses at the starting gate, are subject to life's false starts. The courts cannot erase the world's imperfections.

The Georgia Supreme Court in Georgia High School Ass'n v. Waddell (1981) 248 Ga. 542 [285 S.E.2d 7], decided it was without authority to review the decision of a football referee regarding the outcome of the game. The court stated that the referee's decision did not present a justiciable controversy. Nor does the decision of the spelling bee officials present a justiciable controversy here.

Our decision at least keeps plaintiff's bucket of water from being added to the tidal wave of litigation that has engulfed our courts.

* * *

As for the judgment of the trial court, we'll spell it out. A-F-I-R-M-E-D. Appellant is to pay respondent's costs on appeal.

Ericson v. Playgirl, Inc.,

Court of Appeals of California, Second Appellate District, Division Two, 1977
73 Cal.App.3d 850

FLEMING, ACTING P. J.

Were damages awarded here for breach of contract speculative and conjectural, or were they clearly ascertainable and reasonably certain, both in nature and in origin? The breach of contract arose from the following circumstances: plaintiff John Ericson, in order to boost his career as an actor, agreed that defendant Playgirl, Inc. could publish without compensation as the centerfold of its January 1974 issue of Playgirl photographs of Ericson posing naked at Lion Country Safari. No immediate career boost to Ericson resulted from the publication. In April 1974 defendant wished to use the pictures again for its annual edition entitled Best of Playgirl, a publication with half the circulation of Playgirl and without advertising. Ericson agreed to a rerun of his pictures in Best of Playgirl on two conditions: that certain of them be cropped to more modest exposure, and that Ericson's photograph occupy a quarter of the front cover, which would contain photographs of five other persons on its remaining three-quarters. Defendant honored the first of these conditions but not the second, in that as the result of an editorial mixup Ericson's photograph did not appear on the cover of Best of Playgirl. Ericson thereupon sued for damages, not for invasion of privacy from unauthorized publication of his pictures, but for loss of the publicity he would have received if defendant had put Ericson's picture on the cover as it had agreed to do.

All witnesses testified that the front cover of a magazine is not for sale, that a publisher reserves exclusive control over the front cover because its format is crucial to circulation, that consequently it is impossible to quote a direct price for front cover space. Witnesses also agreed that a picture on the front cover of a national magazine can provide valuable publicity for an actor or entertainer, but that it is difficult to put a price on this publicity. Analogies were sought in the cost of advertising space inside and on the back cover of national magazines. In July 1974 a full-page advertisement in Playgirl cost $7,500 to $8,000, a quarter page $2,500, and the back cover $11,000. However, Best of Playgirl carried no advertising and enjoyed only half the circulation of its parent magazine.

The trial court awarded plaintiff damages of $12,500, expressly basing its award on the testimony of Richard Cook, western advertising manager for TV Guide. According to Cook, the value to an entertainer of an appearance on the cover of a national magazine is "probably close to $50,000, and I base that on this: That magazine lays on the newsstand, a lot of people that never buy it see it, and everybody that does buy it certainly sees it." Cook said that the circulation of a magazine affects the value of a cover appearance, as does the magazine's demographics, i.e., the specific audience it reaches. He based his opinion on his knowledge of Playgirl, for he had no knowledge of the circulation, demographics, or even existence of Best of Playgirl. He also quantified his opinion by stating that if the picture only occupied a quarter of the cover instead of the full cover, the value of the appearance would be only a fourth of $50,000, which was the figure used by the trial court in fixing plaintiff's damages for loss of publicity at $12,500.

I

On appeal the sole substantial issue is that of damages, for it is clear the parties entered a contract which defendant breached.

In reviewing the issue of damages we first note that the cause of action is for breach of contract and not for a tort such as invasion of privacy. Defendant is not charged with committing a civil wrong but merely with failing to keep its promise. From this classification of the action as breach of contract, three important consequences affecting the measure of damages follow:

1. Damages may not be punitive or exemplary and may not be imposed as a form of chastisement (Civ. Code, § 3294).

2. Damages are limited to losses that might reasonably be contemplated or foreseen by the parties. (Civ. Code, §§ 3300, 3358; Hadley v. Baxendale (1854) 156 Eng. Rep. 145.)

3. Damages must be clearly ascertainable and reasonably certain, both in their nature and origin. (Civ. Code, § 3301.)

In each of these respects damages for breach of contract differ from damages in tort (see Civ. Code, §§ 3294, 3333); accordingly, tort precedents on the measure of damages have no direct relevancy here. Of limited application, too, is the tort rule that when calculation of the fact and amount of damages has been made difficult by defendant's wrong, courts will adopt whatever means are at hand to right the wrong. (Bigelow v. R.K.O. Radio Pictures (1946) 327 U.S. 251, 265-266 [90 L.Ed. 652, 660-661, 66 S.Ct. 574]; Zinn v. Ex-Cell-O-Corp. (1944) 24 Cal.2d 290, 297-298 [149 P.2d 177]; cf. Cal. Lettuce Growers, Inc. v. Union Sugar Co. (1955) 45 Cal.2d 474, 486-487 [289 P.2d 785, 49 A.L.R.2d 496].)

Plaintiff's claim of damages for breach of contract was based entirely on the loss of general publicity he would have received by having his photograph appear, alongside those of five others, on the cover of Best of Playgirl. Plaintiff proved that advertising is expensive to buy, that publicity has value for an actor. But what he did not prove was that loss of publicity as the result of his nonappearance on the cover of Best of Playgirl did in fact damage him in any substantial way or in any specific amount. Plaintiff's claim sharply contrasts with those few breach of contract cases that have found damages for loss of publicity reasonably certain and reasonably calculable, as in refusals to continue an advertising contract. In such cases the court has assessed damages at the market value of the advertising, less the agreed contract price. (See Metropolitan Broadcasting Corporation v. Lebowitz (D.C.Cir. 1961) 293 F.2d 524 [110 App.D.C. 336, 90 A.L.R.2d 1193]; Annot., 90 A.L.R.2d 1199.) Plaintiff's claim for damages more closely resembles those which have been held speculative and conjectural, as in the analogous cases of Jones v. San Bernardino Real Estate Board (1959) 168 Cal.App.2d 661, 665 [336 P.2d 606], where the court declined to award purely conjectural damages for loss of commissions, contacts, business associations, and clientele allegedly occasioned by plaintiff's expulsion from a local realty board; and of Fisher v. Hampton (1975) 44 Cal.App.3d 741 [118 Cal.Rptr. 811], where the court rejected an award of damages for defendant's failure to drill a $35,000 oil well when geological reports opined that oil would not be found and no evidence whatever established that plaintiff had been damaged. Under normal legal rules plaintiff's claim for damages failed to satisfy the requirements of reasonable foreseeability (Civ. Code, § 3300) and reasonable certainty (Civ. Code, § 3301), and therefore took on a punitive hue (Civ. Code, § 3294).

II

Plaintiff, however, contends that special rules of foreseeability and certainty of damages apply to loss of publicity by actors, entertainers, and other performing artists dependent upon public patronage for the success of their careers. In substance, plaintiff argues that for artists the loss of any kind of publicity is harmful and detrimental to their careers; hence for them any loss of publicity in breach of contract is compensable in damages. In order to evaluate this contention we must consider the nature and kind of publicity that plaintiff has lost.

All persons who offer personal services to the general public rely on goodwill to establish and maintain custom (cf. Bus. & Prof. Code, § 14100), and at first blush it seems reasonable to assume that the better known they are, the more likely they are to attract custom. But to be accurate we must make this assumption more precise. We must ask the question—better known for what? A lawyer who is a famous yachtsman may not necessarily attract legal business; a dentist world-renowned as a mountain climber may not necessarily improve his practice of dentistry as a consequence of his renown; a hairdresser who swims the Catalina Channel in record time may not necessarily increase the patronage of her beauty salon. For publicity to be of value and result in custom it must relate to the specific aspect of the human activity that is involved. General publicity bears little relation to the repute that leads to custom and trade, for it is specific reputation that brings about gain or loss of business. (Cf. Civ. Code, §§ 46, subd. 3, 48a, subd. 4(b).) It follows that damages for loss of publicity in breach of contract must be tied to loss of publicity for some particular event, such as a musical concert or a prize fight, or loss of publicity for some continuing activity, such as the conduct of a specific business at a specific location or the practice of a particular skill or art. Consequently, damages from loss of general publicity alone will almost always be wholly speculative and conjectural.

Plaintiff, however, insists that actors and performing artists fall in a special category apart from other purveyors of personal services. He argues that an actor needs an audience to perform; that an actor must be visible to patrons of his art to become successful; that only by becoming publicly visible can an actor become favorably known to patrons of his art and to producers of dramatic productions who provide him with employment; therefore all publicity is valuable to an actor, and the loss by an actor of any publicity is injurious and damaging. To a considerable extent the argument is sound—except for the breadth of its final conclusion. In our view it is not any kind of publicity, celebrity, or notoriety that is valuable to an artist's career, but instead the publicity which is valuable to the artist is publicity related to the performance of his art. Publicity of this sort, gained by the performance or production of his art, is the type of publicity that creates good will, reputation, and custom, and which taken at the flood leads to fame and fortune. Hence the importance to actors of appearances on the stage and screen, to musicians of appearances in concerts, and to writers and composers of credits for the works they have written or composed. Loss of publicity of this type as a result of breach of contract is compensable to an actor, musician, or writer, because the lost publicity is directly connected with the performance of his art, grows out of his profession, and directly affects his earning power.

The compensability in damages for an artist's loss of publicity in connection with his art as a result of breach of contract was established by a series of English cases that culminated in Herbert Clayton and Jack Waller Ld. v. Oliver [1930] A.C. 209. In that case the House of Lords squarely held that an actor whose contract of employment has been breached has a cause of action not only for loss of salary but for loss of publicity resulting from the denial of the opportunity to appear in public in his professional capacity. California has adopted the English rule in Colvig v. R.K.O. General, Inc. (1965) 232 Cal.App.2d 56 [42 Cal.Rptr. 473]. But an examination of the cases allowing recovery of damages for loss of publicity as a result of breach of contract discloses that in each instance the lost publicity grew out of the loss of the artist's exercise of his profession, i.e.,

loss of the opportunity to act, to broadcast, to sing, to conduct an orchestra, to enter-
tain; or resulted from the loss of credit to the artist for professional services connected
with a particular work, i.e., a script, play, musical composition, design, production,
and the like. Publicity in both these categories performs a similar function in that it
permits patrons and producers to evaluate the artist's merits in connection with the
performance of his art. Damages for the loss of such publicity does not present insuper-
able difficulties in calculation, for the artist's future earnings can be directly correlated
to his box office appeal or to his known record of successes. But even here proof of
damages from loss of publicity must be reasonably certain and specific, and those
claims that appear speculative and conjectural are rejected. For example, in Zorich v.
Petroff (1957) 152 Cal.App.2d 806, 811 [313 P.2d 118], the court declined to award
damages to an associate producer of a motion picture for defendant's failure to give him
screen credit. In that case the motion picture was a failure, no evidence of actual damage was introduced, and the court opined that screen credit, if given, might have turned
out to be a liability rather than an asset.

 A yawning gulf exists between the cases that involve loss of professional publicity and
the instant case in which plaintiff complains of loss of mere general publicity that bears
no relation to the practice of his art. His situation is comparable to that of an actor who
hopes to obtain wide publicity by cutting the ribbon for the opening of a new resort-
hotel complex, by sponsoring a golf or tennis tournament, by presenting the winning
trophy at the national horse show, or by acting as master of ceremonies at a televised political dinner. Each of these activities may generate wide publicity that conceivably could
bring the artist to the attention of patrons and producers of his art and thus lead to professional employment. Yet none of it bears any relation to the practice of his art. Plaintiff's argument, in essence, is that for an actor all publicity is valuable, and the loss of any
publicity as a result of breach of contract is compensable. Carried to this point, we think
his claim for damages becomes wholly speculative. It is possible, as plaintiff suggests, that
a television programmer might have seen his photograph on the cover of Best of Playgirl,
might have scheduled plaintiff for a talk show, and that a motion picture producer viewing the talk show might recall plaintiff's past performances, and decide to offer him a role
in his next production. But it is equally plausible to speculate that plaintiff might have
been hurt professionally rather than helped by having his picture appear on the cover of
Best of Playgirl, that a motion picture producer whose attention had been drawn by the
cover of the magazine to its contents depicting plaintiff posing naked in Lion Country
Safari might dismiss plaintiff from serious consideration for a role in his next production.
The speculative and conjectural nature of such possibilities speaks for itself.

 Assessment of the value of general publicity unrelated to professional performance takes us on a random walk whose destination is as unpredictable as the lottery
and the roulette wheel. When, as at bench, damages to earning capacity and loss of
professional publicity in the practice of one's art are not involved, we think recovery
of compensable damages for loss of publicity is barred by the Civil Code requirement that damages for breach of contract be clearly foreseeable and clearly ascertainable. (§§ 3300, 3301.) Plaintiff relies heavily on the somewhat analogous case of
Leavy v. Cooney (1963) 214 Cal.App.2d 496 [29 Cal.Rptr. 580]. In that case Leavy,
the prosecutor in the notorious Chessman case, appeared as narrator and participant
in a motion picture depicting the prosecution and imprisonment of Chessman,
under an agreement that the picture would be shown only on television as a news
broadcast and not in motion picture theaters. Defendant breached that agreement.
In affirming an award of compensatory damages of $7,500 to plaintiff, the court

pointed out that plaintiff's professional reputation could well have been damaged by the publicity occasioned by the breach of contract, that it was within the jury's discretion to assess the detriment caused. (214 Cal.App.2d at pp. 501-502.) Two critical factors distinguish Leavy from the cause before us: First, the publicity in Leavy intimately and directly related to the prosecutor's practice of his profession. Second, the publicity was unwanted, and defendant's conduct constituted the tort of invasion of privacy as well as breach of contract. At bench, the gist of plaintiff's claim is the precise opposite, for he seeks damages for loss of wanted publicity. No injury to personal rights and no relation to professional activities are involved. We conclude that the damages awarded by the trial court are speculative and conjectural, and that plaintiff failed to establish any ascertainable loss for which he is entitled to compensatory damages.

III

Plaintiff, however, is entitled to recover nominal damages for breach of contract. We evaluate plaintiff's right to nominal damages by analogy to Civil Code section 3344, which provides minimum statutory damages of $300 for knowing commercial use of a person's name or likeness without his consent. The statute's obvious purpose is to specify an amount for nominal damages in situations where actual damages are impossible to assess. Accordingly, although we find no support for any assessment of compensatory damages in plaintiff's favor because of the wholly speculative nature of the detriment suffered by plaintiff as a result of his nonappearance on a fourth of the cover of Best of Playgirl, plaintiff is entitled to nominal damages for breach of contract, which we fix in the sum of $300.

The judgment is modified to reduce the amount of damages to $300, and, as so modified, the judgment is affirmed. Costs on appeal to plaintiff.

Compton, J., and Beach, J., concurred.

Afterthoughts

No damages can be recovered for a breach of contract which are not clearly ascertainable in both their nature and origin. (Cal.Civ.Code § 3301) For other examples, see *Jones v. San Bernardino Real Estate Board* (1959) 168 Cal.App.2d 661, 665 [336 P.2d 606], where the court declined to award purely conjectural damages for loss of commissions, contacts, business associations, and clientele allegedly occasioned by plaintiff's expulsion from a local realty board, and *Fisher v. Hampton* (1975) 44 Cal.App.3d 741 [118 Cal.Rptr. 811], where the court rejected an award of damages for defendant's failure to drill a $35,000 oil well when geological reports opined that oil would not be found and no evidence whatever established that plaintiff had been damaged.

Damages must be reasonable. Plaintiff cannot recover a greater amount as damages than he or she could have gained by the full performance of the contract. In other words, the injured party should not be in a better position as a result of the breach than he or she would have been if the contract had been fully performed. (Cal.Civ.Code §3358.)

Measure of Damages for Breach of Specific Types of Contracts

Breach of Employment Contract

A wrongfully discharged or terminated employee is entitled to recover monetary damages caused by the breach. Damages for breach of the employment contract are the amount of compensation agreed upon for the period determined to be a reasonable period that plaintiff's employment would have continued but for the breach of the employment contract less any compensation actually earned by the employee during that period.(*Parker v. Twentieth Century-Fox* (1970) 3 Cal.3d 176, 181-182)

Employee Cannot Recover for Damages That Could Have Been Avoided

An employee who was damaged as a result of a breach of an employment contract by the employer has a duty to take steps to minimize the loss by making a reasonable effort to find comparable employment. If the employee through reasonable efforts could have found comparable employment, any amount that the employee could reasonably have earned by obtaining comparable employment through reasonable efforts shall be deducted from the amount of damages awarded to employee. (*Parker v. Twentieth Century-Fox, supra,* 3 Cal.3d 176, 181-182)

Sale of Land-Buyer's Damages

The measure of damages for a breach of contract to sell an interest in real estate is:

(1) The price paid,

(2) Expenses properly incurred in examining the title and preparing the necessary papers,

(3) The difference between the price agreed to be paid and the fair market value of the estate agreed to be conveyed at the time of the breach,

(4) The expenses properly incurred in preparing to enter upon the land,

(5) Consequential damages, and

(6) Interest from the date of the breach. (Cal.Civ.Code § 3306)

Sale of Land-Seller's Damages

The measure of damages for a breach of contract to purchase an interest in real estate is:

(1) The excess of the amount which would have been due the seller under the contract over the fair market value of the property to him or her,

(2) Interest from the date of the breach,

(3) Consequential damages. (Cal.Civ.Code § 3307)

The correct legal formula to measure the loss of bargain damages as to real property when the buyer breaches is the excess of the contract price over the value of the real property to the seller at the date of breach. (Cal.Civ. Code, §3307; *Royer v. Carter*, 37 Cal.2d 544.) Loss of bargain damages should be calculated on an all-cash-to-seller basis. Any promissory note must be converted to present case value. (*Abrams v. Motter* (1970) 3 Cal.App.3d 828, 83 Cal.Rptr. 855.)

Interest on Damages

Civil Code sections 3289(a) and (b) set forth the interest rate due upon breach of a contract, other than a promissory note secured by a deed of trust upon real estate. Generally, if a contract does not stipulate a legal rate of interest, the contract shall bear interest at a rate of 10 percent per annum after a breach.

Buyer's Damages for Seller's Breach of Contract for Sale of Goods

Allied Canners & Packers, Inc. v. Victor Packing Co.,
Court of Appeals of California, First Appellate District, Division Two, 1984
162 Cal.App.3d 905

ROUSE, J.

Allied Canners & Packers, Inc. (Allied) appeals from a judgment entered in its favor, following a trial to the court, in an action for damages for breach of two sales contracts. It contends that the trial court erroneously determined that it was a broker rather than a buyer under the contracts and therefore failed to apply the proper measure of damages specified in the California Uniform Commercial Code (Commercial Code). We determine that Allied was a buyer within the meaning of the Commercial Code but conclude that under the facts and circumstances of this case the trial court awarded the proper amount of damages.

The facts initially giving rise to the controversy are essentially undisputed. Allied is a corporation engaged in the business of exporting dry, canned and frozen food products. Its principal place of business is San Francisco. Respondent, Victor Packing Company (Victor), is engaged in the business of packing and processing fruits and is located in Fresno. On September 3, 1976, Allied entered into a contract with Victor whereby Victor was to sell and deliver five containers (each holding 37,500 pounds) of select Natural Thompson Seedless (NTS) raisins, to be delivered FOB at the Port of Oakland during the month of October, 1976, at a time and to a vessel later to be designated by Allied. On September 8, 1976, the parties entered into a second contract whereby Victor agreed to sell and deliver an additional five containers of NTS raisins on the same terms.

* * *

In this case, Allied had contracts to sell the raisins to Japanese firms. * * * Allied's contracts with Victor provided for Victor to sell the raisins at 29.75 cents per pound with a discount of 4 percent.

Allied characterizes the 4 percent as "the standard trade discount" while Victor characterizes it as a "commission." Regardless of the characterization, the parties agree that

Allied was to realize a gain of $4,462.50 in the transaction. Although the record is not entirely clear as to the terms of Allied's contracts with the Japanese firms, it appears that Allied was to net 29.75 cents per pound on the raisins, since its total gain was to be $4,462.50.

Heavy rains during the night of September 9, 1976, severely damaged the raisin crop which was drying on the ground, adversely affecting the supply of raisins in the Fresno area. * * * Victor notified Allied that it would not deliver the raisins as required by the contracts. Victor conceded that it thereby breached those contracts.

Allied did not cover by purchasing raisins on the open market.

* * *

Allied argued at trial, and contends on appeal, that it was the buyer under its contracts with Victor and therefore entitled to damages pursuant to Commercial Code section 2713, subdivision (1), which provides: "Subject to the provisions of this division with respect to proof of market price (Section 2723), the measure of damages for nondelivery or repudiation by the seller is the difference between the market price at the time when the buyer learned of the breach and the contract price together with any incidental and consequential damages provided in this division (Section 2715), but less expenses saved in consequence of the seller's breach." This is section 2-713, subdivision (1), of the 1962 Official Text of the Uniform Commercial Code (Uniform Code) without change. (See 23A West's Ann. Cal. U. Com. Code (1964 ed.) p. 628.

Allied contends that pursuant to section 2713, subdivision (1), it is entitled to damages in the amount of $150,281.25, representing the difference between the contract price of 29.75 cents per pound and a market price of 87 cents per pound for 262,500 pounds (seven containers) of NTS raisins. The trial court, however, refused to apply section 2713 because it determined, purportedly as a matter of fact, that Allied was a broker, not a buyer, and therefore not subject to the provisions of the Commercial Code governing a buyer's remedies for breach of contract by a seller. The court concluded that Allied was damaged only to the extent of its lost "commission" as a broker in the sum of $4,462.50. Judgment for that amount was entered in Allied's favor.

While we perceive that the trial court was attempting to limit Allied's damages to those actually suffered, and felt that application of the formula set forth in section 2713, subdivision (1), would result in a windfall to Allied, it could not properly do so on the basis that Allied was not a "buyer" within the meaning of the Commercial Code. Although Victor urges that this case turns upon whether there is substantial evidence to support the trial court's "finding" that Allied was a broker not a buyer, we believe that whether Allied was a broker or a buyer is a conclusion of law to be drawn from the pertinent facts in this case, which are basically undisputed. (See 6 Witkin, Cal. Procedure (1971 ed.) Appeal, §210, pp. 4200, 4201 ["Existence of the legal relationship of agency or independent contract, and the scope of employment, are questions of law"], and cases there cited.)

Section 2103, subdivision (1)(a), defines buyer as follows: "'Buyer' means a person who buys or contracts to buy goods." The contracts between Allied and Victor mention only those two parties and provide that Victor was to ship the raisins to Allied at the dock in Oakland. Victor did not even know the name of Shoei. Certainly, had Victor shipped the raisins but Allied not paid for them, logic dictates that Victor would have sued Allied for payment as the buyer.

Victor argues that Allied was not buying for its own account because Shoei was sending it a letter of credit to pay for Shoei's purchase of the raisins. Nevertheless, the evidence is uncontroverted that Allied would be sent an invoice from Victor in such transactions, and Allied would pay Victor with a check drawn on its general company account.

In essence, Victor is arguing that, because Allied had already contracted to sell the raisins to another, it was not a buyer in its transaction with Victor. As the manager of RAC testified at trial, "An exporter is a person [who] buys raisins and sells them to somebody else." Certainly it is not uncommon for an exporter to have "back-to-back" contracts, one to buy and the other to sell. Such entities are often referred to as "middlemen" or persons having "forward contracts" in discussions of buyer and seller remedies under the Uniform Code. (See, e.g., White & Summers, Uniform Commercial Code (2d ed. 1980) §6-4, p. 224; Simon & Novack, Limiting the Buyer's Market Damages to Lost Profits: A Challenge to the Enforceability of Market Contracts (1979) 92 Harv.L.Rev. 1395, 1404 (hereafter cited as Market Damages).)

We conclude that Allied was a buyer in its contract with Victor and that it had a "forward contract" to sell the raisins to Shoei. As such, the remedies provided to a buyer by the Commercial Code are applicable to it. Thus, we turn to a consideration of the correct application of such remedies in this case.

A buyer's primary remedies for nondelivery of goods by a seller are provided by sections 2712 ("cover" damages), 2713 (damages when buyer has not covered), 2715 (incidental and consequential damages), and sections 2502 and 2716 (replevin or specific performance under certain circumstances). Of these sections, only the provisions of sections 2712, 2713 and 2715 are pertinent to our discussion here.

Section 2712 provides: "(1) After a breach within [§2711, which specifies, inter alia, remedies available upon nondelivery or repudiation] the buyer may 'cover' by making in good faith and without unreasonable delay any reasonable purchase of or contract to purchase goods in substitution for those due from the seller. [¶] (2) The buyer may recover from the seller as damages the difference between the cost of cover and the contract price together with any incidental or consequential damages as hereinafter defined (Section 2715), but less expenses saved in consequence of the seller's breach. [¶] (3) Failure of the buyer to effect cover within this section does not bar him from any other remedy." Section 2713, subdivision (1), set forth in full at page 909, ante, provides that the measure of damages when the buyer has not covered is the difference between the market price when the buyer learned of the breach and the contract price, together with incidental and consequential damages. Section 2715, subdivision (2)(a), provides that consequential damages include "[a]ny loss resulting from general or particular requirements and needs of which the seller at the time of contracting had reason to know and which could not reasonably be prevented by cover or otherwise...."

Sections 2-712 and 2-713 of the Uniform Code are sometimes referred to as "cover" and "hypothetical cover," since the former involves an actual entry into the market by the buyer while the latter does not. (See Childres, Buyer's Remedies: The Danger of Section 2-713 (1978) 72 Nw.U.L.Rev. 837, 841 [applying those terms] (hereafter cited as Buyer's Remedies); Peters, Remedies for Breach of Contracts Relating to the Sale of Goods Under the Uniform Commercial Code: A Roadmap For Article Two (1963) 73 Yale L.J. 199, 259 [market under section 2-713 is "purely theoretical"] (hereafter cited as Remedies for Breach of Contracts).) It has been recognized that the use of the market- price contract-price formula under section 2-713 does not, absent pure accident, result in a damage award reflecting the buyer's actual loss. (Buyer's Remedies, supra, at pp. 841-842; Remedies for Breach of Contracts, supra, at p. 259; Market Damages, supra, 92 Harv.L.Rev. 1395 et seq.; White & Summers, Uniform Commercial Code, supra, at p. 224.)

For example, in this case it is agreed that Allied's actual lost profit on the transaction was $4,462.50, while application of the market-contract price formula would yield damages of approximately $150,000. In Market Damages, supra, Simon and Novack describe the courts as divided on the issue of whether market damages, even though in excess of the plaintiff's loss, are appropriate for a supplier's breach of his delivery obligations and observe: "Strangely enough, each view has generally tended to disregard the arguments, and even the existence, of the opposing view. These two rival bodies of law, imposing in appearance, have passed each other like silent ships in the night." (92 Harv.L.Rev. 1395, 1397.) In Buyer's Remedies, supra, Professor Childres similarly points out that the courts have generally not undertaken any real analysis of the competing considerations involved in determining the correct measure of damages in such circumstances. (72 Nw.U.L.Rev. 837, 844 et seq.) We shall undertake such an analysis.

Professors White and Summers, after noting their belief that "the Code drafters did not by [section 2-713] intend to put the buyer in the same position as performance would have" (White & Summers, Uniform Commercial Code, supra, at p. 224), advance two possible explanations for the section. First, they suggest that it is simply a historical anomaly: "Since cover was not a recognized remedy under pre-Code law, it made sense under that law to say that the contract-market formula put buyer in the same position as performance would have on the assumption that the buyer would purchase substitute goods. If things worked right, the market price would approximate the cost of the substitute goods and buyer would be put 'in the same position.... ' But under the Code, 2-712 does this job with greater precision, and 2-713 reigns over only those cases in which the buyer does not purchase a substitute. Perhaps the drafters retained 2-713 not out of a belief in its appropriateness, but out of fear that they would be dismissed as iconoclasts had they proposed that the court in noncover cases simply award the buyer any economic loss proximately caused by seller's breach." (Ibid)

They conclude, however, that probably the best explanation for section 2-713 "is that it is a statutory liquidated damage clause, a breach inhibitor the payout of which need bear no close relation to plaintiff's actual loss. "(White & Summers, Uniform Commercial Code, supra, at p. 225.) They then observe that this explanation conflicts with the policy set forth in section 1-106, which provides in subdivision (1): "The remedies provided by this code shall be liberally administered to the end that the aggrieved party may be put in as good a position as if the other party had fully performed but neither consequential or special nor penal damages may be had except as specifically provided in this code or by other rule of law." They find section 2-713 consistent, however, with a belief that plaintiffs recover too little and too infrequently for the law of contracts to be effective, and offer no suggestion for resolution of the conflict. (Ibid)

In her article Remedies for Breach of Contracts, supra, then-Professor Peters states: "Perhaps it is misleading to think of the market-contract formula as a device for the measurement of damages.... An alternative way of looking at market-contract is to view this differential as a statutory liquidated damages clause, rather than as an effort to calculate actual losses. If it is useful in every case to hold the party in breach to some baseline liability, in order to encourage faithful adherence to contractual obligations, perhaps market fluctuations furnish as good a standard as any." (73 Yale L.J. 199, 259.) She does not discuss the conflict between the market-contract formula and the "only as good a position as performance" policy embodied in section 1-106.

Simon and Novack state: "While it is generally recognized that the automatic invocation of market damages may sometimes overcompensate the plaintiff, a variety of arguments have been employed by commentators and courts to justify this result: the desirability of maintaining a uniform rule and of facilitating settlements; the public interest in encouraging contract performance and the proper functioning of the market; the prevention of defendant's unjust enrichment; the restoration of the very 'value' promised to plaintiff; and the inherent difficulty and complexity of proving actual economic losses not encompassed within the contract terms." (Fns. omitted; Market Damages, supra, 92 Harv. L.Rev. 1395, 1403.) That a defendant not be unjustly enriched by a bad faith breach is a concern widely shared by commentators and courts. (Id, at p. 1406, fn. 51, and cases there cited.)

Viewing section 2-713 as, in effect, a statutory provision for liquidated damages, it is necessary for us to determine whether a damage award to a buyer who has not covered is ever appropriately limited to the buyer's actual economic loss which is below the damages produced by the market-contract formula, and, if so, whether the present case presents a situation in which the damages should be so limited.

One view is that section 2-713 of the Uniform Code, or a substantively similar statutory provision, establishes the principle that a buyer's resale contract and damage claims made thereunder are irrelevant to an award of damages, and that damages therefore cannot be limited to a plaintiff's actual economic loss. (See 11 Williston, Contracts (3d ed. 1968) §1388 [Uniform Code]; Coombs and Company of Ogden v. Reed (1956) 5 Utah2d 419 [303 P.2d 1097] [Uniform Sales Act]; Brightwater Paper Co. v. Monadnock Paper Mills (1st Cir. 1947) 161 F.2d 869 [Massachusetts Sales Act then in effect]; Goldfarb v. Campe Corporation (1917) 99 Misc. 475 [164 N.Y.S. 583] [New York Sales Act then in effect].) Simon and Novack, while favoring that view, concede that it can be argued that the provision of section 1-106 that an aggrieved party be put "'in as good a position as if the other party had fully performed'" calls for an opposite conclusion. (Market Damages, supra, 92 Harv.L.Rev. 1395, 1412-1413, fn. 71.)

Although we find no cases discussing the interaction of section 1-106 and section 2-713, we note that some pre-Uniform Code cases held that a limitation to actual losses should be placed upon the market price-contract price measure of damages under general contract principles. (See, e.g., Foss v. Heineman (1910) 144 Wis. 146 [128 N.W. 881]; Isaacson v. Crean (1917) 165 N.Y.S. 218; Texas Co. v. Pensacola Maritime Corporation (5th Cir. 1922) 279 Fed. 19.) One author on the subject has apparently concluded that such a limitation is appropriate under the Uniform Code when the plaintiff-buyer has a resale contract and the existence of the resale contract is known to the defendant-seller: "It may be supposed ... that the buyer was bound by a contract made before the breach to deliver to a third person the very goods which the buyer expected to obtain from the seller, and the price under the resale contract may be less than the market price at the time of the breach. If the reason generally given for the rule permitting the recovery of additional damage because of an advantageous resale contract existing and known to the defendant when he contracted be applied, namely, that such consequential damages are allowed because the parties supposedly contract for them, it would follow that in every case the damage that the defendant might normally expect to follow from breach of his contract should be recovered even though the plaintiff actually suffered less damage than the difference between the contract price and the market price." (4 Anderson, Uniform Commercial Code (3d ed. 1983) §2-711:15, pp. 430-431.)

The only California case directly applying section 2713 is Gerwin v. Southeastern Cal. Assn. of Seventh Day Adventists (1971) 14 Cal.App.3d 209 [92 Cal.Rptr. 111]. There the plaintiff had contracted to purchase bar and restaurant equipment which he planned to use in a hotel he had recently acquired. The seller failed to deliver the equipment, and plaintiff, who had not covered, was awarded damages of $15,000 as the difference between the contract price and the market price of the equipment. The plaintiff had not covered because substitute items were not available at prices within his financial ability. (Id, at pp. 218-219.) Presumably, after recovering his damage award, the plaintiff in Gerwin paid it out to purchase other equipment. That case is inapposite to the present case because the plaintiff there had no resale contract which limited his liability and defined the actual profit he expected to make through the acquisition of the items covered by the sales contract.

We conclude that in the circumstances of this case—in which the seller knew that the buyer had a resale contract (necessarily so because raisins would not be released by RAC unless Allied provided it with the name of the buyer in its forward contract), the buyer has not been able to show that it will be liable in damages to the buyer on its forward contract, and there has been no finding of bad faith on the part of the seller—the policy of section 1106, subdivision (1), that the aggrieved party be put in as good a position as if the other party had performed, requires that the award of damages to the buyer be limited to its actual loss, the amount it expected to make on the transaction. We note that in the context of a cover case under section 2712, a Court of Appeal has recently approved the use of section 1106 to limit damages to the amount that would put the plaintiff in as good a position as if the defendant had performed. (Sun Maid Raisin Growers v. Victor Packing Co. (1983) 146 Cal.App.3d 787, 792 [194 Cal.Rptr. 612].)

We need not determine in this case what degree of bad faith on the part of a breaching seller might warrant the award of market-contract price damages without limitation, in circumstances otherwise similar to those involved here, in order to prevent unjust enrichment to a seller who deliberately breaches in order to take advantage of a rising market. Although Allied implies that Victor was guilty of bad faith here because after its breach it allowed another packer to acquire reserve raisins to which it was entitled at 36.25 cents per pound, rather than acquiring the raisins and delivering them to Allied, the record is simply not clear on Victor's situation following the rains. It does appear clear, however, that, as the trial court found, the rains caused a severe problem, and Victor made substantial efforts to persuade RAC to release reserve raisins to it in spite of its failure to get its check to RAC before 8:30 a.m. on September 10, 1976. We do not deem this record one to support an inference that windfall damages must be awarded the buyer to prevent unjust enrichment to a deliberately breaching seller. (Compare Sun Maid Raisin Growers v. Victor Packing Co., supra, 146 Cal.App.3d 787 [where, in a case coincidentally involving Victor, Victor was expressly found by the trial court to have engaged in bad faith by gambling on the market price of raisins in deciding whether to perform its contracts to sell raisins to Sun Maid].)

The judgment is affirmed. Each party is to bear its own costs on appeal.

Kline, P. J., and Smith, J., concurred.

Sun-Maid Raisin Growers v. Victor Packing Co.
Court of Appeals of California, Fifth Appellate District, 1983
146 Cal.App.3d 787, 194 Cal.Rptr. 612

FRANSON, Acting P. J.

I. The Case

Plaintiff and respondent Sun-Maid Raisin Growers of California (hereinafter Sun-Maid) filed a complaint against defendants and appellants Victor Packing Company and Pyramid Packing Company (hereinafter appellants or Victor). The complaint for injunctive relief, specific performance and damages alleged appellants had breached agreements to sell Sun-Maid 1,800 tons of raisins from the 1975 raisin crop by repudiating the contracts and refusing to deliver 610 tons of raisins which remained to be delivered under the contracts. The repudiation allegedly occurred on August 10, 1976.

After a court trial, judgment was issued in favor of Sun-Maid, holding appellants jointly liable for damages of $247,383, and Victor additionally liable for damages of $59,956, for a total of $307,339. In addition, Sun-Maid recovered its costs of suit. Findings of fact and conclusions of law were filed. After denial of appellants' motion for new trial, a timely appeal was filed.

* * *

V. Damages Were Foreseeable

Appellants' precise argument on appeal is that the damages award of $295,339.40 for lost profits is excessive because "the amount of lost profits was unforeseeable by either party when the contracts were formed," citing Hadley v. Baxendale (1854) 9 Ex. 341, 156 Eng.Rep. 145. According to appellants, the foreseeability requirement applies not only to the fact that some profits might be lost as a result of the breach but also to the amount of profits thereby lost. Thus, "the foreseeability of extraordinary profits must itself be proved, even if the fact of ordinary … profits is either presumed or otherwise proved to be within the parties' contemplation." Appellants hinge their argument on the fact that the new crop in September was reduced in quantity and quality by "disastrous" rains which resulted in an extraordinary increase in the market price of raisins in November and December 1976.

Preliminarily, we observe that appellants made no foreseeability objection to Sun-Maid's evidence of damages at trial. It was only in appellants' posttrial brief that they argued the point. Furthermore, appellants filed no objections to Sun-Maid's proposed findings on damages (Nos. 42, 43 and 44) and made no request for a specific finding on the foreseeability question.

We also observe that unless it can be ruled on as a matter of law, the question whether the buyer's consequential damages were foreseeable by the seller is one of fact to be determined by the trier of fact. (See Annot. (1979) 96 A.L.R.3d 299, 329, § 4b.) If supported by the evidence, the decision cannot be overturned on appeal.

The basic measure of damages for a seller's nondelivery or repudiation is the difference between the market price and the contract price. (Cal. U. Com. Code, § 2713.) The market price to be used as the basis of the calculation is the market to which a buyer would normally go to effect cover. (§ 2713, subd. (2); 1 Cal. Commercial Law (Cont.Ed.Bar 1966) § 12.15, pp. 562-563.) Market price is measured as of the time the buyer learned of the breach—in this case August 10—at which time he could be expected to seek cover. (§ 2713, subd. (1).)

If evidence of a price prevailing at the appropriate time or place "is not readily available," the price prevailing within a reasonable time before or after may be used. (§ 2723, subd. (2).)

In addition to the difference between the market price and the contract price, the buyer can recover incidental damages such as expenses of cover (§ 2715, subd. (1)) and consequential damages such as lost profits (§ 2715, subd. (2)(a)) to the extent they could not have been avoided by cover. The inability to cover after a prompt and reasonable effort to do so is a prerequisite to recovery of consequential damages. (Ibid) If the buyer is only able to cover in part, he is entitled to the net cost of cover (the difference between the cover price and the contract price plus expenses) together with any consequential damages as hereinafter defined (§ 2715) but less expenses saved in consequence of the seller's breach (§ 2712).

Under section 2715, subdivision (2)(a), consequential damages include "[a]ny loss resulting from general or particular requirements and needs of which the seller at the time of contracting had reason to know and which could not reasonably be prevented by cover or otherwise; ..." The "reason to know" language concerning the buyer's particular requirements and needs arises from Hadley v. Baxendale, supra, 9 Ex. 347, 156 Eng.Rep. 145 (see Dunn, Recovery of Damages for Lost Profits in California (1974-75) 9 U.S.F.L.Rev. 415). The code, however, has imposed an objective rather than a subjective standard in determining whether the seller should have anticipated the buyer's needs. Thus, actual knowledge by the seller of the buyer's requirements is not required. The only requirement under section 2715, subdivision (2)(a), is that the seller reasonably should have been expected to know of the buyer's exposure to loss. (Id, at pp. 420-421.)

Furthermore, comment 6 to section 2715 provides that if the seller knows that the buyer is in the business of reselling the goods, the seller is charged with knowledge that the buyer will be selling the goods in anticipation of a profit. "Absent a contractual provision against consequential damages a seller in breach [will] therefore always be liable for the buyer's resulting loss of profit." (1 Cal. Commercial Law, supra, § 12.20, p. 568, citingStott v. Johnston (1951) 36 Cal.2d 864 [229 P.2d 348, 28 A.L.R.2d 580].)

Finally, a buyer's failure to take any other steps by which the loss could reasonably have been prevented bars him from recovering consequential damages. (§ 2715, subd. (2)(a).) This is merely a codification of the rule that the buyer must attempt to minimize damages. (1 Witkin, Summary of Cal. Law (8th ed. 1973) Contracts, §§ 639-640, 670-674.)

In the present case, the evidence fully supports the finding that after appellants' breach of the contract on August 10, 1976, Sun-Maid acted in good faith in a commercially reasonable manner and was able to cover by purchase of only some 200 tons of substitute raisins at a cost of 43 cents per pound. ($860 per packed weight ton.) There were no other natural Thompson seedless free tonnage raisins available for purchase in the market at or within a reasonable time after appellants' breach. Although the evidence indicates that Sun-Maid actually was able to purchase an additional 410 tons of raisins after the September rainfall in their efforts to effect cover, these were badly damaged raisins which had to be reconditioned at a substantial cost to bring them up to market condition. According to Sun-Maid, if the trial court had used the total cost of cover of the full 610 tons as the measure of damages rather than lost profits on resale, their damages would have totaled $377,720.

Although the trial court did not specify why it determined damages by calculating lost profits instead of the cost of cover (no findings were requested), the court probably found that damages should be limited to the amount that would have put Sun-Maid in "as good a position as if the other party had fully performed." (§ 1106.) Thus, Sun-Maid was awarded the lesser of the actual cost of cover (treating the reconditioning of the 410 tons as a cost) and the loss of prospective profits.

In contending the foreseeability requirement applies to the amount of the lost profits and not just to the fact of lost profits, appellants apparently acknowledge that they knew at the time of contracting that Sun-Maid would be reselling the raisins to its customers in the domestic market. Appellants have no alternative to this concession since they were experienced packers and knew that Sun-Maid marketed raisins year round in the domestic market. They also knew that Sun-Maid substituted reserve raisins into their free tonnage in place of appellants' raisins which were shipped to Japan. Furthermore, appellants must be presumed to have known that if they did not deliver the full quota of raisins provided under the contracts (1,800 tons) by the end of the crop year or before such reasonable time as thereafter might be agreed to, Sun-Maid would be forced to go into the market to attempt to cover its then existing orders for sale of raisins. This is exactly what occurred. When Peterson called Sahatdjian on August 10 and requested some 38 tons of raisins and Sahatdjian refused the order, Peterson stated, "Well, we have orders here to fill; and I'll have to tell Frank Light about it." Within five minutes, Light called Sahatdjian and demanded to know what was going on. Sahatdjian again refused to deliver as requested but said he "would be glad" to deliver when the new crop came in.

A reasonable inference arises that apart from appellants' breach of contract, they intended to fulfill their obligations to Sun-Maid by acquiring raisins from the new crop which would be available in October. The fact that Sun-Maid requested only 38 tons on August 10 suggests that Sun-Maid also understood that appellants intended to deliver the balance of the raisins from the new crop.

The contemplation of the parties in August was consistent with Sun-Maid's industry-wide announcement in November 1975 that it needed raisins for sale in the domestic market "through 1976."

When the contract for sale involves repeated occasions for performance by either party with the knowledge of the nature of the performance and opportunity for objection to it by the other, any performance accepted or acquiesced in without objection shall be relevant to determining the meaning of the agreement. (§ 2208, subd. (1).) Since appellants had delivered only 1, 190 tons by August and the amount of each delivery had been within their discretion, Sun-Maid's reliance on appellants' future performance of the contract by accepting orders from the domestic market must have been within the parties' contemplation. Thus, appellants had "reason to know" that their failure to deliver the 610 tons before the new crop came in would result in lost profits on resales by Sun-Maid.

Finally, there is no showing that Sun-Maid's evidence of the price of raisins on December 1, which was used by the trial court to measure damages, did not accurately reflect the true state of the domestic market before the September crop was produced when free tonnage raisins were unavailable. The December price was a reasonable alternative market price to the "not readily available" price on August 10 as required by section 2723, subdivision (2).

Appellants nonetheless contend they should not be liable for damages based on the extraordinarily high price of raisins in the fall of 1976 which was caused by the "disastrous" rains in September. These rains reportedly caused a 50 percent loss of the new crop which with the lack of a substantial carryover of 1975 raisins drove the market price from approximately $860 per packed weight ton to over $1,600 per packed weight ton.

Appellants do not assert the doctrines of impossibility or impracticability of performance as a defense. (§ 2615.) This is understandable since the nondelivery of raisins was not caused by the failure of a presupposed condition (continuance of the $860 per ton market price) but solely by appellants' failure to deliver the 610 tons of raisins during the 1975 crop year. This is where the trial court's findings of appellants' bad faith become pertinent. A reasonable inference may be drawn that from early spring appellants were gambling on the market price of raisins in deciding whether to perform their contracts with Sun-Maid. If the price would fall below the contract price, appellants would buy raisins and deliver them to Sun-Maid. If the market price went substantially above the contract price, appellants would sit tight. While we cannot read Sahatdjian's mind during the late spring and summer months, we can surmise that he speculated that the market price would remain below the contract price after the current crop year so that he could purchase new raisins for delivery to Sun-Maid at the contract price. He threw the dice and lost.

The possibility of "disastrous" rain damage to the 1976 raisin crop was clearly foreseeable to appellants. Such rains have occurred at sporadic intervals since raisins have been grown in the San Joaquin Valley. Raisin packers fully understand the great risk in contracting to sell raisins at a fixed price over a period of time extending into the next crop year. The market price may go up or down depending on consumer demand and the supply and quality of raisins. If the seller does not have sufficient inventory to fulfill his delivery obligations within the time initially required or as subsequently modified by the parties, he will have to go into the market to purchase raisins. The fact that he may be surprised by an extraordinary rise in the market price does not mean that the buyer's prospective profits on resale are unforeseeable as a matter of law.

Conclusion

Once the trial court found that the contracts did not end either by March 1 or June 30, appellants were required to deliver the balance of the raisins by September 1 or by such further time as the parties would have agreed to if the contracts had not been breached on August 10. Sun-Maid's damages for the cost of cover and lost profits on prospective resale were the natural, foreseeable and inevitable result of appellants' failure to deliver according to the contracts.

The judgment is affirmed.

Woolpert, J., and Martin, J., concurred.

Liquidated Damages

The parties may agree in advance to the amount of damages that will be imposed in the event of a breach. Such an agreement is known as a liquidated damage clause. The validity of a clause for liquidated damages requires that the parties to the contract "agree therein upon an amount which shall be presumed to be the amount of damages sustained by a breach thereof...." This amount must represent the result of a reasonable endeavor by the parties to estimate a fair average compensation for any loss that may be sustained. (*Rice v. Schmid* (1941) 18 Cal.2d 382, 386 [115 P.2d 498, 138 A.L.R. 589]; Restatement Second Contracts § 356)" (*Better Food Mkts. v. Amer. Dist. Teleg. Co.*, (1953) 40 Cal.2d 179, 186-187.) A provision in a contract liquidating the damages for the breach of the contract is valid unless the party seeking to invalidate the provision establishes that the provision was unreasonable under the circumstances existing at the time the contract was made. (Cal.Civ.Code § 1671(b).)

Chapter 6

Contract Interpretation

The Parol Evidence Rule

Where the parties have reduced their agreement to a final written form, which they intend to be the complete statement of their agreement, it is said that the agreement is "integrated." The parol evidence rule prohibits the introduction of any extrinsic evidence, whether oral or written, to vary, alter or add to the terms of an integrated written instrument. (*Tahoe National Bank v. Phillips* (1971) 4 Cal.3d 11, 23 [92 Cal.Rptr. 704, 480 P.2d 320].) The rule comes into operation when there is a single and final written agreement setting forth the understanding of the parties. When that takes place, prior and contemporaneous negotiations, oral or written, are excluded; or, as it is sometimes said, the written agreement supersedes these prior or contemporaneous negotiations.

Masterson v. Sine
Supreme Court of California, 1968
68 Cal.2d 222

TRAYNOR, C. J.

Dallas Masterson and his wife Rebecca owned a ranch as tenants in common. On February 25, 1958, they conveyed it to Medora and Lu Sine by a grant deed "Reserving unto the Grantors herein an option to purchase the above described property on or before February 25, 1968" for the "same consideration as being paid heretofore plus their depreciation value of any improvements Grantees may add to the property from and after two and a half years from this date." Medora is Dallas' sister and Lu's wife. Since the conveyance Dallas has been adjudged bankrupt. His trustee in bankruptcy and Rebecca brought this declaratory relief action to establish their right to enforce the option.

The case was tried without a jury. Over defendants' objection the trial court ... determined that the parol evidence rule precluded admission of extrinsic evidence offered by defendants to show that the parties wanted the property kept in the Masterson family and that the option was therefore personal to the grantors and could not be exercised by the trustee in bankruptcy.

The court entered judgment for plaintiffs, declaring their right to exercise the option ...

Defendants appeal. They contend that extrinsic evidence (as to the option provision's) meaning should not have been admitted. The trial court properly refused to frustrate the obviously declared intention of the grantors to reserve an option to repurchase by an overly meticulous insistence on completeness and clarity of written expression.... It properly admitted extrinsic evidence to explain the language of the deed ... to the end that the consideration for the option would appear with sufficient certainty to permit specific enforcement.... The trial court erred, however, in excluding the extrinsic evidence that the option was personal to the grantors and therefore non-assignable.

When the parties to a written contract have agreed to it as an "integration"—a complete and final embodiment of the terms of an agreement—parol evidence cannot be used to add to or vary its terms. When only part of the agreement is integrated, the same rule applies to that part, but parol evidence may be used to prove elements of the agreement not reduced to writing.

The crucial issue in determining whether there has been an integration is whether the parties intended their writing to serve as the exclusive embodiment of their agreement. The instrument itself may help to resolve that issue. It may state, for example, that "there are no previous understandings or agreements not contained in the writing," and thus express the parties' "intention to nullify antecedent understandings or agreements." (See 3 Corbin, Contracts (1960) § 578, p. 411.) Any such collateral agreement itself must be examined, however, to determine whether the parties intended the subjects of negotiation it deals with to be included in, excluded from, or otherwise affected by the writing. Circumstances at the time of the writing may also aid in the determination of such integration. (See 3 Corbin, Contracts (1960) §§ 582-584; McCormick, Evidence (1954) § 216, p. 441; 9 Wigmore Evidence (3d ed. 1940) § 2430, p. 98, § 2431, pp. 102-103; Witkin, Cal. Evidence (2d ed. 1966) § 721; Schwartz v. Shapiro, supra, 229 Cal.App.2d 238, 251, fn. 8; contra, 4 Williston, Contracts (3d ed. 1961) § 633, pp. 1014-1016.)

California cases have stated that whether there was an integration is to be determined solely from the face of the instrument and that the question for the court is whether it "appears to be a complete ... agreement...." (See Ferguson v. Koch (1928) 204 Cal. 342, 346 [268 P. 342, 58 A.L.R. 1176]; Harrison v. McCormick, supra, 89 Cal. 327, 330.) Neither of these strict formulations of the rule, however, has been consistently applied. The requirement that the writing must appear incomplete on its face has been repudiated in many cases where parol evidence was admitted "to prove the existence of a separate oral agreement as to any matter on which the document is silent and which is not inconsistent with its terms"—even though the instrument appeared to state a complete agreement.... Even under the rule that the writing alone is to be consulted, it was found necessary to examine the alleged collateral agreement before concluding that proof of it was precluded by the writing alone. (See 3 Corbin, Contracts (1960) § 582, pp. 444-446.) It is therefore evident that "The conception of a writing as wholly and intrinsically self- determinative of the parties' intent to make it a sole memorial of one or seven or twenty-seven subjects of negotiation is an impossible one." (9 Wigmore, Evidence (3d ed. 1940) § 2431, p. 103.) For example, a promissory note given by a debtor to his creditor may integrate all their present contractual rights and obligations, or it may be only a minor part of an underlying executory contract that would never be discovered by examining the face of the note.

In formulating the rule governing parol evidence, several policies must be accommodated. One policy is based on the assumption that written evidence is more accurate than human memory. (Germain Fruit Co. v. J. K. Armsby Co. (1908) 153 Cal. 585, 595 [96 P. 319].) This policy, however, can be adequately served by excluding parol evidence of agreements that directly contradict the writing. Another policy is based on the fear that fraud or unintentional invention by witnesses interested in the outcome of the litigation will mislead the finder of facts. (German Fruit Co. v. J. K. Armsby Co., supra, 153 Cal. 585, 596; Mitchill v. Lath (1928) 247 N.Y. 377, 388 [160 N.E. 646, 68 A.L.R. 239] [dissenting opinion by Lehman, J.]; see 9 Wigmore, Evidence (3d ed. 1940) § 2431, p. 102; Murray, The Parol Evidence Rule: A Clarification (1966) 4 Duquesne L.Rev. 337,

338- 339.) McCormick has suggested that the party urging the spoken as against the written word is most often the economic underdog, threatened by severe hardship if the writing is enforced. In his view the parol evidence rule arose to allow the court to control the tendency of the jury to find through sympathy and without a dispassionate assessment of the probability of fraud or faulty memory that the parties made an oral agreement collateral to the written contract, or that preliminary tentative agreements were not abandoned when omitted from the writing. (See McCormick, Evidence (1954) §210.) He recognizes, however, that if this theory were adopted in disregard of all other considerations, it would lead to the exclusion of testimony concerning oral agreements whenever there is a writing and thereby often defeat the true intent of the parties. (See McCormick, op. cit. supra, §216, p. 441.)

Evidence of oral collateral agreements should be excluded only when the fact finder is likely to be misled. The rule must therefore be based on the credibility of the evidence. One such standard, adopted by section 240(1)(b) of the Restatement of Contracts, permits proof of a collateral agreement if it "is such an agreement as might naturally be made as a separate agreement by parties situated as were the parties to the written contract." (Italics added; see McCormick, Evidence (1954) §216, p. 441; see also 3 Corbin, Contracts (1960) §583, p. 475, §594, pp. 568-569; 4 Williston, Contracts (3d ed. 1961) §638, pp. 1039-1045.) The draftsmen of the Uniform Commercial Code would exclude the evidence in still fewer instances: "If the additional terms are such that, if agreed upon, they would certainly have been included in the document in the view of the court, then evidence of their alleged making must be kept from the trier of fact." (Com. 3, §2-202, italics added.)

The option clause in the deed in the present case does not explicitly provide that it contains the complete agreement, and the deed is silent on the question of assignability. Moreover, the difficulty of accommodating the formalized structure of a deed to the insertion of collateral agreements makes it less likely that all the terms of such an agreement were included.... The statement of the reservation of the option might well have been placed in the recorded deed solely to preserve the grantors' rights against any possible future purchasers, and this function could well be served without any mention of the parties' agreement that the option was personal. There is nothing in the record to indicate that the parties to this family transaction, through experience in land transactions or otherwise, had any warning of the disadvantages of failing to put the whole agreement in the deed. This case is one, therefore, in which it can be said that a collateral agreement such as that alleged "might naturally be made as a separate agreement." A fortiori, the case is not one in which the parties "would certainly" have included the collateral agreement in the deed.

It is contended, however, that an option agreement is ordinarily presumed to be assignable if it contains no provisions forbidding its transfer or indicating that its performance involves elements personal to the parties.... The fact that there is a written memorandum, however, does not necessarily preclude parol evidence rebutting a term that the law would otherwise presume. In American Industrial Sales Corp. v. Airscope, Inc., supra, 44 Cal.2d 393, 397-398, we held it proper to admit parol evidence of a contemporaneous collateral agreement as to the place of payment of a note, even though it contradicted the presumption that a note, silent as to the place of payment, is payable where the creditor resides. (For other examples of this approach, see Richter v. Union Land etc. Co. (1900) 129 Cal. 367, 375 [62 P. 39] [presumption of time of delivery rebutted by parol evidence]; Wolters v. King (1897) 119 Cal. 172, 175-176 [51 P. 35] [presumption of time of payment rebutted by parol evidence]; Mangini v. Wolfschmidt,

Ltd., supra, 165 Cal.App.2d 192, 198-201 [presumption of duration of an agency contract rebutted by parol evidence]; Zinn v. Ex- Cell-O Corp. (1957) 148 Cal.App.2d 56, 73-74 [306 P.2d 1017]; see also Rest., Contracts, § 240, com. c.) Of course a statute may preclude parol evidence to rebut a statutory presumption. (E. G. Neff v. Ernst (1957) 48 Cal.2d 628, 635 [311 P.2d 489] [commenting on Civ. Code, § 1112]; Kilfoy v. Fritz (1954) 125 Cal.App.2d 291, 293-294 [270 P.2d 579] [applying Deering's Gen. Laws, 1937, Act. 652, § 15(a)]; see also Com. Code, § 9-318, subd. (4).) Here, however, there is no such statute. In the absence of a controlling statute the parties may provide that a contract right or duty is nontransferable.... Moreover, even when there is no explicit agreement—written or oral—that contractual duties shall be personal, courts will effectuate a presumed intent to that effect if the circumstances indicate that performance by a substituted person would be different from that contracted for ...

In the present case defendants offered evidence that the parties agreed that the option was not assignable in order to keep the property in the Masterson family. The trial court erred in excluding that evidence.

The judgment is reversed.

Peters, J., Tobriner, J., Mosk, J., and Sullivan, J., concurred.

BURKE, J.

I dissent. The majority opinion: (1) Undermines the parol evidence rule as we have known it in this state since at least 1872 by declaring that parol evidence should have been admitted by the trial court to show that a written option, absolute and unrestricted in form, was intended to be limited and nonassignable; transferable to the trustee in bankruptcy.

Delta Dynamics, Inc. v. Arioto

Supreme Court of California, 1968
69 Cal.2d 525, 46 P.2d 785, 72 Cal.Rptr. 785

TRAYNOR, C. J.

Plaintiff Delta Dynamics, Inc. developed a trigger lock for use as a safety device on firearms. On March 23, 1961, it entered into a contract with defendants, partners doing business as the Pixey Distributing Co., for the distribution and sale of the locks throughout the United States. * * * Delta agreed to manufacture or arrange for the manufacture of the locks and to supply them to Pixey, which it appointed as exclusive distributor. Pixey agreed to pay for the locks at specified prices. Pixey promised to promote the locks diligently and "to sell not less than 50,000 units within one year from the date of delivery of the initial order" and not less than 100,000 units in each of the succeeding four years. "Should Pixey fail to distribute in any one year the minimum number of devices to be distributed by it ... this agreement shall be subject to termination" by Delta on 30 days' notice. The contract also provided that "In the event of breach of this agreement by either party, the party prevailing in any action for damages or enforcement of the terms of this Agreement shall be entitled to reasonable attorneys' fees."

Pixey ordered and paid for 10,000 locks, and Delta delivered them in August 1961. In October 1961 Pixey executed a written purchase order requesting Delta to supply 10,000 additional locks to be delivered "as needed." Pixey never requested delivery of that order, however, and it did not order any of the 30,000 additional locks needed to meet the 50,000 quota for the first year. On October 1, 1962, Delta terminated the agreement.

Thereafter it brought this action to recover damages for Pixey's failure to purchase the first year's quota.

After a nonjury trial the court entered judgment for Delta. It interpreted the contract as requiring Pixey to purchase 50,000 locks in the first year, which commenced with the initial delivery of 10,000 locks, and rejected Pixey's defense that Delta's exclusive remedy for Pixey's failure to meet the quota was the right to terminate the contract. Pixey appeals.

* * *

Since Pixey agreed to buy the locks from Delta, the only source of supply, its promise to sell 50,000 locks to third parties clearly implied a promise to buy that number from Delta, and the trial court correctly so found.

Pixey contends, however, that the termination clause made Delta's right to terminate the contract Delta's exclusive remedy for Pixey's failure to meet the annual quota and that the trial court erred in refusing to admit extrinsic evidence offered to prove that the termination clause had that meaning.

"The test of admissibility of extrinsic evidence to explain the meaning of a written instrument is not whether it appears to the court to be plain and unambiguous on its face, but whether the offered evidence is relevant to prove a meaning to which the language of the instrument is reasonably susceptible." To determine whether offered evidence is relevant to prove such a meaning the court must consider all credible evidence offered to prove the intention of the parties. "If the court decides, after considering this evidence, that the language of a contract, in the light of all the circumstances, 'is fairly susceptible of either one of the two interpretations contended for …' [citations], extrinsic evidence to prove either of such meanings is admissible." (Pacific Gas & Elec. Co. v. G. W. Thomas Drayage etc. Co. (1968) ante, pp. 33, 40 [69 Cal.Rptr. 561, 442 P.2d 641].)

In the present case the parties may have included the termination clause to spell out with specificity the condition on which Delta would be excused from further performance under the contract, or to set forth the exclusive remedy for a failure to meet the quota in any year, or for both such purposes. That clause is therefore reasonably susceptible of the meaning contended for by Pixey, namely, that it expresses the parties' determination that Delta's sole remedy for Pixey's failure to meet a quota was to terminate the contract. There is nothing in the rest of the contract to preclude that interpretation. It does not render meaningless the provision for the recovery of attorneys' fees in the event of an action for damages for breach of the contract, for the attorneys' fees provision would still have full effect with respect to other breaches of the contract. Accordingly, the trial court committed prejudicial error by excluding extrinsic evidence offered to prove the meaning of the termination clause contended for by Pixey. The judgment must therefore be reversed.

* * *

Although the termination clause is reasonably susceptible of a meaning that precludes that remedy in the absence of extrinsic evidence, we believe it should not be given that meaning but should be interpreted only as a statement of the condition on which Delta could terminate the contract.

The judgment is reversed.

Peters, J., Tobriner, J., and Sullivan, J., concurred.

MOSK, J.

I dissent.

Both on the basis of the four corners of the contract and the context in which the interrogation proceeded, the trial court properly excluded parol evidence.

* * *

It is hornbook law that conversations, discussions and negotiations culminating in a written instrument are not admissible in evidence. Indeed, since 1872 Civil Code section 1625 (amended in 1905), has provided that the "execution of a contract in writing, whether the law requires it to be written or not, supersedes all the negotiations or stipulations concerning its matter which preceded or accompanied the execution of the instrument."

* * *

Once again this court adopts a course leading toward emasculation of the parol evidence rule. During this very year Masterson v. Sine (1968) 68 Cal.2d 222 [65 Cal.Rptr. 545, 436 P.2d 561], and Pacific Gas & Elec. Co. v. G. W. Thomas Drayage etc. Co. (1968) ante, p. 33 [69 Cal.Rptr. 561, 442 P.2d 641], have contributed toward that result. Although I had misgivings at the time, I must confess to joining the majority in both of those cases. Now, however, that the majority deem negotiations leading to execution of contracts admissible, the trend has become so unmistakably ominous that I must urge a halt.

It can be contended that there may be no evil per se in considering testimony about every discussion and conversation prior to and contemporaneous with the signing of a written instrument and that social utility may result in some circumstances. The problem, however, is that which devolves upon members of the bar who are commissioned by clients to prepare a written instrument able to withstand future assaults. Given two experienced businessmen dealing at arm's length, both represented by competent counsel, it has become virtually impossible under recently evolving rules of evidence to draft a written contract that will produce predictable results in court. The written word, heretofore deemed immutable, is now at all times subject to alteration by self-serving recitals based upon fading memories of antecedent events. This, I submit, is a serious impediment to the certainty required in commercial transactions.

I would affirm the judgment.

Trident Center v. Connecticut General Life Ins. Co.
U.S. Court of Appeal Ninth Circuit (Cal.), 1988
847 F.2d 564

KOZINSKI, CIRCUIT JUDGE:

The parties to this transaction are, by any standard, highly sophisticated business people: Plaintiff is a partnership consisting of an insurance company and two of Los Angeles' largest and most prestigious law firms; defendant is another insurance company. Dealing at arm's length and from positions of roughly equal bargaining strength, they negotiated a commercial loan amounting to more than $56 million. The contract documents are lengthy and detailed; they squarely address the precise issue that is the subject of this dispute; to all who read English, they appear to resolve the issue fully and conclusively.

Plaintiff nevertheless argues here, as it did below, that it is entitled to introduce extrinsic evidence that the contract means something other than what it says. This case therefore presents the question whether parties in California can ever draft a contract that is proof to parol evidence. Somewhat surprisingly, the answer is no.

Facts

The facts are rather simple. Sometime in 1983 Security First Life Insurance Company and the law firms of Mitchell, Silberberg & Knupp and Manatt, Phelps, Rothenberg & Tunney formed a limited partnership for the purpose of constructing an office building complex on Olympic Boulevard in West Los Angeles. The partnership, Trident Center, the plaintiff herein, sought and obtained financing for the project from defendant, Connecticut General Life Insurance Company. The loan documents provide for a loan of $56,500,000 at 12 1/4 percent interest for a term of 15 years, secured by a deed of trust on the project. The promissory note provides that "[m]aker shall not have the right to prepay the principal amount hereof in whole or in part" for the first 12 years. Note at 6. In years 13-15, the loan may be prepaid, subject to a sliding prepayment fee. The note also provides that in case of a default during years 1-12, Connecticut General has the option of accelerating the note and adding a 10 percent prepayment fee.

Everything was copacetic for a few years until interest rates began to drop. The 12 1/4 percent rate that had seemed reasonable in 1983 compared unfavorably with 1987 market rates and Trident started looking for ways of refinancing the loan to take advantage of the lower rates. Connecticut General was unwilling to oblige, insisting that the loan could not be prepaid for the first 12 years of its life, that is, until January 1996.

Trident then brought suit in state court seeking a declaration that it was entitled to prepay the loan now, subject only to a 10 percent prepayment fee. Connecticut General promptly removed to federal court and brought a motion to dismiss, claiming that the loan documents clearly and unambiguously precluded prepayment during the first 12 years. The district court agreed and dismissed Trident's complaint. The court also "*sua sponte,* sanction[ed] the plaintiff for the filing of a frivolous lawsuit." Order of Dismissal, No. CV 87-2712 JMI (Kx), at 3 (C.D. Cal. June 8, 1987). Trident appeals both aspects of the district court's ruling.

Discussion

I

Trident makes two arguments as to why the district court's ruling is wrong. First, it contends that the language of the contract is ambiguous and proffers a construction that it believes supports its position. Second, Trident argues that, under California law, even seemingly unambiguous contracts are subject to modification by parol or extrinsic evidence. Trident faults the district court for denying it the opportunity to present evidence that the contract language did not accurately reflect the parties' intentions.

A. The Contract

As noted earlier, the promissory note provides that Trident "shall not have the right to prepay the principal amount hereof in whole or in part before January 1996." Note at 6. It is difficult to imagine language that more clearly or unambiguously expresses the idea that Trident may not unilaterally prepay the loan during its first 12 years. Trident, however, argues that there is an ambiguity because another clause of the note provides that "[i]n the event of a prepayment resulting from a default hereunder or the Deed of Trust prior to January 10, 1996 the prepayment fee will be ten percent (10%)." Note at 6-7. Trident interprets this clause as giving it the option of prepaying the loan if only it is willing to incur the prepayment fee.

We reject Trident's argument out of hand. In the first place, its proffered interpretation would result in a contradiction between two clauses of the contract; the default clause would swallow up the clause prohibiting Trident from prepaying during the first 12 years of the contract. The normal rule of construction, of course, is that courts must interpret contracts, if possible, so as to avoid internal conflict. *See Brobeck, Phleger & Harrison v. Telex Corp.,* 602 F.2d 866, 872 (9th Cir.), *cert. denied,* 444 U.S. 981, 100 S.Ct. 483, 62 L.Ed.2d 407 (1979) (California law); Cal.Civ.Proc.Code § 1858 (West 1983); 4 S. Williston, *A Treatise on the Law of Contracts* § 618, at 714-15 (3d ed. 1961); *id.* § 624, at 825.

In any event, the clause on which Trident relies is not on its face reasonably susceptible to Trident's proffered interpretation. Whether to accelerate repayment of the loan in the event of default is entirely Connecticut General's decision. The contract makes this clear at several points. *See* Note at 4 ("in each such event [of default], the entire principal indebtedness, or so much thereof as may remain unpaid at the time, shall, *at the option of Holder,* become due and payable immediately" (emphasis added)); *id.* at 7 ("[i]n the event Holder exercises its *option to accelerate* the maturity hereof ..." (emphasis added)); Deed of Trust ¶ 2.01, at 25 ("in each such event [of default], Beneficiary *may* declare all sums secured hereby immediately due and payable ..." (emphasis added)). Even if Connecticut General decides to declare a default and accelerate, it "may rescind any notice of breach or default." *Id.* ¶ 2.02, at 26. Finally, Connecticut General has the option of doing nothing at all: "Beneficiary reserves the right at its sole option to waive noncompliance by Trustor with any of the conditions or covenants to be performed by Trustor hereunder." *Id.* ¶ 3.02, at 29.

Once again, it is difficult to imagine language that could more clearly assign to Connecticut General the exclusive right to decide whether to declare a default, whether and when to accelerate, and whether, having chosen to take advantage of any of its remedies, to rescind the process before its completion.

Trident nevertheless argues that it is entitled to precipitate a default and insist on acceleration by tendering the balance due on the note plus the 10 percent prepayment fee. The contract language, cited above, leaves no room for this construction. It is true, of course, that Trident is free to stop making payments, which may then cause Connecticut General to declare a default and accelerate. But that is not to say that Connecticut General would be required to so respond. The contract quite clearly gives Connecticut General other options: It may choose to waive the default, or to take advantage of some other remedy such as the right to collect "all the income, rents, royalties, revenue, issues, profits, and proceeds of the Property." Deed of Trust ¶ 1.18, at 22. By interpreting the contract as Trident suggests, we would ignore those provisions giving Connecticut General, not Trident, the exclusive right to decide how, when and whether the contract will be terminated upon default during the first 12 years.

Trident's position is that the prepayment fee must either be a fee imposed as part of an "alternative method of performance" or "a liquidated damages provision specifying the amount of damages payable by Trident in the event that it defaults by prepaying the ... loan." Appellant's Reply Brief at 12-13. Trident contends that if the prepayment fee is instead read as a provision for liquidated damages triggered by any default whatsoever, it would be invalid as a penalty because it would not be a reasonable estimate of the likely injury to Connecticut General resulting from most types of default: "[I]f, for example, Trident were to default on the payment of a single installment, a fee of 10% of the outstanding balance of the loan would not qualify as a valid liquidated damages payment." *Id.* at 8.

California law is unsettled on this point and it may be that Connecticut General could not enforce the 10 percent fee in the event of certain defaults by Trident. *See gen-*

erally 1 H. Miller & M. Starr, *Current Law of California Real Estate* §3:71 n. 12 (Supp.1987). But the contract assigns to Connecticut General alone the right to decide whether and under what circumstances to seek the prepayment fee. Connecticut General may well attempt to enforce the fee only in circumstances where it is valid. What the contract clearly does not provide is what Trident suggests. If the parties had wanted to give Trident the option of prepaying with a 10 percent fee, they certainly could have done so expressly.

In effect, Trident is attempting to obtain judicial sterilization of its intended default. But defaults are messy things; they are supposed to be. Once the maker of a note secured by a deed of trust defaults, its credit rating may deteriorate; attempts at favorable refinancing may be thwarted by the need to meet the trustee's sale schedule; its cash flow may be impaired if the beneficiary takes advantage of the assignment of rents remedy; default provisions in its loan agreements with other lenders may be triggered. Fear of these repercussions is strong medicine that keeps debtors from shirking their obligations when interest rates go down and they become disenchanted with their loans. That Trident is willing to suffer the cost and delay of a lawsuit, rather than simply defaulting, shows far better than anything we might say that these provisions are having their intended effect. We decline Trident's invitation to truncate the lender's remedies and deprive Connecticut General of its bargained-for protection.

B. Extrinsic Evidence

Trident argues in the alternative that, even if the language of the contract appears to be unambiguous, the deal the parties actually struck is in fact quite different. It wishes to offer extrinsic evidence that the parties had agreed Trident could prepay at any time within the first 12 years by tendering the full amount plus a 10 percent prepayment fee. As discussed above, this is an interpretation to which the contract, as written, is not reasonably susceptible. Under traditional contract principles, extrinsic evidence is inadmissible to interpret, vary or add to the terms of an unambiguous integrated written instrument. *See* 4 S. Williston, *supra* p. 5, §631, at 948- 49; 2 B. Witkin, *California Evidence* §981, at 926 (3d ed. 1986).

Trident points out, however, that California does not follow the traditional rule. Two decades ago the California Supreme Court in *Pacific Gas & Electric Co. v. G.W. Thomas Drayage & Rigging Co.,* 69 Cal.2d 33, 442 P.2d 641, 69 Cal.Rptr. 561 (1968), turned its back on the notion that a contract can ever have a plain meaning discernible by a court without resort to extrinsic evidence. The court reasoned that contractual obligations flow not from the words of the contract, but from the intention of the parties. "Accordingly," the court stated, "the exclusion of relevant, extrinsic, evidence to explain the meaning of a written instrument could be justified only if it were feasible to determine the meaning the parties gave to the words from the instrument alone." 69 Cal.2d at 38, 442 P.2d 641, 69 Cal.Rptr. 561. This, the California Supreme Court concluded, is impossible: "If words had absolute and constant referents, it might be possible to discover contractual intention in the words themselves and in the manner in which they were arranged. Words, however, do not have absolute and constant referents." *Id.* In the same vein, the court noted that "[t]he exclusion of testimony that might contradict the linguistic background of the judge reflects a judicial belief in the possibility of perfect verbal expression. This belief is a remnant of a primitive faith in the inherent potency and inherent meaning of words." *Id.* at 37, 442 P.2d 641, 69 Cal.Rptr. 561 (citation and footnotes omitted).

Under *Pacific Gas,* it matters not how clearly a contract is written, nor how completely it is integrated, nor how carefully it is negotiated, nor how squarely it addresses the issue before the court: the contract cannot be rendered impervious to attack by parol evidence. If one side is willing to claim that the parties intended one thing but the agreement provides for another, the court must consider extrinsic evidence of possible ambiguity. If that evidence raises the specter of ambiguity where there was none before, the contract language is displaced and the intention of the parties must be divined from self-serving testimony offered by partisan witnesses whose recollection is hazy from passage of time and colored by their conflicting interests. *See Delta Dynamics, Inc. v. Arioto,* 69 Cal.2d 525, 532, 446 P.2d 785, 72 Cal.Rptr. 785 (1968) (Mosk, J., dissenting). We question whether this approach is more likely to divulge the original intention of the parties than reliance on the seemingly clear words they agreed upon at the time. *See generally Morta v. Korea Ins. Co.,* 840 F.2d 1452, 1460 (9th Cir.1988).

Pacific Gas casts a long shadow of uncertainty over all transactions negotiated and executed under the law of California. As this case illustrates, even when the transaction is very sizeable, even if it involves only sophisticated parties, even if it was negotiated with the aid of counsel, even if it results in contract language that is devoid of ambiguity, costly and protracted litigation cannot be avoided if one party has a strong enough motive for challenging the contract. While this rule creates much business for lawyers and an occasional windfall to some clients, it leads only to frustration and delay for most litigants and clogs already overburdened courts.

It also chips away at the foundation of our legal system. By giving credence to the idea that words are inadequate to express concepts, *Pacific Gas* undermines the basic principle that language provides a meaningful constraint on public and private conduct. If we are unwilling to say that parties, dealing face to face, can come up with language that binds them, how can we send anyone to jail for violating statutes consisting of mere words lacking "absolute and constant referents"? How can courts ever enforce decrees, not written in language understandable to all, but encoded in a dialect reflecting only the "linguistic background of the judge"? Can lower courts ever be faulted for failing to carry out the mandate of higher courts when "perfect verbal expression" is impossible? Are all attempts to develop the law in a reasoned and principled fashion doomed to failure as "remnant[s] of a primitive faith in the inherent potency and inherent meaning of words"?

Be that as it may. While we have our doubts about the wisdom of Pacific *Gas,* we have no difficulty understanding its meaning, even without extrinsic evidence to guide us. As we read the rule in California, we must reverse and remand to the district court in order to give plaintiff an opportunity to present extrinsic evidence as to the intention of the parties in drafting the contract. It may not be a wise rule we are applying, but it is a rule that binds us. *Erie R.R. Co. v. Tompkins,* 304 U.S. 64, 78, 58 S.Ct. 817, 822, 82 L.Ed. 1188 (1938).

II

* * *

Having reversed the district court on its substantive ruling, we must, of course, also reverse it as to the award of sanctions. While we share the district judge's impatience with this litigation, we would suggest that his irritation may have been misdirected. It is difficult to blame plaintiff and its lawyers for bringing this lawsuit. With this much money at stake, they would have been foolish not to pursue all remedies available to them under the applicable law. At fault, it seems to us, are not the parties and their lawyers but the legal system that encourages this kind of lawsuit. By holding that language has no objective meaning, and that contracts mean only what courts ultimately say they do, *Pacific Gas* invites precisely this type of lawsuit. With the benefit of 20 years of hindsight, the California Supreme Court may wish to revisit the issue. If it does so, we commend to it the facts of this case as a paradigmatic example of why the traditional rule, based on centuries of experience, reflects the far wiser approach.

Conclusion

The judgment of the district court is REVERSED. The case is REMANDED for reinstatement of the complaint and further proceedings in accordance with this opinion. The parties shall bear their own costs on appeal.

A. Kemp Fisheries, Inc. v. Castle & Cooke, Inc., Bumble Bee Seafoods Div.

U.S. Court of Appeal Ninth Circuit (Wash.) 1989
852 F.2d 493,

EUGENE A. WRIGHT, Circuit Judge:

In this case we consider whether the court properly admitted parol evidence to determine the terms of the Charter Agreement between A. Kemp Fisheries, Inc. and Bumble Bee Samoa, Inc., a subsidiary of Castle & Cooke, Inc. We conclude that the court applied the parol evidence rule incorrectly and reverse its judgment.

Background

A. Kemp Fisheries Inc. and Bumble Bee Samoa, Inc., a fully owned subsidiary of Castle & Cooke, Inc., agreed that Kemp would charter, with an option to purchase, the M/V CITY OF SAN DIEGO. Kemp needed the vessel to fish for herring and salmon in Alaska from April to August 1983. In February of that year they signed a letter of intent that incorporated certain telexes exchanged in their negotiations. This letter served as their agreement "[p]ending preparation and execution of final documentation required for the bareboat charter and option to purchase." To compensate Bumble Bee for removing the vessel from the market Kemp paid a nonrefundable deposit of $50,000.

After reviewing drafts of the agreement with Kemp's attorney, Bumble Bee sent the final bare boat Charter Agreement late in March. Louis Kemp, the charterer's president, found that the agreement differed from his understanding of the arrangement. Specifically, he understood that Bumble Bee had agreed that the engines would be in good working order and had represented orally that the freezing system would meet Kemp's specific needs. The agreement contained no such provisions and in fact, disclaimed all warranties, express or implied. Despite his reservations, Kemp signed it without voicing his concerns to Bumble Bee. He took the vessel in early April and sailed to Alaska for the May herring season.

In the midst of herring season, two of the three auxiliary engines that powered the SAN DIEGO's freezing system broke down. After repairing one engine, Kemp switched from freezing to curing the herring because it lacked confidence that the engine would last. Kemp sold the cured herring for a price below that for frozen herring.

In preparation for salmon season at the end of June, Kemp repaired the auxiliary engines and rented an additional engine. Although the engines were operating at full power and suffered no breakdowns, the salmon froze in a block and the flesh was "honey combed." Kemp's buyer rejected most of it. Kemp took it to a shore-based freezing plant in Bellingham where it was thawed and refrozen. It sold the salmon for 75 cents a pound, 50 cents less than the price it would have received for properly frozen salmon.

Kemp sued Bumble Bee and Castle & Cooke in admiralty for breach of the Charter Agreement, intentional and negligent misrepresentation, estoppel, and rescission. It claimed that Bumble Bee agreed to provide engines in good working order and represented that the freezing system would meet its specific needs.

The trial judge found that the Charter Agreement signed in March was ambiguous and admitted parol evidence to clarify the parties' intent. She concluded that the letter of intent and referenced telexes reflected the parties' final intent and indicated that no other negotiations would occur. From evidence of their negotiations, she found that Bumble Bee warranted the vessel to be seaworthy and the engines to be in good working condition, and represented orally that the vessel's freezing system could meet Kemp's specific requirements. She held Bumble Bee liable for all of Kemp's damages because the "inability of the M/V CITY OF SAN DIEGO to freeze herring and salmon within the parameters specified by Bumble Bee is solely the result of Bumble Bee's breach of warranties." Bumble Bee appeals.

Analysis

I.

Parol Evidence

In the Charter Agreement, the parties agreed that "the Charter Party shall be governed by and enforced under the laws of the State of California." We apply California law in our analysis.

The parol evidence rule provides:

> When the parties to a written contract have agreed to it as an "integration"—a complete and final embodiment of the terms of an agreement—parol evidence cannot be used to add to or vary its terms. When only part of the agreement is integrated, the same rule applies to that part, but parol evidence may be used to prove elements of the agreement not reduced to writing. *Masterson v. Sine,* 68 Cal.2d 222, 65 Cal. Rptr. 545, 547, 436 P.2d 561 (1968) (citations omitted). *See also* Cal.Civ.Code § 1625, Cal.Code Civ.P. § 1856(a), and *Battery Steamship Corp. v. Refineria Panama, S.A.,* 513 F.2d 735, 738 (2d Cir.1975) (the federal common law parol evidence rule).

If a contract is integrated, the parol evidence rule operates to exclude evidence that is not "relevant to prove a meaning to which the language of the instrument is reasonably susceptible." *Pacific Gas and Elec. Co. v. G.W. Thomas Drayage & R. Co.,* 69 Cal.2d 33, 69 Cal.Rptr. 561, 564, 442 P.2d 641, 644 (1968). "[E]xtrinsic evidence is not admissible to add to, detract from, or vary the terms of a written contract." *Id.* 69 Cal.Rptr. at 565, 442 P.2d at 645. If a contract is not integrated, the parol evidence rule does not apply. The court can admit all evidence relevant to the parties' intent, including negotiations and prior agreements.

"The crucial issue in determining whether there has been an integration is whether the parties intended their writings to serve as the exclusive embodiment of their agreement." *Marani v. Jackson,* 183 Cal.App.3d 695, 228 Cal.Rptr. 518, 521 (1 Dist. 1986) (quoting *Salyer Grain & Milling Co. v. Henson,* 13 Cal.App.3d 493, 91 Cal.Rptr. 847 (5 Dist.1970)). To make this determination, the court considers: the language and completeness of the written agreement and whether it contains an integration clause, the terms of the alleged agreement and whether they contradict those in the writing, whether the agreement might naturally be made as a separate agreement, and whether the jury might be misled by the introduction of the parol testimony. A court also considers the circumstances surrounding the transaction and its subject matter, nature and object. *Marani,* 228 Cal.Rptr. at 522 (citations omitted).

A. Integration

The Charter Agreement is an integrated contract. The agreement itself is complete and comprehensive. It covers in great detail the various rights and responsibilities of the parties. Although the Charter does not contain an integration clause, the letter of intent shows clearly that the parties intended that the Charter would be the "final documentation" of their agreement.

The alleged agreements regarding the warranties of the vessel's seaworthiness, engines, and freezing system are not collateral agreements that would normally be made in a separate contract. These alleged understandings directly contradict the Charter's waiver of all warranties. In addition, the agreement specifies Bumble Bee's responsibility for testing and repairing the freezing system and preparing the vessel for Kemp. If Bumble Bee warranted the freezing system and the engines, the Charter Agreement would typically provide that.

The circumstances surrounding this transaction also support our conclusion that the contract is integrated. Kemp and Bumble Bee are corporations familiar with business transactions. Kemp's attorney reviewed the Charter with Bumble Bee in the month before it signed. Bumble Bee incorporated some of Kemp's changes into the final Charter presented in March. Kemp had ample opportunity to express its understanding of the deal. Nothing suggests that this agreement was not recognized by both parties as final and complete.

B. Ambiguity

The judge admitted parol evidence to resolve ambiguities and contradictions within sub-paragraphs 3B, E and F. Sub-paragraph 3B provides:

> B. Prior to delivery of the Vessel, Owner shall maintain the Vessel in good condition and shall cause the Vessel to be surveyed, on its own account, by a competent surveyor chosen by Owner, which survey shall show that the Vessel meets TA 2003 insurance requirements and is in all respects tight, staunch, strong and seaworthy.

Sub-paragraphs 3E and F provide:

> E. Delivery to Charterer shall constitute full performance by Owner of all of Owner's obligations hereunder, and thereafter Charterer shall not be entitled to make or assert any claim against Owner on account of any representations or warranties, express or implied, with respect to the Vessel. F. Charterer's acceptance of delivery of the Vessel, its equipment, gear and non-consumable stores shall constitute conclusive evidence that the same have been inspected by Charterer and are accepted by Charterer as suitable for the intended use hereunder and, as between the parties, the seaworthiness and suitability of the Vessel, its equipment, gear and non-consumable stores are deemed admitted.

The judge construed sub-paragraph 3B as an express warranty of seaworthiness and sub-paragraphs 3E and F as a waiver of that warranty. To resolve this conflict, she turned to parol evidence.

The court erred. The parol evidence rule requires that courts consider extrinsic evidence to determine whether the contract is ambiguous. *Drayage,* 69 Cal.Rptr. at 565-66, 442 P.2d at 645-46 ("[R]ational interpretation requires at least a preliminary consideration of all credible evidence offered to prove the intention of the parties."); *Trident Center v. Connecticut General Life Ins. Co.,* 847 F.2d 564, 569 (9th Cir.1988). But if the extrinsic evidence advances an interpretation to which the language of the contract is not reasonably susceptible, the evidence is not admissible. *Drayage,* 69 Cal.Rptr. at 564, 442 P.2d at 644: "The test of admissibility of extrinsic evidence to explain the meaning of a written instrument is … whether the offered evidence is relevant to prove a meaning to which the language of the instrument is reasonably susceptible." *Cf. Trident,* at 570 n. 6. The Charter Agreement is not "reasonably susceptible" to the court's interpretation that it warrants the seaworthiness of the vessel, the condition of the engines, and the capacity of the freezing system.

Sub-paragraph 3B concerns the condition of the vessel prior to delivery. It imposes on Bumble Bee an obligation to maintain the vessel in "good," not seaworthy condition, and to see that a "competent surveyor" surveys it to show that it is "tight, staunch, strong and seaworthy" for insurance purposes. It guarantees neither the accuracy of the survey nor the seaworthiness of the vessel.

Sub-paragraphs 3E and F address Bumble Bee's obligations after delivery. They provide that once Kemp accepts delivery, Bumble Bee's responsibility for the condition of the vessel ceases. They make clear that Kemp's acceptance of delivery releases Bumble Bee from responsibility for the vessel's condition and cannot be interpreted reasonably to warrant seaworthiness.

Nor should the court similarly have admitted evidence that Bumble Bee warranted the condition of the engines and the capacity of the freezing system. Paragraphs 3B, E and F do not even mention the engines or the freezing system and are not "reasonably susceptible" to that interpretation.

The court erred in admitting parol evidence and in enforcing warranties of seaworthiness, the engines, and freezing capacity. The Charter Agreement contains none of these warranties.

* * *

Conclusion

The judgment is REVERSED and is rendered for the defendant. The Charter Agreement is an integrated contract and contained all the parties' agreements. It is not ambiguous and the court erred in admitting parol evidence on the warranty of seaworthiness, the capacity of the freezing system, and the engines. * * * Bumble Bee is not liable for Kemp's losses.

Afterthoughts

The execution of a contract in writing, whether the law requires it to be written or not, supersedes all the negotiations or stipulations concerning its matter which preceded or accompanied the execution of the instrument. (Cal.Civ.Code § 1625) Terms set forth in a writing intended by the parties as a final expression of their agreement with respect to such terms as are included therein may not be contradicted by evidence of any prior agreement or of a contemporaneous oral agreement. (Cal.Code.Civ.Proc. §1856 (a).)

Where a mistake or imperfection of the writing is put in issue by the pleadings, the Parol Evidence Rule does not exclude evidence relevant to that issue. In other words, the Parol Evidence Rule does not bar evidence of mistake with respect to the written agreement. (Cal.Code.Civ.Proc. §1856 (e).)

The terms set forth in a writing intended by the parties as a final expression of their agreement may be explained or supplemented by evidence of consistent additional terms unless the writing is intended also as a complete and exclusive statement of the terms of the agreement. (Cal.Code.Civ.Proc. §1856 (b).) Similarly, the terms set forth in a writing intended by the parties as a final expression of their agreement may be explained or supplemented by course of dealing or usage of trade or by course of performance. (Cal.Code.Civ.Proc. §1856 (c).)

In a trial, it is the judge and not the jury who determines whether the parties intended the writing to be a final expression of their agreement with respect to such terms as are included therein and whether the writing is intended also as a complete and exclusive statement of the terms of the agreement. (Cal.Code.Civ.Proc. §1856 (d).)

Drafting Tip—Merger or Integration Clauses

While it is not completely conclusive on the question of whether the parties intended the writing to be the final, full and complete expression of their agreement, the presence of a "merger" or "integration" clause declaring that intention is strong evidence of that fact. A typical "merger clause" might be written as follows:

"This Agreement and the exhibits attached hereto contain the entire agreement of the parties with respect to the subject matter of this Agreement, and supersede all prior negotiations, agreements and understandings with respect thereto. This Agreement may only be amended by a written document duly executed by all parties."

General Rules of Contract Interpretation

Meaning of Contract Ascertained from Four Corners of Instrument

Where contract language is clear and explicit and does not lead to an absurd result, a court will ascertain contractual intent from the written provisions of the contract itself and go no further. The language of a contract is to govern its interpretation, if the language is clear and explicit, and does not involve an absurdity. (Cal.Civ. Code §1638) When a contract is reduced to writing, the intention of the parties is to be ascertained from the writing alone, if possible. (Cal.Civ.Code §1639)

The interpretation of the writing is a question of law for the court. (*Parsons v. Bristol Development Co.* (1965) 62 Cal.2d 861 at pp. 864-866.)

Contract Construed Most Strictly against Drafter

Any ambiguities caused by the drafter of the contract must be resolved against the drafter or the party employing him or her. In cases of uncertainty the language of a contract should be interpreted most strongly against the party who caused the uncertainty to exist. (Cal.Civ.Code § 1654).

Words Used Given Their Ordinary Meaning

The words of a contract are to be understood in their ordinary and popular sense, rather than according to their strict legal meaning, unless used by the parties in a technical sense, or unless a special meaning is given to them by usage, in which case the latter must be followed. (Cal.Civ.Code § 1644.)

Filling Gaps

"At Will" Employment

Historically, in the absence of a specified term or length of employment, an employee could be fired or terminated for any reason at all or for no reason at all. This is known as employment "at will." However, termination of an "at will" employee for a reason that violates public policy is a wrongful termination. According to a recent count, 43 jurisdictions have adopted the so-called "retaliatory discharge" cause of action as a restraint on the employer's historical at-will power of termination. For example, an employee who states a wrongful discharge claim for having refused to join a criminal conspiracy in violation of the antitrust laws (cf. Tameny v. Atlantic Richfield Co. (1980) 27 Cal.3d 167 [164 Cal.Rptr. 839, 610 P.2d 1330, 9 A.L.R.4th 314]), or for having resisted efforts to induce him to give false information in a public investigation of sexual harassment charges filed by a co-worker (cf. Gantt v. Sentry Insurance (1992) 1 Cal.4th 1083, 1095 [4 Cal.Rptr.2d 874, 824 P.2d 680].), is provided a remedy in tort not only to compensate the individual plaintiff for the loss of employment but as an indirect means of vindicating the underlying fundamental public policy itself. Unlike some other jurisdictions that have refused to extend the tort of retaliatory discharge to "in-house" counsel, California permits in-house counsel to bring a claim for retaliatory discharge against their employer.

General Dynamics Corp. v. Superior Court (Rose)
Supreme Court of California, 1994
7 Cal.4th 1164, 32 Cal.Rptr.2d 1; 876 P.2d 487

ARABIAN, J.

We granted review to consider an attorney's status as "in-house" counsel as it affects the right to pursue claims for damages following an allegedly wrongful termination of employment. Specifically, we are asked to decide whether an attorney's status as an employee bars the pursuit of implied-in-fact contract and retaliatory discharge tort causes of action against the employer that are commonly the subject of suits by non-attorney employees who assert the same claims.

We conclude that, because so-called "just cause" contractual claims are unlikely to implicate values central to the attorney-client relationship, there is no valid reason why an in-house attorney should not be permitted to pursue such a contract claim in the same way as the nonattorney employee. * * * As will appear, we conclude that there is no reason inherent in the nature of an attorney's role as in-house counsel to a corporation that in itself precludes the maintenance of a retaliatory discharge claim, provided it can be established without breaching the attorney-client privilege or unduly endangering the values lying at the heart of the professional relationship.

Although the effect of the attorney-client relationship is to produce a remedy more limited than that available to the nonattorney employee, the similarities between the position of in-house attorneys and their nonattorney colleagues nevertheless justify an analogous cause of action. The complete economic dependence of in-house attorneys on their employers is indistinguishable from that of nonattorney employees who are entitled to pursue a retaliatory discharge remedy. Moreover, as we explain, the position of in-house counsel is especially sensitive to those fundamental ethical imperatives derived from an attorney's professional duties, as well as organizational pressures to ignore or subvert them. On balance, these considerations favor allowing a tort claim for discharges for reasons that contravene an attorney's mandatory ethical obligations or for which a non-attorney employee could maintain such a claim and a statute or ethical code provision permits the attorney to depart from the usual rule that client matters remain confidential.

The trial courts have at their disposal several measures to minimize or eliminate the potential untoward effects on both the attorney-client privilege and the interests of the client-employer resulting from the litigation of such wrongful termination claims by in-house counsel. Thus, we also hold that, in those instances where the attorney-employee's retaliatory discharge claim is incapable of complete resolution without breaching the attorney-client privilege, the suit may not proceed. That result, however, is rarely, if ever, appropriate where, as in this case, the litigation is still at the pleadings stage.

I

Andrew Rose, an attorney, began working for General Dynamics Corporation (hereafter General Dynamics) as a 27-year-old contract administrator at its Pomona plant in 1978. He progressed steadily within the organization, earning repeated commendations and, after 14 years with the company, was in line to become a division vice-president and general counsel. On June 24, 1991, he was fired, abruptly and wrongfully.

So Rose alleged in the complaint for damages that began this litigation. The complaint also alleged that although the stated reason for his discharge was a loss of the company's confidence in Rose's ability to represent vigorously its interests, the "real" reasons motivating his firing had more to do with an attempt by company officials to cover up widespread drug use among the General Dynamics work force, a refusal to investigate the mysterious "bugging" of the office of the company's chief of security, and the displeasure of company officials over certain legal advice Rose had given them, rather than any loss of confidence in his legal ability or commitment to the company's interests.

The complaint relied on two main theories of relief. First, it alleged that General Dynamics had, by its conduct and other assurances, impliedly represented to Rose over the years that he was subject to discharge only for "good cause," a condition that the complaint alleged was not present in the circumstances under which he was fired. Second, the complaint alleged that Rose was actually fired for cumulative reasons, all of which violated fundamental public policies: in part because he spearheaded an investigation into employee drug use at the Pomona plant (an investigation, the complaint alleged, that led to the termination of more than 60 General Dynamics employees), in part because he protested the company's failure to investigate the bugging of the office of the chief of security (allegedly a criminal offense and, since it involved a major defense contractor, a serious breach of national security), and in part as a result of advising General Dynamics officials that the company's salary policy with respect to the compensation paid a certain class of employees might be in violation of the federal Fair Labor Standards Act, possibly exposing the firm to several hundred million dollars in backpay claims.

General Dynamics filed a general demurrer to the complaint, asserting that Rose had failed to state a claim for relief. Because he had been employed as an in-house attorney, the company contended, Rose was subject to discharge at any time, "for any reason or for no reason." The trial court overruled the demurrer and the Court of Appeal denied General Dynamics's ensuing petition for a writ of mandate, ruling that, at least at the pleading stage, the complaint was sufficient to survive a general demurrer as to both theories of relief.

II

* * *

The growth in the number and role of in-house counsel has brought with it a widening recognition of the descriptive inadequacy of the nineteenth century model of the lawyer's place and role in society-one based predominantly on the small to middle-sized firm of like-minded attorneys whose economic fortunes were not tethered to the good will of a single client -and of the social and legal consequences that have accompanied that transformation. Unlike the law firm partner, who typically possesses a significant measure of economic independence and professional distance derived from a multiple client base, the economic fate of in-house attorneys is tied directly to a single employer, at whose sufferance they serve. Thus, from an economic standpoint, the dependence of in-house counsel is indistinguishable from that of other corporate managers or senior executives who also owe their livelihoods, career goals and satisfaction to a single organizational employer.

Moreover, the professional relationship between the in-house attorney and the client is not the "one shot" undertaking-drafting a will, say, or handling a piece of litigation-characteristic of the outside law firm. Instead, the corporate attorney-employee, operating in a heavily regulated medium, often takes on a larger advisory and compliance role, anticipating potential legal problems, advising on possible solutions, and generally assisting the corporation in achieving its business aims while minimizing entanglement in the increasingly complex legal web that regulates organizational conduct in our society. This expansion in the scope and stature of in-house counsel's work, together with an inevitably close professional identification with the fortunes and objectives of the corporate employer, can easily subject the in-house attorney to unusual pressures to conform to organizational goals, pressures that are qualitatively different from those imposed on the outside lawyer. Even the most dedicated professionals, their economic and professional fate allied with that of the business organizations they serve, may be irresistibly tempted to cut corners by bending the ethical norms that regulate an attorney's professional conduct.

Indeed, the analogy of in-house counsel's position to that of his or her lay colleagues in the executive suite is inexact only because, as a licensed professional, an attorney labors under unique ethical imperatives that exceed those of the corporate executive who seeks, say, a tort remedy after being terminated for refusing to join a conspiracy to violate the antitrust laws. (See, e.g., Tameny v. Atlantic Richfield Co. (1980) 27 Cal.3d 167 [164 Cal.Rptr. 839, 610 P.2d 1330, 9 A.L.R.4th 314] [Tameny].) We turn, then, to a consideration of the effects of in-house counsel's professional role and ethical duties on access to judicial remedies for alleged wrongful termination that are available to the nonattorney colleague.

III

A

If there is a unifying theme in this conflict, it is the claim of General Dynamics that our opinion in Fracasse v. Brent (1972) 6 Cal.3d 784 [100 Cal.Rptr. 385, 494 P.2d 9] (Fracasse) is dispositive of all issues tendered against it by Rose in his complaint. Because Fracasse cloaks the client in an unfettered, absolute right to discharge an attorney at any time and for any reason, General Dynamics argues, the complaint cannot state a claim against the company that is judicially cognizable; the trial court should thus have sustained General Dynamics's demurrer without leave to amend.

* * *

Although the core proposition established by our opinion in Fracasse, supra, 6 Cal.3d at page 790, affirming the trial court, undoubtedly remains valid-we concluded that "a client should have both the right and the power at any time to discharge his attorney with or without cause"-our holding in that case does not support the sweeping scope urged for it by General Dynamics. It should be evident to anyone reading our opinion in Fracasse that we confronted there one of the most common of the traditional forms of the lawyer-client relationship: the potential claimant who seeks redress by hiring an independent professional to prosecute her claim for personal injuries.

Our holdings in that case were expressly founded on the recognition that a client who retains an attorney to prosecute a personal injury action under a contingent fee agreement "may and often is very likely to be a person of limited means for whom the contingent fee arrangement offers the only realistic hope of establishing a legal claim." (Fracasse, supra, 6 Cal.3d at p. 792.)

* * *

In stating that "the client's power to discharge an attorney, with or without cause, is absolute...," we relied on the provisions of Code of Civil Procedure section 284, permitting a change of attorneys in "an action or special proceeding." (Fracasse, supra, 6 Cal.3d at p. 790; see also Santa Clara County Counsel Attys. Assn. v. Woodside (1994) 7 Cal.4th 525, 555 [28 Cal.Rptr.2d 617, 869 P.2d 1142].) In light of the specific hazards confronting the contingent fee plaintiff who has lost confidence in his or her attorney-notably the risk of guessing wrong whether cause for discharge existed and thereby losing "73 1/3 percent of a recovered judgment" we concluded that it "should be sufficient that the client has, for whatever reason, lost faith in the attorney, to establish 'cause' for discharging him." (Fracasse, supra, 6 Cal.3d at p. 790.) Finally, we reasoned that, "since the attorney agreed initially to take his chances on recovering any fee whatever, we believe that the fact that the success of the litigation is no longer under his control is insufficient to justify imposing a new and more onerous burden on the client." (Id. at p. 792.) "It follows," we concluded, "that the attorney will be denied compensation in the event such recovery is not obtained." (Ibid.)

Entwined with our concern for the specific risks facing the contingent-fee plaintiff who has lost faith in her attorney was an underlying perception that, whatever the circumstances, no client should be forced to suffer representation by an attorney in whom that confidence and trust lying at the heart of a fiduciary relationship has been lost. It is not surprising, given this chain of reasoning, that our opinion in Fracasse, supra, 6 Cal.3d 784, should establish as bedrock law what remains probably the central value of the lawyer-client relationship-the primacy of fiducial values and its corollary: the unilateral right of the client to sever the professional relationship at any time and for any reason.

That rule, which we reaffirm today, some 22 years after our decision in Fracasse, supra, 6 Cal.3d 784, does not mean, however, that the "absolute" right of the personal injury client to discharge unilaterally his attorney permits all clients to terminate the attorney-client relationship under all circumstances without consequence. The sources of contract and tort claims in wrongful termination cases are analytically distinct from the circumstances confronting the contingent-fee plaintiff that propelled our analysis in Fracasse. Given these disparate origins, it is unlikely that the client's undoubted power to discharge the attorney at will is one that can be invoked under all circumstances without consequence.

* * *

Additionally, General Dynamics' claim of an unqualified immunity from any liability for terminating in-house counsel is inconsistent with the law in other areas, notably claims grounded in alleged violations of antidiscrimination laws and statutory rights to public collective bargaining. (See, e.g., Hishon v. King & Spalding (1984) 467 U.S. 69 [81 L.Ed.2d 59, 104 S.Ct. 2229] [federal civil rights laws apply to law firm partnership decisions]; Golightly-Howell v. Oil, Chemical & Atomic Workers (D.Colo. 1992) 806 F.Supp. 921, 924 ["[B]ecause Title VII prohibits discrimination based on race or sex, it prohibits such discrimination against one employed as in-house counsel."]; Santa Clara County Counsel Attys. Assn. v. Woodside, supra, 7 Cal.4th 525 [Meyers-Milias-Brown Act creates an exception to the general rule that a client may discharge an attorney at will].)

Indeed, General Dynamics's complete reliance on Fracasse, supra, 6 Cal.3d 784, as dispositive of Rose's claims proves too much. If, as a matter of legal doctrine, the client's right of discharge can be invoked without consequence in all circumstances, it might easily produce unconscionable results. Suppose an attorney in New York responds to a professional advertisement seeking an assistant general counsel for a corporation headquartered in Los Angeles. A series of negotiations ensues and the parties execute a written contract under which the employer agrees to hire the attorney to perform legal work as a full time employee for an agreed salary. Suppose further that the agreement provides that the attorney can only be terminated for specified reasons. The newly hired lawyer-employee then sells his house, moves family and goods across the country, buys a new home, enrolls his children in local schools, and begins his new employment. Three months later, he is summarily fired by the company for reasons that are not among those stipulated in the employment contract. To insist in the face of such egregious circumstances that our opinion in Fracasse, supra, 6 Cal.3d 784, immunizes the employer by providing an "absolute" right to discharge the employee with complete impunity, foreclosing suit on the contract terms, would compel us to embrace an intuitively unjust, even outrageous, result on the basis of a holding expressly shaped by the unique concerns confronting the contingent fee personal injury client who has lost faith in counsel.

* * *

Given the circumstances of attorney and client in the typical contingent fee personal injury case-well illustrated by the facts in Fracasse, supra, 6 Cal.3d 784 -we reached a resolution of competing claims tailored to the strengths of the interests of the parties: securing the client's right of unilateral discharge while recognizing that, in light of the speculative nature of contingent fee claims, the discharged attorney was fairly compensated by payment of the reasonable value of his services in the event of a recovery on the client's behalf. In sum, our language in Fracasse, supra, 6 Cal.3d 784, should not be read as standing for more than its context and rationale will reasonably support.

B

How does the fundamental rule of the client's unilateral power of discharge announced in Fracasse, supra, 6 Cal.3d 784, apply in the circumstances of this case? First, Rose's complaint does not contest the right of General Dynamics to terminate a member of its corporate legal department at any time or for any reason, nor could it. It simply asserts that there is a cost to be paid for such an action under the circumstances alleged in the complaint-either in lost wages and related damages in the case of the implied-in-fact contract claim, or as tort damages in the case of the public policy tort claim. (Cf. Howard v. Babcock (1994) 6 Cal.4th 409, 419 [25 Cal.Rptr.2d 80, 863 P.2d 150] [law firm "non-compete" agreement "attaches an economic consequence to a departing partner's unrestricted choice to pursue a particular kind of practice."].) In neither case, however, is the client's power to rid itself of an attorney in whom it has lost confidence thwarted. To the extent that General Dynamics's claim that its "unfettered" right to discharge a member of its corporate legal department means that it may do so without liability of any kind under all circumstances, that is not, and never has been, the law of this state.

* * *

We turn to a consideration of the merits of plaintiff's claims that his termination breached an implied-in-fact agreement with General Dynamics and violated fundamental public policies, as well as the possible limitations on the vitality of such claims when brought by in-house counsel.

IV

As the name suggests, an implied-in-fact contract claim as a limitation on an employer's historical at-will power to terminate one of its employees is rooted in the conduct of the parties to the employment relationship itself. As such, it is a branch of the law of contracts and subject to the time-honored notion that contractual bargains ought to be enforced unless there is some imperative-generally rooted in policies external to the employment relationship-that prevents a court from doing so. At this stage of the litigation, General Dynamics' facial challenge to Rose's implied-in-fact contract claim does not attack the factual accuracy of the allegations of the complaint. It would, of course, be inappropriate to do so in a demurrer testing the legal sufficiency of the plaintiff's theory of relief.

* * *

Perhaps the overriding distinction between Fracasse, supra, 6 Cal.3d 784, and this case lies in the allegations of the complaint that the plaintiff was hired as a "career oriented" employee with an expectation of permanent employment, provided his performance was satisfactory; that he was promised job security and substantial retirement benefits; that he regularly received outstanding performance reviews, promotions, salary increases, and commendations throughout his 14-year tenure; and that the company abruptly terminated him without adhering to its published discharge procedures.

These pleadings, we conclude, adequately allege that a "course of conduct, including various oral representations, created a reasonable expectation" that the plaintiff would not be terminated without good cause. (Foley v. Interactive Data Corp. (1988) 47 Cal.3d 654, 675 [254 Cal.Rptr. 211, 765 P.2d 373] [hereafter Foley].) The factual allegations of the complaint being sufficient to withstand a general demurrer, we see no reason in policy, at least at the outset, why the plaintiff's status as an in-house attorney should operate to defeat his contract claim. It is true, as we have just affirmed, that General Dynamics has a right to discharge any member of its general counsel's staff in whom it has lost confidence. That right does not mean, however, that it may do so without honoring antecedent contractual obligations to discharge an attorney-employee only on the occurrence of specified conditions.

In short, implied-in-fact limitations being a species of contract, no reason appears why an employer that elects to limit its at-will freedom to terminate the employment relationship with in-house counsel should not be held to the terms of its bargain. The Minnesota Supreme Court has put the nub of the matter succinctly: "The fact remains … that the in-house attorney is also a company employee, and we see no reason to deny the job security aspects of the employer-employee relationship if this can be done without violence to the integrity of the attorney-client relationship. For matters of compensation, promotion, and tenure, inside counsel are ordinarily subject to the same administrative personnel supervision as other company employees. These personnel arrangements differ from the traditional scenario of the self-employed attorney representing a client; and these differences are such, we think, that the elements of client trust and attorney autonomy are less likely to be implicated in the employer-employee aspect of the in-house counsel status." (Nordling v. Northern States Power Co. (Minn. 1991) 478 N.W.2d 498, 502; see also Mourad v. Automobile Club Ins. Ass'n (1991) 186 Mich.App. 715 [465 N.W.2d 395, 400] [Senior in-house counsel, fired for refusing to permit nonattorney employees of his insurance company employer to supervise outside counsel representing the company's insureds, sought damages alleging the company's practice violated the Code of Professional Responsibility and that his discharge breached an implied just-cause term of his employment contract. Held: by hiring plaintiff as an attorney, defendants "knew or should have known that plaintiff was bound by the code of professional conduct and incorporated this fact in creating a just-cause employment contract."].)

We agree that, as creatures of contract, implied-in-fact limitations on a client-employer's right to discharge in-house counsel are not likely to present issues implicating the distinctive values subserved by the attorney-client relationship. Such suits can thus for the most part be treated as implied-in-fact claims brought by the nonattorney employee.

* * *

V

* * *

There is a substantial counterargument against permitting the pursuit of a retaliatory discharge tort claim by in-house counsel, one that also inheres in the essential nature of the attorney's professional role. Indeed, in the handful of reported cases dealing with the question, a majority of courts have refused to permit the maintenance of such suits on the ground that they pose too great a threat to the attorney-client relationship. This rationale is well illustrated in a trio of recent cases, each holding as a matter of law that retaliatory discharge suits by in-house counsel are not maintainable.

The leading opinion is perhaps Balla v. Gambro, Inc. (1991) 145 Ill.2d 492 [164 Ill.Dec. 892, 584 N.E.2d 104, 16 A.L.R.5th 1000] (hereafter Balla), a case in which the general counsel of an Illinois distributor of German-made dialysis equipment sued his employer for wrongful discharge, complaining that he had learned internally of major defects in several dialysis machines shipped to his employer for distribution in the American market, defects which put users at serious risk of uremic poisoning. He advised his superiors to reject the machines as not in compliance with Food and Drug Administration (FDA) regulations and as potentially dangerous to consumers. On later learning that company officials had accepted delivery of the units for sale to a customer " 'who buys only on price,' " plaintiff confronted the company president and told him that he would "do whatever necessary to stop the sale of the dialyzers." (Id. at p. 106.)

After being abruptly fired two weeks later, the lawyer-employee reported the equipment defects to FDA officials the following day; they seized the machines as "adulterated" within the meaning of the federal act and the employee filed a damage action for retaliatory discharge, contending that he was fired for reasons that contravened a fundamental public policy. (584 N.E.2d at pp. 106-107.) The Illinois Supreme Court agreed that plaintiff's discharge "was in contravention of a clearly mandated public policy.... As we have stated before, '[t]here is no public policy more important or more fundamental than the one favoring the effective protection of the lives and property of citizens.' " (Id. at pp. 107-108.) The court declined, however, to permit the plaintiff to maintain a retaliatory discharge action because he "was not just an employee of [defendant], but also general counsel for [defendant]." (Id. at p. 108.)

* * *

Those courts that have declined to permit in-house counsel to pursue retaliatory discharge claims-in Balla, Herbster, and Willy-have rested their conclusion on two distinct grounds: First, because the fiducial qualities of their professional calling pervade the attorney-client relationship-"lawyers are different." It is essential to the proper functioning of the lawyer's role that the client be assured that matters disclosed to counsel in confidence remain sacrosanct; to permit in-house attorneys to file suit against their clients can only harm that relationship. Second, to the extent that the retaliatory discharge tort rests on underpinnings designed to secure fundamental public policies, a tort remedy for in-house counsel is redundant-such attorneys are under an ethical obligation to sever their professional relationship with the erring client in any event-meaning, in the case of in-house counsel, resigning their employment.

D

There is no doubt that the Illinois courts in Balla, supra, 584 N.E.2d 104, and Herbster, supra, 501 N.E.2d 343, grappled conscientiously with the conflicting values presented by cases such as this one. If their reasoning and conclusions can be faulted, it is because one searches in vain for a principled link between the ethical duties of the in-house attorney and the courts' refusal to grant such an employee a tort remedy under conditions that directly implicate those professional obligations. As more than one critic of these opinions has pointed out, both cases appear to reflect not only an unspoken adherence to an anachronistic model of the attorney's place and role in contemporary society, but an inverted view of the consequences of the in-house attorney's essential professional role.

As one authoritative commentator on lawyers' ethics, criticizing the court's decision in Balla, supra, 584 N.E.2d 104, has written, "It is clear that there would have been a right of action had the employee not been a lawyer. It thus seems bizarre that a lawyer employee, who has affirmative duties concerning the administration of justice, should be denied redress for discharge resulting from trying to carry out those very duties. A good beginning point for analysis may well be the client's normal and broad right to discharge the lawyer, but that cannot be the ending point as well, for the lawyer-client relationship exists in a context of other law regulating both parties to that relationship, including the lawyer's duties to third persons, the courts, and the government." (1 Hazard & Hodes, The Law of Lawyering, supra, § 1.16.206 at p. 477, fns. omitted.)

Granted the priest-like license to receive the most intimate and damning disclosures of the client, granted the sanctity of the professional privilege, granted the uniquely influential position attorneys occupy in our society, it is precisely because of that role that attorneys should be accorded a retaliatory discharge remedy in those instances in which mandatory ethical norms embodied in the Rules of Professional Conduct collide with illegitimate demands of the employer and the attorney insists on adhering to his or her clear professional duty. It is, after all, the office of the retaliatory discharge tort to vindicate fundamental public policies by encouraging employees to act in ways that advance them. By providing the employee with a remedy in tort damages for resisting socially damaging organizational conduct, the courts mitigate the otherwise considerable economic and cultural pressures on the individual employee to silently conform.

* * *

In addition, the emphasis by the Balla, Herbster and Willy courts on the "remedy" of the in-house attorney's duty of "withdrawal" strikes us as illusory. Courts do not require nonlawyer employees to quietly surrender their jobs rather than "go along" with an employer's unlawful demands. Indeed, the retaliatory discharge tort claim is designed to encourage and support precisely the opposite reaction. Why, then, did the courts in these three cases content themselves with the bland announcement that the only "choice" of an attorney confronted with an employer's demand that he violate his professional oath by committing, say, a criminal act, is to voluntarily withdraw from employment, a course fraught with the possibility of economic catastrophe and professional banishment?

Whatever the reason, the withdrawal "remedy" fails to confront seriously the extraordinarily high cost that resignation entails. More importantly, it is virtually certain that, without the prospect of limited judicial access, in-house attorneys-especially those in mid-career who occupy senior positions -confronted with the dilemma of choosing between adhering to professional ethical norms and surrendering to the employer's unethical demands will almost always find silence the better part of valor. Declining to provide a limited remedy under defined circumstances will thus almost certainly foster a degradation of in-house counsel's professional stature.

E

In addition to retaliatory discharge claims founded on allegations that an in-house attorney was terminated for refusing to violate a mandatory ethical duty embodied in the Rules of Professional Conduct, judicial access ought logically extend to those limited circumstances in which in-house counsel's nonattorney colleagues would be permitted to pursue a retaliatory discharge claim and governing professional rules or statutes expressly remove the requirement of attorney confidentiality. Thus, in determining whether an in-house attorney has a retaliatory discharge claim against his or her employer, a court must first ask whether the attorney was discharged for following a mandatory ethical obligation prescribed by professional rule or statute. If, for example, in-house counsel is asked to commit a crime, or to engage in an act of moral turpitude that would subject him to disbarment (see, e.g., Bus. & Prof. Code, §§ 6101, 6106 * * * and is discharged for refusing to engage in such an act, counsel would have been discharged for adhering to a mandatory ethical obligation; under most circumstances, the attorney would have a retaliatory discharge cause of action against the employer.

If, on the other hand, the conduct in which the attorney has engaged is merely ethically permissible, but not required by statute or ethical code, then the inquiry facing the court is slightly more complex. Under these circumstances, a court must resolve two questions: First, whether the employer's conduct is of the kind that would give rise to a retaliatory discharge action by a nonattorney employee under Gantt v. Sentry Insurance, supra, 1 Cal.4th 1083, and related cases; second, the court must determine whether some statute or ethical rule, such as the statutory exceptions to the attorney-client privilege codified in the Evidence Code (see id., §§ 956-958) specifically permits the attorney to depart from the usual requirement of confidentiality with respect to the client-employer and engage in the "nonfiduciary" conduct for which he was terminated.

We emphasize the limited scope of our conclusion that in-house counsel may state a cause of action in tort for retaliatory discharge. The lawyer's high duty of fidelity to the interests of the client work against a tort remedy that is coextensive with that available to the nonattorney employee. Although claims by in-house attorneys are cognate to those we approved in Foley, supra, 47 Cal.3d 654, the underlying rationale differs somewhat, being grounded in the attorney's obligation to adhere to ethical norms specific to the profession. The cause of action is thus one designed to support in-house counsel in remaining faithful to those fundamental public policies reflected in the governing ethical code when carrying out professional assignments.

* * *

VI

Applying the principles developed above to the complaint in this case, it is evident that as noted, ante, at page 1178, plaintiff's first claim-for breach of an implied-in-fact just-cause agreement-adequately pleads the essential elements of the cause of action. It is less clear, however, that the allegations in support of relief under plaintiff's retaliatory discharge theory are sufficient. Plaintiff nowhere alleges that the conduct which allegedly led to his termination was required or supported by any requirement of our Rules of Professional Conduct or a relevant statute. This omission is not surprising, however, in light of the fact that no court of this state has previously addressed the precise question presented by this case in a published opinion. In drawing up the complaint, plaintiff apparently proceeded on the assumption that the scope of retaliatory discharge claims by in-house counsel is coextensive with that of other corporate employees. We have, of course, concluded that that view is too expansive.

In light of our ruling, we believe the fairest resolution is to direct that the matter be remanded to the trial court and that plaintiff be permitted to amend his complaint against General Dynamics in accordance with the views we have expressed. It should go without saying that nothing we have said is intended to intimate in any way a view of the merits of this action.

Conclusion

The judgment of the Court of Appeal is affirmed and the cause is remanded to that court with directions to order further proceedings in accordance with the views expressed herein.

Lucas, C. J., Mosk, J., Kennard, J., Baxter, J., George, J., and Turner, J.

Usage of Trade

Technical words in a contract must "be interpreted as usually understood by persons in the profession or business to which they relate, unless clearly used in a different sense." (Cal.Civ.Code § 1645,) A contract is to be interpreted according to the law and usage of the place where it is to be performed or, if it does not indicate a place of performance, according to the law and usage of the place where it is made. (Cal.Civ.Code § 1646)

Ermolieff v. R. K. O. Radio Pictures

Supreme Court of California, 1942
19 Cal.2d 543, 122 P.2d 3

CARTER, J.

Plaintiff and defendant are producers and distributors in the motion picture industry. Plaintiff was the owner and producer of a foreign language motion picture entitled "Michael Strogoff," based on a novel by Jules Verne, which prior to July 6, 1936, he had produced in the German and French languages. On that date the parties entered into a contract in which plaintiff granted to defendant the exclusive right to produce and distribute an English version of that picture in only those "countries or territories of the world" listed on an exhibit annexed to the contract. On the exhibit is listed among other places "The United Kingdom." Plaintiff reserved the rights in the picture in both foreign and English language in all countries or territories not listed in the exhibit. The contract was modified in December, 1936, and September, 1937, to add other countries or territories to the list. Plaintiff commenced the instant action on May 8, 1940, pleading the contract and its modifications and alleging that defendant had produced an English version of the picture under the title "Soldier and a Lady" in the United States and elsewhere; and that a controversy has arisen between the parties as to the countries and territories granted to defendant and those reserved by plaintiff under the contract and its modifications. Those allegations were admitted by defendant and it alleges that the only controversy between the parties is with respect to the area referred to as "The United Kingdom"; that the only dispute is whether "The United Kingdom," in which the contract grants rights to defendant, includes Eire or the Irish Free State; and that there is a custom and usage in the motion picture industry that that term does include Eire and that such usage is a part of the contract. Both the complaint and the answer pray for declaratory relief, namely, a declaration of their rights with respect to those areas embraced in the contract which are in dispute.

It was stipulated that the sole issue with respect to the territory embraced in the contract was whether defendant or plaintiff held the rights in the picture in Eire, which in turn depended upon whether The United Kingdom included Eire; that defendant did distribute the picture in Eire, and that The United Kingdom, from a political and legal viewpoint, did not include Eire, the latter being independent from it.

* * *

In the instant case plaintiff in his complaint claimed a controversy with respect to the respective rights of the parties under the contract. Defendant in its answer set forth with particularity the controversy as being whether The United Kingdom included Eire. It was stipulated that that was the sole controversy and the case was tried on that issue. The court denied defendant's claim that the case was not within the purview of section 1060 and granted declaratory relief. While it is true that defendant has already distributed pictures in Eire, it is also true that if plaintiff is correct in his assertion that Eire is not included in The United Kingdom, he has reserved the right in the contract to distribute pictures there. If defendant is correct it has the right to make a further distribution of pictures in Eire. Defendant's contention must therefore fail.

Defendant asserts, however, that the judgment must be reversed because of the granting of plaintiff's motion to strike defendant's evidence that according to the custom and usage of the moving picture industry Eire is included in The United Kingdom. With that contention we agree. Both plaintiff and defendant are engaged in the business of producing and distributing moving pictures and rights in connection therewith. Defendant's evidence consisted of the testimony of several witnesses familiar with the distribution of motion pictures to the effect that in contracts covering the rights to produce pictures the general custom and usage was that the term "The United Kingdom" included Eire, the Irish Free State. Plaintiff's motion to strike out all of that evidence on the ground that it was incompetent, irrelevant and immaterial was granted. Plaintiff, reserving his objection to defendant's evidence, offered contrary evidence concerning such custom and usage.

The correct rule with reference to the admissibility of evidence as to trade usage under the circumstances here presented is that while words in a contract are ordinarily to be construed according to their plain, ordinary, popular or legal meaning, as the case may be, yet if in reference to the subject matter of the contract, particular expressions have by trade usage acquired a different meaning, and both parties are engaged in that trade, the parties to the contract are deemed to have used them according to their different and peculiar sense as shown by such trade usage. Parol evidence is admissible to establish the trade usage, and that is true even though the words are in their ordinary or legal meaning entirely unambiguous, inasmuch as by reason of the usage the words are used by the parties in a different sense. (See Code of Civil Procedure, sec. 1861; Civil Code, secs. 1644, 1646, 1655; Jenny Lind Co. v. Bower & Co., 11 Cal. 194; Callahan v. Stanley, 57 Cal. 476; Higgins v. California Petroleum etc. Co., 120 Cal. 629 [52 P. 1080]; Caro v. Mattei, 39 Cal.App. 253 [178 P. 537]; Wigmore on Evidence, vol. IX, sec. 2463, p. 204; Restatement, Contracts, secs. 246, 248; 89 A.L.R. 1228.) The basis of this rule is that to accomplish a purpose of paramount importance in interpretation of documents, namely, to ascertain the true intent of the parties, it may well be said that the usage evidence does not alter the contract of the parties, but on the contrary gives the effect to the words there used as intended by the parties. The usage becomes a part of the contract in aid of its correct interpretation.

Plaintiff relies upon such cases as Brant v. California Dairies, Inc., 4 Cal.2d 128 [48 PaCal.2d 13], and Wells v. Union Oil Co., 25 Cal.App.2d 165 [76 PaCal.2d 696], as announcing a rule contrary to the one above stated. However, in those cases evidence of custom or usage was not offered, and no contention was made therein that the words employed in the contracts there involved had any other than their ordinary, popular or legal meaning in reference to the subject matter of said contracts. That is not the case here. Plaintiff also cites other authorities. In New York Cent. R. R. Co. v. Frank H. Buck Co., 2 Cal.2d 384 [41 PaCal.2d 547], and the cases therein cited, the rule stated is merely that where the terms of the contract are expressly and directly contrary to the precise subject matter embraced in the custom or usage, parol evidence of that custom or usage is not admissible. The provision in the contract was tantamount to a clause that custom or usage shall not be a part of the contract. They did not involve a situation where the evidence was introduced to define a term in the contract. In the case at bar it cannot be said that there was a provision of that character. The contract stated that the defendant's rights existed only in the countries or territories listed in the annexed exhibit and plaintiff reserved the rights in all other countries or territories. "Territories" is a more comprehensive term than countries, and may well include more than one political entity or nation. The term "The United Kingdom" as a territory or area, does not necessarily limit that area to a political entity known as The United Kingdom. The fact that it is expressly stipulated in the contract that defendant has no rights in any countries not named in the exhibit, does not alter the situation. It falls short of being tantamount to an express and direct agreement that Eire shall not be considered as included in The United Kingdom. The door is still open to evidence of custom and usage with reference to the scope of The United Kingdom. The foregoing comments are equally applicable to the other cases cited by plaintiff, namely, Withers v. Moore, 140 Cal. 591 [74 P. 159]; May v. American Trust Co., 135 Cal.App. 385 [27 PaCal.2d 101]; Brandenstein v. Jackling, 99 Cal.App. 438 [278 P. 880]; Fish v. Correll, 4 Cal.App. 521 [88 P. 489], and California Jewelry Co. v. Provident Loan Assn., 6 Cal.App.2d 506 [45 PaCal.2d 271].

Plaintiff urges that since judicial notice may be taken and it was stipulated that Eire is independent of The United Kingdom and not a part thereof, the custom and usage evidence is not admissible to contradict that stipulation or notice. That notice and stipulation add nothing material to the situation. In any case where a word in a contract had an unquestioned common meaning there could be no dispute as to that common meaning, but the custom and usage is evidence of the peculiar sense in which it was used. The stipulation would add nothing that was not already plain on the face of the contract.

It is contended that the parties placed a practical construction on the contract which negatived presence of custom and usage as a part thereof. The contract was modified on December 1, 1936, and September 8, 1937, to include countries not mentioned in the original contract. Eire was not among the added areas and nothing was said therein with reference to the territory embraced by The United Kingdom. Malta and Gibraltar which are political subdivisions of The United Kingdom were added. It does not necessarily follow that these modifications constituted a construction of the contract by the parties to the effect that Eire was not included in the term "The United Kingdom," nor that evidence of custom or usage was removed from the picture. Indeed, it may reasonably follow from those modifications that the criterion to be used in construing the area embraced within The United Kingdom was not the political or legal boundaries thereof. It may well be said to indicate an uncertainty as to the extent of the area embraced by that term because upon plaintiff's present reasoning The United Kingdom is circumscribed by the political and legal boundaries thereof. That being the case, there would be no occasion for the modification because Malta and Gibraltar being political subdivisions of The United Kingdom would be embraced in the contract as originally written. For those reasons, it is also a fair inference to conclude, that the parties because of the modifications, had some meaning in their mind for the term "The United Kingdom," other than that territory which is a political and legal part thereof.

Finally, plaintiff asserts that the custom and usage evidence was inadmissible because a custom and usage to be available must be known by the parties or so generally known that knowledge must be presumed, citing Security Commercial & Savings Bank of San Diego v. Southern Trust & Commerce Bank, 74 Cal.App. 734 [241 P. 945]. But in this case defendant's excluded evidence showed that the custom was general in the moving picture industry and both parties were engaged in the production of motion pictures. As plaintiff expresses it in his brief, "Respondent (plaintiff) is a world famous producer." It is stated in Restatement, Contracts, section 248, page 352:

> Where both parties to a transaction are engaged in the same occupation, or belong to the same group of persons, the usages of that occupation or group are operative, unless one of the parties knows or has reason to know that the other party has an inconsistent intention.

Plaintiff further urges in support of the exclusion of the evidence of usage; that the witnesses were biased, that it was a "low quality of proof," that it was insufficient and the like. These are matters that go to the weight of the evidence, rather than to its admissibility. With that we are not concerned. There is no necessity for a detailed analysis of the evidence. It is clear that the trial court did not purport to weigh or evaluate that evidence. It disregarded it in toto as is evinced by its order striking it out. On retrial of the action, if the parties so desire, the trial court may consider and give such weight to such evidence as may be introduced.

The judgment is reversed.

Gibson, C.J., Shenk, J., Curtis, J., Edmonds, J., Houser, J., and Traynor, J., concurred.

Higgins v. California Petroleum & Asphalt Co. et al.

Supreme Court of California, 1898
120 Cal. 629, 52 P. 1080

TEMPLE, J.

Plaintiff brought this action to recover certain royalties on certain bituminous rock and liquid asphaltum mined by defendants, for which they agreed to pay 'the sum of fifty cents per ton for each and every gross ton.' The trial court found 'that the term 'gross ton,' as used in the lease, * * * means two thousand two hundred and forty,' and gave judgment for plaintiff accordingly. From this judgment, plaintiff appeals on the judgment roll alone. His contention is that the ton contemplated by the contract is a ton of two thousand pounds. A contract of precisely the same terms in respect of the question now presented, was before this court in Higgins v. Asphalt Co., 109 Cal. 304, 41 Pac. 1087. It was held in that case that the ton referred to, upon the facts as they there appeared, was 'equal to two thousand pounds avoirdupois, and no more.' The only question involved here is whether the finding above quoted supports the judgment. Appellant claims that this 'is simply a conclusion of law based upon the contract,' and, * * * 'if a finding of fact, it is error, as it is found from the contract itself.' By section 3215 of the Political Code it is provided that 'twenty hundred weight constitute a ton.' The contention of appellant is that the statute defines the meaning and use of the word 'ton' (section 3215, Pol. Code); and that the lease is unambiguous, and cannot be explained or contradicted by parol evidence. Therefore, there could have been no evidence at the trial justifying the finding of the court that the phrase 'gross ton,' used in the lease, meant a long ton of 2,240 pounds.

Some decisions are cited apparently holding that a contract of this nature must be conclusively presumed to refer to the statutory weights and measures, at least in the absence of a direct and express reference in the contract to a different standard; and in this connection it is argued that the adjective 'gross' does not refer to measure,—that is, to the number of pounds in the ton,—but to the condition of the commodity when weighed, to wit, that the crude and unrefined asphalt is to be weighed, and not the refined product. I think the question is entirely settled by section 1861 of the Code of Civil Procedure, which reads as follows: 'The terms of a writing are presumed to have been used in their primary and general acceptation, but evidence is nevertheless admissible that they have a local, technical or otherwise peculiar signification, and were so used and understood in the particular instance, in which case the agreement must be construed accordingly.' I know no reason why this rule would not apply as well to a statutory weight or measure as to any other term used in a writing. Suppose there had been a bill of exceptions in this case, showing that upon the trial it was proven (1) that there was a usage throughout the state among all dealing in asphaltum that the crude material was dealt in according to a gross ton of 2,240 pounds; (2) that there was a custom to the same effect in Santa Barbara county; that in fact, by the usage and custom, the phrase 'gross ton' is always used to indicate the long ton, just as, by commercial usage, the last phrase is used to indicate that 2,240 pounds is meant; (3) that the parties, acting under this very contract, had in numerous settlements recognized the fact that 'gross ton' meant the long ton, and not the statutory ton. And we might add to this that there had been previous contracts between these same parties, of the same general character, but in which the phrase had been so defined. Would not such evidence have been admissible, and would it not have supported the finding? I think it would.

Of course, appellant would contend that, even under section 1861, such evidence cannot be received, unless the contract expressly indicates a local, technical, or peculiar signification. But the section plainly provides that it may be shown by evidence that the language is used in a technical, local, or peculiar sense, and not merely that evidence may be introduced to show what such meaning is when language is so used. This view is somewhat strengthened by the fact, as shown in respondents' brief, that the phrase 'gross ton' is often used in lieu of the phrase 'long ton,' with which we are all familiar in commercial reports, and which always indicates a ton containing 2,240 pounds. It is said that in the case of Higgins v. Asphalt Co., supra, this identical lease was construed, and that it was between the same parties. Possibly, had the evidence been brought up on this appeal, we would now construe it in the same way. But that case does not constitute the law of this case, and here we are asked to decide whether there could possibly have been evidence which would have sustained the finding objected to. I think the finding was not necessarily a mere conclusion of law,—that is, a construction of the language of the lease,—but may have been based upon evidence. Judgment affirmed.

We concur: HENSHAW, J.; McFARLAND, J.

Chapter 7

Performance & Breach

Conditions Precedent, Subsequent and Concurrent

A condition is a fact, an event, the happening or non-happening of which creates or extinguishes a duty on the part of a promisor. A condition which creates a duty is a condition precedent. (Cal.Civ.Code § 1436) A condition which extinguishes a duty is a condition subsequent. (Cal.Civ.Code § 1438) Conditions concurrent are those which are mutually dependent, and are to be performed at the same time. (Cal.Civ.Code § 1437)

A contractual obligation is conditional when the rights or duties of any party thereto depend upon the occurrence of an uncertain event. (Cal.Civ.Code § 1434.) Hence, a person who makes an absolute or unconditional promise, supported by a sufficient consideration, is bound to perform when the time for performance arrives. A person who makes a conditional promise, supported by a sufficient consideration, is bound to perform only if the condition precedent occurs or is relieved from the duty to perform if the condition subsequent occurs.

A promise may be dependent upon the happening or performance of more than one condition, in which event, the person to whom the promise is made must perform all conditions precedent before any duty to perform arises. (1 Witkin, Summary of Cal. Law, (9th ed. 1987) Contracts, § 721.)

Express and Constructive (Implied) Conditions

A condition may be express, implied in fact, or implied in law. (1 Witkin, Summary of Cal. Law, (9th ed. 1987) Contracts, § 722, 739-752.) An express condition is one explicitly agreed to and placed in the contract by the parties. A constructive condition (sometimes called an implied condition) is a condition that is imposed by law in order to do justice. Express conditions must be literally performed and are not subject to the doctrine of substantial performance. Constructive conditions may be satisfied by substantial performance.

173

Pittman v. Canham

California Court of Appeal, Second District Division Six, 1992
2 Cal.App.4th 556, 3 Cal.Rptr.2d 340

GILBERT, J.

When is a contract no longer a contract? When it contains concurrent conditions and neither party tenders timely performance. Unlike love or taxes, concurrent conditions do not last forever.

We hold that where a contract creates concurrent conditions and neither party tenders timely performance, both parties are discharged. We affirm the judgment.

Facts

Jeffrey A. Pittman was a licensed real estate broker. In 1987 he contacted Lily V. Canham, then 85 years old, to purchase a parcel of property she owned in San Luis Obispo County. After many telephone calls to Canham between May and November 1987, she agreed to sell a 56-acre parcel to Pittman for $250,000.

Pittman drafted the contract dated November 24, 1987, and deposited $1,000 in escrow. The contract called for a further deposit of $24,000 in cash, with the balance of the purchase price to be paid by a note secured by a deed of trust on the property. Closing of escrow was to be within 30 days. The contract provided that "[t]ime is of the essence. All modification or extensions shall be in writing signed by the parties."

The parties executed escrow instructions that provided: "Time is of the essence of these instructions. If this escrow is not in condition to close by the Time Limit Date of December 24, 1987 and written demand for cancellation is received by you from any principal to this escrow after said date, you shall act in accordance with [other provisions of the instructions].... [¶] If no demand for cancellation is made, you will proceed to close this escrow when the principals have complied with the escrow instructions." Paragraph 2 of section 4 of the instructions provided, however, that the instructions were not intended to amend, modify or supersede the contract.

About the second week of December Canham gave a signed copy of the escrow instructions to Pittman for delivery to escrow. With the instructions, Canham included a signed deed to the property. The escrow company pointed out, however, that the deed had not been notarized. When Pittman contacted Canham, she told him she would have it notarized at an escrow company near her home.

The December 24 closing date came and went. Canham had not tendered a notarized deed nor had Pittman tendered $24,000, a promissory note or deed of trust.

By March 1988, Canham had been contacted by another broker who wanted to list the property. On March 21 she told Pittman she wanted $10,000 per acre. Pittman embarked on an effort to find out what a fair price for the property was.

In May 1988, Canham told Pittman that she had entered into a contract with other purchasers to buy the property for $600,000. Pittman wrote a letter demanding that she perform on his contract, but she sold the property to the other buyers.

Pittman sued Canham for breach of contract. At trial he attributed the difference in the $250,000 he offered Canham and the $600,000 sales price six months later to an escalating real estate market.

At the end of Pittman's case, Canham moved for a judgment of nonsuit. (Code Civ. Proc., § 581c.) A ruling on the motion was reserved, however, until all the evidence was presented. After the presentation of the evidence, the court granted the motion on the ground that time was of the essence of the contract and neither party tendered performance. The court also gave a statement of decision in which it found that Pittman and not Canham was responsible for the delay in performance, that Canham had not waived time for performance, and that Pittman defaulted when he failed to tender the purchase money, note and deed of trust by December 24, 1987.

Discussion

Pittman contends the trial court erred in finding he was in default for failing to tender the purchase money note and deed of trust. He concedes that the result reached by the trial court would be proper if his performance had been a condition precedent, but he points out that here the contract provision requiring Canham to deliver a recordable deed into escrow and the provision requiring him to deposit money, a note and a deed of trust are concurrent conditions. Pittman claims that unlike the failure to perform a condition precedent, the failure of both parties to perform concurrent conditions does not automatically terminate the contract, but that one party must tender performance before the other party is in default. (Citing Chan v. Title Ins. & Trust Co. (1952) 39 Cal.2d 253 [246 P.2d 632]; Rubin v. Fuchs (1969) 1 Cal.3d 50 [81 Cal.Rptr. 373, 459 P.2d 925]; 1 Miller & Starr, Cal. Real Estate (2d ed. 1989) § 1:135, p. 488.)

Concurrent conditions are conditions precedent which are mutually dependent, and the only important difference between a concurrent condition and a condition precedent is that the condition precedent must be performed before another duty arises, whereas a tender of performance is sufficient in the case of a concurrent condition. (1 Witkin, Summary of Cal. Law (9th ed. 1987) Contracts, § 737, pp. 667-668.)

Contrary to Pittman's assertion, the failure of both parties to perform concurrent conditions does not leave the contract open for an indefinite period so that either party can tender performance at his leisure. The failure of both parties to perform concurrent conditions during the time for performance results in a discharge of both parties' duty to perform. Thus, where the parties have made time the essence of the contract, at the expiration of time without tender by either party, both parties are discharged. (3A Corbin on Contracts (1960) § 663, p. 181.) Here, because time was made the essence of the contract, the failure of both parties to tender performance by December 24, 1987, discharged both from performing. Neither party can hold the other in default and no cause of action to enforce the contract arises. (See Pitt v. Mallalieu (1948) 85 Cal.App.2d 77, 81 [192 P.2d 24].)

Pittman relies on the portion of the escrow instructions that states: "Time is of the essence of these instructions.... If this escrow is not in condition to close by the Time Limit Date of December 24, 1987 and ... [i]f no demand for cancellation is made, you will proceed to close this escrow when the principals have complied with the escrow instructions." He claims this provision shows that time was not truly of the essence in this transaction.

But it is difficult to see how a paragraph that begins with the words "[t]ime is of the essence" could reasonably be construed as meaning time is not truly of the essence. The provision relied on by Pittman merely instructs the escrow holder not to cancel escrow on its own initiative, but to close escrow should the parties voluntarily and notwithstanding discharge mutually decide to perform. As we read the paragraph, it does not purport to give a party the unilateral right to demand performance after the time for performance has passed. Such a construction would render meaningless the parties' agreement that time is of the essence.

We appreciate the reluctance of a buyer to act first by placing money into escrow. But in a contract with concurrent conditions, the buyer and seller cannot keep saying to one another, "No, you first." Ultimately, in such a case, the buyer seeking enforcement comes in second; he loses.

Chan v. Title Ins. & Trust Co., supra, 39 Cal.2d 253, is of no help to Pittman. There, the court found no default because time for performance had been waived. (Id., at p. 256.) Here, the trial court held that there has been no waiver, and there is nothing in the record that requires us to disturb that finding.

Nor is Pittman aided by Rubin v. Fuchs, supra, 1 Cal.3d 50. There, buyer promised to deposit cash and a purchase money deed of trust before the date set for close of escrow. Seller promised to record a tract map prior to that date. Recordation of the tract map would supply the legal description for the deed of trust. Seller, however, did not record the tract map, and buyer could therefore not deposit a deed of trust.

Our Supreme Court held that seller could not rescind for buyer's failure to perform because seller's performance was necessarily precedent to performance by the buyer. (Rubin v. Fuchs, supra, 1 Cal.3d 50, 54.) Here there was no impediment to Pittman's tender of performance.

Canham requests sanctions for a frivolous appeal. But sanctions should be used most sparingly to deter only the most egregious conduct. (In re Marriage of Flaherty (1982) 31 Cal.3d 637, 651 [183 Cal.Rptr. 508, 646 P.2d 179].) This appeal does not qualify for sanctions.

The judgment is affirmed. Costs are awarded to Canham.

Stone (S. J.), P. J., and Yegan, J., concurred.

Parsons v. Bristol Development Co.

Supreme Court of California, 1965.
62 Cal.2d 861

TRAYNOR, C. J.

In December 1960 defendant Bristol Development Company entered into a written contract with plaintiff engaging him as an architect to design an office building for a lot in Santa Ana and to assist in supervising construction. Plaintiff's services were to be performed in two phases. He completed phase one, drafting preliminary plans and specifications, on January 20, 1961, and Bristol paid him $600.

The dispute concerns Bristol's obligation to pay plaintiff under phase two of the contract. The contract provided that "a condition precedent to any duty or obligation on the part of the Owner [Bristol] to commence, continue or complete Phase 2 or to pay Architect any fee therefor, shall be the obtaining of economically satisfactory financing arrangements which will enable Owner, in its sole judgment, to construct the project at a cost which in the absolute decision of the Owner shall be economically feasible." It further provided that when Bristol notified plaintiff to proceed with phase two it should pay him an estimated 25 per cent of his fee, and that it would be obligated to pay the remaining 75 per cent "only from construction loan funds."

Using plaintiff's preliminary plans and specifications, Bristol obtained from a contractor an estimate of $1,020,850 as the cost of construction, including the architect's fee of 6 per cent. On the basis of this estimate, it received an offer from a savings and loan company for a construction loan upon condition that it show clear title to the Santa Ana lot and execute a first trust deed in favor of the loan company.

Shortly after obtaining this offer from the loan company, Bristol wrote plaintiff on March 14, 1961, to proceed under phase two of the contract. In accordance with the contract, Bristol paid plaintiff $12,000, an estimated 25 per cent of his total fee. Thereafter, plaintiff began to draft final plans and specifications for the building.

Bristol, however, was compelled to abandon the project because it was unable to show clear title to the Santa Ana lot and thus meet the requirements for obtaining a construction loan. Bristol's title became subject to dispute on May 23, 1961, when defendant James Freeman filed an action against Bristol claiming an adverse title. (Freeman had previously conveyed the Santa Ana lot to Bristol on October 1, 1960, with the understanding that Bristol would construct an office building upon the lot and pay Freeman an annuity.) On August 15, 1961, Bristol notified plaintiff to stop work on the project.

Plaintiff brought an action against Bristol and Freeman to recover for services performed under the contract and to foreclose a mechanic's lien on the Santa Ana lot. The trial court, sitting without a jury, found that Bristol's obligation to make further payment under the contract was conditioned upon the existence of construction loan funds. On the ground that this condition to plaintiff's right to further payment was not satisfied, the court entered judgment for defendants. Plaintiff appeals.

The trial court properly admitted evidence extrinsic to the written instrument to determine the circumstances under which the parties contracted and the purpose of the contract. (Code Civ. Proc., § 1860; Civ. Code, § 1647; see Corbin, The Interpretation of Words and the Parol Evidence Rule, 50 Cornell L.Q. 161.) There is no conflict in that evidence. Bristol contends, however, that an appellate court is compelled to accept any reasonable interpretation of a written instrument adopted by a trial court whether or not extrinsic evidence has been introduced to interpret the instrument and whether or not that evidence, if any, is in conflict. We do not agree with this contention.

Since there has been confusion concerning the rules for appellate review of the interpretation of written instruments (see Estate of Platt, 21 Cal.2d 343, 352 [131 P.2d 825] [concurring opinion]; Estate of Shannon, 231 Cal.App.2d 886, 889-890 [42 Cal.Rptr. 278]), it is appropriate here to define the scope of such review.

The interpretation of a written instrument, even though it involves what might properly be called questions of fact (see Thayer, Preliminary Treatise on Evidence, pp. 202-204), is essentially a judicial function to be exercised according to the generally accepted canons of interpretation so that the purposes of the instrument may be given effect. (See Civ. Code, §§ 1635-1661; Code Civ. Proc., §§ 1856-1866.) Extrinsic evidence is "admissible to interpret the instrument, but not to give it a meaning to which it is not reasonably susceptible" (Coast Bank v. Minderhout, 61 Cal.2d 311, 315 [38 Cal.Rptr. 505, 392 P.2d 265]; Nofziger v. Holman, 61 Cal.2d 526, 528 [39 Cal.Rptr. 384, 393 P.2d 696]; Imbach v. Schultz, 58 Cal.2d 858, 860 [27 Cal.Rptr. 160, 377 P.2d 272]), and it is the instrument itself that must be given effect. (Civ. Code, §§ 1638, 1639; Code Civ. Proc., § 1856.) It is therefore solely a judicial function to interpret a written instrument unless the interpretation turns upon the credibility of extrinsic evidence. Accordingly, "An appellate court is not bound by a construction of the contract based solely upon the terms of the written instrument without the aid of evidence [citations], where there is no conflict in the evidence [citations], or a determination has been made upon incompetent evidence [citation]." (Estate of Platt, 21 Cal.2d 343, 352 [131 P.2d 825]. Accord,

Moore v. Wood, 26 Cal.2d 621, 629-630 [160 P.2d 772]; Western Coal & Mining Co. v. Jones, 27 Cal.2d 819, 826-827 [167 P.2d 719, 164 A.L.R. 685]; Estate of Wunderle, 30 Cal.2d 274, 280 [181 P.2d 874]; Estate of Fleming, 31 Cal.2d 514, 523 [190 P.2d 611]; Meyer v. State Board of Equalization, 42 Cal.2d 376, 381 [267 P.2d 257].)

It is true that cases have said that even in the absence of extrinsic evidence the trial court's interpretation of a written instrument must be accepted "if such interpretation is reasonable, or if [it] is one of two or more reasonable constructions of the instrument" (Prickett v. Royal Ins. Co., 56 Cal.2d 234, 237 [14 Cal.Rptr. 675, 363 P.2d 907, 86 A.L.R.2d 711]; Lundin v. Hallmark Productions, Inc. 161 Cal.App.2d 698, 701 [327 P.2d 166]), or if it is "equally tenable" with the appellate court's interpretation (Estate of Northcutt, 16 Cal.2d 683, 690 [107 P.2d 607]; accord, Estate of Cuneo, 60 Cal.2d 196, 201 [32 Cal.Rptr. 409, 384 P.2d 1]). Such statements are not in conflict with Estate of Platt, supra, 21 Cal.2d 343, if they are interpreted, as they should be, to mean only that an appellate court must determine that the trial court's interpretation is erroneous before it may properly reverse a judgment. (See Estate of Shannon, 231 Cal.App.2d 886, 893 [42 Cal.Rptr. 278].) They do not mean that the appellate court is absolved of its duty to interpret the instrument.

Since there is no conflict in the extrinsic evidence in the present case we must make an independent determination of the meaning of the contract. After providing for payment of an estimated 25 per cent of plaintiff's fee upon written notice to proceed with phase two, paragraph 4 of the contract makes the following provisions for payment:

"4. . . .

"(a) . . .

"(b) Upon completion of final working plans, specifications and engineering, or authorized commencement of construction, whichever is later, a sum equal to Seventy-Five (75%) Per Cent of the fee for services in Phase 2, less all previous payments made on account of fee; provided, however, that this payment shall be made only from construction loan funds.

"(c) The balance of the fee shall be paid in equal monthly payments commencing with the first day of the month following payments as set forth in Paragraph 4(b); provided, however, that Ten (10%) Per Cent of the fee based upon the reasonable estimated cost of construction shall be withheld until thirty (30) days after the Notice of Completion of the project has been filed.

"(d) If any work designed or specified by the Architect is abandoned of [sic] suspended in whole or in part, the Architect is to be paid forthwith to the extent that his services have been rendered under the preceding terms of this paragraph. Should such abandonment or suspension occur before the Architect has completed any particular phase of the work which entitles him to a partial payment as aforesaid, the Architect's fee shall be prorated based upon the percentage of the work completed under that particular phase and shall be payable forthwith."

Invoking the provision that "payment shall be made only from construction loan funds," Bristol contends that since such funds were not obtained it is obligated to pay plaintiff no more than he has already received under the contract.

Plaintiff, on the other hand, contends that he performed 95 per cent of his work on phase two and is entitled to that portion of his fee under subdivision (d) of paragraph 4 less the previous payment he received. He contends that subdivision (d) is a "savings clause" designed to secure partial payment if, for any reason, including the lack of funds, the project was abandoned or suspended, plaintiff would limit the construction loan condition to subdivision (b), for it provides "that this payment shall be made only from construction loan funds" (emphasis added), whereas the other subdivisions are not expressly so conditioned.

The construction loan condition, however, cannot reasonably be limited to subdivision (b), for subdivisions (c) and (d) both refer to the terms of subdivision (b) and must therefore be interpreted with reference to those terms. Thus, the "balance of the fee" payable "in equal monthly payments" under subdivision (c) necessarily refers to the preceding subdivisions of paragraph 4. In the absence of evidence to the contrary, subdivision (d), upon which plaintiff relies, must likewise be interpreted to incorporate the construction loan condition (Civ. Code, § 1641), for it makes explicit reference to payment under preceding subdivisions by language such as "under the preceding terms" and "partial payment as aforesaid." Subdivision (d) merely provides for accelerated payment upon the happening of a contingency. It contemplates, however, that construction shall have begun, for it provides for prorated payment upon the abandonment or suspension in whole or in part of "any work designed or specified by the Architect." Implicit in the scheme is the purpose to provide, after initial payments, for a series of payments from construction loan funds, with accelerated payment from such funds in the event that construction was abandoned or suspended. Although plaintiff was guaranteed an estimated 25 per cent of his fee if the project was frustrated before construction, further payment was contemplated only upon the commencement of construction. This interpretation is supported by evidence that plaintiff knew that Bristol's ability to undertake construction turned upon the availability of loan funds. Accordingly, the trial court properly determined that payments beyond an estimated 25 per cent of plaintiff's fee for phase two were to be made only from construction loan funds.

When "payment of money is to be made from a specific fund, and not otherwise, the failure of such fund will defeat the right of recovery." (Rains v. Arnett, 189 Cal.App.2d 337, 347 [11 Cal.Rptr. 299].) Although there are exceptions to this rule, plaintiff has neither alleged nor proved facts that entitle him to recover on the ground of any exception.

Each party to a contract has a duty to do what the contract presupposes he will do to accomplish its purpose. (Bewick v. Mecham, 26 Cal.2d 92, 99 [156 P.2d 757, 157 A.L.R. 1277].) Thus, "A party who prevents fulfillment of a condition of his own obligation ... cannot rely on such condition to defeat his liability." (Bewick v. Mecham, supra, 26 Cal.2d at p. 99; Pacific Venture Corp. v. Huey, 15 Cal.2d 711, 717 [104 P.2d 641].)plaintiff, however, has not shown that Bristol failed to make the proper and reasonable efforts that were contemplated to secure the loan from which he was to be paid. (Cf. Rosenheim v. Howze, 179 Cal. 309 [176 P. 456].) The risk that a loan might not be obtained even though Bristol acted properly and in good faith was a risk clearly anticipated even though the reason the loan failed may not have been foreseen.

Nor has plaintiff established grounds for applying the doctrine of equitable estoppel to deny Bristol the right to invoke the construction loan condition. (See Code Civ. Proc., § 1962, subd. 3.) If, by its letter of March 14, asking plaintiff to proceed with his work under phase two of the contract, Bristol had induced plaintiff to believe that funds had been obtained, and if plaintiff had reasonably relied upon such representation, Bristol could not invoke the condition to defeat its contractual liability. Reasonable reliance resulting in a foreseeable prejudicial change in position is the essence of equitable estoppel, and therefore a compelling basis for preventing a party from invoking a condition that he represented as being satisfied. (See Crestline Mobile Homes Mfg. Co. v. Pacific Finance Corp., 54 Cal.2d 773, 778-781 [8 Cal.Rptr. 448, 356 P.2d 192]; cf. Drennan v. Star Paving Co., 51 Cal.2d 409, 414-415 [333 P.2d 757].) Bristol, however, did not represent that funds had been obtained, and plaintiff did not reasonably rely upon the existence of construction loan funds when he undertook work under phase two of the contract. A representative of Bristol told plaintiff before he began phase two of his work that although Bristol would be able to pay plaintiff $12,000, an estimated 25 per cent of his fee, "they would not be able to proceed unless actual construction funds were obtained." Plaintiff, knowing that funds had not been obtained, nevertheless chose to proceed with his work on the project.

Finally, plaintiff has not shown that Bristol breached the duty to give him notice when it became clear that construction funds could not be obtained. Without such funds the purpose of the contract would have been frustrated and plaintiff could not have been paid the balance of his fee. Plaintiff therefore would have been excused from performing so long as there was a reasonable doubt as to his compensation. Whether or not such funds were obtained was a matter peculiarly within Bristol's knowledge. Accordingly, Bristol had a duty to notify plaintiff that the project was imperiled when Freeman filed his action against Bristol on May 23, for Bristol then knew or should have known that it would be unable to obtain a loan. Plaintiff, however, has not shown that he failed to receive such notice, and even if it is assumed that he had no notice, he did not prove the extent to which he suffered damages by continuing to work after he should have received notice.

The judgment is affirmed.

McComb, J., Peters, J., Tobriner, J., Peek, J., Mosk, J., and Burke, J., concurred.

Beverly Way Associates v. Barham

California Court of Appeal Second District, Division Four, 1990
226 Cal.App.3d 49, 276 Cal.Rptr. 240

EPSTEIN, J.

This case presents a single principal issue for resolution. It is whether, in a contract for the sale of real estate, the buyer's communicated rejection of a "satisfaction" condition precedent to its obligation to purchase terminates the contract so that the buyer cannot later waive the condition and enforce the agreement. We conclude that it does. We therefore affirm the decision of the trial court, which reached the same conclusion in its order sustaining a demurrer to the buyer's suit to enforce the contract.

Factual and Procedural Summary

This case reaches us on the basis of a successful assertion of a general demurrer without leave to amend. "In assessing the sufficiency of a complaint against a general demurrer, we must treat the demurrer as admitting all material facts properly pleaded." (Glaire v. LaLanne-Paris Health Spa, Inc. (1974) 12 Cal.3d 915, 918 [117 Cal.Rptr. 541, 528 P.2d 357].) Since the demurrer was sustained without leave to amend, we are also mindful of the policy that "the allegations of the complaint must be liberally construed with a view to obtaining substantial justice among the parties." (Youngman v. Nevada Irrigation Dist. (1969) 70 Cal.2d 240, 244-245 [74 Cal.Rptr. 398, 449 P.2d 462].)

The verified complaint in this case incorporates a series of documents by reference that thoroughly chronicle the agreement of the parties. The following summary is based on that pleading, including its incorporated annexes.

In July 1988, the defendant Phyllis Barham (seller) owned a residential building in Long Beach. On July 7, 1988, she executed a contract to sell the building to plaintiff, Beverly Way Associates, a California general partnership (buyer). The purchase price was $3.9 million. The contract provided for the opening of escrow and for a closing within 60 days thereafter. There was no "time is of the essence" provision.

Paragraph 5 of the agreement (contingencies) provided that the "Buyer's obligations to purchase the Property shall be conditioned upon" approval by the buyer of a number of specified inspections and documents, and delivery of clear title and conveyance documents at the close of escrow. The most important provision in the agreement, for purposes of our review, is paragraph 5(a) (Approval by Buyer of Inspection and Documents). The initial portion of that provision states:

"Buyer (and Buyer's consultants) shall have twenty-eight (28) business days after receipt of each of the following items in which to inspect and approve (and Seller shall immediately upon acceptance of this offer deliver to Buyer true copies of the following documents and access to Property to inspect) and it shall be a condition to Buyer's obligation to close escrow that Buyer shall have approved...." There follows a listing of seven categories of matters to be approved. The fourth of these includes a certified ALTA survey of the property showing all improvements thereon and the location of all exceptions to the title referred to in the preliminary title report.

Although the 60-day provision in the contract would have had escrow close by mid-September, the parties continued to take actions called for under the agreement for a considerable time thereafter. The seller furnished the material required in paragraph 5 on November 15, 1988. On December 2, 1988, a date well within the 28-day period for buyer approval, the buyer wrote the seller rejecting the land survey.

The buyer's letter recites that it had received the survey delivered by the seller, and advised that, "We reluctantly disapprove of the matters disclosed on the Survey and relating to the Property." The following six paragraphs describe the reasons for the rejection in detail. The principal concern appeared to be that a concrete electrical room was constructed on one of the garage parking spaces, and that this reduced the parking spaces to a number below the amount shown on the tract map. According to the buyer's letter, "This fact and its implications represent a serious matter affecting the lawful use, value, title, utility, financeability and marketability of the Property."

The letter continued with an expression of hope that the problems just recited could be surmounted with "some effort, additional time and expense." Rather than cancel, the buyer proposed "some alternatives to keep the deal alive."

Two alternatives were put forward. The first proposed that the seller give the buyer an option until July 1, 1989, to purchase the property for the original price. In return, the seller would have the right to recover $50,000 of the $75,000 deposited in escrow in the event that the buyer should fail to exercise the option.

The second alternative would have reconstructed the agreement into a lease-purchase arrangement, under which the buyer would take possession of the property and pay rent to the seller, and would have an option to purchase "before a certain specified date."

The letter closed with a request to the seller to "advise as to how you wish to proceed with this transaction."

According to the complaint, there was no further communication between the parties until February 2, 1989. On that date, the buyer sent the second letter pertinent to the case. In this correspondence, it advised that, "We are prepared to waive our objections to such items and to proceed to close escrow within 45 days of Ms. Barham's confirmation to us and to escrow that this will be satisfactory to Ms. Barham." The reference to "such items" was to the problems discussed in the December 2, 1988, letter.

The seller then instructed escrow to immediately prepare cancellation instructions and to transmit them to the parties for their inspection. The buyer demanded that seller go forward with the original sale transaction. The seller refused, and the buyer sued for specific performance. (May 19, 1989.) It also filed a lis pendens. The seller demurred and moved to expunge the lis pendens. The demurrer and motion were heard together on July 21, 1989. The demurrer was sustained. The trial court concluded that, "By disapproving the survey on December 12, 1988, plaintiff buyer terminated the contract and cannot sue on same. The court is satisfied that, if plaintiff were granted leave to amend, it would not plead around exhibit D." (The Dec. 2, 1988, letter.) The court therefore declined to grant leave to amend. It also expunged the lis pendens. This appeal followed.

Discussion

Both sides to this appeal treat the buyer's right of approval under paragraph 5 of the contract as a condition precedent in favor of the buyer. They are quite correct in that characterization.

Section 1436 of the Civil Code (a part of the original 1872 codification) defines a condition precedent as one "which is to be performed before some right dependent thereon accrues, or some act dependent thereon is performed." Although the Restatement avoids the terms "condition precedent" and "condition subsequent," preferring the word "condition" alone to define the former concept (see Rest.2d Contracts, § 224, com. e), the definition it provides is essentially the same for purposes of the issue in this case: "A condition is an event, not certain to occur, which must occur, unless its non-occurrence is excused, before performance under a contract becomes due." (Rest.2d, Contracts, § 224.) This is consistent with the view of the text writers (see 5 Williston, Contracts (3d ed. 1961) §§ 666A, 675A, pp. 141, 189; 3A Corbin, Contracts (1960) § 647, p. 102; 1 Witkin, Summary of Cal. Law (9th ed. 1987) Contracts, § 729, p. 659) and with the national majority view (see Annot., Sale of Realty-Conditions-Financing (1962) 81 A.L.R.2d 1338). It also is consistent with the California authorities. (See Mattei v. Hopper (1958) 51 Cal.2d 119, 122 [330 P.2d 625]; Kadner v. Shields (1971) 20 Cal.App.3d 251, 257 [97 Cal.Rptr. 742].) Finally, we find it significant that the contract language tracks the California statutory definition of a condition precedent as well as the Restatement definition. Paragraph 5(a) specifically provides that "it shall be a condition to Buyer's obligation to close escrow that Buyer shall have approved" of the items specified in the further provisions of the subparagraph, including the property survey.

We turn to an examination of the nature of the buyer's power to approve the condition precedent and to the effect of its disapproval.

Most of the textual and case material on "satisfaction" conditions precedent turns on whether an objective or subjective standard is to be used in reviewing the reasonableness of its exercise, whether good faith is required, and whether such clauses render agreements that include them unenforceable. (See Rest. 2d, Contracts, § 228 (objective standard preferred); 5 Williston, supra, 675A (honest judgment required; contracts generally upheld); Mattei v. Hopper, supra, 51 Cal.2d 119 (contracts not illusory).) We put these issues to one side, since neither party questions the reasonableness, under any standard, of the buyer's exercise of its approval authority in the December 2, 1988, letter, let alone its good faith in doing so.

The effect of a buyer's power to approve documentation required in a contract for the purchase of real estate "is to give the buyer an option not to consummate the purchase if it fails to meet the condition," at least so long as the buyer acts reasonably and in the exercise of good faith. (Crescenta Valley Moose Lodge v. Bunt (1970) 8 Cal.App.3d 682, 687 [87 Cal.Rptr. 428].) Stated another way, the contract gives the buyer the "power and privilege" of termination in the event that it reasonably concludes that the condition has not been fulfilled. (See Mattei v. Hopper, supra, 51 Cal.2d at p. 122 ["satisfactory" lease]; see also Fowler v. Ross (1983) 142 Cal.App.3d 472, 478 [191 Cal.Rptr. 183] [effect of failure of condition that buyer obtain financing was termination of contract, even though contract did not include language that specifically so provided].)

Under the California rule, the holder of a formal option loses the right to exercise it once it has communicated a formal rejection, and this is so even though the purported exercise occurs within the time specified in the option agreement. (Landberg v. Landberg (1972) 24 Cal.App.3d 742, 757 [101 Cal.Rptr. 335].) If anything, the situation of a party who has a power to approve or disapprove a condition precedent and also exercises it by disapproval, presents an a fortiori case.

Except for the judicial gloss that the power of rejection must be exercised reasonably, the party having the power to approve or reject is in the same position as a contract offeree. It is hornbook law that an unequivocal rejection by an offeree, communicated to the offeror, terminates the offer; even if the offeror does no further act, the offeree cannot later purport to accept the offer and thereby create enforceable contractual rights against the offeror. (See Rest.2d, Contracts, § 38, illus. 1, and authority cited in Reporter's Note; 1 Witkin, Summary of Cal. Law, supra, § 172.)

There can be no question but that the buyer exercised its power of disapproval in this case. The December 2, 1988, letter said so expressly ("[w]e reluctantly disapprove the matter disclosed on the Survey and relating to the Property"). This rejection, communicated to the seller, terminated the contract. It left the buyer with no power to create obligations against the seller by a late "waiver" of its objections and acceptance of the proffered documentation.

The fact that the buyer considered the existing contract to be at an end is reflected not only in the unequivocal language of its disapproval, which we have quoted, but also by its effort to keep the "deal alive" by proposing two entirely new formulations that were novel to the agreement of the parties: an option to purchase, and a lease-purchase arrangement. It may be inferred that the buyer was hoping to find a way to acquire the property, but it cannot be doubted that it was unwilling to do so on the basis of what had been presented by the seller.

The buyer presents several arguments in aid of its position that its February 2, 1989, "waiver" and acceptance letter bound the seller to go through with the deal. None of them has merit.

The buyer points out that the contract did not contain a "time is of the essence" clause. From that it argues that it could exercise its power to approve or waive the paragraph 5 documentation within a "reasonable" time, and that whether its doing so two and one-half months after the documents were furnished (instead of within twenty-eight days, as the contract provided) was reasonable is a question of fact. Given the procedural posture of the case, this may be allowed. But it is irrelevant because the buyer exercised its power by rejecting the documentation. The case is entirely different from a simple failure to accept or reject for a period beyond a time specified in the agreement.

For the same reason, we cannot credit the buyer's purported waiver of the objections it had raised in the December 2, 1988, letter. That letter did more than express a concern about the land survey; it disapproved the survey. Approval of the survey was an express condition precedent to the buyer's obligation to perform. The February 2, 1989, letter is consistent with this result. It did not unequivocally do anything. Instead, it stated that the buyer was "prepared" to waive its objection to the survey, and to proceed to close escrow within 45 days of the seller's confirmation that this would be satisfactory to her, and it asked whether it was satisfactory to her. This language reads far more like a renewed offer for a contract than an assertion that the parties have an agreement to which the seller is still bound.

The buyer also argues that since the contract does not specify the effect a failure to approve the documentation, it cannot be concluded that the effect was to terminate the agreement, and that parol evidence should be admitted on that issue. This argument suffers from the same infirmity as buyer's other contentions. The buyer did not just fail to approve the documentation; it disapproved it. Absent a contrary agreement, the legal effect of that act was to terminate the contract. The verified pleading contains no suggestion of a contrary agreement, and none is presented to us in the arguments of the parties. Given that, we see no basis for parol evidence.

As we have seen, the trial court sustained the demurrer without leave to amend because it did not believe that the buyer could plead around the December 2, 1988, rejection letter. Nor do we, and nothing to the contrary has been suggested in the briefs. We conclude that the trial court correctly resolved the issues before it.

Disposition

The order of dismissal is affirmed. Respondent shall have her costs on appeal.

Woods (A. M.), P. J., and Goertzen, J., concurred.

Real Estate Brokers and Conditions

A common type of listing agreement is one wherein the broker agrees to produce a buyer ready, willing and able to purchase the described property on the terms and conditions set forth in the listing and the seller agrees to accept the offer on the terms set forth in the agreement. Under such an agreement, it is well settled the broker's commission is earned upon the production of a ready, willing and able buyer. The broker or agent is ordinarily entitled to the commission when he produces a purchaser, ready, able and willing to buy the property for the price and on the terms specified by the principal, regardless of whether a valid contract of sale is entered into by the buyer and seller, or whether the sale is ever consummated. (See, *Seck v. Foulks* (1972,) 25 Cal.App.3d 556, 571-572) Production of a buyer ready, willing and able to purchase on the seller's terms is a condition precedent to the broker's right to a commission.

Condition or Promise?

Dependent and Independent Promises

Unless the parties clearly express a contrary intent, the law presumes that mutual promises in a contract are dependent. In other words, the law constructs or implies a condition that performance by one party is a condition precedent to the duty of the other party to perform. The parties can avoid this presumption by agreeing that each party's duty to perform is independent of the other party's duty. Why would the parties want to do that? Consider this example: the typical fire insurance policy is subject to at least two conditions; that there be a loss by fire and that the insurance premiums be paid up. A lender who holds a mortgage on the structure might find itself without security for its loan if the insurance company could site the owner/mortgagor's failure to timely make premium payments as a failure of condition when a claim is made against the policy. To afford even greater protection to the secured creditor, it became customary to modify the loss payable clause to provide that the lender's coverage could not be forfeited by the act or default of any other person. This modified provision came to be known as a standard mortgage clause. Insurance companies have used standard mortgage clauses in real estate fire insurance policies since at least 1878. (See, e.g., *Witherow v. United American Ins. Co.* (1929) 101 Cal.App. 334.) In effect it means that the duty to pay the mortgagee in the event of a loss is independent of the duty of the mortgagor to pay premiums.

"Pay If Paid" or "Pay When Paid?"

Wm. R. Clarke Corp. v. Safeco Ins. Co.

Supreme Court of California, 1997
15 Cal.4th 882, 64 Cal.Rptr.2d 578; 938 P.2d 372

KENNARD, J.

In recent years, general contractors in California have begun to insert "pay if paid" provisions into their agreements with subcontractors. A pay if paid provision makes payment by the owner to the general contractor a condition precedent to the general contractor's obligation to pay the subcontractor for work the subcontractor has performed.

In other jurisdictions, the majority view is that, if reasonably possible, clauses in construction subcontracts stating that the subcontractor will be paid when the general contractor is paid will not be construed as establishing true conditions precedent, but rather as merely fixing the usual time for payment to the subcontractor, with the implied understanding that the subcontractor in any event has an unconditional right to payment within a reasonable time. (See, e.g., Koch v. Construction Technology, Inc. (Tenn. 1996) 924 S.W.2d 68; Power & Pollution Svcs. v. Suburban Piping (1991) 74 Ohio App.3d 89 [598 N.E.2d 69]; OBS Co., Inc. v. Pace Const. Corp. (Fla. 1990) 558 So.2d 404; Southern St. Masonry v. J.A. Jones Const. (La. 1987) 507 So.2d 198; Thos. J. Dyer Co. v. Bishop International Engineering Co. (6th Cir. 1962) 303 F.2d 655.) This approach has been followed in California. (Yamanishi v. Bleily & Collishaw, Inc. (1972) 29 Cal.App.3d 457, 462463 [105 Cal.Rptr. 580]; see also Rubin v. Fuchs (1969) 1 Cal.3d 50, 53 [81 Cal.Rptr. 373, 459 P.2d 925] [stating that "provisions of a contract will not be construed as conditions precedent in the absence of language plainly requiring such construction"].) A contract clause that has been construed in this fashion is sometimes referred to as a "pay when paid" rather than a "pay if paid" provision. (See Kirksey, "Minimum Decencies"-A Proposed Resolution of the "Pay-When-Paid"/"Pay-If-Paid" Dichotomy (Jan. 1992) Construction Law. 1.)

If it is not reasonably possible to construe the contractual provision as other than a condition precedent, then courts must decide whether public policy permits enforcement of a contractual provision that may result in the subcontractor's forfeiting all right to payment for work performed. The high court of New York has concluded that a true pay if paid provision in a subcontract for construction work is void as against public policy. (West-Fair Elec. v. Aetna Cas. & Sur. Co. (1995) 87 N.Y.2d 148, 157 [638 N.Y.S.2d 394, 398, 661 N.E.2d 967, 971].) In Illinois, North Carolina, and Wisconsin, pay if paid provisions have been declared void and unenforceable by statute. (770 Ill. Comp. Stat. Ann. 60/21; N.C. Gen. Stat. §22C-2 (1991); Wis. Stat. §779.135.) The validity of a true pay if paid provision presents a question of first impression in this court.

We granted review in this case to determine whether a subcontractor may collect on a general contractor's payment bond for work it has performed under a contract containing a pay if paid provision when the owner has not paid the general contractor. We conclude that pay if paid provisions like the one at issue here are contrary to the public policy of this state and therefore unenforceable because they effect an impermissible indirect waiver or forfeiture of the subcontractors' constitutionally protected mechanic's lien rights in the event of nonpayment by the owner. Because they are unenforceable, pay if paid provisions in construction subcontracts do not insulate either general contractors or their payment bond sureties from their contractual obligations to pay subcontractors for work performed.

I. Facts

In 1990, the owner of a commercial building in Los Angeles entered into a contract with Keller Construction Co., Ltd. (Keller), as general contractor, for rehabilitation work on the building. Keller in turn entered into subcontracts for this project with, among others, Wm. R. Clarke Corporation, Barsotti's, Inc., Garvin Fire Protection Systems, Inc., and Church and Larsen, Inc. (collectively, the subcontractors). Each subcontract contained a pay if paid provision and three of the four subcontracts also included an addendum reiterating the pay if paid limitation yet also purporting to preserve the subcontractors' mechanic's lien rights and to make those rights the subcontractors' "sole remedy" in the event the owner failed to pay Keller.

At the owner's insistence, and pursuant to the terms of the general contract, Keller obtained a labor and material payment bond from defendant Safeco Insurance Company of America (Safeco) to protect the owner from mechanic's lien claims by subcontractors and material suppliers. The bond recited that it was a payment bond as defined in Civil Code section 3096 and that it had been executed to comply with title 15 (Works of Improvement) of the Civil Code. The bond stated that Keller, as principal, and Safeco, as surety, "are held and firmly bound unto any and all persons who perform labor upon or bestow skill or other necessary services on, or furnish materials or lease equipment to be used or consumed in, or furnish appliances, teams, or power contributing to the work described in [the general contract between the owner and Keller], a copy of which contract is or may be attached hereto, and is hereby referred to, in the sum of" $16.5 million. The bond further stated: "Now, Therefore, the Condition of This Obligation Is Such, That if the Principal shall pay, or cause to be paid in full, the claims of all persons performing labor upon or bestowing skill or other necessary services on, or furnishing materials or leasing equipment to be used or consumed in or furnishing appliances, teams or power contributing to such work, then this obligation shall be void; otherwise to remain in full force and effect." In the final provision relevant here, the bond stated: "No suit, action or proceeding may be maintained on this bond unless the person claiming hereunder shall previously have either, recorded a mechanic's lien claim pursuant to Title 15, Works of Improvement, of the Civil Code of the State of California or given notice to the Surety on this bond before the expiration of the time prescribed in said statute for recording a lien." The bond was duly executed by the authorized agents of Keller and Safeco, and it was duly recorded.

After substantial work had been completed on the project, the owner stopped making payments to Keller, apparently as a result of the owner's insolvency. Keller then declined to pay the subcontractors, which recorded mechanic's liens and filed separate actions against Safeco seeking recovery under the payment bond. The actions were deemed related and were assigned to the same judge for all purposes. Three of the actions were resolved by summary judgment, the fourth by trial to the court. In each action, the trial court granted judgment for the subcontractors and against Safeco. Safeco appealed from each judgment. After consolidating the appeals, the Court of Appeal affirmed each judgment against Safeco.

II. Analysis and Resolution

Safeco argues here, as it did in the trial court and in the Court of Appeal, that its obligation under the payment bond never matured because the liability of a surety on a private works payment bond is no greater than that of its principal, and Keller, the principal on the payment bond issued by Safeco, never incurred any obligation to pay the subcontractors for their work because a condition precedent to Keller's contractual obligation to pay the subcontractors-that Keller receive payment from the owner for the subcontractors' work-was never satisfied. Safeco's argument thus assumes the validity of the pay if paid provisions in the subcontracts, under which payment from the owner to Keller was a condition precedent to Keller's obligation to pay the subcontractors. As will appear, we conclude that the assumption is false.

Our state Constitution provides: "Mechanics, persons furnishing materials, artisans, and laborers of every class, shall have a lien upon the property upon which they have bestowed labor or furnished material for the value of such labor done and material furnished; and the Legislature shall provide, by law, for the speedy and efficient enforcement of such liens." (Cal. Const., art. XIV, § 3.) As this court has said, "The mechanic's lien is the only creditors' remedy stemming from constitutional command and our courts 'have uniformly classified the mechanics' lien laws as remedial legislation, to be liberally construed for the protection of laborers and materialmen.' [Citation.]" (Hutnick v. United States Fidelity & Guaranty Co. (1988) 47 Cal.3d 456, 462 [253 Cal.Rptr. 236, 763 P.2d 1326].) "[S]tate policy strongly supports the preservation of laws which give the laborer and materialman security for their claims." (Connolly Development, Inc. v. Superior Court (1976) 17 Cal.3d 803, 827 [132 Cal.Rptr. 477, 553 P.2d 637].)

By law, a subcontractor may not waive its mechanic's lien rights except under certain specified circumstances. Subdivision (a) of Civil Code section 3262 provides: "Neither the owner nor original contractor by any term of their contract, or otherwise, shall waive, affect, or impair the claims and liens of other persons whether with or without notice except by their written consent, and any term of the contract to that effect shall be null and void. Any written consent given by any claimant pursuant to this subdivision shall be null, void, and unenforceable unless and until the claimant executes and delivers a waiver and release. Such a waiver and release shall be binding and effective to release the owner, construction lender, and surety on a payment bond from claims and liens only if the waiver and release follows substantially one of the forms set forth in this section and is signed by the claimant or his or her authorized agent, and, in the case of a conditional release, there is evidence of payment to the claimant. Evidence of payment may be by the claimant's endorsement on a single or joint payee check which has been paid by the bank upon which it was drawn or by written acknowledgment of payment given by the claimant."

Subdivision (d) of Civil Code section 3262 provides that a waiver and release of mechanic's lien rights "shall be null, void and unenforceable unless it follows substantially the following forms in the following circumstances:...." The subdivision then lists the text of four lien waivers: (1) a conditional waiver and release upon progress payment; (2) an unconditional waiver and release upon progress payment; (3) a conditional waiver and release upon final payment; and (4) an unconditional waiver and release upon final payment. Thus, under our mechanic's lien law, waiver and release of mechanic's lien rights is permitted only in conjunction with payment, or a promise of payment, and a conditional release is effective only if the claimant is actually paid. (See Cal. Mechanics' Liens and Other Remedies (Cont.Ed.Bar 1988) § 4.21, p. 200.)

Safeco argues that a pay if paid provision in a construction subcontract does not violate Civil Code section 3262's anti-waiver provisions because, under Civil Code section 3140 (limiting a subcontractor's recovery on a mechanic's lien claim to "such amount as may be due him according to the terms of his contract"), mechanic's lien remedies are available only to subcontractors whose payment rights have vested under the terms of their contracts. Absent a contractual right to payment, a subcontractor has no mechanic's lien remedy to enforce. In Safeco's view, a mechanic's lien is merely one remedy that is granted to subcontractors to enforce a contractual right to payment. Absent such a contractual right, there can be no remedy. Thus, according to Safeco, the subcontractors have not waived their mechanic's lien remedy. Rather, they never acquired the contractual payment right that is a necessary precondition to the enforcement of any mechanic's lien remedy.

Strictly speaking, Safeco is correct. A pay if paid provision in a construction agreement does not take the form of a waiver of mechanic's lien rights. Yet "[t]he law respects form less than substance" (Civ. Code, § 3528), and a pay if paid provision is in substance a waiver of mechanic's lien rights because it has the same practical effect as an express waiver of those rights.

The New York high court put it this way: "As the owner here has become insolvent, the owner may never make another contract payment to the general contractor. Because the lack of future payments by the owner is virtually certain, [the plaintiff subcontractor's] right to receive payment has been indefinitely postponed, and plaintiff has effectively waived its right to enforce its mechanics' liens. The waiver has occurred by operation of the pay-when-paid provision because mechanics' liens may not be enforced until a debt becomes due and payable." (West-Fair Elec. v. Aetna Cas. & Sur. Co., supra, 87 N.Y.2d at p. 158 [638 N.Y.S.2d at p. 398, 661 N.E.2d at p. 971].)

We may agree with Safeco that a pay if paid provision is not precisely a waiver of mechanic's lien rights and yet conclude that a pay if paid provision is void because it violates the public policy that underlies the anti-waiver provisions of the mechanic's lien laws. The Legislature's carefully articulated anti-waiver scheme would amount to little if parties to construction contracts could circumvent it by means of pay if paid provisions having effects indistinguishable from waivers prohibited under Civil Code section 3262.

Safeco advances several arguments against the conclusion that pay if paid provisions in construction subcontracts are void as against public policy. We consider these arguments in turn.

Safeco argues that it is established law in this state that pay if paid provisions in construction subcontracts are valid and enforceable. The authority Safeco cites for this proposition is Michel & Pfeffer v. Oceanside Properties, Inc. (1976) 61 Cal.App.3d 433 [132 Cal.Rptr. 179], which we find to be distinguishable. There, under a modification of the subcontractor's agreement with the general contractor, the subcontractor agreed to accept as payment for the final 15 percent of the contract price a pro rata interest in funds the general contractor would receive from either a secured promissory note or the proceeds of an intended sale of the project property. The Court of Appeal concluded that under this agreement the subcontractor had no right to the final payment until the general contractor received funds from one of the two designated sources. (Id. at p. 441.) The Court of Appeal further reasoned that because the general contractor had not received funds from either source, the general contractor was not in default on its agreement, and the subcontractor therefore could not yet recover its final payment either by proceeding against the surety on a payment bond or by foreclosing a mechanic's lien on the project property. (Ibid.)

Although the agreement provision at issue in Michel & Pfeffer v. Oceanside Properties, Inc., supra, 61 Cal.App.3d 433, raises some of the same concerns as a pay if paid provision, it was not such a provision. Nothing in the Court of Appeal's opinion suggests that the final payment to the subcontractor could be delayed indefinitely, nor did the Court of Appeal consider whether, if so, the provision there at issue violated the public policy underlying the anti-waiver provisions of Civil Code section 3262. Accordingly, we do not find the Court of Appeal's decision in that case relevant or helpful in deciding the issue presented here, and Safeco's reliance upon it is misplaced.

In defense of pay if paid provisions, Safeco argues strenuously that the public policy against waivers of mechanic's lien rights is not the only public policy at issue, and that this court should consider also the fundamental public policy served by freedom of contract. Safeco argues that pay if paid provisions should be held valid because they permit general contractors and subcontractors to allocate the risk of owner insolvency in a mutually agreeable manner.

Safeco's argument assumes that the sole purpose and effect of a pay if paid provision in a subcontract is to allocate the risk of owner insolvency. But the provisions at issue here were not so limited. As noted above, the pay if paid provision in each subcontract made the owner's payment to Keller a condition precedent of Keller's obligation to pay the subcontractor "regardless of the reason for Owner's nonpayment, whether attributable to the fault of the Owner, Contractor, Subcontractor or due to any other cause."

In any event, we find Safeco's "freedom of contract" argument unpersuasive in this context. By closely and carefully circumscribing subcontractors' freedom to waive mechanic's lien rights, and by forbidding waivers not accompanied by payment, or a promise of payment, the Legislature has already determined that there are policy considerations here that override the value of freedom of contract. We merely recognize and enforce that legislative policy determination.

Moreover, it is doubtful that enforcement of the pay if paid provisions at issue in this case would be fully consistent with the intent of the contracting parties. All but one of the subcontracts at issue here contained an addendum purporting to reserve mechanic's lien rights and remedies. This addendum is evidence of a contractual intent to allow the subcontractors, in the event of the owner's default in its payment obligations to the general contractor, to obtain payment for work performed by foreclosing mechanic's liens on the project property. Yet the pay if paid provision makes this impossible, because the amount due and unpaid under the subcontract is the measure of the subcontractors' mechanic's liens. Had the subcontractors understood that this reservation of rights was illusory (because under Civil Code section 3140 their recovery on their mechanic's lien claims would be limited to amounts due under their subcontracts), they might never have entered into the subcontracts. In short, the allocation of risks and remedies contemplated by the subcontracts appears to be a statutory impossibility, and this lawsuit must necessarily determine which contracting party will have its expectations frustrated.

In this court, in its consolidated reply brief on the merits, Safeco for the first time has taken the position that "it is not necessary for any party improving real property to establish the validity of a contract claim in order to have a mechanic's lien" and that "[t]he reference in the mechanic's lien laws to the contract price merely is used to set a limit on the amount of a mechanic's lien, rather than to create a condition precedent to the validity of the lien." Safeco appears to argue, in other words, that pay if paid provisions do not preclude the assertion of mechanic's lien claims, and therefore are not against public policy. Safeco cites no authority for this assertion, which is inconsistent with the position Safeco took initially in this court in its brief on the merits. We reject this new position as being contrary to the language of Civil Code section 3140, which provides that a subcontractor's mechanic's lien claim is for "only such amount as may be due him according to the terms of his contract." This statutory language does not merely refer to the contract price; rather, it refers to and incorporates all of "the terms of [the] contract" to determine the amount that is "due" under the subcontract, making this contractually due amount the measure of the subcontractor's mechanic's lien claim.

Safeco's argument fails in another respect as well. Were we to adopt Safeco's proposed construction of Civil Code section 3140, and thereby to conclude that the pay if paid provision merely bars the subcontractors' contract claims against Keller, while fully preserving their mechanic's lien claims (and thus not violating the public policy underlying the anti-waiver provisions of the mechanic's lien laws), this conclusion would not assist either Safeco or Keller because both are obligated by the payment bond to pay all valid mechanic's lien claims. If the subcontractors have valid mechanic's lien claims, as posited by Safeco's argument, then those claims are necessarily enforceable against the payment bond.

Seeking to escape from this inexorable logic, Safeco argues that it incurred no liability on the bond because a surety's obligation on a payment bond is only to answer for the default of its principal. As Safeco observes, the very definition of a surety is "one who promises to answer for the debt, default, or miscarriage of another, or hypothecates property as security therefor." (Civ. Code, § 2787.) Absent a default by the principal, the surety incurs no liability. In this connection, Safeco relies also on Civil Code section 2809, which states that a surety's obligation "must be neither larger in amount nor in other respects more burdensome than that of the principal." Safeco argues that its obligation under the payment bond is simply to answer for any default by Keller in the performance of its contractual payment obligations to the subcontractors. Because payment by the owner was a condition precedent to Keller's contractual payment obligations to the subcontractors, and because that condition was not met, Keller was not in default of any contractual payment obligation to the sub-contractors. Therefore, reasons Safeco, as a surety it incurred no liability on the payment bond.

The fallacy of this reasoning (apart from its erroneous assumption that the pay if paid provisions are valid and enforceable and its reliance on a strained construction of Civil Code section 3140) is that it considers only Keller's contractual liability under the subcontracts, while ignoring Keller's separate and independent liability as principal and co-obligor on the payment bond. Keller's contract with the owner required it to obtain a payment bond, the purpose of which is "to create an additional fund or security for the satisfaction of lien claimants [citations], and also to limit the owner's liability to the contract price [citation]...." (Sudden Lumber Co. v. Singer (1930) 103 Cal.App. 386, 390 [284 P. 477]; accord, Simpson v. Bergmann (1932) 125 Cal.App. 1, 12 [13 P.2d 531].) The payment bond at issue here refers to Keller's contract with the owner, but makes no mention of the subcontracts. The operative language of the bond states that "[Keller], as Principal, and [Safeco], as Surety, are held and firmly bound unto any and all persons who perform labor upon ... the work described in" the general contract.

Keller's obligation under the bond is measured by the terms of the bond and the statutes referenced in the bond. (Southern Heaters Corp. v. N. Y. Cas. Co. (1953) 120 Cal.App.2d 377, 379 [260 P.2d 1048].) Under the bond, Keller assumed an obligation to pay the lien claims of any and all persons, including subcontractors, that performed work on the project identified in the general contract. Liability on the bond thus extends not only to those with whom Keller has entered into subcontracts, but to "everyone who has a right to claim a lien" (Myers v. Alta Construction Co. (1951) 37 Cal.2d 739, 743 [235 P.2d 1]; see also Hammond Lumber Co. v. Willis (1915) 171 Cal. 565, 568-569 [153 P. 947]; Union Asphalt, Inc. v. Planet Ins. Co. (1994) 21 Cal.App.4th 1762 [27 Cal.Rptr.2d 371]). And the liability on the bond to pay mechanic's lien claims fell equally on Keller as principal and Safeco as surety. (See, e.g., Code Civ. Proc., § 996.410, subd. (a) [stating that "[t]he beneficiary may enforce the liability on a bond against both the principal and sureties"].) Thus, the default for which Safeco promised to answer was Keller's default under the bond and not Keller's default under the subcontracts.

We find nothing to the contrary in Flickinger v. Swedlow Engineering Co. (1955) 45 Cal.2d 388 [289 P.2d 214] (Flickinger) or in Lewis & Queen v. N. M. Ball Sons (1957) 48 Cal.2d 141 [308 P.2d 713] (Lewis).

Flickinger, supra, 45 Cal.2d 388, concerned a subcontract for work on a state highway project. The subcontractor was a licensed contractor who later assigned the benefits of the contract to a partnership composed of himself and another licensed contractor. After the work was completed, the general contractor sued both the partnership and the individual partners, who responded with a cross-complaint against the general contractor. The trial court entered judgment that neither party take anything on their opposing claims, and this judgment became final. The original subcontractor then sued the general contractor and its payment bond sureties, arguing a legal theory of recovery different from the one he had unsuccessfully urged by cross-complaint in the earlier action. The trial court granted judgment for the subcontractor, and the general contractor appealed. This court reversed, holding that the subcontractor could and should have asserted any claim arising from the subcontract in the earlier action, and that the claim was therefore barred.

Rejecting the subcontractor's argument that this bar was not good against the payment bond surety, who was not a party to the earlier action, this court stated: "[A]ny right which plaintiff might have had to recover upon the bond was necessarily dependent upon plaintiff's right to recover upon his contract with [the general contractor]. While he had the option to file a cross-complaint on the bond and thereby bring in the surety as a party in the prior action [citation], he was clearly compelled to assert by way of counterclaim, in said prior action, any right which he had against [the general contractor] under the contract which was the basis of [the general contractor]'s prior action. [Citation.] Having omitted to assert directly in that action his alleged rights under the contract, but having elected to assert his alleged rights upon an alleged acount stated with the resulting adverse final judgment on the merits, plaintiff is now barred from relitigating his alleged rights under the contract as the basis for an action against [the general contractor] as the principal on the bond. And as such defense to this action is available to [the general contractor] as the principal, it is likewise available to ... the surety on the bond." (Flickinger, supra, 45 Cal.2d 388, 394.)

In Lewis, supra, 48 Cal.2d 141, a state road construction contract prohibited the general contractor from subcontracting more than 50 percent of the work. Attempting to circumvent this requirement, the general contractor purported to enter into separate equipment rental and subcontract agreements with a partnership that did not have a contractor's license. Later, the partnership sued the general contractor and its payment bond sureties for money due under the rental agreements. The trial court denied recovery. On the partnership's appeal, this court affirmed, relying on Business and Professions Code section 7031, which bars unlicensed contractors from bringing any action for compensation for work requiring a license. After concluding that the partnership could not recover from the general contractor because the rental agreement was a sham and the partnership was actually seeking recovery for work requiring a license, this court considered the partnership's claim against the payment bond sureties. This court noted that Business and Professions Code section 7031 bars not only an unlicensed contractor's action for breach of contract, but also its action to foreclose a mechanic's lien. This court then stated: "The obligation of the sureties on defendant's bonds was not to pay for labor merely by virtue of the fact that it had been expended on [the public work]. It was an obligation to pay only if plaintiff established, without reference to the bond, a legal and valid claim for compensation." (Lewis, supra, 48 Cal.2d 141, 155, citing, inter alia, Flickinger, supra, 45 Cal.2d 388, 393-394.)

Flickinger, supra, 45 Cal.2d 388, and Lewis, supra, 48 Cal.2d 141, both stand for the proposition that a claimant on a labor and material payment bond must "establish[], without reference to the bond, a legal and valid claim for compensation" (id. at p. 155). That proposition is in no way inconsistent with our conclusion here that the payment bond obligates Keller to pay the subcontractors' valid mechanic's lien claims, because a mechanic's lien claim is "a legal and valid claim for compensation." Where the bond is conditioned, as is the Safeco bond at issue here, on the payment of mechanic's lien claims on a particular private work, Flickinger and Lewis require only that a claimant on the bond establish, without reference to the terms of the bond, a legal and valid mechanic's lien claim for that project. Neither Flickinger nor Lewis, nor any other case that has come to our attention, has addressed Safeco's hypothesized situation, in which a subcontractor is able to establish, without reference to the terms of a payment bond, a legal and valid mechanic's lien claim but not a legal and valid claim for breach of contract.

One more appellate decision requires our attention. In Kalfountzos v. Hartford Fire Ins. Co. (1995) 37 Cal.App.4th 1655 [44 Cal.Rptr.2d 714] (Kalfountzos), the Court of Appeal applied the rule of law established in Flickinger, supra, 45 Cal.2d 388, and Lewis, supra, 48 Cal.2d 141. In Kalfountzos, the issue presented was whether a surety on a public works payment bond could assert the defenses and setoffs of a principal whose corporate powers had been suspended for nonpayment of franchise fees. Concluding that the surety could assert the defenses of its principal, the Court of Appeal stated: "The surety must pay on the bond only if the claimant establishes, without reference to the bond, a legal obligation on the part of the principal to pay." (Kalfountzos, supra, 37 Cal.App.4th 1655, 1659, italics added.) The italicized language goes beyond the rule of law declared in Flickinger, supra, 45 Cal.2d 388, and Lewis, supra, 48 Cal.2d 141, on which the Court of Appeal purported to rely, because it requires the claimant on the bond to establish, without reference to the bond, a claim for compensation that is not only legal and valid, but also one that the bond principal would otherwise be obligated to pay. To the extent that Kalfountzos implies that the principal on a payment bond incurs no liability on the bond unless it has a separate payment obligation, contractual or otherwise, the statement is incorrect and is hereby disapproved. When a general contractor executes a statutory labor and material payment bond as principal, the obligation on the bond is not limited to the subcontractors and material suppliers with which the general contractor has executed valid contracts, but extends also to lower tier subcontractors and material suppliers with which the general contractor has no privity of contract, and to which the general contractor owes no payment obligation apart from the bond, provided only that they have valid lien claims for that project. (Myers v. Alta Construction Co., supra, 37 Cal.2d 739, 743; Hammond Lumber Co. v. Willis, supra, 171 Cal. 565, 568-569; Union Asphalt, Inc. v. Planet Ins. Co., supra, 21 Cal.App.4th 1762.)

III. Conclusion

Having concluded that a general contractor's liability to a subcontractor for work performed may not be made contingent on the owner's payment to the general contractor, we conclude that Keller was liable to the subcontractors under their subcontracts for the work they performed and that Safeco, as Keller's surety, was likewise liable on the payment bond.

The judgment of the Court of Appeal is affirmed, and the matter is remanded for further proceedings consistent with this opinion.

George, C. J., Werdegar, J., and Brown, J., concurred.

Chin, J. dissented. (Mosk and Baxter, JJ., concurred in the dissent.)

Excuse of Condition

Performance of a condition precedent is excused when:

(1) The other party refuses to perform his or her own promise, or

(2) The other party prevents or makes impossible the performance of the condition precedent, or

(3) The condition is waived, or

(4) Performance of the condition is impossible, unlawful, or impractical, or

(5) Requiring performance of the condition would substantially frustrate the object or effect of the contract. (See, Cal.Civ.Code § 1441)

(See also, 1 Witkin, Summary of Cal. Law (9th ed. 1987) Contracts, §§ 764-790.)

If a party to an obligation gives notice to another, before the latter is in default, that he or she will not perform the same upon his part, and does not retract such notice before the time at which performance upon his part is due, such other party is entitled to enforce the obligation without previously performing or offering to perform any conditions upon his part in favor of the former party. (Cal.Civ.Code § 1440)

Failure of Consideration

If one party materially fails to perform his or her promise, or materially delays performance, the other party's duty is discharged. However, a slight or partial delay or failure to perform does not discharge or end the other party's duty to perform.

In determining whether a failure to perform is material, the trier of fact is to consider:

(1) The extent of the actual performance or preparation;

(2) The good faith, or lack thereof, of the defaulting party;

(3) The hardship, if any, resulting to the defaulting party; and

(4) The adequacy of damages to compensate the other party for the default.

A duty to perform is discharged or ended by a material failure of consideration even though the party owing the duty is unaware of the failure or has breached his or her own promise. (See, 1 Witkin, Summary of Cal. Law (9th ed. 1987) Contracts, §§ 757-759, 761.)

Drafting Tip — "Time Is of the Essence"

Delay in performance is material only if time of performance is of the essence, that is, if prompt performance is, by the express language of the contract or by its very nature, a vital matter. A late or delayed performance does not ordinarily give rise to a material breach. If the parties intend that a prompt performance is necessary or that failure to perform in a timely manner shall constitute a breach they should insert the following language into their agreement:

Time is of the essence for the completion of the work described in this contract. It is anticipated by the parties that all work described herein will be completed within 30 days of the date of execution, and that any delay in the completion of the work described herein shall constitute a material breach of this contract.

Tender

A tender is an offer of performance. An effective tender has the effect of placing the party to whom the tender is made in default if such person refuses to accept the offer of performance.

To be effective, the tender must:

(1) Be of full and unconditional performance; A party entitled under the contract to the performance of a condition precedent or concurrent may, however, make an

offer of performance dependent upon due performance of the condition precedent or concurrent;

(2) Be made by the party making the tender or by some person on his or her behalf and with that party's consent;

(3) Be made to the party to whom the tender is due or some other person authorized by such party to receive or collect what is due;

(4) Be made at a place appointed by the party to whom the tender is due or a place where the person authorized by that party can be found or if he she cannot be found, at any place within the state;

(5) Be timely; and

(6) Be made in good faith. (See, 1 Witkin, Summary of Cal. Law (9th ed. 1987) Contracts, §§ 714-716.)

Breach of Contract — Essential Elements

An unjustified or unexcused failure to perform a contract is a breach.

The essential elements of such a claim are:

(1) The existence of a valid contract between the parties;

(2) Plaintiff's performance, unless excused;

(3) Defendant's unjustified or unexcused failure to perform; and

(4) Plaintiff had the ability to perform; and

(5) Damages to plaintiff caused by the breach. (See, 1 Witkin, Summary of Cal. Law (9th ed. 1987) Contracts, § 791)

Total and Partial Breach

A breach of contract may be total or partial. If the breach is total, the injured party has the right to terminate the contract. If the breach is partial, there is no such right. A total breach occurs if the breach is material. Materiality depends upon the importance or seriousness of the breach and the probability of the injured party obtaining substantial performance. A slight breach at the outset of performance justifies termination and constitutes a total breach. After substantial commencement of performance, a slight breach which does not materially impact upon the contract, does not justify termination, and does not constitute a total breach. Any breach of contract, whether total or partial, causing measurable injury, gives rise to a cause of action for damages. (See, 1 Witkin, Summary of Cal. Law (9th ed. 1987) Contracts, §§ 791, 795.)

Repudiation and Anticipatory Breach

An unjustified or unexcused failure to perform a contractual duty at the time performance is due is an actual breach. A repudiation (which is a positive, unequivocal statement of an intention not to perform) that occurs before the time when performance is due gives rise to an anticipatory breach. When an anticipatory breach occurs, the injured party may either sue immediately, or wait until the time for performance and then exercise his or her rights for actual breach of contract.

An anticipatory repudiation or breach may be express or implied. A person who expressly repudiates the contract by an unequivocal refusal to perform commits an express anticipatory breach or repudiation. A person, who puts it out of his or her power to perform the promise commits an implied anticipatory breach or repudiation. (See, 1 Witkin, Summary of Cal. Law (9th ed. 1987) Contracts, §§ 805-808.)

Although an anticipatory breach or repudiation of a contract by one party permits the other party to sue for damages without performing or offering to perform its own obligations, this does not mean damages can be recovered without evidence that, but for the defendant's breach, the plaintiff would have had the ability to perform. (*Dickey v. Kuhn* (1930) 106 Cal.App. 300, 303-304 [289 P. 242]) In other words, plaintiff must be able to prove that he was ready, willing and able to perform in order to recover damages.

Waiver of Breach

Instead of treating a breach as a termination of the contract, the injured party may waive the breach by electing to treat the contract as still alive and remaining ready and able to perform on his or her own part, thereby limiting the claim to damages caused by the breach. (Cal.Comm.Code § 2-607(3)(a). A waiver may be express or implied. It is implied when the injured party continues to perform with knowledge of the other's breach and accepts further performance from the breaching party following the breach. (See, 1 Witkin, Summary of Cal. Law (9th ed. 1987) Contracts, §§ 800-801.)

Drafting Tip — Avoiding Waivers of Breach

If a party desires to avoid the consequences of an implied waiver, he or she may wish to insert the following language into the written agreement:

> *The failure by one party to require performance of any provision shall not affect that party's right to require performance at any time thereafter, nor shall a waiver of any breach or default of this Contract constitute a waiver of any subsequent breach or default or a waiver of the provision itself.*

Rescission

Rescission is the cancellation of a contract by mutual agreement of the parties. How free should the parties be to rescind or abandon their agreement? There is justified concern for the effects of an overly indulgent rescission policy on the stability of bargains. "The power to cancel a contract is a most extraordinary power. It is one which should be exercised with great caution — nay, I may say, with great reluctance — unless in a clear case. A too free use of this power would render all business uncertain, and, as has been said, make the length of a chancellor's foot the measure of individual rights. The greatest liberty of making contracts is essential to the business interests of the country. In general, the parties must look out for themselves." (*Colton v. Stanford* (1980) 82 Cal. 351, 398 [23 P. 16].)

Chapter 8

Mistake, Impossibility of Performance and Frustration of Purpose

Mistake

Donovan v. RRL Corp.
Supreme Court of California, 2001
26 Cal.4th 261, 109 Cal.Rptr.2d 807; 27 P.3d 702

[Facts are set forth at page 31.]

Having concluded that defendant's advertisement for the sale of the Jaguar automobile constituted an offer that was accepted by plaintiff's tender of the advertised price, and that the resulting contract satisfied the statute of frauds, we next consider whether defendant can avoid enforcement of the contract on the ground of mistake.

A party may rescind a contract if his or her consent was given by mistake. (Civ. Code, § 1689, subd. (b)(1).) A factual mistake by one party to a contract, or unilateral mistake, affords a ground for rescission in some circumstances. Civil Code section 1577 states in relevant part: "Mistake of fact is a mistake, not caused by the neglect of a legal duty on the part of the person making the mistake, and consisting in: [¶] 1. An unconscious ignorance or forgetfulness of a fact past or present, material to the contract...."

The Court of Appeal determined that defendant's error did not constitute a mistake of fact within the meaning of Civil Code section 1577. In support of this determination, the court relied upon the following principle: "[A] unilateral misinterpretation of contractual terms, without knowledge by the other party at the time of contract, does not constitute a mistake under either Civil Code section 1577 [mistake of fact] or 1578 [mistake of law]." (*Hedging Concepts, Inc. v. First Alliance Mortgage Co.* (1996) 41 Cal.App.4th 1410, 1422 (*Hedging Concepts*).)

The foregoing principle has no application to the present case. In *Hedging Concepts*, the plaintiff believed that he would fulfill his contractual obligations by introducing potential business prospects to the defendant. The contract, however, required the plaintiff to procure a completed business arrangement. The Court of Appeal held that the plaintiff's subjective misinterpretation of the terms of the contract constituted, at most, a mistake of law. Because the defendant was unaware of the plaintiff's misunderstanding at the time of the contract, the court held that rescission was not a proper remedy. (*Hedging Concepts, supra*, 41 Cal.App.4th at pp. 1418-1422; citing 1 Witkin, *supra*,

Contracts, § 379, pp. 345-346 [relief for unilateral mistake of law is authorized only where one party knows of, does not correct, and takes advantage or enjoys the benefit of another party's mistake].) Defendant's mistake in the present case, in contrast, did not consist of a subjective misinterpretation of a contract term, but rather resulted from an unconscious ignorance that the Daily Pilot advertisement set forth an incorrect price for the automobile. Defendant's lack of knowledge regarding the typographical error in the advertised price of the vehicle cannot be considered a mistake of law. Defendant's error constituted a mistake of fact, and the Court of Appeal erred in concluding otherwise. As we shall explain, the Court of Appeal also erred to the extent it suggested that a unilateral mistake of fact affords a ground for rescission only where the other party is aware of the mistake.

Under the first Restatement of Contracts, unilateral mistake did not render a contract voidable unless the other party knew of or caused the mistake. (1 Witkin, *supra*, Contracts, § 370, p. 337; see Rest., Contracts, § 503.) In *Germain etc. Co. v. Western Union etc. Co.* (1902) 137 Cal. 598, 602, this court endorsed a rule similar to that of the first Restatement. Our opinion indicated that a seller's price quotation erroneously transcribed and delivered by a telegraph company contractually could bind the seller to the incorrect price, unless the buyer knew or had reason to suspect that a mistake had been made. Some decisions of the Court of Appeal have adhered to the approach of the original Restatement. (See, e.g., *Conservatorship of O'Connor* (1996) 48 Cal.App.4th 1076, 1097-1098, and cases cited therein.) Plaintiff also advocates this approach and contends that rescission is unavailable to defendant, because plaintiff was unaware of the mistaken price in defendant's advertisement when he accepted the offer.

The Court of Appeal decisions reciting the traditional rule do not recognize that in *M. F. Kemper Const. Co. v. City of L. A.* (1951) 37 Cal.2d 696, 701 (*Kemper*), we acknowledged but rejected a strict application of the foregoing Restatement rule regarding unilateral mistake of fact. The plaintiff in *Kemper* inadvertently omitted a $301,769 item from its bid for the defendant city's public works project—approximately one-third of the total contract price. After discovering the mistake several hours later, the plaintiff immediately notified the city and subsequently withdrew its bid. Nevertheless, the city accepted the erroneous bid, contending that rescission of the offer was unavailable for the plaintiff's unilateral mistake.

Our decision in *Kemper* recognized that the bid, when opened and announced, resulted in an irrevocable option contract conferring upon the city a right to accept the bid, and that the plaintiff could not withdraw its bid unless the requirements for rescission of this option contract were satisfied. (*Kemper, supra*, "37 Cal.2d at pp. 700, 704.) We stated: "Rescission may be had for mistake of fact if the mistake is material to the contract and was not the result of neglect of a legal duty, if enforcement of the contract as made would be unconscionable, and if the other party can be placed in statu quo. [Citations.]" (*Id.* at p. 701.) Although the city knew of the plaintiff's mistake before it accepted the bid, and this circumstance was relevant to our determination that requiring the plaintiff to perform at the mistaken bid price would be unconscionable (*id.* at pp. 702-703), we authorized rescission of the city's option contract even though the city had not known of or contributed to the mistake before it opened the bid.

Similarly, in *Elsinore Union etc. Sch. Dist. v. Kastorff* (1960) 54 Cal.2d 380 (*Elsinore*), we authorized the rescission of an erroneous bid even where the contractor had assured the public agency, after the agency inquired, that his figures were accurate, and where the agency already had accepted the bid before it was aware of the mistake. In this situation, the other party clearly had no reason to know of the contractor's mistake before it accepted the bid.

The decisions in *Kemper* and *Elsinore* establish that California law does not adhere to the original Restatement's requirements for rescission based upon unilateral mistake of fact—i.c., only in circumstances where the other party knew of the mistake or caused the mistake. Consistent with the decisions in *Kemper* and *Elsinore*, the Restatement Second of Contracts authorizes rescission for a unilateral mistake of fact where "the effect of the mistake is such that enforcement of the contract would be unconscionable." (Rest.2d Contracts, § 153, subd. (a).) fn. 6 The comment following this section recognizes "a growing willingness to allow avoidance where the consequences of the mistake are so grave that enforcement of the contract would be unconscionable." (*Id.*, com. a, p. 394.) Indeed, two of the illustrations recognizing this additional ground for rescission in the Restatement Second of Contracts are based in part upon this court's decisions in *Kemper* and *Elsinore*. (Rest.2d Contracts, § 153, com. c, illus. 1, 3, pp. 395, 396, and Reporter's Note, pp. 400-401; see also *Schultz v. County of Contra Costa* (1984) 157 Cal.App.3d 242, 249-250 [applying section 153, subdivision (a), of the Restatement Second of Contracts], disagreed with on another ground in *Van Petten v. County of San Diego* (1995) 38 Cal.App.4th 43, 50-51; 1 Witkin, *supra*, Contracts, § 370, p. 337 [reciting the rule of the same Restatement provision].) Although the most common types of mistakes falling within this category occur in bids on construction contracts, section 153 of the Restatement Second of Contracts is not limited to such cases. (Rest.2d Contracts, § 153, com. b, p. 395.)

Because the rule in section 153, subdivision (a), of the Restatement Second of Contracts, authorizing rescission for unilateral mistake of fact where enforcement would be unconscionable, is consistent with our previous decisions, we adopt the rule as California law. As the author of one treatise recognized more than 40 years ago, the decisions that are inconsistent with the traditional rule "are too numerous and too appealing to the sense of justice to be disregarded." (3 Corbin, Contracts (1960) § 608, p. 675, fn. omitted.) We reject plaintiff's contention and the Court of Appeal's conclusion that, because plaintiff was unaware of defendant's unilateral mistake, the mistake does not provide a ground to avoid enforcement of the contract.

Having concluded that a contract properly may be rescinded on the ground of unilateral mistake of fact as set forth in section 153, subdivision (a), of the Restatement Second of Contracts, we next consider whether the requirements of that provision, construed in light of our previous decisions, are satisfied in the present case. Where the plaintiff has no reason to know of and does not cause the defendant's unilateral mistake of fact, the defendant must establish the following facts to obtain rescission of the contract: (1) the defendant made a mistake regarding a basic assumption upon which the defendant made the contract; (2) the mistake has a material effect upon the agreed exchange of performances that is adverse to the defendant; (3) the defendant does not bear the risk of the mistake; and (4) the effect of the mistake is such that enforcement of the contract would be unconscionable. We shall consider each of these requirements below.

A significant error in the price term of a contract constitutes a mistake regarding a basic assumption upon which the contract is made, and such a mistake ordinarily has a material effect adverse to the mistaken party. (See, e.g., *Elsinore, supra*, 54 Cal.2d at p. 389 [7 percent error in contract price]; *Lemoge Electric v. County of San Mateo* (1956) 46 Cal.2d 659, 661-662 [6 percent error]; *Kemper, supra*, 37 Cal.2d at p. 702 [28 percent error]; *Brunzell Const. Co. v. G. J. Weisbrod, Inc.* (1955) 134 Cal.App.2d 278, 286 [20 percent error]; Rest.2d Contracts, § 152, com. b, illus. 3, p. 387 [27 percent error].) In establishing a material mistake regarding a basic assumption of the contract, the defendant must show that the resulting imbalance in the agreed exchange is so severe that it would be unfair to require the defendant to perform. (Rest.2d Contracts, § 152, com. c, p. 388.) Ordinarily, a defendant can satisfy this requirement by showing that the exchange not only is less desirable for the defendant, but also is more advantageous to the other party. (*Ibid.*)

Measured against this standard, defendant's mistake in the contract for the sale of the Jaguar automobile constitutes a material mistake regarding a basic assumption upon which it made the contract. Enforcing the contract with the mistaken price of $25,995 would require defendant to sell the vehicle to plaintiff for $12,000 less than the intended advertised price of $37,995—an error amounting to 32 percent of the price defendant intended. The exchange of performances would be substantially less desirable for defendant and more desirable for plaintiff. Plaintiff implicitly concedes that defendant's mistake was material.

The parties and amici curiae vigorously dispute, however, whether defendant should bear the risk of its mistake. Section 154 of the Restatement Second of Contracts states: "A party bears the risk of a mistake when [¶] (a) the risk is allocated to him by agreement of the parties, or [¶] (b) he is aware, at the time the contract is made, that he has only limited knowledge with respect to the facts to which the mistake relates but treats his limited knowledge as sufficient, or [¶] (c) the risk is allocated to him by the court on the ground that it is reasonable in the circumstances to do so." Neither of the first two factors applies here. Thus, we must determine whether it is reasonable under the circumstances to allocate to defendant the risk of the mistake in the advertisement.

Civil Code section 1577, as well as our prior decisions, instructs that the risk of a mistake must be allocated to a party where the mistake results from that party's neglect of a legal duty. (*Kemper, supra,* "37 Cal.2d at p. 701.) It is well established, however, that ordinary negligence does not constitute neglect of a legal duty within the meaning of Civil Code section 1577. (*Kemper, supra,* "37 Cal.2d at p. 702.) For example, we have described a careless but significant mistake in the computation of the contract price as the type of error that sometimes will occur in the conduct of reasonable and cautious businesspersons, and such an error does not necessarily amount to neglect of legal duty that would bar equitable relief. (*Ibid.*; see also *Sun 'n Sand, Inc. v. United California Bank* (1978) 21 Cal.3d 671, 700-701 (plur. opn. of Mosk, J.); *Elsinore, supra,* "54 Cal.2d at pp. 388-389.)

A concept similar to neglect of a legal duty is described in section 157 of the Restatement Second of Contracts, which addresses situations in which a party's fault precludes relief for mistake. Only where the mistake results from "a failure to act in good faith and in accordance with reasonable standards of fair dealing" is rescission unavailable. (Rest.2d Contracts, § 157.) This section, consistent with the California decisions cited in the preceding paragraph, provides that a mistaken party's failure to exercise due care does not necessarily bar rescission under the rule set forth in section 153.

"The mere fact that a mistaken party could have avoided the mistake by the exercise of reasonable care does not preclude ... avoidance ... [on the ground of mistake]. Indeed, since a party can often avoid a mistake by the exercise of such care, the availability of relief would be severely circumscribed if he were to be barred by his negligence. Nevertheless, in *extreme cases* the mistaken party's fault is a proper ground for denying him relief for a mistake that he otherwise could have avoided.... [T]he rule is stated in terms of good faith and fair dealing.... [A] failure to act in good faith and in accordance with reasonable standards of fair dealing during pre-contractual negotiations does not amount to a breach. Nevertheless, under the rule stated in this Section, the failure bars a mistaken party from relief based on a mistake that otherwise would not have been made. During the negotiation stage each party is held to a degree of responsibility appropriate to the justifiable expectations of the other. The terms 'good faith' and 'fair dealing' are used, in this context, in much the same sense as in ... Uniform Commercial Code § 1-203." (Rest.2d Contracts, § 157, com. a, pp. 416-417, Section 1201, subdivision (19), of the California Uniform Commercial Code defines "good faith," as used in section 1203 of that code, as "honesty in fact in the conduct or transaction concerned."

Because of its erroneous conclusion that defendant's error was not a mistake of fact, the Court of Appeal did not reach the question whether the mistake resulted from defendant's neglect of a legal duty. The Court of Appeal did make an independent finding of fact on appeal that, in light of the statutory duties imposed upon automobile dealers, defendant's failure to review the proof sheet for the advertisement constituted *negligence*. This finding, however, was relevant only to the Court of Appeal's determination that defendant's concurrent negligence rendered it unnecessary for the court to consider the application of *Germain etc. Co. v. Western Union etc. Co.*, *supra*, 137 Cal. 598, to the present case, because *Germain* involved a mistaken offer resulting solely from the negligence of an intermediary. In any event, as established above, ordinary negligence does not constitute the neglect of a legal duty within the meaning of Civil Code section 1577 and the governing decisions. (See also 3 Corbin, Contracts, *supra*, § 606, pp. 649-656 [negligence is no bar to relief from unilateral mistake if other party can be placed in statu quo].) Accordingly, we shall consider in the first instance whether defendant's mistake resulted from its neglect of a legal duty, barring the remedy of rescission.

Plaintiff contends that section 11713.1(e) imposes a legal duty upon licensed automobile dealers to ensure that their advertisements containing sale prices are accurate. As established above, section 11713.1(e) provides that it is a violation of the Vehicle Code for a dealer to "[f]ail to sell a vehicle to any person at the advertised total price ... while the vehicle remains unsold, unless the advertisement states the advertised total price is good only for a specified time and the time has elapsed." Plaintiff also relies upon Vehicle Code section 11713, subdivision (a), which provides that a[licensed dealer shall not "[m]ake or disseminate ... in any newspaper ... any statement which is untrue or misleading and which is known, or which by the exercise of reasonable care should be known, to be untrue or misleading...." According to plaintiff, defendant's alleged violation of the duties arising from these statutes also constitutes the neglect of a legal duty within the meaning of Civil Code section 1577.

Even if we were to conclude that the foregoing statutes impose a duty of care upon automobile dealers to ensure that prices in an advertisement are accurate, a violation of such a duty would not necessarily preclude the availability of equitable relief. Our prior decisions instruct that the circumstance that a statute imposes a duty of care does not establish that the violation of such a duty constitutes "the neglect of a legal duty" (Civ. Code, § 1577) that would preclude rescission for a unilateral mistake of fact.

In *Sun 'n Sand, Inc. v. United California Bank, supra*, 21 Cal.3d 671, for example, a bank contended that a customer's violation of its statutory duty to examine bank statements and returned checks for alterations or forgeries (Cal. U. Com. Code, § 4406) constituted the neglect of a legal duty within the meaning of Civil Code section 1577, thus barring relief for the customer's mistake of fact. We rejected the bank's defense: "It does not follow ... that breach of this duty by failure to exercise reasonable care in discharging it constitutes the 'neglect of a legal duty' such that a cause of action for mistake of fact must be barred.... We have ... recognized on a number of occasions that 'ordinary negligence does not constitute the neglect of a legal duty as that term is used in section 1577 of the Civil Code.' [Citations.] The rule developed in these cases reflects a determination that the 'neglect of a legal duty' qualification derives content from equitable considerations and principles, and that it would be inequitable to bar relief for mistake because of the breach of a duty of care when the [other] party … suffers no loss. That [the plaintiff] may have failed to exercise care in examining its bank statements is thus not a sufficient basis for denying it equitable relief for mistake." (*Sun 'n Sand, Inc. v. United California Bank, supra,* 21 Cal.3d at pp. 700-701 (plur. opn. of Mosk, J.); see *id.* at p. 709 (conc. & dis. opn. of Sullivan, J.) [agreeing with conclusion of plur. opn. on this claim].)

Plaintiff also seeks to preclude relief for defendant's mistake on the ground that defendant's alleged violation of Vehicle Code section 11713.1(e) constitutes negligence per se pursuant to Evidence Code section 669, which provides that an individual's violation of a statute can lead to a presumption that he or she failed to exercise due care. As we have seen, however, a failure to exercise due care, by itself, does not constitute the neglect of a legal duty. Without evidence of bad faith on the part of defendant, its alleged violation of any duty of care arising from section 11713.1(e) constitutes, at most, ordinary negligence. Accordingly, a negligent violation of any duty imposed by section 11713.1(e) does not constitute the neglect of a legal duty or a sufficient basis for denying defendant equitable relief for its good faith mistake.

In a related claim, plaintiff contends that section 11713.1(e) imposes upon automobile dealers an absolute obligation to sell a vehicle at the advertised price—notwithstanding any mistake regarding the price, or the circumstances under which the mistake was made—and that this statute therefore supplants the common law regarding rescission of contracts and eliminates the defense of mistake. Allowing automobile dealers to avoid contracts because of carelessness in proofreading advertisements, plaintiff asserts, would undermine the legislative intent and public policy favoring the protection of consumers and ensuring accuracy in advertisements.

Plaintiff's contention regarding the effect of section 11713.1(e) upon the common law is inconsistent with our prior decisions. In *Moorpark, supra,* 54 Cal.3d 921, we held that a statute supplying the parameters for the price term of a contract, and requiring one party to perform certain acts as part of the process of making the contract, "does not remove the contract-making process from the purview of the common law unless the Legislature intends to occupy the field." (*Id.* at p. 929.) Our decision in *Moorpark* indicated that where a statutory scheme neither explicitly defines an offer nor, by the breadth of its regulation, implicitly supplants the common law of contracts, general common law principles govern the question whether an effective legal offer has been made. (*Id.* at p. 930.)

Section 11713.1(e) does not eliminate mistake as a ground for rescission of the contract, as plaintiff contends. The statute is part of a regulatory scheme that subjects licensed dealers to potential discipline for a violation of the duties set forth therein. As in *Moorpark, supra,* 54 Cal.3d 921, nothing in section 11713.1(e) or the regulatory scheme reflects a legislative intent completely to remove the contract-making process from the purview of the common law. At most, section 11713.1(e) reflects an intent to *supplement* contract law by establishing a ceiling for the price term of a contract for the sale of an advertised vehicle. Therefore, the common law, including the law governing mistake, remains applicable.

In *Kemper, supra,* 37 Cal.2d 696, we rejected a contention similar to that advanced by plaintiff. Relying upon a charter provision that "no bid shall be withdrawn" after being opened and declared, the city maintained that the public interest precluded the contractor from having the right to rescind its bid for mistake. Our decision stated that the offer remained subject to rescission upon proper equitable grounds, and that prior cases did not recognize any distinction between public and private contracts with regard to the right of equitable relief. (*Id.* at p. 704.) In support of this statement, we quoted from *Moffett, Hodgkins & C. Co. v. Rochester* (1900) 178 U.S. 373, 386, which had rejected a similar argument, as follows: " 'If the [city is] correct in [its] contention[,] there is absolutely no redress for a bidder for public work, no matter how aggravated or palpable his blunder. The moment his proposal is opened by the executive board he is held as in a grasp of steel. There is no remedy, no escape. If, through an error of his clerk, he has agreed to do work worth a million dollars for ten dollars, he must be held to the strict letter of his contract, while equity stands by with folded hands and sees him driven to bankruptcy. The [city's] position admits of no compromise, no exception, no middle ground.' "

In *Kemper* we further rejected the city's contention that a statement in the official bid form that bidders " 'will not be released on account of errors' " (*Kemper, supra,* "37 Cal.2d at p. 703) required all contractors to waive the right to seek relief for mistake. Our decision recognized a distinction between mere mechanical or clerical errors in tabulating or transcribing figures, on the one hand, and errors of judgment, on the other. "Where a person is denied relief because of an error in judgment, the agreement which is enforced is the one he intended to make, whereas if he is denied relief from a clerical error, he is forced to perform an agreement he had no intention of making.... If we were to give the language the sweeping construction contended for by the city, it would mean holding that the contractor intended to assume the risk of a clerical error no matter in what circumstances it might occur or how serious it might be. Such interpretation is contrary to common sense and ordinary business understanding and would result in the loss of heretofore well-established equitable rights to relief from certain types of mistake." (*Id.* at pp. 703-704.)

As in the foregoing cases, if we were to accept plaintiff's position that section 11713.1(e), by requiring a dealer to sell a vehicle at the advertised price, necessarily precludes relief for mistake, and that the dealer always must be held to the strict terms of a contract arising from an advertisement, we would be holding that the dealer intended to assume the risk of all typographical errors in advertisements, no matter how serious the error and regardless of the circumstances in which the error was made. For example, if an automobile dealer proofread an advertisement but, through carelessness, failed to detect a typographical error listing a $75,000 automobile for sale at $75, the defense of mistake would be unavailable to the dealer.

The trial court expressed a similar concern when it posed the following hypothetical to plaintiff. "The perennial mistakes in ads are infinite. You can move the decimal point over two, three places, so you are selling a $1,000,000 item for $100, any ridiculous example you can think of. [¶] If your theory is correct, that a printout would constitute an unconditional offer to sell, would that same result be attained if we had one of these mistakes, where some printer, instead of printing a million, left off some of the zeros, put in a thousand, and you are selling a million dollar yacht, and it came out to a thousand dollars, would a person be entitled, under your theory of the law, to say here's my thousand bucks, and I would like to sail away?" Consistent with his contention that the violation of section 11713.1(e) constitutes the neglect of a legal duty, plaintiff responded that the answer to the court's hypothetical is "yes." Plaintiff reiterated his position in this regard at oral argument in this court.

Giving such an effect to section 11713.1(e), however, "is contrary to common sense and ordinary business understanding and would result in the loss of heretofore well-established equitable rights to relief from certain types of mistake." (*Kemper, supra,* "37 Cal.2d at p. 704.) Although this statute obviously reflects an important public policy of protecting consumers from injury caused by unscrupulous dealers who publish deceptive advertisements (see *Ford Dealers Assn. v. Department of Motor Vehicles* (1982) 32 Cal.3d 347, 356), and establishes that automobile dealers that violate the statute can suffer the suspension or revocation of their licenses, there is no indication in the statutory scheme that the Legislature intended to impose such an absolute *contractual* obligation upon automobile dealers who make an honest mistake. Therefore, absent evidence of bad faith, the violation of any obligation imposed by this statute does not constitute the neglect of a legal duty that precludes rescission for unilateral mistake of fact.

The municipal court made an express finding of fact that "the mistake on the part of [defendant] was made in good faith[;] it was an honest mistake, not intended to deceive the public...." The Court of Appeal correctly recognized that "[w]e must, of course, accept the trial court's finding that there was a 'good faith' mistake that caused the error in the advertisement." The evidence presented at trial compellingly supports this finding.

Defendant regularly advertises in five local newspapers. Defendant's advertising manager, Crystal Wadsworth, testified that ordinarily she meets with Kristen Berman, a representative of the Daily Pilot, on Tuesdays, Wednesdays, and Thursdays to review proof sheets of the advertisement that will appear in the newspaper the following weekend. When Wadsworth met with Berman on Wednesday, April 23, 1997, defendant's proposed advertisement listed a 1995 Jaguar XJ6 Vanden Plas without specifying a price, as it had the preceding week. On Thursday, April 24, a sales manager instructed Wadsworth to substitute a 1994 Jaguar XJ6 with a price of $25,995. The same day, Wadsworth met with Berman and conveyed to her this new information. Wadsworth did not expect to see another proof sheet reflecting this change, however, because she does not work on Friday, and the Daily Pilot goes to press on Friday and the edition in question came out on Saturday, April 26.

Berman testified that the revised advertisement was prepared by the composing department of the Daily Pilot. Berman proofread the advertisement, as she does all advertisements for which she is responsible, but Berman did not notice that it listed the 1995 Jaguar XJ6 Vanden Plas for sale at $25,995, instead of listing the 1994 Jaguar at that price. Both Berman and Wadsworth first learned of the mistake on Monday, April 28, 1997. Defendant's sales manager first became aware of the mistake after plaintiff attempted to purchase the automobile on Sunday, April 27. Berman confirmed in a letter of retraction that Berman's proofreading error had led to the mistake in the advertisement.

Defendant's erroneous advertisement in the Daily Pilot listed 16 used automobiles for sale. Each of the advertisements prepared for several newspapers in late April 1997, except for the one in the Daily Pilot, correctly identified the 1994 Jaguar XJ6 for sale at a price of $25,995. In May 1997, defendant's advertisements in several newspapers listed the 1995 Jaguar XJ6] Vanden Plas for sale at $37,995, and defendant subsequently sold the automobile for $38,399. Defendant had paid $35,000 for the vehicle.

Evidence at trial established that defendant adheres to the following procedures when an incorrect advertisement is discovered. Defendant immediately contacts the newspaper and requests a letter of retraction. Copies of any erroneous advertisements are provided to the sales staff, the error is explained to them, and the mistake is circled in red and posted on a bulletin board at the dealership. The sales staff informs customers of any advertising errors of which they are aware.

No evidence presented at trial suggested that defendant knew of the mistake before plaintiff attempted to purchase the automobile, that defendant intended to mislead customers, or that it had adopted a practice of deliberate indifference regarding errors in advertisements. Wadsworth regularly reviews proof sheets for the numerous advertisements placed by defendant, and representatives of the newspapers, including the Daily Pilot, also proofread defendant's advertisements to ensure they are accurate. Defendant follows procedures for notifying its sales staff and customers of errors of which it becomes aware. The uncontradicted evidence established that the Daily Pilot made the proofreading error resulting in defendant's mistake.

Defendant's fault consisted of failing to review a proof sheet reflecting the change made on Thursday, April 24, 1997, and/or the actual advertisement appearing in the April 26 edition of the Daily Pilot—choosing instead to rely upon the Daily Pilot's advertising staff to proofread the revised version. Although, as the Court of Appeal found, such an omission might constitute negligence, it does not involve a breach of defendant's duty of good faith and fair dealing that should preclude equitable relief for mistake. In these circumstances, it would not be reasonable for this court to allocate the risk of the mistake to defendant.

As indicated above, the Restatement Second of Contracts provides that during the negotiation stage of a contract "each party is held to a degree of responsibility appropriate to the justifiable expectations of the other." (Rest.2d Contracts, § 157, com. a, p. 417.) No consumer reasonably can expect 100 percent accuracy in each and every price appearing in countless automobile advertisements listing numerous vehicles for sale. The degree of responsibility plaintiff asks this court to impose upon automobile dealers would amount to strict contract liability for any typographical error in the price of an advertised automobile, no matter how serious the error or how blameless the dealer. We are unaware of any other situation in which an individual or business is held to such a standard under the law of contracts. Defendant's good faith, isolated mistake does not constitute the type of extreme case in which its fault constitutes the neglect of a legal duty that bars equitable relief. Therefore, whether or not defendant's failure to sell the automobile to plaintiff could amount to a violation of section 11713.1(e)—an issue that is not before us—defendant's conduct in the present case does not preclude rescission.

* * *

Having determined that defendant satisfied the requirements for rescission of the contract on the ground of unilateral mistake of fact, we conclude that the municipal court correctly entered judgment in defendant's favor.

V

The judgment of the Court of Appeal is reversed.

Kennard, J., Chin, J., and Brown, J., concurred.

Werdegar, J., dissented with Baxter, J., concurring

Afterthoughts

California Civil Code section 1577 does not include language regarding allocation of the risk of mistake to one party, but rather excludes from the definition of "mistake of fact" any mistake resulting from the neglect of a legal duty. Pursuant to section 1577 and the Restatement Second of Contracts section 157, the neglect of a legal duty amounting to a breach of the duty of good faith and fair dealing bars relief from mistake, whether or not the other party has reason to know of the mistake.

An apparent consent is not real or free when obtained through mistake. (Cal.Civ.Code § 1567) Mistake may be either of fact or law. (Cal.Civ.Code § 1576)

Mistake of fact is a mistake not caused by the neglect of a legal duty on the part of the person making the mistake, and consisting in:

(1) An unconscious ignorance or forgetfulness of a fact past or present, material to the contract; or,

(2) Belief in the present existence of a thing material to the contract, which does not exist, or in the past existence of such a thing, which has not existed. (Cal.Civ.Code § 1577)

Mistake of law constitutes a mistake only when it arises from:

(1) A misapprehension of the law by all parties, all supposing that they knew and understood it, and all making substantially the same mistake as to the law; or,

(2) A misapprehension of the law by one party, of which the others are aware at the time of contracting, but which they do not rectify. (Cal.Civ.Code § 1578)

On the purported sale of personal property the parties to the proposed contract are not bound where it appears that each of them is honestly mistaken or in error with reference to the identity of the subject-matter of the contract. In other words, in such circumstances, no enforceable sale has taken place. (*Smith v. Zimbalist* (1934) 2 Cal.App.2d 324)

Impossibility or Impracticability of Performance

The general rule is that in contracts in which performance depends on the continued existence of a given person or thing, an implied condition is that the perishing of the person or thing shall excuse performance. A thing is impossible in legal contemplation when it is not practicable; and a thing is impracticable when it can only be done at an excessive and unreasonable cost. (*City of Vernon v. City of Los Angeles* (1955) 45 Cal.2d 710, 720.) In other words, "impossibility" is defined as not only strict impossibility but as impracticability because of extreme and unreasonable difficulty, expense, injury, or loss involved. "Impossibility" is the traditional term used in such a situation however, both the Restatement Second and the Uniform Commercial Code now use the term "impracticability." (See, Rest.2d Contracts, § 261; Cal.Comm.Code § 2-615) Temporary impossibility of the character which, if it should become permanent, would discharge a promisor's entire contractual duty, operates as a permanent discharge if performance after the impossibility ceases would impose a substantially greater burden upon the promisor; otherwise, the duty is suspended while the impossibility exists. (*Autry v. Republic Productions, Inc.* (1947) 30 Cal.2d 144)

Cazares v. Saenz

Court of Appeals of California, Fourth Appellate District, Division One, 1989
208 Cal.App.3d 279 , 256 Cal.Rptr. 209

WIENER, Acting P. J.

On one level, the issue in this case is simply one of attorney's fees. Are plaintiffs Roy Cazares and Thomas Tosdal, former partners in the law firm of Cazares & Tosdal, entitled to one-half of a contingent fee promised them by defendant Phil Saenz when he associated the firm on a particular personal injury case, notwithstanding that Cazares became a municipal court judge before the case was settled? More fundamentally, however, the issue before us requires that we review not only the nature of contingent attorney fee arrangements but also basic contract law regarding frustration of purpose, incapacitation of parties to a contract, and the proper measure of quantum meruit recovery in such circumstances. We decide that where one member of a two-person law firm becomes incapable of performing on a contract of association with another lawyer, the obligations of the parties to the contract are discharged if it was contemplated that the incapacitated attorney would perform substantial services under the agreement. We therefore hold that Cazares and Tosdal are not entitled to 50 percent of the contingent fee as provided in the association agreement. They may, however, recover the reasonable value of the legal services rendered before Cazares's incapacitation, prorated on the basis of the original contract price.

Factual and Procedural Background

Defendant Phil Saenz was an attorney of limited experience in November 1978 when he was contacted by the Mexican consulate in San Diego regarding a serious accident involving a Mexican national, Raul Gutierrez. Gutierrez had been burned after touching a power line owned by San Diego Gas & Electric Company (SDG&E). He retained Saenz to represent him in a lawsuit against SDG&E and other defendants. The written retainer agreement authorized Saenz to "retain co-counsel if he deems it necessary" and provided that "[a]ttorney fees shall be 33 1/3% of the net recovery; i.e., after all costs and medical expenses."

Saenz shared office space with the law firm of Cazares & Tosdal, which was composed of partners Roy Cazares and Thomas Tosdal, the plaintiffs in this action. In September 1979, Saenz agreed with Cazares to associate Cazares & Tosdal on the Gutierrez case. According to Saenz, he wanted to work with Cazares because Cazares spoke Spanish and could communicate directly with Gutierrez and because he (Saenz) respected Cazares's work in the Mexican-American community. In contrast, Saenz did not feel comfortable with Tosdal: "Basically, he was an Anglo, a surfer. In my opinion, he was just too liberal for me...." Saenz testified he had no reason to doubt Tosdal's competence as a lawyer. In fact, Saenz did not object to Tosdal's working on the case as long as he (Saenz) had nothing to do with him.

Cazares, on behalf of his firm, and Saenz agreed Saenz would continue to maintain client contact with Gutierrez and would handle a pending immigration matter to prevent Gutierrez from being deported. Saenz also wanted to actively assist in the preparation and trial of the case as a learning experience. Cazares & Tosdal was to handle most of the legal work on the case. Saenz and Cazares orally agreed they would evenly divide the contingent fee on the Gutierrez case. Both Cazares and Saenz testified they expected and assumed Cazares would prosecute the case to its conclusion.

Gutierrez's complaint filed in November 1979 listed both Saenz and Cazares & Tosdal as counsel of record. During the next two and one-half years, Cazares performed most of the legal work in the case. Saenz maintained client contact, performed miscellaneous tasks and attended depositions including some defense depositions which Cazares did not attend. For all intents and purposes Tosdal performed no work on the case. Neither Cazares nor Saenz kept time records.

In June 1981, the Cazares & Tosdal partnership dissolved. The two partners decided to retain some cases, including the Gutierrez matter, as partnership assets. No formal substitution of counsel was filed in the case. Cazares and Saenz moved to a new office and continued to work on the case together for the next year.

In May 1982 Cazares was appointed a municipal court judge. Cazares urged Saenz to seek Tosdal's help in prosecuting the Gutierrez case. Saenz refused. In January 1983 Tosdal wrote Saenz stating that he remained "ready, willing and available to assist you in any aspect of the preparation of the case in which you may desire my aid."

Saenz never responded to Tosdal's offer. Instead, he associated an experienced personal injury attorney, Isam Khoury, to assist him on the Gutierrez case. Saenz also hired a young attorney, Dan Mazella, to do some research work.

In April 1983, Saenz settled the Gutierrez case for $1.1 million, entitling him to a fee slightly in excess of $366,000. Out of that fee, Saenz paid Khoury $40,000 and Mazella $7,000 for their work on the case. About two weeks later, Saenz visited Cazares and offered to pay him $40,000 for his work on the case. Cazares declined, claiming Saenz owed the now defunct Cazares & Tosdal partnership more than $183,000. This litigation ensued.

The case was tried to a referee by stipulation. (See Code Civ. Proc., § 638.) The referee concluded in pertinent part as follows: "The partnership of Tosdal and Cazares entered into an agreement with Saenz, which was in effect a joint venture agreement. The partnership performed fully up until the time Cazares took the bench. At that time, Saenz rejected any help from the remaining partner, therefore preventing the performance by the partnership in further prosecution of the case. The case of Jewel v. Boxer, 156 Cal.App.3d 171 would appear to govern. The joint venture entered into by [the] partnership [with] Saenz entitled the partnership to receive 50% of the fees received by Defendant Saenz." The referee went on to conclude that Saenz was entitled to deduct the $47,000 paid to Khoury and Mazella before calculating the 50 percent due Cazares and Tosdal. Accordingly, judgment was entered in favor of Cazares and Tosdal in the amount of $159,833.00 plus interest.

Discussion

I

The initial question is whether Saenz breached the association agreement with Cazares & Tosdal when, after Cazares's appointment to the municipal court, he refused to work with Tosdal on the Gutierrez case. Here, the referee in effect held that Saenz was obligated to accept Tosdal as a substitute for Cazares even though the record firmly establishes both parties to the association agreement contemplated that most if not all of the work on the Gutierrez case would be performed by Cazares. We conclude that Saenz acted within his rights in refusing to work with Tosdal after Cazares became a judge

Where a contract contemplates the personal services of a party, performance is excused when that party dies or becomes otherwise incapable of performing. (Rest.2d Contracts, §§ 261, 262; 1 Witkin, Summary of Cal. Law (9th ed. 1987) Contracts, § 782, p. 705.) Here, the parties contemplated Cazares would personally perform the firm's obligations under the contract with Saenz, which he in fact did for two and one-half years after the execution of the contract. Cazares became legally incapable of performing the contract after his appointment to the bench. (See State Bar of California v. Superior Court (1929) 207 Cal. 323, 337 [278 P. 432].) Of course, the contract was not between Saenz and Cazares but between Saenz and the firm of Cazares & Tosdal; thus, performance by the firm was not technically impossible. Nonetheless, the Restatement

Second of Contracts, section 262 addresses this issue because its language is not limited to the death or incapacity of a party to the contract: "If the existence of a particular person is necessary for the performance of a duty, his death or such incapacity as makes performance impracticable is an event the non-occurrence of which was a basic assumption on which the contract was made." (Italics added.) Here, both Saenz and Cazares testified that Cazares's prosecution of the case to completion was a "basic assumption on which the contract was made."

We have been unable to locate any cases—California or otherwise—addressing this issue in the context of an association agreement between lawyers. A similar situation occurs, however, whenever a client hires a firm of lawyers with the expectation of obtaining the services of a particular attorney. Of course under California law, a client may discharge an attorney at any time for any reason; there is no requirement that the discharge be for "cause." The client's only obligation is to compensate the discharged attorney in quantum meruit for the reasonable value of any services rendered. (Fracasse v. Brent (1972) 6 Cal.3d 784, 790-791 [100 Cal.Rptr. 385, 494 P.2d 9].) Thus, if the relationship with Cazares & Tosdal had been terminated by Gutierrez rather than Saenz, there would be no question that the termination was proper.

It is unnecessary in this case for us to decide whether the rights of an attorney acting on behalf of the client in associating other counsel mirror the client's broad rights under Fracasse. Even before Fracasse, when good cause was required to discharge an attorney (see Zurich G. A. & L. Ins. Co., Ltd. v. Kinsler (1938) 12 Cal.2d 98, 100-101 [81 P.2d 913]; Baldwin v. Bennett (1854) 4 Cal. 392, 393), the rule was that where a client contracts with a law firm to obtain the services of a particular attorney and that attorney dies or becomes incapacitated, the client at his option may discharge the firm subject only to the obligation to compensate the firm for the reasonable value of services rendered before the discharge. (See Little v. Caldwell (1894) 101 Cal. 553, 559-560 [36 P. 107]; see also, e.g., Felt v. Mitchell (1909) 44 Ind.App. 96 [88 N.E. 723, 723-724]; Clifton v. Clark, Hood & Co. (1904) 83 Miss. 446 [36 So. 251, 253]; Green County v. Lewis (1914) 157 Ky. 490 [163 S.W. 489, 493]; Speiser, Attorneys' Fees (1973) §4:44, p. 196.) We see no reason why a similar rule should not apply when an attorney on behalf of a client enters into an association agreement with another firm of lawyers. A lawyer who associates a firm on a specific case in order to obtain the services of a particular professional colleague is certainly no less likely than the client to be relying on that colleague's unique legal talents. Here, in fact, Gutierrez specifically delegated to Saenz the discretion to associate co-counsel "if he deem[ed] it necessary." (Ante, p. 282.)

It may be helpful to consider a hypothetical situation in which the roles here were reversed, i.e., if Saenz sought to compel Tosdal to perform after Cazares was appointed to the bench. One of the illustrations to Restatement Second of Contracts, section 262 addresses this precise situation, stating the rule that the death or incapacity of one partner discharges the firm's obligations under the contract. At least where the contract contemplates the unique personal services of a firm member, the rationale of the illustration necessarily leads to the conclusion that the obligations of the party retaining the firm are also discharged in such a situation.

* * *

Disposition

The judgment is reversed. The case is remanded to the superior court for further proceedings consistent with this opinion.

Benke, J., and Nares, J., concurred.

Crop Failures

Squillante v. California Lands, Inc.,

California Court of Appeal, Fourth Appellate District, 1935
5 Cal.App.2d 89, 42 P.2d 81

ALLYN, J., pro tem.

Plaintiff brought suit for damages for breach of contract to buy ten carloads of Zinfandel grapes "of good quality and color and of good sugar content" from the defendant. The agreement was made through an exchange of telegrams after the plaintiff had inspected defendant's vineyards and arranged that the grapes be packed by a certain packer and under defendant's brand. Five cars were delivered and then, due to heat damage, defendant was unable to harvest or ship any further grapes of the quality agreed upon. Plaintiff was so notified and in due course this action was brought and judgment given for the defendant. The defendant was a grower and not a dealer in grapes except in so far as was necessary to dispose of its own products.

Upon this appeal plaintiff submits that defendant was not relieved from its obligation to deliver the grapes by the crop losses caused by adverse weather conditions and hence that it was error to admit evidence on this issue. It is argued that the contract was a general undertaking to sell grapes of a given quality which the seller was to have ready at all events when delivery was due. This might well be true if the defendant were in the general business of packing and selling grapes (Eskew v. California Fruit Exchange, 203 Cal. 257 [263 P. 804]), but it is apparent here that the parties intended the sale and purchase of ten cars of grapes of a particular quality to be grown and produced in the vineyards of the defendant, to be packed by a named packer under the defendant's established brand which was used by it in marketing its own products. The sale being of a designated quality of a specific variety of grapes growing or to be grown in specific vineyards, and these vineyards being so far affected by extraordinary heat conditions that they did not produce sufficient grapes of the variety and quality named to comply with the contract, the defendant could be compelled to perform the contract only so far as it was possible for it so to do. It could not be compelled to perform impossibilities nor was it liable in damages for a failure to comply with its contract resulting from vis major not attributable to any fault on its part (Ontario Deciduous Fruit Growers Assn. v. Cutting Fruit Packing Co., 134 Cal. 21 [66 P. 28, 86 Am.St.Rep. 231, 53 L.R.A. 681]; Operators' Oil Co. v. Barbre, 65 Fed.2d 857, 861).

The finding of the trial court on this issue is conclusive and is sufficient to sustain the judgment for the defendant. It is therefore unnecessary to review the questions raised as to the measure and proof of damages. They have been considered and found insufficient to justify a reversal.

The judgment is therefore affirmed.

Barnard, P. J., and Marks, J., concurred.

Drafting Tip — *Force Majeure* Clauses

A *force majeure* clause is an exculpatory clause inserted into a contract that excuses performance upon the occurrence of an event beyond a party's control. A typical such clause might read:

The Company shall not be liable for any failure in the performance of its obligations under this agreement which may result from strikes or acts of labor unions, fires, floods, earthquakes, or acts of God, war or other contingencies beyond its control.

Frustration of Purpose

Where a party's principal purpose is frustrated by the occurrence of an event, the non-occurrence of which was a basic assumption on which the contract was made, the duty of performance is discharged. (Restatement, Second Contracts § 265.) The doctrine of frustration addresses situations where, because of the occurrence of an unforeseen supervening event, one party's performance becomes virtually worthless to the other.

Lloyd v. Murphy

Supreme Court of California, 1944
25 Cal.2d 48, 153 P.2d 47

TRAYNOR, J.

On August 4, 1941, plaintiff leased to defendant for a five-year term beginning September 15, 1941, certain premises located at the corner of Almont Drive and Wilshire Boulevard in the city of Beverly Hills, Los Angeles County, "for the sole purpose of conducting thereon the business of displaying and selling new automobiles (including the servicing and repairing thereof and of selling the petroleum products of a major oil company) and for no other purpose whatsoever without the written consent of the lessor" except "to make an occasional sale of a used automobile." Defendant agreed not to sublease or assign without plaintiffs' written consent. On January 1, 1942, the federal government ordered that the sale of new automobiles be discontinued. It modified this order on January 8, 1942, to permit sales to those engaged in military activities, and on January 20, 1942, it established a system of priorities restricting sales to persons having preferential ratings of A-1-j or higher. On March 10, 1942, defendant explained the effect of these restrictions on his business to one of the plaintiffs authorized to act for the others, who orally waived the restrictions in the lease as to use and subleasing and offered to reduce the rent if defendant should be unable to operate profitably. Nevertheless defendant vacated the premises on March 15, 1942, giving oral notice of repudiation of the lease to plaintiffs, which was followed by a written notice on March 24, 1942. Plaintiffs affirmed in writing on March 26th their oral waiver and, failing to persuade defendant to perform his obligations, they rented the property to other tenants pursuant to their powers under the lease in order to mitigate damages. On May 11, 1942, plaintiffs brought this action praying for declaratory relief to determine their rights under the lease, and for judgment for unpaid rent. Following a trial on the merits, the court found that the leased premises were located on one of the main traffic arteries of Los Angeles County; that they were equipped with gasoline pumps and in general adapted for the maintenance of an automobile service station; that they contained a one-story storeroom adapted to many commercial purposes; that plaintiffs had waived the restrictions in the lease and granted defendant the right to use the premises for any legitimate purpose and to sublease to any responsible party; that defendant continues to carry on the business of selling and servicing automobiles at two other places. Defendant testified that at one of these locations he sold new automobiles exclusively and when asked if he were aware that many new automobile dealers were continuing in business replied: "Sure. It is just the location that I couldn't make a go, though, of automobiles." Although there was no finding to that effect, defendant estimated in response to inquiry by his counsel, that 90 per cent of his gross volume of business was new car sales and 10 per cent gasoline sales. The trial court held that war conditions had not terminated defendant's obligations under the lease and gave judgment for plaintiffs, declaring the lease as modified by plaintiffs' waiver to be in full force and effect, and ordered defendant to pay the unpaid rent with interest, less amounts received by plaintiffs from re- renting. Defendant brought this appeal, contending that the purpose for which the premises were leased was frustrated by the restrictions placed on the sale of new automobiles by the federal government, thereby terminating his duties under the lease.

Although commercial frustration was first recognized as an excuse for nonperformance of a contractual duty by the courts of England (Krell v. Henry [1903] 2 K.B. 740 [C.A.]; Blakely v. Muller, 19 T.L.R. 186 [K. B.]; see McElroy and Williams, The Coronation Cases, 4 Mod.L.Rev. 241) its soundness has been questioned by those courts (see Maritime National Fish, Ltd., v. Ocean Trawlers, Ltd. [1935] A.C. 524, 528-29, 56 L.Q.Rev. 324, arguing that Krell v. Henry, supra, was a misapplication of Taylor v. Caldwell, 3 B.&S 826 [1863], the leading case on impossibility as an excuse for nonperformance), and they have refused to apply the doctrine to leases on the ground that an estate is conveyed to the lessee, which carries with it all risks (Swift v. McBean, 166 L.T.Rep. 87 [1942] 1 K.B. 375; Whitehall Court v. Ettlinger, 122 L.T.Rep. 540, (1920) 1 K.B. 680, [1919] 89 L.J. [K.B.] N.S. 126; 137 A.L.R. 1199, 1224; see collection and discussion on English cases in Wood v. Bartolino, ___ N.M. ___ [146 P.2d 883, 886-87]). Many courts, therefore, in the United States have held that the tenant bears all risks as owner of the estate (Cusack v. Pratt, 78 Colo. 28 [239 P. 22, 44 A.L.R. 55]; Yellow Cab Co. v. Stafford-Smith Co., 320 Ill. 294 [150 N.E. 670, 43 A.L.R. 1173]), but the modern cases have recognized that the defense may be available in a proper case, even in a lease. As the author declares in 6 Williston, Contracts (rev. ed. 1938), § 1955, pp. 5485-87,

> The fact that lease is a conveyance and not simply a continuing contract and the numerous authorities enforcing liability to pay rent in spite of destruction of leased premises, however, have made it difficult to give relief. That the tenant has been relieved, nevertheless, in several cases indicates the gravitation of the law toward a recognition of the principle that fortuitous destruction of the value of performance wholly outside the contemplation of the parties may excuse a promisor even in a lease....

> Even more clearly with respect to leases than in regard to ordinary contracts the applicability of the doctrine of frustration depends on the total or nearly total destruction of the purpose for which, in the contemplation of both parties, the transaction was entered into.

The principles of frustration have been repeatedly applied to leases by the courts of this state (Brown v. Oshiro, 58 Cal.App.2d 190 [136 P.2d 29]; Davidson v. Goldstein, 58 Cal.App.2d Supp. 909 [136 P.2d 665]; Grace v. Croninger, 12 Cal.App.2d 603 [55 P.2d 940]; Knoblaugh v. McKinney, 5 Cal.App.2d 339 [42 P.2d 332]; Industrial Development & Land Co. v. Goldschmidt, 56 Cal.App. 507 [206 P. 134]; Burke v. San Francisco Breweries, Ltd., 21 Cal.App. 198 [131 P. 83]) and the question is whether the excuse for nonperformance is applicable under the facts of the present case.

Although the doctrine of frustration is akin to the doctrine of impossibility of performance (see Civ. Code, §1511; 6 Cal.Jur. 435-450; 4 Cal.Jur. Ten-year Supp. 187-192; Taylor v. Caldwell, supra) since both have developed from the commercial necessity of excusing performance in cases of extreme hardship, frustration is not a form of impossibility even under the modern definition of that term, which includes not only cases of physical impossibility but also cases of extreme impracticability of performance (see Mineral Park Land Co. v. Howard, 172 Cal. 289, 293 [156 P. 458, L.R.A. 1916F 1]; Christin v. Superior Court, 9 Cal.2d 526, 533 [71 P.2d 205, 112 A.L.R. 1153]; 6 Williston, op.cit. supra, §1935, p. 5419; Rest., Contracts, §454, comment a., and Cal.Ann. p. 254). Performance remains possible but the expected value of performance to the party seeking to be excused has been destroyed by a fortuitous event, which supervenes to cause an actual but not literal failure of consideration (Krell v. Henry, supra; Blakely v. Muller, supra; Marks Realty Co. v. Hotel Hermitage Co., 170 App.Div. 484 [156 N.Y.S. 179]; 6 Williston, op. Cit. Supra, §§1935, 1954, pp. 5477, 5480; Restatement, Contracts, §288).

The question in cases involving frustration is whether the equities of the case, considered in the light of sound public policy, require placing the risk of a disruption or complete destruction of the contract equilibrium on defendant or plaintiff under the circumstances of a given case (Fibrosa Spolka Akcyjina v. Fairbairn Lawson Combe Barbour, Ltd. [1942], 167 L.T.R. [H.L.] 101, 112-113; see Smith, Some Practical Aspects of the Doctrine of Impossibility, 32 Ill.L.Rev. 672, 675; Patterson, Constructive Conditions in Contracts, 42 Columb.L.Rev. 903, 949; 27 Cal.L.Rev. 461), and the answer depends on whether an unanticipated circumstance, the risk of which should not be fairly thrown on the promisor, has made performance vitally different from what was reasonably to be expected (6 Williston, op.cit. supra, §1963, p. 5511; Restatement, Contracts, §454). The purpose of a contract is to place the risks of performance upon the promisor, and the relation of the parties, terms of the contract, and circumstances surrounding its formation must be examined to determine whether it can be fairly inferred that the risk of the event that has supervened to cause the alleged frustration was not reasonably foreseeable. If it was foreseeable there should have been provision for it in the contract, and the absence of such a provision gives rise to the inference that the risk was assumed.

The doctrine of frustration has been limited to cases of extreme hardship so that businessmen, who must make their arrangements in advance, can rely with certainty on their contracts (Anglo-Northern Trading Co. v. Emlyn Jones and Williams, 2 K.B. 78; 137 A.L.R. 1199, 1216-1221). The courts have required a promisor seeking to excuse himself from performance of his obligations to prove that the risk of the frustrating event was not reasonably foreseeable and that the value of counterperformance is totally or nearly totally destroyed, for frustration is no defense if it was foreseeable or controllable by the promisor, or if counterperformance remains valuable. (La Cumbre Golf & Country Club v. Santa Barbara Hotel Co., 205 Cal. 422, 425 [271 P. 476]; Johnson v. Atkins, 53 Cal.App.2d 430, 434 [127 P.2d 1027]; Grace v. Croninger, 12 Cal.App2d 603, 606-607 [55 P.2d 940]; Industrial Development & Land Co. v. Goldschmidt, 56 Cal.App. 507, 511 [206 P. 134]; Burke v. San Francisco Breweries, Ltd., 21 Cal.App. 198, 201 [131 P. 83]; Megan v. Updike Grain Corp. (C.C.A. 8), 94 F.2d 551, 553; Herne Bay Steamboat Co. v. Hutton [1903], 2 K.B. 683; Leiston Gas Co. v. Leiston Cum Sizewell Urban District Council [1916], 2 K.B. 428; Raner v. Goldberg, 244 N.Y. 438 [155 N.E. 733]; 6 Williston, op. Cit. Supra, §§1939, 1955, 1963; Restatement, Contracts, §288.)

Thus laws or other governmental acts that make performance unprofitable or more difficult or expensive do not excuse the duty to perform a contractual obligation (Sample v. Fresno Flume etc. Co., 129 Cal. 222, 228 [61 P. 1085]; Klauber v. San Diego St. Car Co., 95 Cal. 353 [30 P. 555]; Texas Co. v. Hogarth Shipping Co., 256 U.S. 619, 630 [41 S.Ct. 612, 65 L.Ed. 1123]; Columbus Ry. Power & Light Co. v. Columbus, 249 U.S. 399, 414 [39 S.Ct. 349, 63 L.Ed. 669]; Thomson v. Thomson, 315 Ill. 521, 527 [146 N.E. 451]; Commonwealth v. Bader, 271 Pa. 308, 312 [114 A. 266]; Commonwealth v. Neff, 271 Pa. 312, 314 [114 A. 267]; London & Lancashire Ind. Co. v. Columbiana County, 107 OhioSt. 51, 64 [140 N.E. 672]; see 6 Williston, op. Cit. Supra, §§ 1955, 1963, pp. 5507-09). It is settled that if parties have contracted with reference to a state of war or have contemplated the risks arising from it, they may not invoke the doctrine of frustration to escape their obligations Northern Pac. Ry. Co. v. American Trading Co., 195 U.S. 439, 467-68 [25 S.Ct. 84, 49 L.Ed. 269]; Primos Chemical Co. v. Fulton Steel Corp. (D.C.N.Y.), 266 F. 945, 948; Krulewitch v. National Importing & Trading Co., 195 App.Div. 544 [186 N.Y.S. 838, 840]; Smith v. Morse, 20 La.Ann. 220, 222; Lithflux Mineral & Chem. Works v. Jordan, 217 Ill.App. 64, 68; Medeiros v. Hill, 8 Bing. 231, 131 Eng.Rep. 390, 392; Bolckow V. & Co. v. Compania Minera de Sierra Minera, 115 L.T.R. [K.B.] 745, 747).

At the time the lease in the present case was executed the National Defense Act (Public Act No. 671 of the 76th Congress [54 Stats. 601], § 2A), approved June 28, 1940, authorizing the President to allocate materials and mobilize industry for national defense, had been law for more than a year. The automotive industry was in the process of conversion to supply the needs of our growing mechanized army and to meet lend-laase commitments. Iceland and Greenland had been occupied by the army. Automobile sales were soaring because the public anticipated that production would soon be restricted. These facts were commonly known and it cannot be said that the risk of war and its consequences necessitating restriction of the production and sale of automobiles was so remote a contingency that its risk could not be foreseen by defendant, an experienced automobile dealer. Indeed, the conditions prevailing at the time the lease was executed, and the absence of any provision in the lease contracting against the effect of war, gives rise to the inference that the risk was assumed. Defendant has therefore failed to prove that the possibility of war and its consequences on the production and sale of new automobiles was an unanticipated circumstance wholly outside the contemplation of the parties.

Nor has defendant sustained the burden of proving that the value of the lease has been destroyed. The sale of automobiles was not made impossible or illegal but merely restricted and if governmental regulation does not entirely prohibit the business to be carried on in the leased premises but only limits or restricts it, thereby making it less profitable and more difficult to continue, the lease is not terminated or the lessee excused from further performance (Brown v. Oshiro, supra, p. 194; Davidson v. Goldstein, supra, p. 918; Grace v. Croninger, supra, p. 607; Industrial Development & Land Co. v. Goldschmidt, supra; Burke v. San Francisco Brewing Co., supra, p. 202; First National Bank of New Rochelle v. Fairchester Oil Co., 267 App.Div. 281 [45 N.Y.S.2d 532, 533]; Robitzek Inv. Co., Inc. v. Colonial Beacon Oil Co., 265 App.Div. 749 [40 N.Y.S.2d 819, 824]; Colonial Operating Corp. v. Hannon Sales & Service, Inc., 265 App.Div. 411 [39 N.Y.S.2d 217, 220]; Byrnes v. Balcom, 265 App.Div. 268 [38 N.Y.S.2d 801, 803]; Deibler v. Bernard Bros. Inc., 385 Ill. 610 [53 N.E.2d 450, 453]; Wood v. Bartolino, ___ N.M. ___ [146 P.2d 883, 886, 888, 890]). Defendant may use the premises for the purpose for which they were leased. New automobiles and gasoline continue to be sold. Indeed, defendant testified that he continued to sell new automobiles exclusively at another location in the same county.

Defendant contends that the lease is restrictive and that the government orders therefore destroyed its value and frustrated its purpose. Provisions that prohibit subleasing or other uses than those specified affect the value of a lease and are to be considered in determining whether its purpose has been frustrated or its value destroyed (see Owens, The Effect of the War Upon the Rights and Liabilities of Parties to a Contract, 19 California State Bar Journal 132, 143). It must not be forgotten, however, that "The landlord has not covenanted that the tenant shall have the right to carry on the contemplated business or that the business to which the premises are by their nature or by the terms of the lease restricted shall be profitable enough to enable the tenant to pay the rent but has imposed a condition for his own benefit; and, certainly, unless and until he chooses to take advantage of it, the tenant is not deprived of the use of the premises." (6 Williston, Contracts, op. Cit. Supra, § 1955, p. 5485; see, also, People v. Klopstock, 24 Cal.2d 897, 901 [151 P.2d 641].)

In the present lease plaintiffs reserved the rights that defendant should not use the premises for other purposes than those specified in the lease or sublease without plaintiff's written consent. Far from preventing other uses or subleasing they waived these rights, enabling defendant to use the premises for any legitimate purpose and to sublease them to any responsible tenant. This waiver is significant in view of the location of the premises on a main traffic artery in Los Angeles County and their adaptability for many commercial purposes. The value of these rights is attested by the fact that the premises were rented soon after defendants vacated them. It is therefore clear that the governmental restrictions on the sale of new cars have not destroyed the value of the lease. Furthermore, plaintiffs offered to lower the rent if defendant should be unable to operate profitably, and their conduct was at all times fair and cooperative.

The consequences of applying the doctrine of frustration to a leasehold involving less than a total or nearly total destruction of the value of the leased premises would be undesirable. Confusion would result from different decisions purporting to define "substantial" frustration. Litigation would be encouraged by the repudiation of leases when lessees found their businesses less profitable because of the regulations attendant upon a national emergency. Many leases have been affected in varying degrees by the widespread governmental regulations necessitated by war conditions.

The cases that defendant relies upon are consistent with the conclusion reached herein. In Industrial Development & Land Co. v. Goldschmidt, supra, the lease provided that the premises should not be used other than as a saloon. When national prohibition made the sale of alcoholic beverages illegal, the court excused the tenant from further performance on the theory of illegality or impossibility by a change in domestic law. The doctrine of frustration might have been applied, since the purpose for which the property was leased was totally destroyed and there was nothing to show that the value of the lease was not thereby totally destroyed. In the present case the purpose was not destroyed but only restricted, and plaintiffs proved that the lease was valuable to defendant. In Grace v. Croninger, supra, the lease was for the purpose of conducting a "saloon and cigar store and for no other purpose" with provision for subleasing a portion of the premises for bootblack purposes. The monthly rental was $650. It was clear that prohibition destroyed the main purpose of the lease, but since the premises could be used for bootblack and cigar store purposes, the lessee was not excused from his duty to pay the rent. In the present case new automobiles and gasoline may be sold under the lease as executed and any legitimate business may be conducted or the premises may be subleased under the lease as modified by plaintiff's waiver. Colonial Operating Corp. v. Hannon Sales & Service, Inc., 34 N.Y.S.2d 116, was reversed in 265 App.Div. 411 [39 N.Y.S.2d 217, and Signal Land Corp. v. Loecher, 35 N.Y.S.2d 25; Schantz v. American Auto Supply Co., Inc., 178 Misc. 909 [36 N.Y.S.2d 747]; and Canrock Realty Corp. v. Vim Electric Co., Inc., 37 N.Y.S.2d 139, involved government orders that totally destroyed the possibility of selling the products for which the premises were leased. No case has been cited by defendant or disclosed by research in which an appellate court has excused a lessee from performance of his duty to pay rent when the purpose of the lease has not been totally destroyed or its accomplishment rendered extremely impracticable or where it has been shown that the lease remains valuable to the lessee.

The judgment is affirmed.

Gibson, C.J., Shenk, J., Curtis, J., Edmonds, J., Carter, J., and Schauer, J., concurred.

20th Century Lites, Inc. v. Goodman
California Superior Court, Appellate Department, 1944
64 Cal.App.2d Supp. 938

KINCAID, J.

This appeal arises out of an action commenced by plaintiff to recover certain monthly payments claimed due under a written contract whereby plaintiff leased neon sign installations to defendant in consideration of agreed payments to be made by defendant for the contractual period. The defendant, among other defenses, alleges that by reason of the governmental order of August 5, 1942, prohibiting the illumination of all outside neon or lighting equipment between the hours of sunset and sunrise, he has been prevented, without fault on his part, from using such installations during the nighttime, and that such use was the desired object and effect contemplated by the parties at the time of the execution of the contract.

The lease contract of September 3, 1941, is one wherein plaintiff retains the title to the neon signs and tubing which it installed and maintained on the exterior of defendant's "drive-in" restaurant. The court found from the evidence that the parties had each performed all terms and conditions of the contract to August 4, 1942; that on August 5, 1942, the Government of the United States, as an emergency war measure, ordered a cessation of all outside lighting, including neon illuminated signs, at all hours between sunset and sunrise, covering the district in which defendant's place of business is located; that said proclamation of cessation has, during all the time in question, remained in full force and effect, and that, because of this fact, the defendant has been prevented from illuminating such signs during such hours; that subsequent to August 5, 1942, defendant offered to surrender to plaintiff such contract, to terminate same, and to permit plaintiff to remove such signs, but plaintiff refused to accept the offer and thereafter, beginning September 1, 1942, defendant failed to pay the monthly rental payments in the contract set forth.

The trial court properly concluded and found that, by reason of such governmental proclamation, the desired object or effect that the parties to the contract intended to attain at the time it was entered into, was frustrated without the fault of either party on and after August 5, 1942, and that defendant was harmed thereby. It further found that on and after said date both parties to said contract were excused from any further performance of any one of the terms or conditions thereof, and that said contract thereupon terminated.

The legal principles which are here applicable are set forth in the case of Johnson v. Atkins (1942), 53 Cal.App.2d 430, 433 [127 P.2d 1027], wherein the court quotes with approval from Restatement of the Law of Contracts, section 288, as follows: "'Where the assumed possibility of a desired object or effect to be attained by either party to a contract forms the basis on which both parties enter into it, and this object or effect is or surely will be frustrated, a promisor who is without fault in causing the frustration, and who is harmed thereby, is discharged from the duty of performing his promise unless a contrary intention appears.'" To the same general effect such decision further quotes (p. 434), from 13 Corpus Juris 642: "'Where from the nature of the contract it is evident that the parties contracted on the basis of the continued existence of the person or thing, condition or state of things, to which it relates, the subsequent perishing of the person or thing, or cessation of existence of the condition, will excuse the performance, a condition to such effect being implied, in spite of the fact that the promise may have been unqualified.'" These principles are apparently recognized by Civil Code, section 1511, subdivision 1. Among the California cases in support thereof are Johnson v. Atkins (supra); H. Hackfeld & Co. v. Castle (1921), 186 Cal. 53 [198 P. 1041]; and La Cumbre G. & Co. Club v. Santa Barbara Hotel Co. (1928), 205 Cal. 422 [271 P. 476].

Plaintiff contends that the foregoing principles of law, which have been called the doctrine of commercial frustration, are inapplicable under the terms and conditions of the contract made by the parties herein; that the contractual provisions for block lettering of the signs, thus making them visible in the daytime when they are not illuminated, and the availability of the illumination of the sign during daylight as well as dark hours, demonstrate that there has been no destruction of the subject matter of the contract and that the desired object was not completely frustrated. It argues that the enforced termination of illumination of the signs during the night hours caused only a condition rendering the transaction less attractive and less profitable to defendant.

In considering the soundness of plaintiff's position, it is first necessary to examine the contract in order to ascertain the nature of the "desired object or effect to be attained" by the transaction which the agreement represents. The contract describes the thing leased to defendant as an "electrical advertising display." The defendant is required to use it at his place of business and not elsewhere. Ordinarily, words of a contract are to be understood in their ordinary or popular sense. (Civ. Code, § 1644.) Webster's New International Dictionary defines the noun "display" as "An opening or unfolding; exhibition; manifestation. Ostentatious show; exhibition for effect; parade." When qualified by the adjective "electrical" it becomes an electrical exhibition or electrical manifestation. In order to be an electrical display, it must use electricity, in which event it then becomes illuminated and is an "electrical advertising display." Unelectrified, it is merely a display. While illuminated, it would remain as a sign, still it would not be the "electrical advertising display" which the contract called for and which manifestly was the "desired object or effect to be attained."

The contract is silent as to what hours of the day or night the signs were to be illuminated, although it requires the use of the "electrical advertising display" for a period of thirty-six months. The absence from the contract of any provision fixing hours of the day or night during which the sign is to be illuminated does not create an uncertainty. The parol evidence was inadmissible for the purpose of interpreting any such claimed uncertainty, but it was properly admitted to show a state of facts to which the doctrine of commercial frustration was applicable. The cases do not hold that such facts must appear on the face of the contract, and the purpose of proving them is not to vary the terms of the contract itself, but to show that a state of facts has arisen which results in its termination. The evidence is admissible, not for the purpose of inserting in the contract a provision requiring the defendant to use the sign at night or forbidding him to use it at any other time, but only to show that its illumination at night was the desired object to be obtained by the parties, and that the possibility of such illumination formed the basis on which both parties entered into the contract.

The defendant testified that he had never at any time illuminated the signs in the daytime, and that at the time of his negotiations with plaintiff's representative for such signs defendant advised plaintiff that he was interested in a neon sign for nighttime illumination for his place of business, which he needed because he was "blocked off more or less on a side street." Plaintiff's agent then demonstrated a tube which he said was a much larger and brighter neon tube than the ordinary one, and that by installing it in the tower of the building, it would give illumination at night from a great distance and would bring traffic into his place. Such a tube was ultimately installed as a part of the display.

It is apparent, therefore, that the "desired object or effect to be obtained" by defendant in his hiring of the "electrical advertising display" was the dual purpose of illuminating the exterior of his place of business at night, and the advertising thereof by means of the electrically illuminated signs during the nighttime, whereby passing trade would be notified of the presence of his place of business and would be attracted thereto. The merely incidental facts, that it remained physically possible to illuminate the display with electricity in the daytime and the signs were visible even though unlighted during the daylight hours, are of such inconsequential moment as to have no effect on the application of the rule.

When considered with the fact that all of such neon installations were on the exterior of the building, the required termination of the use of electricity in such signs, between the hours of sunset and sunrise, constituted a "cessation of existence of the condition" which was the "desired object or effect" and was the essential, primary and principal basis for which the signs were rented. The court's finding that such were the facts is substantially supported by the evidence.

We cannot agree with plaintiff's contention that the doctrine of commercial frustration may not be applied unless the defendant can show that the legal prohibition of the use to which the electrical equipment may be put was complete and that such use was entirely prevented for any purpose permitted under the contract of letting. The weight of authority in the United States is to the contrary, and is to the effect that such doctrine may be invoked whenever official governmental action prevents the hirer from using the property for the primary and principal purpose for which it was hired. In such event the contract of hiring is terminated even though other incidental uses might remain available for the thing hired.

Such governmental proclamation having, without the fault of either party to the contract, frustrated the "desired object or effect to be obtained," the doctrine of commercial frustration is applied through the means of implying a condition to exist in the contract whereby under such circumstances as are here found, the parties shall be excused from any further performance of its terms. This rule is cited in Johnson v. Atkins (supra, p. 431), wherein an excerpt from the case of Straus v. Kazemekas, 100 Conn. 581 [124 A. 234, 238] is quoted as follows: "'Where from the nature of the contract and the surrounding circumstances the parties from the beginning must have known that it could not be fullfilled unless when the time for fulfillment arrived, some particular thing or condition of things continued to exist so that they must be deemed, when entering into the contract, to have contemplated such continuing existence as the foundation of what was to be done; in the absence of any express or implied warranty that such thing or condition of things shall exist the contract is to be construed as subject to an implied condition that the parties shall be excused in case, before breach, performance becomes impossible or the purpose of the contract frustrated from such thing or condition ceasing to exist without default of either of the parties. 12 A.L.R. 1275.'"

The lease contract herein contains no provisions with regard to the contingencies here considered. The right to illuminate the signs at night being the primary foundation essential to the desirability and usefulness of the contract, the termination of that right under the conditions here found results in a situation wherein the contract must be deemed subject to the implied condition that the parties had in mind, at the inception of the contract, that such primary foundation should be continuing in existence. Such being the case the trial court properly held that from and after August 5, 1942, the contract was terminated and both parties thereto were excused from further performance.

Plaintiff argues that, even conceding the facts above referred to as being true, the doctrine of commercial frustration cannot be invoked in this case, because of the fact that it has been put to an expense in manufacturing and installing the signs; that the termination of the contract on such grounds would violate the principles of equity. It relies strongly on the case of San Joaquin L. & P. Corp. v. Costaloupes (1929), 96 Cal.App. 322 [274 P. 84], in support of this contention. The latter case may be distinguished from the one here under consideration, as the court there held the contract to be one to deliver electrical energy to a certain described piece of land irrespective of its use. Although a fire had destroyed the factory wherein it had been contemplated that the electricity would be used, the court said (p. 327): "All that appears here is that by reason of the premises the defendants could not use any more power or light in these particular buildings, but if at any time they chose to rebuild or make other use or application of the light and power they could have enforced their right of delivery of electrical energy." This is a vastly different situation than is presented by the contract and the facts of our case. Here, the plaintiff agreed to furnish an "electrical advertising display" which contemplated its being continuously operable by electrified illumination at night. Furthermore, the defendant was not in the position of the user of electricity in the cited case, in that he could not relieve his situation by any voluntary act of his own, such as rebuilding his factory or making other use of the hired product. The facts herein are such as to prohibit the application of this exception to the general rule.

The defendant, by way of petition for rehearing, for the first time advanced the proposition that, because of the governmental order of November 1, 1943, abolishing the dim-out requirements, the effect of such dim-out regulation was to merely suspend, rather than terminate, the contract during the approximately fourteen months' existence of such regulation. Rehearing was granted, and this proposition was argued and considered.

Such is not the rule in cases where the doctrine of commercial frustration applies. On the application of such doctrine, the promisor "is discharged from the duty of performing his promise ..." (Johnson v. Atkins, supra, p. 434.) (Italics added.) On page 433, we find, " ... such a frustration brings the contract to an end forthwith, without more and automatically."

This rule has been recognized by the United States Supreme Court in the case of Allanwilde Transport Corp. v. Vacuum Oil Co. (1918), 248 U.S. 377 [39 S.Ct. 147, 63 L.Ed. 312], where it was urged that the government's embargo on ships leaving American ports during a part of World War I, because of the enemy submarine menace, constituted but a temporary impediment, and therefore did not terminate the contract. In holding to the contrary, the court said: "The duration was of indefinite extent. Necessarily, the embargo would be continued as long as the cause of its imposition,—that is, the submarine menace,—and that, as far as then could be inferred, would be the duration of the war, of which there could be no estimate or reliable speculation. The condition was, therefore, so far permanent as naturally and justifiably to determine business judgment and action depending upon it."

The cases where the doctrine of commercial frustration, with its immediate termination of the obligations of the promisor applies, are to be distinguished from that type of case wherein such doctrine is inapplicable and the governmental embargo or regulation is not a permanent prohibition but is temporary only. The case of United States Trading Corp. v. Newmark G. Co. (1922), 56 Cal.App. 176, 186 [205 P. 29], is of the latter class, and does not conflict with the rule heretofore enunciated.

The judgment is affirmed, respondent to recover his costs of appeal.

Shaw, J., and Fox, J., concurred.

Afterthoughts

Although the doctrines of frustration and impossibility are akin, frustration is not a form of impossibility of performance. It more properly relates to the consideration for performance. Under it, performance remains possible, but is excused whenever a fortuitous event supervenes to cause a failure of the consideration or a practically total destruction of the expected value of the performance. (*20th Century Lites, Inc. v. Goodman*, *supra*, 64 Cal.App.2d Supp. 938 [149 P.2d 88]; Restatement Second of Contracts, §265.)

Chapter 9

Third Party Rights

Third Party Beneficiary Contracts

A contract, made expressly for the benefit of a third person, may be enforced by him at any time before the parties thereto rescind it. (Civ. Code, § 1559.)

Johnson v. Holmes Tuttle Lincoln-Mercury
California Court of Appeal, Second District, Division Three, 1958
160 Cal.App.2d 290, 325 P.2d 193

VALLEE, J.

Appeal from a judgment for plaintiffs as third party beneficiaries of an oral agreement to procure public liability and property damage insurance.

The agreement is alleged to have been entered into between Holmes Tuttle Lincoln-Mercury, Inc., called defendant, and Phillip R. Caldera and his wife, Ruth, in connection with the purchase by the Calderas of a new Mercury automobile from defendant on November 23, 1953.

On December 11, 1953, about three weeks after the Calderas purchased the car, Phillip Caldera was involved in an accident with the Mercury. Plaintiffs, Willie Mae Johnson and Fletcher Jones, a passenger, were injured and Johnson's car was damaged.

Separate actions were filed by plaintiffs against Phillip Caldera. Judgments were entered May 23, 1955, in favor of plaintiff Johnson for $4,413.89, and in favor of plaintiff Jones for $2,070. These judgments remain unsatisfied.

Plaintiffs allege defendant, by its salesman Harry Rozany, had agreed with Caldera at the time the Mercury was purchased to procure "full coverage" insurance for Caldera, including public liability and property damage, for the operation of the Mercury; both Caldera and defendant understood the insurance was to be obtained for the usual term and for no less than the minimum legal limits; defendant failed to obtain the public liability and property damage insurance after Caldera had performed all of the terms of the agreement on his part. The prayer is for the amounts of the judgments obtained against Caldera with interest. In a jury trial the verdict was for plaintiffs as prayed. Defendant appeals from the judgment which followed.

On November 23, 1953, Caldera appeared with his wife, Ruth, at the showroom of defendant for the purpose of purchasing a new Mercury. One of defendant's salesmen, Harry Rozany, approached the Calderas and discussed with them the prospective purchase of a new Mercury like the one then in the showroom. After about five minutes Rozany took them to a "closing room" where terms were discussed for about an hour and the purchase consummated. The Calderas told Rozany they had a 1948 Chevrolet as a trade- in and $900 cash as a down payment. They indicated they could not afford to make payments of over $80 a month on the balance. During the discussion Caldera told Rozany he wanted "full coverage insurance," and Rozany replied, "Oh, yes, you are getting it." Rozany made out the papers and sold them "another insurance," a policy by which the insurer engaged to pay the balance of the purchase price of the car in the event of the death or disability of Caldera. The premium of $2.50 to $3.00 a month was to be included in the installment payments. Rozany computed the figures in the transaction on "scratch paper." He had Caldera sign the car order and the conditional sale contract in blank. Rozany took the papers "upstairs," saying he was going to complete filling them out.

About December 2, 1953, Mrs. Caldera received by mail a copy of the conditional sale contract dated December 1, 1953, which showed fire, theft, comprehensive, and $50 deductible collision insurance thereon, but which made no reference to public liability and property damage insurance. Mrs. Caldera read only the figures. She called defendant to talk to Rozany but as he was not there she did not talk to him or to anyone. Caldera did not see this copy of the conditional sale contract received by Mrs. Caldera. Neither of the Calderas saw the original sales order until after the first of the year when Caldera went to put in the new certificate of registration and discovered the folded document with the stamped notation "No liability insurance sold on this car," which had been placed in the registration holster and fastened on the wheel by Rozany shortly after he had returned to the closing room with the approved order at the time of the purchase. Caldera first learned he had no public liability and property damage insurance after his wife went to the office of Olympic Insurance Company "to find out about the insurance." That company had issued the collision policy dated December 15, 1953, which the Calderas received December 17, 1953, four days after the accident.

To Caldera, who was 36 years old, employed as a mechanic, and who had been through the ninth grade in school, "full coverage insurance" meant everything that is supposed to be in insurance, including public liability and property damage. The public liability and property damage insurance on the 1948 Chevrolet automobile used as a trade-in had expired in August of 1953, and Caldera testified that since it was an old car and they intended trading it in on a new one any day he thought there was no use in renewing it.

Defendant had a licensed insurance department. Its salesman, Rozany, had been a new car salesman there about three years, during which time he had sold about 300 cars, and on at least one occasion the sale involved the purchase of public liability and property damage insurance. Rozany's experience as a new car salesman was continuous from 1937.

Plaintiffs' expert witness, James P. Bennett, an experienced insurance salesman, testified over objection of defendant that the term "full coverage" when used by a layman meant in the automobile insurance business insurance against damage to his car and against damage caused by his car; it would include a term of one year, basic limits of $5,000 for injuries to one person, $10,000 for injuries to all persons in one accident, and $5,000 for property damage, as well as $500 medical payments. The premium for such insurance by one using his car to travel to and from work in the particular territory in which Caldera drove would be $63. He also testified there was sufficient information on the purchaser's statement which was signed by Caldera to order the coverage, so long as he had the sales order to identify the car.

Defendant first asserts the evidence does not support the implied finding of the jury that there was a contract to procure public liability and property damage insurance between Caldera and defendant; nor does the evidence support the implied finding that plaintiffs were third party beneficiaries of a contract between Caldera and defendant. It is argued there was no consideration paid by Caldera for defendant's agreement to procure full coverage insurance, including public liability and property damage. The agreement alleged and proved was that in consideration of Caldera's purchasing the Mercury defendant would procure full coverage insurance, including public liability and property damage. Mutual promises constitute consideration. (Civ. Code, § 1605; El Rio Oils v. Pacific Coast Asphalt Co., 95 Cal.App. 2d 186, 193 [213 P.2d 1]; 12 Cal.Jur.2d 498, § 266; Rest., Contracts, § 77.) A single consideration may support several counterpromises. (H. S. Crocker Co., Inc. v. McFaddin, 148 Cal.App.2d 639, 645 [307 P.2d 429].)

It is interesting to note that the conditional sale contract which Caldera signed in blank recites a total contract balance due of $2,505.73. The policy received by Caldera shows the amount of the contract as $2,598.73, a difference of $93. The insurer must have obtained the contract figure from defendant. The uncontradicted evidence shows that the cost of public liability and property damage in basic limits plus $500 medical payments coverage was $63. Figuring the transaction with one year's premiums in advance as Rozany did with the other coverages, the total charges equal the $93 difference.

The evidence recited, contrary to defendant's claim, shows there was a meeting of minds. It is argued that because Rozany testified he did not know what the term "full coverage" meant there could be no meeting of minds. The jury was not compelled to believe Rozany. He was thoroughly impeached. The jury may have inferred his knowledge from his experience. He had been a new car salesman since 1937, three years with defendant, and had sold around 300 cars "or better." Defendant was a licensed insurance broker with an insurance department operated in connection with its auto sales business. Rozany told Mrs. Caldera full coverage "includes everything."

Referring to the testimony of the witness Bennett, which was admitted over its objection, defendant argues it was erroneously admitted in that it was proof of custom and usage for the purpose of creating a contract, which may not be done. Custom and usage was not relied on to create a contract. It was admitted for the purpose of explaining and interpreting the phrase, "full coverage," and for that purpose it was admissible. (Code Civ. Proc., § 1870, subd. 12.) Furthermore, the testimony was in effect merely a statement of the law which every person is presumed to know and of which the court could take judicial notice. (Veh. Code, § 415.)

Defendant contends plaintiffs were not third party beneficiaries. "A contract, made expressly for the benefit of a third person, may be enforced by him at any time before the parties thereto rescind it." (Civ. Code, § 1559.) Where one person for a valuable consideration engages with another to do some act for the benefit of a third person, and the agreement thus made has not been rescinded, the party for whose benefit the contract or promise was made, or who would enjoy the benefit of the act, may maintain an action against the promisor for the breach of his engagement. While the contract remains unrescinded, the relations of the parties are the same as though the promise had been made directly to the third party. Although the party for whose benefit the promise was made was not cognizant of it when made, it is, if adopted by him, deemed to have been made to him. He may sue on the promise. Where a promise is made to benefit a third party on the happening of a certain contingency, the third party may enforce the contract on the occurrence of that contingency. (12 Cal.Jur.2d 493, § 261.) The action by a third party beneficiary for the breach of the promisor's engagement does not rest on the ground of any actual or supposed relationship between the parties but on the broad and more satisfactory basis that the law, operating on the acts of the parties, creates the duty, establishes a privity, and implies the promise and obligation on which the action is founded. (Washer v. Independent Min. & Dev. Co., 142 Cal. 702, 708-9 [76 P. 654].)

It is not necessary that the beneficiary be named and identified as an individual; a third party may enforce a contract if he can show he is a member of a class for whose benefit it was made. (Calhoun v. Downs, 211 Cal. 766, 770-1 [297 P. 548]; Garratt v. Baker, 5 Cal.2d 745, 748 [56 P.2d 225]; Shell v. Schmidt, 126 Cal.App.2d 279, 290 [272 P.2d 82]; Woodhead Lbr. Co. v. E. G. Niemann Inv., 99 Cal.App. 456, 459 [278 P. 913].) It is no objection to the maintenance of an action by a third party that a suit might be brought also against the one to whom the promise was made. (Malone v. Crescent City M. & T. Co., 77 Cal. 38, 44 [18 P. 858].)

The test for determining whether a contract was made for the benefit of a third person is whether an intent to benefit a third person appears from the terms of the contract. (Le Ballister v. Redwood Theatres, Inc., 1 Cal.App.2d 447, 449 [36 P.2d 827].) If the terms of the contract necessarily require the promisor to confer a benefit on a third person, then the contract, and hence the parties thereto, contemplate a benefit to the third person. The parties are presumed to intend the consequences of a performance of the contract. [15] It is held that a person injured may sue on a contract for the benefit of all members of the public who are so injured since the happening of the injury sufficiently determines his identity and right of action. (Levy v. Daniels' U-Drive Auto Renting Co., 108 Conn. 333 [143 A. 163, 165, 61 A.L.R. 846].)

Section 11580 of the Insurance Code reads:

"A policy insuring against losses set forth in subdivision (a) shall not be issued or delivered to any person in this State unless it contains the provisions set forth in subdivision (b). Such policy, whether or not actually containing such provisions, shall be construed as if such provisions were embodied therein.

"(a) Unless it contains such provisions, the following policies of insurance shall not be thus issued or delivered:

"(1) Against loss or damage resulting from liability for injury suffered by another person other than a policy of workmen's compensation insurance.

"(2) Against loss of or damage to property caused by draught animals or any vehicle, and for which the insured is liable.

"(b) Such policy shall not be thus issued or delivered to any person in this State unless it contains all the following provisions:

"(1) A provision that the insolvency or bankruptcy of the insured will not release the insurer from the payment of damages for injury sustained or loss occasioned during the life of such policy.

"(2) A provision that whenever judgment is secured against the insured or the executor or administrator of a deceased insured in an action based upon bodily injury, death, or property damage, then an action may be brought against the insurer on the policy and subject to its terms and limitations, by such judgment creditor to recover on the judgment."

The statute is a part of every policy and creates a contractual relation which inures to the benefit of any and every person who might be negligently injured by the insured as completely as if such injured person had been specifically named in the policy. (Malmgren v. Southwestern A. Ins. Co., 201 Cal. 29, 33 [255 P. 512]; Bias v. Ohio Farmers Indemnity Co., 28 Cal.App.2d 14, 16 [81 P.2d 1057].) The primary purpose of the statute is to protect an injured person when the insured is bankrupt or insolvent. (Hynding v. Home Acc. Ins. Co., 214 Cal. 743, 746 [7 P.2d 999, 85 A.L.R. 13].) The complaint here alleges Caldera is insolvent and there was evidence to that effect. The statute in effect makes the tortfeasee a creditor beneficiary. It makes the benefit of the policy available to the creditor beneficiary tortfeasee. (See 27 Cal.L.Rev. 497, 529.)

In James Stewart & Co. v. Law, 149 Tex. 392 [233 S.W.2d 558, 22 A.L.R.2d 639], a corporation—the owner—entered into a contract with a contractor for the erection of certain buildings. The contract expressly obligated the contractor to maintain certain insurance, and also provided that in case any part of the contract was sublet by the contractor the latter should require of its subcontractor the maintenance of automobile liability insurance. The contractor sublet part of the work to a subcontractor who in turn contracted with a truck owner for the hauling of gravel in connection with the performance of his subcontract. Neither the contractor nor the subcontractor required his respective subcontractor to carry automobile insurance and none was carried by the truck owner. While hauling gravel, the latter injured an employee of the owner, and the employee brought suit against the contractor to recover damages on the theory that the contractor had breached its contract with the owner by failing to see that all subcontractors carried automobile liability insurance, and that he, the employee, was a third party beneficiary of such contract. The court held the injured employee was a third party beneficiary under the contract and as such entitled to maintain suit against the contractor.

Buckley v. Gray, 110 Cal. 339 [42 P. 900, 52 Am.St.Rep. 88, 31 L.R.A. 862], relied on by defendant, was overruled in Biakanja v. Irving, 49 Cal.2d 647, 651 [320 P.2d 16].

There is no escape from the conclusion that the agreement between defendant and Caldera was not for the sole benefit of the latter but that it was intended to inure to the benefit of third persons who might be protected by a full coverage policy. (Cf. Goff v. Ladd, 161 Cal. 257, 258 [118 P. 792]; French v. Farmer, 178 Cal. 218, 221 [172 P. 1102]; Sunset Lumber Co. v. Smith, 91 Cal.App. 746, 750-751 [267 P. 738]. See anno.: 81 A.L.R. 1271; 26 Cal.L.Rev. 627.) The intent to confer a benefit on anyone to whom Caldera might become liable as a result of a hazard incident to ownership and operation of the Mercury is obvious. This is precisely what Caldera wanted as a means of obtaining a benefit to himself. It must have been in the contemplation of the parties when Rozany agreed to procure public liability and property damage insurance that injury to third persons might result from ownership and operation of the Mercury. It was reasonable for the jury to infer that Caldera, in making the agreement with defendant, desired and intended that such persons be protected in the event of an accident with the Mercury. The jury's finding that there was a third party beneficiary contract breached by defendant to plaintiffs' damage is amply supported by the record.

The action is for breach of an oral contract to procure insurance; it is not based on fraud, as defendant asserts. Proof of fraud was merely incidental to proof of the contract. Defendant filed a general and special demurrer to the complaint which was overruled. Error is asserted. It is said there is no "allegation that the alleged agreement was for the express benefit of plaintiffs." Sufficient facts are alleged to show that it was for plaintiffs' benefit. While there are some uncertainties in the complaint, no prejudice is shown. Depositions were taken before trial, the cause was fully and fairly tried, defendant does not claim surprise, and the error, if any, in overruling the special demurrer did not affect defendant's substantial rights in any way.

Other points made do not require discussion.

Affirmed.

Shinn, P. J., and Wood (Parker), J., concurred.

Lucas v. Hamm

Supreme Court of California, 1961
56 Cal.2d 583, 364 P.2d 685, 15 Cal.Rptr. 821

GIBSON, C. J.

Plaintiffs, who are some of the beneficiaries under the will of Eugene H. Emmick, deceased, brought this action for damages against defendant L. S. Hamm, an attorney at law who had been engaged by the testator to prepare the will. They have appealed from a judgment of dismissal entered after an order sustaining a general demurrer to the second amended complaint without leave to amend.

The allegations of the first and second causes of action are summarized as follows: Defendant agreed with the testator, for a consideration, to prepare a will and codicils thereto for him by which plaintiffs were to be designated as beneficiaries of a trust provided for by paragraph Eighth of the will and were to receive 15 per cent of the residue as specified in that paragraph. Defendant, in violation of instructions and in breach of his contract, negligently prepared testamentary instruments containing phraseology that was invalid by virtue of section 715.2 and former sections 715.1 and 716 of the Civil Code relating to restraints on alienation and the rule against perpetuities. Paragraph Eighth of these instruments "transmitted" the residual estate in trust and provided that the "trust shall cease and terminate at 12 o'clock noon on a day five years after the date upon which the order distributing the trust property to the trustee is made by the Court having jurisdiction over the probation of this will." After the death of the testator the instruments were admitted to probate. Subsequently defendant, as draftsman of the instruments and as counsel of record for the executors, advised plaintiffs in writing that the residual trust provision was invalid and that plaintiffs would be deprived of the entire amount to which they would have been entitled if the provision had been valid unless they made a settlement with the blood relatives of the testator under which plaintiffs would receive a lesser amount than that provided for them by the testator. As the direct and proximate result of the negligence of defendant and his breach of contract in preparing the testamentary instruments and the written advice referred to above, plaintiffs were compelled to enter into a settlement under which they received a share of the estate amounting to $75,000 less than the sum which they would have received pursuant to testamentary instruments drafted in accordance with the directions of the testator.

* * *

It was held in Buckley v. Gray, 110 Cal. 339 [42 P. 900, 52 Am.St.Rep. 88, 31 L.R.A. 862], that an attorney who made a mistake in drafting a will was not liable for negligence or breach of contract to a person named in the will who was deprived of benefits as a result of the error. The court stated that an attorney is liable to his client alone with respect to actions based on negligence in the conduct of his professional duties, and it was reasoned that there could be no recovery for mere negligence where there was no privity by contract or otherwise between the defendant and the person injured. (110 Cal. at pp. 342-343.) The court further concluded that there could be no recovery on the theory of a contract for the benefit of a third person, because the contract with the attorney was not expressly for the plaintiff's benefit and the testatrix only remotely intended the plaintiff to be benefited as a result of the contract. (110 Cal. at pp. 346-347.) For the reasons hereinafter stated the case is overruled.

The reasoning underlying the denial of tort liability in the Buckley case, i.e., the stringent privity test, was rejected in Biakanja v. Irving, 49 Cal.2d 647, 648-650 [320 P.2d 16, 65 A.L.R.2d 1358], where we held that a notary public who, although not authorized to practice law, prepared a will but negligently failed to direct proper attestation was liable in tort to an intended beneficiary who was damaged because of the invalidity of the instrument. It was pointed out that since 1895, when Buckley was decided, the rule that in the absence of privity there was no liability for negligence committed in the performance of a contract had been greatly liberalized. (49 Cal.2d at p. 649.) In restating the rule it was said that the determination whether in a specific case the defendant will be held liable to a third person not in privity is a matter of policy and involves the balancing of various factors, among which are the extent to which the transaction was intended to affect the plaintiff, the foreseeability of harm to him, the degree of certainty that the plaintiff suffered injury, the closeness of the connection between the defendant's conduct and the injury, and the policy of preventing future harm. (49 Cal.2d at p. 650.) The same general principle must be applied in determining whether a beneficiary is entitled to bring an action for negligence in the drafting of a will when the instrument is drafted by an attorney rather than by a person not authorized to practice law.

Many of the factors which led to the conclusion that the notary public involved in Biakanja was liable are equally applicable here. As in Biakanja, one of the main purposes which the transaction between defendant and the testator intended to accomplish was to provide for the transfer of property to plaintiffs; the damage to plaintiffs in the event of invalidity of the bequest was clearly foreseeable; it became certain, upon the death of the testator without change of the will, that plaintiffs would have received the intended benefits but for the asserted negligence of defendant; and if persons such as plaintiffs are not permitted to recover for the loss resulting from negligence of the draftsman, no one would be able to do so and the policy of preventing future harm would be impaired.

Since defendant was authorized to practice the profession of an attorney, we must consider an additional factor not present in Biakanja, namely, whether the recognition of liability to beneficiaries of wills negligently drawn by attorneys would impose an undue burden on the profession. Although in some situations liability could be large and unpredictable in amount, this is also true of an attorney's liability to his client. We are of the view that the extension of his liability to beneficiaries injured by a negligently drawn will does not place an undue burden on the profession, particularly when we take into consideration that a contrary conclusion would cause the innocent beneficiary to bear the loss. The fact that the notary public involved in Biakanja was guilty of unauthorized practice of the law was only a minor factor in determining that he was liable, and the absence of the factor in the present case does not justify reaching a different result.

It follows that the lack of privity between plaintiffs and defendant does not preclude plaintiffs from maintaining an action in tort against defendant.

Neither do we agree with the holding in Buckley that beneficiaries damaged by an error in the drafting of a will cannot recover from the draftsman on the theory that they are third-party beneficiaries of the contract between him and the testator. Obviously the main purpose of a contract for the drafting of a will is to accomplish the future transfer of the estate of the testator to the beneficiaries named in the will, and therefore it seems improper to hold, as was done in Buckley, that the testator intended only "remotely" to benefit those persons. It is true that under a contract for the benefit of a third person performance is usually to be rendered directly to the beneficiary, but this is not necessarily the case. (See Rest., Contracts, § 133, comment d; 2 Williston on Contracts (3d ed. 1959) 829.) For example, where a life insurance policy lapsed because a bank failed to perform its agreement to pay the premiums out of the insured's bank account, it was held that after the insured's death the beneficiaries could recover against the bank as third-party beneficiaries. (Walker Bank & Trust Co. v. First Security Corp., 9 Utah 2d 215 [341 P.2d 944, 945 et seq.].)persons who had agreed to procure liability insurance for the protection of the promisees but did not do so were also held liable to injured persons who would have been covered by the insurance, the courts stating that all persons who might be injured were third-party beneficiaries of the contracts to procure insurance. (Johnson v. Holmes Tuttle Lincoln-Merc., 160 Cal.App.2d 290, 296 et seq. [325 P.2d 193]; James Stewart & Co. v. Law, 149 Tex. 392 [233 S.W.2d 558, 561-562, 22 A.L.R.2d 639].) Since, in a situation like those presented here and in the Buckley case, the main purpose of the testator in making his agreement with the attorney is to benefit the persons named in his will and this intent can be effectuated, in the event of a breach by the attorney, only by giving the beneficiaries a right of action, we should recognize, as a matter of policy, that they are entitled to recover as third-party beneficiaries. (See 2 Williston on Contracts (3d ed. 1959) pp. 843-844; 4 Corbin on Contracts (1951) pp. 8, 20.)

Section 1559 of the Civil Code, which provides for enforcement by a third person of a contract made "expressly" for his benefit, does not preclude this result. The effect of the section is to exclude enforcement by persons who are only incidentally or remotely benefited. (See Hartman Ranch Co. v. Associated Oil Co., 10 Cal.2d 232, 244 [73 P.2d 1163]; cf. 4 Corbin on Contracts (1951) pp. 23-24.) As we have seen, a contract for the drafting of a will unmistakably shows the intent of the testator to benefit the persons to be named in the will, and the attorney must necessarily understand this.

Defendant relies on language in Smith v. Anglo- California Trust Co., 205 Cal. 496, 502 [271 P. 898], and Fruitvale Canning Co. v. Cotton, 115 Cal.App.2d 622, 625 [252 P.2d 953], that to permit a third person to bring an action on a contract there must be "an intent clearly manifested by the promisor" to secure some benefit to the third person. This language, which was not necessary to the decision in either of the cases, is unfortunate. Insofar as intent to benefit a third person is important in determining his right to bring an action under a contract, it is sufficient that the promisor must have understood that the promisee had such intent. (Cf. Rest., Contracts, § 133, subds. 1(a) and 1(b); 4 Corbin on Contracts (1951) pp. 16-18; 2 Williston on Contracts (3d ed. 1959) pp. 836-839.) No specific manifestation by the promisor of an intent to benefit the third person is required. The language relied on by defendant is disapproved to the extent that it is inconsistent with these views.

We conclude that intended beneficiaries of a will who lose their testamentary rights because of failure of the attorney who drew the will to properly fulfill his obligations under his contract with the testator may recover as third-party beneficiaries.

* * *

The judgment is affirmed.

Traynor, J., Schauer, J., McComb, J., Peters, J., White, J., and Dooling, J., concurred.

Schauer v. Mandarin Gems of Cal.

California Court of Appeal, Fourth District, Division 3, 2005
125 Cal.App.4th 949

IKOLA, J.

Sarah Jane Schauer (plaintiff) appeals from a judgment of dismissal in favor of Mandarin Gems of California, Inc., dba Black, Starr & Frost (defendant) after the court sustained defendant's demurrer to plaintiff's second amended complaint without leave to amend. Plaintiff sought to recover on various theories based on her discovery that a diamond ring given to her as an engagement gift prior to her marriage to her now former husband, Darin Erstad, allegedly was not worth the $43,000 he paid defendant for it in 1999. Erstad is not a party to this action.

We reverse the judgment and remand. We conclude plaintiff has standing as a third party beneficiary of the sales contract between Erstad and defendant, and she has adequately pleaded a contract cause of action based on allegations of defendant's breach of express warranty. Defendant must answer to that claim. In all other respects, the pleading is defective and cannot be cured by amendment.

Facts

Our factual summary "accepts as true the facts alleged in the complaint, together with facts that may be implied or inferred from those expressly alleged." (*Barnett v. Fireman's Fund Ins. Co.* (2001) 90 Cal.App.4th 500, 505.)

Plaintiff and Erstad went shopping for an engagement ring on August 15, 1999. After looking at diamonds in premier jewelry establishments such as Tiffany and Company and Cartier, they went to defendant's store, where they found a ring that salesperson Joy said featured a 3.01 carat diamond with a clarity grading of "'SI1.'" Erstad bought the ring the same day for $43,121.55. The following month, for insurance purposes, defendant provided Erstad a written appraisal verifying the ring had certain characteristics, including an SI1 clarity rating and an average replacement value of $45,500. Paul Lam, a graduate gemologist with the European Gemological Laboratory (EGL), signed the appraisal.

The couple's subsequent short term marriage was dissolved in a North Dakota judgment awarding each party, "except as otherwise set forth in this Agreement," "the exclusive right, title and possession of all personal property ... which such party now owns, possesses, holds or hereafter acquires." Plaintiff's personal property included the engagement ring given to her by Erstad.

On June 3, 2002, after the divorce, plaintiff had the ring evaluated by the "'Gem Trade Laboratory,'" which gave the diamond a rating of "'SI2' quality," an appraisal with which "multiple other [unidentified] jewelers, including one at [defendant's store]" agreed. That was how plaintiff discovered defendant's alleged misrepresentation, concealment, and breach of express warranty regarding the true clarity of the diamond and its actual worth, which is—on plaintiff's information and belief—some $23,000 less than what Erstad paid for it.

Plaintiff sued defendant on several theories. Three times she attempted to plead her case. * * * The second cause of action, for breach of contract, alleged Erstad and defendant had a written contract under which Erstad agreed to purchase the ring "for the sole and stated purpose of giving it [to] Plaintiff," making plaintiff a third party beneficiary of the sales contract. Defendant breached the contract by delivering an engagement ring that did not conform to the promised SI1 clarity rating.

* * *

Appended to the pleading was a redacted copy of a North Dakota court's judgment filed July 19, 2001, granting Erstad and plaintiff a divorce pursuant to their "Stipulation and Agreement," entitling each party, as noted *ante*, "to the exclusive right, title and possession of all personal property of the parties, joint or several, which such party now owns, possesses, holds or hereafter acquires [*except as otherwise provided in the agreement*]," and awarding the parties their respective "personal effects, clothing and jewelry."

In its general demurrer to the second amended complaint and each cause of action, defendant asserted plaintiff had no viable claim under any theory because: (1) plaintiff was neither the purchaser of the ring nor a third party beneficiary of the contract between defendant and Erstad, who was not alleged to have assigned his rights to plaintiff [.]

* * *

The court again sustained the demurrer, this time without further leave to amend. The judgment of dismissal followed, and plaintiff appeals. As we will explain, the court erred. Although the complaint is fatally defective in some respects, plaintiff is entitled as a matter of law to pursue her contract claim as a third party beneficiary.

Discussion

* * *

We begin with the rule that "[e]very action must be prosecuted in the name of the real party in interest, except as otherwise provided by statute." (Code Civ. Proc., § 367.) Where the complaint shows the plaintiff does not possess the substantive right or standing to prosecute the action, "it is vulnerable to a general demurrer on the ground that it fails to state a cause of action." (*Carsten v. Psychology Examining Com.* (1980) 27 Cal.3d 793, 796; *Cloud v. Northrop Grumman Corp.* (1998) 67 Cal.App.4th 995, 1004.)

The second amended complaint alleges "[d]efendant entered into a written contract with [Erstad] to purchase the subject engagement ring." The attached exhibit shows defendant issued a written appraisal to Erstad. Erstad is clearly a real party in interest, but he has not sued.

Plaintiff contends she, too, is a real party in interest because the North Dakota divorce judgment endowed her with all of Erstad's rights and remedies. As we will explain, this theory is wrong. However, as we will also discuss, plaintiff is correct in asserting she is a third party beneficiary of the sales contract. That status enables her to proceed solely on her contract claim for breach of express warranty.

* * *

Transfer of Erstad's Rights and Remedies to Plaintiff

Plaintiff alleges and argues the North Dakota divorce judgment granted her "the exclusive right, title and possession of all [of her] personal property," including the engagement ring, and the judgment automatically divested Erstad of his substantive rights and transferred or assigned them to her by operation of law. Such is not the case.

Plaintiff undoubtedly owns the ring. (See Civ. Code, § 679 ["The ownership of property is absolute when a single person has the absolute dominion over it, and may use it or dispose of it according to his [or her] pleasure, subject only to general laws"]; see also North Dakota Century Code, section 47-01-01 (2003) ["The ownership of a thing shall mean the right of one or more persons to possess and use it to the exclusion of others. In this code the thing of which there may be ownership is called property"].) But ownership of gifted property, even if awarded in a divorce, does not automatically carry with it ownership of the rights of the person who bought the gift. As will be seen, contrary to plaintiff's hypothesis, the divorce judgment did not give plaintiff the ring embellished with Erstad's rights under the contract or his choses in action.

A cause of action for damages is itself personal property. (See Civ. Code, §953 ["A thing in action is a right to recover money or other personal property by a judicial proceeding"]; *Parker v. Walker* (1992) 5 Cal.App.4th 1173, 1182-1183 ["A cause of action to recover money in damages ... is a chose in action and therefore a form of personal property"]; see also *Iszler v. Jordan* (N.D. 1957) 80 N.W.2d 665, 668-669 [a chose in action is property].) At the time of the divorce judgment, all causes of action that could have been asserted against the jeweler by a buyer of the ring were Erstad's personal property. He was, after all, the purchaser of the ring. The divorce agreement awarded to each party his or her respective personal property, *except as otherwise expressly provided*. The disposition of the ring was expressly provided for in the agreement, i.e., plaintiff was given her jewelry. Any extant choses in action against defendant, however, were *not* expressly provided for in the agreement, therefore, they were *retained* by Erstad as part of his personal property.

To be sure, Erstad could have transferred or assigned *his* rights to legal recourse to plaintiff (see, e.g., *Dixon-Reo Co. v. Horton Motor Co.* (1922) 49 N.D. 304 [191 N.W. 780, 782] [a right arising out of an obligation, i.e., a thing in action, is the property of the person to whom the right is due and may be transferred]), but there are no allegations Erstad either did so or manifested an intention to do so. (See, e.g., *Krusi v. S.J. Amoroso Construction Co.* (2000) 81 Cal.App.4th 995, 1005; *Vaughn v. Dame Construction Co.* (1990) 223 Cal.App.3d 144, 148; see also *Nisewanger v. W.J. Lane Co.* (1947) 75 N.D. 448, 455 [28 N.W.2d 409, 412] [under North Dakota law, when a chose in action is assignable, the clear intent to assign must be established].)

Third Party Beneficiary

The fact that Erstad did not assign or transfer his rights to plaintiff does not mean she is without recourse. For although plaintiff does not have Erstad's rights by virtue of the divorce judgment, she nonetheless has standing in her own right to sue for breach of contract as a third party beneficiary under the allegation, inter alia, that "[d]efendant entered into a written contract with Plaintiff's fiancée [*sic*] to purchase the subject engagement ring for the sole and stated purpose of giving it [to] Plaintiff."

Civil Code section 1559 provides: "A contract, made expressly for the benefit of a third person, may be enforced by him [or her] at any time before the parties thereto rescind it." Because third party beneficiary status is a matter of contract interpretation, a person seeking to enforce a contract as a third party beneficiary "'must plead a contract which was made expressly for his [or her] benefit and one in which it clearly appears that he [or she] was a beneficiary.'" (*California Emergency Physicians Medical Group v. PacifiCare of California* (2003) 111 Cal.App.4th 1127, 1138.)

"Expressly," [as used in the statute and case law,] means "in an express manner; in direct or unmistakable terms; explicitly; definitely; directly.'" [Citations.] '[A]n intent to make the obligation inure to the benefit of the third party must have been clearly manifested by the contracting parties.'" (*Sofias v. Bank of America* (1985) 172 Cal.App.3d 583, 587.) Although this means persons only incidentally or remotely benefited by the contract are not entitled to enforce it, it does not mean both of the contracting parties must intend to benefit the third party: Rather, it means the promisor—in this case, defendant jeweler—"must have understood that the promisee [Erstad] had such intent. [Citations.] No specific manifestation by the promisor of an intent to benefit the third person is required." (*Lucas v. Hamm* (1961) 56 Cal.2d 583, 591; see also, *Johnson v. Superior Court* (2000) 80 Cal.App.4th 1050, 1064-1065; *Don Rose Oil Co., Inc. v. Lindsley* (1984) 160 Cal.App.3d 752, 757, and *Zigas v. Superior Court* (1981) 120 Cal.App.3d 827, 837.)

We conclude the pleading here meets the test of demonstrating plaintiff's standing as a third party beneficiary to enforce the contract between Erstad and defendant. The couple went shopping for an engagement ring. They were together when plaintiff chose the ring she wanted or, as alleged in the complaint, she "caused [the ring] to be purchased for her." Erstad allegedly bought the ring "for the sole and *stated* purpose of giving [the ring]" to plaintiff. (Italics added.) Under the alleged facts, the jeweler *must* have understood Erstad's intent to enter the sales contract for plaintiff's benefit. Thus, plaintiff has adequately pleaded her status as a third party beneficiary, and she is entitled to proceed with her contract claim against defendant to the extent it is not time-barred.

* * *

Rescission

Plaintiff has attempted to plead a separate cause of action for rescission. She is not entitled to that remedy. Civil Code section 1559 provides, "A contract, made expressly for the benefit of a third person, may be *enforced* by him [or her] at any time before *the parties thereto rescind it.*" (Italics added.) But only the parties to the contract may rescind it. Civil Code section 1689 provides, in pertinent part, "(a) A contract may be rescinded if all the *parties* thereto consent. [¶] (b) A *party to a contract* may rescind the contract in the following cases: [¶] (1) If the consent of the *party* rescinding, or of any party *jointly contracting* with him [or her], was given by mistake, or obtained through duress, menace, fraud, or undue influence, exercised by or with the connivance of the *party* as to whom he [or she] rescinds, or of any other *party to the contract jointly interested with such party.* [¶] (2) If the consideration for the obligation of the rescinding *party* fails, in whole or in part, through the fault of the *party* as to whom he [or she] rescinds." (Italics added.)

We have found no cases specifically holding the rescission remedy unavailable to a third party beneficiary, but the proposition is self-evident to a degree that might well explain the absence of precedent. Civil Code section 1559 grants a third party beneficiary the right to *enforce* the contract, not rescind it, and Civil Code section 1689 limits its grant of rescission rights to the contracting parties. Not only do the relevant statutes demand making rescission unavailable to a third party beneficiary, but common sense compels the conclusion. The interest of the third party beneficiary is as the intended recipient of the *benefits* of the contract, and a direct right to those benefits, i.e., specific performance, or damages in lieu thereof, will protect the beneficiary's interests. Rescission, on the other hand, extinguishes a contract between the parties. (Civ. Code, § 1688.) Plaintiff, not having participated in the agreement, not having undertaken any duty or given any consideration, is a stranger to the agreement, with no legitimate interest in voiding it. As a matter of law, without an assignment of Erstad's contract rights, plaintiff cannot rescind the sales contract to which she was not a party.

* * *

Disposition

The judgment is reversed. The case is remanded with directions to the trial court to overrule defendant's demurrer to plaintiff's cause of action for breach of contract and order defendant to answer. In all other respects, the demurrer has been properly sustained without leave to amend. Plaintiff shall recover her costs on appeal.

Rylaarsdam, Acting P. J., and Bedsworth, J., concurred.

Afterthoughts

If a contract is not made expressly for the benefit of a particular third person, such person cannot enforce the contract even though he or she would receive some benefit from the performance of the contract.

It is not necessary that the contract identify the third party by name as long as such third party can show that he or she is one of a class of persons for whose benefit it was made. (*Watson v. Aced* (1957) 156 Cal.App.2d 87, 91-92)

It is not necessary that the intent to benefit the third party be manifested by the promisor; it is sufficient that the promisor understand that the promisee has such intent. (*Lucas v. Hamm, supra,* 56 Cal.2d 583, 589-591, 15 Cal.Rptr. 821, 824-825, 364 P.2d 685, 688-689.)

"Whether a third party is an intended beneficiary or merely an incidental beneficiary to the contract involves construction of the parties' intent gleaned from reading the contract as a whole in light of the circumstances under which it was intended." (*Jones v. Aetna Casualty & Surety Co.* (1994) 26 Cal.App.4th 1717, 1725, 33 Cal.Rptr.2d 291, 296.)

Municipal Contracts and Third Parties

Luis v. Orcutt Town Water Co.

California Court of Appel, Second District Division Four, 1962
204 Cal.App.2d 433

BALTHIS, J.

This action was brought to recover damages resulting from a fire which destroyed the mercantile store of plaintiff Luis in the Town of Orcutt. The second amended complaint (hereinafter referred to as the "complaint") contains six causes of action; three for plaintiff Luis and three for plaintiff Great American Insurance Company (New York); the term "plaintiff" as used in the singular hereafter refers to plaintiff Luis. The claims of the insurance company are derivative from plaintiff Luis and are based upon subrogation by reason of the company's having paid a portion of the loss. The liability of defendants is alleged to be both contractual and tortious.

A demurrer to plaintiffs' complaint was sustained without leave to amend and, after judgment was entered for defendants, plaintiffs appeal. The question presented by the appeal is whether the complaint states facts sufficient to constitute a cause of action against defendants; defendant Union Oil Company of California is referred to herein as "Union" and defendant Orcutt Town Water Company is referred to as "Water Company."

The allegations of the first cause of action of the complaint may be summarized as follows:

Prior to 1940 Union owned and operated a private water system in the Town of Orcutt which also supplied water to third persons for domestic and commercial purposes. The portion of the water system supplying water to third persons in the Town of Orcutt was acquired in 1940 by Water Company with permission of the Public Utilities Commission.

The complaint refers to two contracts between Union and Water Company. The principal agreement provides that Union will supply Water Company with such quantities of water from Union's wells located at Union's property adjoining the Town of Orcutt as Water Company may require for distribution to domestic and commercial consumers within the Town of Orcutt; that said water is to be delivered to Water Company's facilities at Union's Orcutt pump station and that Water Company will maintain and operate the pumps and lines for receiving and transporting the water to its own storage facilities.

Paragraph 2 of the principal agreement provides in part as follows: "Union further agrees to furnish water to Water Company's Orcutt town storage tank from Union's separate high pressure line in case of emergency when Water Company is prevented from or is unable to take water at its connection at Union's Orcutt property."

* * *

The complaint also states that a fire department is maintained in the Town of Orcutt as a volunteer fire department requiring regular annual taxes to be collected by the county. Plaintiff Luis is a resident and taxpayer of Orcutt and was and is a customer of Water Company.

It is further alleged that as a matter of practice and conduct on the part of defendants, the word "emergency" contained in the principal agreement above mentioned was recognized and acknowledged to include emergency by fire and it was further "recognized and acknowledged that the practical method of supplying additional water in the case of emergency by fire would be to open a high pressure valve which existed in the vicinity of a fire hydrant maintained for fire purposes in the vicinity of the Orcutt pump station and which would provide an increase in water from a two inch to a six inch water flow under pressure when said valve was opened." (Complaint, par. VIII.) Defendants advised the local fire officials that in the event water was needed to combat a fire, defendants would open said high-pressure valve at once, but that defendants did not advise the local fire authorities as to the location of said valve. Defendants communicated the various facts to other interested persons including plaintiff.

The complaint then states that plaintiff owned and operated a store building and mercantile business in the Town of Orcutt; that on November 10, 1951, the building and its contents were destroyed by fire; that at the time of fire urgent demand was made upon defendants to supply water to combat the fire but defendants "failed to promptly and immediately operate the valve and delayed in doing so for a highly unreasonable length of time exceeding one hour," and that as a result "plaintiff's building and contents were totally destroyed" (complaint, par. X); that defendants breached the contract and plaintiff has suffered damages in the sum of $140,000.

* * *

In the third cause of action it is alleged that defendants voluntarily assumed an obligation "that in the event of emergency by fire a high pressure valve which existed in the vicinity of a fire hydrant maintained for fire purposes in the vicinity of the Orcutt pump station, and which would provide an increase in water from a two inch to a six inch water flow under pressure when said valve was opened, would be opened immediately upon the occurrence of any such emergency by fire." (Complaint, par. II.) The complaint states that this assumption of obligation by defendants was made known by means of communications to the local officials of the fire district and to other interested persons including plaintiff. One of the individuals responsible for turning on the valve was an employee of Union; the other individual was responsible to both defendants and was unavailable at the time of fire because he was on vacation; no other provision for emergency by fire was made by either defendant or the local fire authorities or by plaintiff; by reason of the failure to provide water for such emergency by fire and because of such negligence plaintiff suffered the property losses mentioned.

* * *

The rule is well established in California that a water company is not liable to one of its consumers for failure to furnish water (or at sufficient pressure) for fire protection unless an express contract for that purpose has been made. Liability for loss resulting from fire is not an incident of the ordinary relation of water distributor and consumer; it can only be created by an express private contract whereby the water company agreed to furnish water as a protection against fire. It is only where the contract calls for water service for the purposes of extinguishing fires that loss of the premises by fire may be compensated in damages as having been reasonably supposed to have been within the contemplation of the parties.

The reasons for the above rule are stated in one of the leading cases (Niehaus Bros. Co. v. Contra Costa etc. Water Co. (1911) 159 Cal. 305, 318-319 [113 P. 375, 36 L.R.A. N.S. 1045], as follows:

"Applying the reasoning of these authorities to the relation between the company and the consumer here ... no obligation to furnish water for fire protection is implied, nor can it be said to exist in the absence of an express contract. Keeping in mind ... that the primary business of a water company is to furnish water as a commodity, and not to extinguish fires, and further recognizing that under the law of this state the defendant is a quasi public corporation engaged in the exercise of a public use and discharging a public duty which would otherwise devolve upon the municipality itself and furnishing water at rates fixed exclusively by the municipality, it would appear plain that it was never contemplated that from the simple relation of distributor and consumer the former undertook to assume liability for failure to furnish water to extinguish fires. In the nature of things the compensation fixed by the municipality has no relation to the assumption of any such liability; that compensation is based on the expense of furnishing water simply as a commodity; liability for destruction of premises to which the company may be required to supply water was not taken into consideration in fixing the rate, nor, we apprehend, was it even thought that any such liability could be imposed by the ordinance, or was to be assumed by the company in doing so."

The court further points out that if a water company were to be held liable for damages resulting from a failure on the part of the water company to supply sufficient water at sufficient pressure to extinguish a fire, it would place upon the water company a staggering insurance burden not covered by the rates charged. The court said at page 321:

It is common knowledge that, notably in large manufacturing centers within municipalities, hydrants are installed on the premises and connected with a public water company's system as a precautionary measure in case of fire. This is particularly true when the enterprise in which the owners are engaged is more readily exposed to danger from fire, either from the inflammable material which is being used in the factories, or on account of the proximity of others which are of that character. The various factories or mills in which hydrants are placed and connections with the public water system made may represent property worth millions of dollars which is subject to danger of destruction by fire and where the water to be used should fire arise is not furnished under any express contract between the parties but is being supplied simply under the ordinance rates as to water and hydrant charges established by law. Of course, if the position of the respondent is correct, then in all these instances a public water company is assuming liability practically as an insurer of millions of dollars worth of property upon which, either from the nature of the business conducted on the premises or the locality in which the property is situated, an insurance company itself would not think of assuming the risk.

* * *

A municipality may not recover damages against a water company for failure to furnish water under sufficient pressure for fire protection (City of Ukiah v. Ukiah Water & Imp. Co. (1904) 142 Cal. 173 [75 P. 773, 100 Am.St.Rep. 107, 64 L.R.A. 231]).

It is helpful to examine the pertinent provisions of the principal contract and to analyze the relationships involved in the instant case.

First to be considered is the fact that there is no contract involved here to which plaintiff Luis is a party. The two agreements referred to in the complaint are between Union and Water Company; the contracts are essentially between the water producer and the water distributor and have nothing to do with the consumer. They refer to the supply and sale of water for "domestic and commercial purposes," not for fire purposes. The contracts are not the type or classification referred to in the exception to the general rule, that is, an express private contract by a consumer with a water company to obtain water service for a particular purpose, fire protection (Niehaus Bros. Co. v. Contra Costa etc. Co., supra, 159 Cal. 305, 312-313).

Further, plaintiff is not an express beneficiary under the principal contract which as pointed out above, is between water supplier and water distributor.

Section 1559, Civil Code, reads: "A contract, made expressly for the benefit of a third person, may be enforced by him at any time before the parties thereto rescind it." This code section has been explained and interpreted by a large number of cases but the most concise statement of the law is found in the Restatement of Contracts, section 133, where third-party beneficiaries are classified as follows:

A person is a donee beneficiary:

"(a) ... if it appears from the terms of the promise in view of the accompanying circumstances that the purpose of the promisee in obtaining the promise of all or part of the performance thereof is to make a gift to the beneficiary or to confer upon him a right against the promisor to some performance neither due nor supposed or asserted to be due from the promisee to the beneficiary." A person is a creditor beneficiary:

"(b) ... if no purpose to make a gift appears from the terms of the promise in view of the accompanying circumstances and performance of the promise will satisfy an actual or supposed or asserted duty of the promisee to the beneficiary, or a right of the beneficiary against the promisee which has been barred by the Statute of Limitations or by a discharge in bankruptcy, or which is unenforceable because of the Statute of Frauds."

A person is an incidental beneficiary:

"(c) … if neither the facts stated in Clause (a) nor those stated in Clause (b) exist."

Although Civil Code section 1559 makes no reference to the different types of beneficiaries, the California cases generally rely on these Restatement classifications (Hartman Ranch Co. v. Associated Oil Co. (1937) 10 Cal.2d 232, 244 [73 P.2d 1163]).

Under the foregoing rules a plaintiff must plead a contract which was made expressly for his benefit and one in which it clearly appears that he was a beneficiary, e.g., Steinberg v. Buchman (1946) 73 Cal.App.2d 605, 609 [167 P.2d 207]. The fortuitous fact that he may have suffered detriment by reason of the nonperformance of the contract does not give him a cause of action. (Shutes v. Cheney (1954) 123 Cal.App.2d 256, 262 [266 P.2d 902].) The test in deciding whether a contract inures to the benefit of a third person is whether an intent to so benefit the third person appears from the terms of the agreement (Le Ballister v. Redwood Theatres, Inc. (1934) 1 Cal.App.2d 447, 448-449 [36 P.2d 827]). Where a claim is made that the parties to an agreement intended to benefit a third party, but no attempt is made to reform the contract nor has any mistake or fraud been alleged, the courts must be guided by the terms of the written instrument (Shutes v. Cheney, supra, 123 Cal.App.2d 256, 261).

We hold that the principal contract involved here, and relied upon by plaintiff for his first and second causes of action, was not made expressly for the benefit of plaintiff; the terms of such agreement do not indicate that the parties to it contemplated or intended expressly to benefit plaintiff Luis, or to protect him against fire losses, or to entitle him to sue upon such agreement. Plaintiff could only be considered a most remote and incidental beneficiary in a relationship not recognized by the law.

* * *

The judgment appealed from is affirmed.

Burke, P. J., and Jefferson, J., concurred.

Vesting of Third Party's Rights

Once the original parties have entered into an enforceable contract may they change or modify it without the consent of the third party beneficiary? The right of the original parties to rescind or modify a third party beneficiary contract, without the assent of the beneficiary, ceases once the beneficiary learns of the contract and assents to it or materially changes his position in justifiable reliance on it or brings suit on it. (Restatement Second Contracts § 311(3).)

Karo v. San Diego Symphony Orchestra Ass'n.
U.S. Court of Appeals, Ninth Circuit (Cal.), 1985
762 F.2d 819,

BOOCHEVER, CIRCUIT JUDGE:

Karo appeals from a district court order dismissing his hybrid suit for breach of a collective bargaining agreement and breach of the duty of fair representation on the ground that he lacked standing. Although Karo is a union member, he is not an employee within the collective bargaining unit. We affirm the dismissal.

Facts

Karo is a percussionist and a member of the Musicians Association of San Diego Local 325, American Federation of Musicians (Local 325). In 1969 he was employed by the San Diego Symphony Orchestra Association (Symphony) as substitute percussionist for one concert, but has not been employed by the Symphony since that time.

On May 4, 1983, Karo filed a complaint against Local 325 and the Symphony (defendants) pursuant to section 301 of the Labor Management Relations Act of 1947 (LMRA), 29 U.S.C. § 185 (1982). The complaint was triggered by Karo's desire to obtain a contract chair in the percussion section of the Symphony. Karo alleged that Local 325 had breached its duty of fair representation by agreeing to a contract modification which bypassed the audition procedures and by failing to act on his grievance concerning the matter; that the Symphony breached the collective bargaining agreement by failing to hold auditions for the percussion chair; and that the Symphony and Local 325 conspired to modify the agreement in order to eliminate auditions so that another musician could be hired for the percussion chair without having to audition.

In 1980 Karo learned that the Symphony had an opening for a percussionist, and that auditions were to be scheduled during the Symphony's 1981-1982 season. At that time the relationship between the Symphony and Local 325 was governed by a collective bargaining agreement entered into on September 1, 1979, which specified the terms and conditions of employment for Local 325 members with the Symphony. Local 325 was recognized as the exclusive representative of Symphony musicians for the purpose of collective bargaining. It is undisputed that although Karo was a union member, he was never a member of the bargaining unit. The agreement, which was to terminate on August 31, 1982, was modified and extended for one year in February 1982.

The audition procedures in the original agreement provided that when a vacancy occurred the Symphony would give fifteen days written notice to the union. The Symphony was required to conduct blind auditions with the players performing behind a screen, and to follow elaborate procedures for impartially selecting the best applicant.

The 1982 modification permitted the Symphony to offer contracts without auditions to noncontract musicians with six years of service within ten years preceding April 10, 1982. Mr. Plank, a noncontract percussionist with the required years of service, was awarded a seat without an audition under this provision.

* * *

II

Standing As a Third Party Beneficiary

Karo further asserts that under California law he has standing to bring an action against the Symphony because he is a third party beneficiary of the collective bargaining agreement.

* * *

California law does not support Karo's position.

California Civil Code § 1559 provides that "[a] contract, made expressly for the benefit of a third party, may be enforced by him at any time before the parties thereto rescind it." A third party qualifies as a beneficiary under a contract if the parties intended to benefit the third party and the terms of the contract make that intent evident. Strauss v. Summerhays, 157 Cal.App.3d 806, 816, 204 Cal.Rptr. 227, 233 (1984); Kirst v. Silna, 103 Cal.App.3d 759, 763, 163 Cal.Rptr. 230, 232 (1980); see also Garcia v. Truck Insurance Exchange, 36 Cal.3d 426, 436-37, 682 P.2d 1100, 1104-05, 204 Cal.Rptr. 435, 439-40 (1984). Although the beneficiary need not be named in the contract, he must be a member of a class referred to and identified in it. Strauss, 157 Cal.App.3d at 816, 204 Cal.Rptr. at 233; Kirst, 103 Cal.App.3d at 763, 163 Cal.Rptr. at 232.

In the instant case, the dispositive provision of the premodified collective bargaining agreement governing audition procedure stated:

When a vacancy occurs, the Employer's Manager shall notify the Union within fifteen (15) days.

Auditions shall be scheduled in accordance with the availability of the Music Director. For each vacancy there shall be as many auditions as necessary to fill the vacancy, but, until the vacancy is filled and subject to the provisions of Section 6.4, there shall be at least two auditions per year (from the date the vacancy occurs).

There is nothing in the agreement which indicates that the audition procedure is for the benefit of nonemployee union members. On its face it is equally applicable to any musician seeking employment with the Symphony. Moreover, there is no indication that the provision was intended to benefit union members rather than the Symphony. But even if Karo could be considered a third party beneficiary of the 1979 agreement he still cannot prevail. The agreement was amended to provide specifically for filling positions without auditions when noncontract musicians had prior service for specified periods. Under the modified agreement Karo had no right to audition for the seat.

The Restatement (Second) of Contracts provides that in the absence of terms in a third party beneficiary contract prohibiting change or modification of a duty to an intended beneficiary, the promisor and promisee retain power to discharge or modify the duty by subsequent agreement. Restatement (Second) of Contracts § 311(1), (2) (1981). The power to modify terminates when the beneficiary materially changes position in justifiable reliance on the promise before receiving notification of the modification. Id. § 311(3). Karo does not allege any such change of position. Thus, assuming that Karo could be regarded as a third party beneficiary under the 1979 contract, no rights he might have acquired thereunder had vested when the contract was modified in 1982. Accordingly the union and Symphony had the power to modify the agreement eliminating the open audition provisions when noncontract musicians had requisite experience for filling the position.

* * *

Conclusion

Karo has no standing to sue the union for breaching a duty of fair representation because he was not a member of the bargaining unit to which such a duty was owed. He does not have standing to sue as a third party beneficiary because he had no vested rights at the time that the agreement was amended. Because the appeal is not frivolous, we decline to award attorney's fees as requested by the Symphony and the Union.

The judgment of dismissal is affirmed.

Assignment

A right arising out of a contract may be transferred by the holder of the right to another person. (Cal.Civ.Code § 1458) Such a transfer is called an *assignment*. The person making the transfer is the *assignor*. The person receiving the transfer is the *assignee*.

Unless some law provides otherwise an assignment may be oral, written, or partly oral and partly written. There need be no consideration for the assignment. If there is consideration, it is a contract of assignment subject to all laws relating to contracts.

A verbal gift is not valid, unless the means of obtaining possession and control of the thing are given, nor if it is capable of delivery, unless there is an actual or symbolical delivery of the thing to the donee. (Cal.Civ.Code § 1147) The delivery of a signed writing expressing an intent to assign makes a gratuitous assignment irrevocable. (*Berl v. Rosenberg* (1959) 169 Cal.App.2d 125, 336 P2d 975)

Whether rights arising out of a contract are assignable depends upon the nature and terms of the contract. Ordinarily, rights are assignable unless (1) the contract expressly or impliedly prohibits an assignment, (2) a statute prohibits an assignment, or (3) performance calls for some personal quality of the person making the promise which materially impairs the non-assigning party's right of obtaining the performance it expected.

A non-assigning party to the contract may waive an objection to an assignment. A waiver may be express or implied. It is implied if the non-assigning party, after learning of the purported assignment, continues to deal with the assignee either by performing to the assignee or by accepting performance from the assignee. (See, 1 Witkin, Summary of Cal. Law, (9th ed. 1987) Contracts, § 921-932)

Where a commercial lease provides for assignment only with the prior consent of the lessor, such consent may be withheld only where the lessor has a commercially reasonable objection to the assignee or the proposed use. (*Kendall v. Ernest Pestana, Inc.* (1985) 40 Cal.3d 488, 220 Cal.Rptr. 818; 709 P.2d 837)

An assignment in violation of a covenant or promise not to assign is not void or ineffective and the only remedy for such violation is an action for breach of the covenant. (*Randal v. Tatum* (1893) 98 Cal. 390)

Assignee Stands in Shoes of Assignor

A written contract for the payment of money or personal property may be transferred. Such a transfer conveys all of the rights of the assignor to the assignee, subject to all equities and defenses existing in favor of the maker or obligor at the time of the assignment. (Cal.Civ.Code § 1459)

Priority of Assignees of the Same Right

As between bona fide assignees of the same right for value without notice, the assignee first giving notice thereof to the obligor in writing has priority. (Cal.Civ.Code § 955.1(b)) In other words, the first to give notice will be the holder of the assigned right.

Delegation

A delegation is an appointment of another person or entity to perform one's duties. In a delegation the person making the appointment remains liable in the event of a breach by the delegate.

Taylor v. Palmer
Supreme Court of California, 1866
31 Cal. 240

By the Court, SANDERSON, J.

* * *

The contract in suit was made by the Superintendent with Smith & Co., who assigned to the plaintiff, by whom the work was performed, and it is next claimed that the contract belongs to that class which the party who is to perform the stipulated work is not permitted to assign by reason of the trust and confidence reposed in his skill and ability by the other contracting party.

* * *

[I]t is clear to us that this contract does not belong to the class suggested. There is nothing in the statute or the contract or the nature of the work suggestive of such a theory. On the contrary, the public generally are invited to bid for and take these contracts regardless of professions, trades or occupations. Aside from the discretion vested in the Board of Supervisors to reject all bids when they deem it for the public good, or the bid of any party who may have proved delinquent or unfaithful in any previous contract with the city, there is no restriction upon the capacity of the contractor. He is not expected nor required to perform the work in person. Were it so, street improvements in San Francisco would make slow progress. Whether he knows anything about road making, or can tell the difference between a mud turnpike and a Nicholson pavement, or whether a sewer should be constructed in the shape of a longitudinal section of an egg shell, or which end of the section should be uppermost, is of no consequence, for the contract is not awarded to him because of his supposed knowledge or skill, but because his bid is the lowest and his bond for the performance of the work in a workmanlike manner and according to the specifications is good. All painters do not paint portraits like Sir Joshua Reynolds, nor landscapes like Claude Lorraine, nor do all writers write dramas like Shakespeare or fiction like Dickens. Rare genius and extraordinary skill are not transferable, and contracts for their employment are therefore personal, and cannot be assigned. But rare genius and extraordinary skill are not indispensable to the workmanlike digging down of a sand hill or the filling up of a depression to a given level, or the construction of brick sewers with manholes and covers, and contracts for such work are not personal, and may be assigned.

* * *

Afterthoughts

Taylor v. Palmer is an old case. Although the court uses the term, "assignment" don't they really mean "delegation?" You will recall that an assignment is a transfer of rights. A delegation is an appointment of another to perform one's duties. The burden of an obligation may be transferred with the consent of the party entitled to its benefit. (Cal.Civ.Code § 1457)

Appendix A

Selected California Contract Statutes

Selected Provisions of the California Civil Code

Table of Contents

PERSONS WITH UNSOUND MIND

§ 38. A person entirely without understanding has no power to make a contract of any kind, but the person is liable for the reasonable value of things furnished to the person necessary for the support of the person or the person's family.

§ 39. (a) A conveyance or other contract of a person of unsound mind, but not entirely without understanding, made before the incapacity of the person has been judicially determined, is subject to rescission, as provided in Chapter 2 (commencing with Section 1688) of Title 5 of Part 2 of Division 3.

(b) A rebuttable presumption affecting the burden of proof that a person is of unsound mind shall exist for purposes of this section if the person is substantially unable to manage his or her own financial resources or resist fraud or undue influence. Substantial inability may not be proved solely by isolated incidents of negligence or improvidence.

§ 40. (a) Subject to Section 1871 of the Probate Code, and subject to Part 1 (commencing with Section 5000) of Division 5 of the Welfare and Institutions Code, after his or her incapacity has been judicially determined a person of unsound mind can make no conveyance or other contract, nor delegate any power or waive any right, until his or her restoration to capacity.

(b) Subject to Sections 1873 to 1876, inclusive, of the Probate Code, the establishment of a conservatorship under Division 4 (commencing with Section 1400) of the Probate Code is a judicial determination of the incapacity of the conservatee for the purposes of this section.

DEFINITION OF OBLIGATIONS

§ 1427. An obligation is a legal duty, by which a person is bound to do or not to do a certain thing.

§ (1428.) Section Fourteen Hundred and Twenty-eight. An obligation arises either from:

One—The contract of the parties; or,

Two—The operation of law. An obligation arising from operation of law may be enforced in the manner provided by law, or by civil action or proceeding.

TRANSFER OF OBLIGATIONS

§ 1457. The burden of an obligation may be transferred with the consent of the party entitled to its benefit, but not otherwise, except as provided by Section 1466.

§ 1458. A right arising out of an obligation is the property of the person to whom it is due, and may be transferred as such.

§ 1459. A non-negotiable written contract for the payment of money or personal property may be transferred by indorsement, in like manner with negotiable instruments. Such indorsement shall transfer all the rights of the assignor under the instrument to the assignee, subject to all equities and defenses existing in favor of the maker at the time of the indorsement.

EXTINCTION OF OBLIGATIONS
PERFORMANCE

§ 1473. Full performance of an obligation, by the party whose duty it is to perform it, or by any other person on his behalf, and with his assent, if accepted by the creditor, extinguishes it.

§ 1474. Performance of an obligation, by one of several persons who are jointly liable under it, extinguishes the liability of all.

§ 1475. An obligation in favor of several persons is extinguished by performance rendered to any of them, except in the case of a deposit made by owners in common, or in joint ownership, which is regulated by the Title on Deposit.

§ 1476. If a creditor, or any one of two or more joint creditors, at any time directs the debtor to perform his obligation in a particular manner, the obligation is extinguished by performance in that manner, even though the creditor does not receive the benefit of such performance.

§ 1477. A partial performance of an indivisible obligation extinguishes a corresponding proportion thereof, if the benefit of such performance is voluntarily retained by the creditor, but not otherwise. If such partial performance is of such a nature that the creditor cannot avoid retaining it without injuring his own property, his retention thereof is not presumed to be voluntary.

§ 1478. Performance of an obligation for the delivery of money only, is called payment.

(§ 1479.) Section Fourteen Hundred and Seventy-nine. Where a debtor, under several obligations to another, does an act, by way of performance, in whole or in part, which is equally applicable to twoor more of such obligations, such performance must be applied as follows:

One—If, at the time of performance, the intention or desire of the debtor that such performance should be applied to the extinction of any particular obligation, be manifested to the creditor, it must be so applied.

Two—If no such application be then made, the creditor, within a reasonable time after such performance, may apply it toward the extinction of any obligation, performance of which was due to him from the debtor at the time of such performance; except that if similar obligations were due to him both individually and as a trustee, he must, unless otherwise directed by the debtor, apply the performance to the extinction of all such obligations in equal proportion; and an application once made by the creditor cannot be rescinded without the consent of (the) debtor.

Three—If neither party makes such application within the time prescribed herein, the performance must be applied to the extinction of obligations in the following order; and, if there be more than one obligation of a particular class, to the extinction of all in that class, ratably:

1. Of interest due at the time of the performance.

2. Of principal due at that time.

3. Of the obligation earliest in date of maturity.

4. Of an obligation not secured by a lien or collateral undertaking.

5. Of an obligation secured by a lien or collateral undertaking.

OFFER OF PERFORMANCE

§ 1485. An obligation is extinguished by an offer of performance, made in conformity to the rules herein prescribed, and with intent to extinguish the obligation.

§ 1486. An offer of partial performance is of no effect.

§ 1487. An offer of performance must be made by the debtor, or by some person on his behalf and with his assent.

§ (1488.) Section Fourteen Hundred and Eighty-eight. An offer of performance must be made to the creditor, or to any one of two or more joint creditors, or to a person authorized by one or more of them to receive or collect what is due under the obligation, if such creditor or authorized person is present at the place where the offer may be made; and if not, wherever the creditor may be found.

§ 1489. In the absence of an express provision to the contrary, an offer of performance may be made, at the option of the debtor:

1. At any place appointed by the creditor; or,

2. Wherever the person to whom the offer ought to be made can be found; or,

3. If such person cannot, with reasonable diligence, be found within this State, and within a reasonable distance from his residence or place of business, or if he evades the debtor, then at his residence or place of business, if the same can, with reasonable diligence, be found within the State; or,

4. If this cannot be done, then at any place within this State.

§ 1490. Where an obligation fixes a time for its performance, an offer of performance must be made at that time, within reasonable hours, and not before nor afterwards.

§ 1491. Where an obligation does not fix the time for its performance, an offer of performance may be made at any time before the debtor, upon a reasonable demand, has refused to perform.

§ 1492. Where delay in performance is capable of exact and entire compensation, and time has not been expressly declared to be of the essence of the obligation, an offer of performance, accompanied with an offer of such compensation, may be made at any time after it is due, but without prejudice to any rights acquired by the creditor, or by any other person, in the meantime.

§ 1493. An offer of performance must be made in good faith, and in such manner as is most likely, under the circumstances, to benefit the creditor.

§ 1494. An offer of performance must be free from any conditions which the creditor is not bound, on his part, to perform.

§ 1495. An offer of performance is of no effect if the person making it is not able and willing to perform according to the offer.

§ 1496. The thing to be delivered, if any, need not in any case be actually produced, upon an offer of performance, unless the offer is accepted.

§ 1497. A thing, when offered by way of performance, must not be mixed with other things from which it cannot be separated immediately and without difficulty.

§ 1498. When a debtor is entitled to the performance of a condition precedent to, or concurrent with, performance on his part, he may make his offer to depend upon the due performance of such condition.

§ 1499. A debtor has a right to require from his creditor a written receipt for any property delivered in performance of his obligation.

§ 1500. An obligation for the payment of money is extinguished by a due offer of payment, if the amount is immediately deposited in the name of the creditor, with some bank or savings and loan association within this state, of good repute, and notice thereof is given to the creditor.

§ 1501. All objections to the mode of an offer of performance, which the creditor has an opportunity to state at the time to the person making the offer, and which could be then obviated by him, are waived by the creditor, if not then stated.

§ 1502. The title to a thing duly offered in performance of an obligation passes to the creditor, if the debtor at the time signifies his intention to that effect.

§ 1503. The person offering a thing, other than money, by way of performance, must, if he means to treat it as belonging to the creditor, retain it as a depositary for hire, until the creditor accepts it, or until he has given reasonable notice to the creditor that he will retain it no longer, and, if with reasonable diligence he can find a suitable depositary therefor, until he has deposited it with such person.

§ 1504. An offer of payment or other performance, duly made, though the title to the thing offered be not transferred to the creditor, stops the running of interest on the obligation, and has the same effect upon all its incidents as a performance thereof.

§ 1505. If anything is given to a creditor by way of performance, which he refuses to accept as such, he is not bound to return it without demand; but if he retains it, he is a gratuitous depositary thereof.

PREVENTION OF PERFORMANCE OR OFFER

§ 1511. The want of performance of an obligation, or of an offer of performance, in whole or in part, or any delay therein, is excused by the following causes, to the extent to which they operate:

1. When such performance or offer is prevented or delayed by the act of the creditor, or by the operation of law, even though there may have been a stipulation that this shall not be an excuse; however, the parties may expressly require in a contract that the party relying on the provisions of this paragraph give written notice to the other party or parties, within a reasonable time after the occurrence of the event excusing performance, of an intention to claim an extension of time or of an intention to bring suit or of any other similar or related intent, provided the requirement of such notice is reasonable and just;

2. When it is prevented or delayed by an irresistible, superhuman cause, or by the act of public enemies of this state or of the United States, unless the parties have expressly agreed to the contrary; or,

3. When the debtor is induced not to make it, by any act of the creditor intended or naturally tending to have that effect, done at or before the time at which such performance or offer may be made, and not rescinded before that time.

(§ 1512.) Section Fifteen Hundred and Twelve. If the performance of an obligation be prevented by the creditor, the debtor is entitled to all the benefits which he would have obtained if it had been performed by both parties.

§ 1514. If performance of an obligation is prevented by any cause excusing performance, other than the act of the creditor, the debtor is entitled to a ratable proportion of the consideration to which he would have been entitled upon full performance, according to the benefit which the creditor receives from the actual performance.

§ 1515. A refusal by a creditor to accept performance, made before an offer thereof, is equivalent to an offer and refusal, unless, before performance is actually due, he gives notice to the debtor of his willingness to accept it.

ACCORD AND SATISFACTION

(§ 1521.) Section Fifteen Hundred and Twenty-one. An accord is an agreement to accept, in extinction of an obligation, something different from or less than that to which the person agreeing to accept is entitled.

§ 1522. Though the parties to an accord are bound to execute it, yet it does not extinguish the obligation until it is fully executed.

§ 1523. Acceptance, by the creditor, of the consideration of an accord extinguishes the obligation, and is called satisfaction.

(§ 1524.) Section Fifteen Hundred and Twenty-four. Part performance of an obligation, either before or after a breach thereof, when expressly accepted by the creditor in writing, in satisfaction, or rendered in pursuance of an agreement in writing for that purpose, though without any new consideration, extinguishes the obligation.

§ 1525. It is the public policy of this State, in the best interests of the taxpayer and of the litigant, to encourage fair dealing and to promote justice by reducing litigated matters to the lowest level of jurisdiction.

In case of a dispute over total money due on a contract and it is conceded by the parties that part of the money is due, the debtor may pay, without condition, the amount conceded to be due, leaving to the other party all remedies to which he might otherwise be entitled as to any balance claimed.

If any conditions are attached to the payment, this section shall not be deemed to have limited the remedies available to the other party under other provisions of law on the original amount claimed.

§ 1526. (a) Where a claim is disputed or unliquidated and a check or draft is tendered by the debtor in settlement thereof in full discharge of the claim, and the words "payment in full" or other words of similar meaning are notated on the check or draft, the acceptance of the check or draft does not constitute an accord and satisfaction if the creditor protests against accepting the tender in full payment by striking out or otherwise deleting that notation or if the acceptance of the check or draft was inadvertent or without knowledge of the notation.

(b) Notwithstanding subdivision (a), the acceptance of a check or draft constitutes an accord and satisfaction if a check or draft is tendered pursuant to a composition or extension agreement between a debtor and its creditors, and pursuant to that composition or extension agreement, all creditors of the same class are accorded similar treatment, and the creditor receives the check or draft with knowledge of the restriction.

A creditor shall be conclusively presumed to have knowledge of the restriction if a creditor either:

(1) Has, previous to the receipt of the check or draft, executed a written consent to the composition or extension agreement.

(2) Has been given, not less than 15 days nor more than 90 days prior to receipt of the check or draft, notice, in writing, that a check or draft will be tendered with a restrictive endorsement and that acceptance and cashing of the check or draft will constitute an accord and satisfaction.

(c) Notwithstanding subdivision (a), the acceptance of a check or draft by a creditor constitutes an accord and satisfaction when the check or draft is issued pursuant to or in conjunction with a release of a claim.

(d) For the purposes of paragraph (2) of subdivision (b), mailing the notice by first-class mail, postage prepaid, addressed to the address shown for the creditor on the debtor's books or such other address as the creditor may designate in writing constitutes notice.

NOVATION

§ 1530. Novation is the substitution of a new obligation for an existing one.

§ 1531. Novation is made:

1. By the substitution of a new obligation between the same parties, with intent to extinguish the old obligation;

2. By the substitution of a new debtor in place of the old one, with intent to release the latter; or,

3. By the substitution of a new creditor in place of the old one, with intent to transfer the rights of the latter to the former.

§ 1532. Novation is made by contract, and is subject to all the rules concerning contracts in general.

(§ 1533.) Section Fifteen Hundred and Thirty-three. When the obligation of a third person, or an order upon such person is accepted in satisfaction, the creditor may rescind such (such) acceptance if the debtor prevents such person from complying with the order, or from fulfilling the obligation; or if, at the time the obligation or order is received, such person is insolvent, and this fact is unknown to the creditor, or if, before the creditor can with reasonable diligence present the order to the person upon whom it is given, he becomes insolvent.

RELEASE

§ 1541. An obligation is extinguished by a release therefrom given to the debtor by the creditor, upon a new consideration, or in writing, with or without new consideration.

(§ 1542.) Section Fifteen Hundred and Forty-two. A general release does not extend to claims which the creditor does not know or suspect to exist in his favor at the time of executing the release, which if known by him must have materially affected his settlement with the debtor.

§ 1542.1. Notwithstanding Section 1542, a provider of health care, as defined in Section 56.05, or its officers, employees, agents, or subcontractors, shall release the state and its officers, employees, and agents, from any claim arising from the defense of the provider of health care by the Attorney General, or other legal counsel provided by the state pursuant to Section 12511.5 of the Government Code.

§ 1543. A release of one of two or more joint debtors does not extinguish the obligations of any of the others, unless they are mere guarantors; nor does it affect their right to contribution from him or her, except as provided in Section 877 of the Code of Civil Procedure.

CONTRACTS
NATURE OF A CONTRACT
DEFINITION

§ 1549. A contract is an agreement to do or not to do a certain thing.

§ 1550. It is essential to the existence of a contract that there should be:

1. Parties capable of contracting;

2. Their consent;

3. A lawful object; and,

4. A sufficient cause or consideration.

PARTIES

§ 1556. All persons are capable of contracting, except minors, persons of unsound mind, and persons deprived of civil rights.

§ 1557. (a) The capacity of a minor to contract is governed by Division 11 (commencing with Section 6500) of the Family Code.

(b) The capacity of a person of unsound mind to contract is governed by Part 1 (commencing with Section 38) of Division 1.

§ 1558. It is essential to the validity of a contract, not only that the parties should exist, but that it should be possible to identify them.

§ 1559. A contract, made expressly for the benefit of a third person, may be enforced by him at any time before the parties thereto rescind it.

CONSENT

§ 1565. The consent of the parties to a contract must be:

1. Free;

2. Mutual; and,

3. Communicated by each to the other.

§ 1566. A consent which is not free is nevertheless not absolutely void, but may be rescinded by the parties, in the manner prescribed by the Chapter on Rescission.

§ 1567. An apparent consent is not real or free when obtained through:

1. Duress;

2. Menace;

3. Fraud;

4. Undue influence; or,

5. Mistake.

§ 1568. Consent is deemed to have been obtained through one of the causes mentioned in the last section only when it would not have been given had such cause not existed.

§ 1569. Duress consists in:

1. Unlawful confinement of the person of the party, or of the husband or wife of such party, or of an ancestor, descendant, or adopted child of such party, husband, or wife;

2. Unlawful detention of the property of any such person; or,

3. Confinement of such person, lawful in form, but fraudulently obtained, or fraudulently made unjustly harrassing or oppressive.

§ 1570. Menace consists in a threat:

1. Of such duress as is specified in Subdivisions 1 and 3 of the last section;

2. Of unlawful and violent injury to the person or property of any such person as is specified in the last section; or,

3. Of injury to the character of any such person.

§ 1571. Fraud is either actual or constructive.

§ 1572. Actual fraud, within the meaning of this Chapter, consists in any of the following acts, committed by a party to the contract, or with his connivance, with intent to deceive another party thereto, or to induce him to enter into the contract:

1. The suggestion, as a fact, of that which is not true, by one who does not believe it to be true;

2. The positive assertion, in a manner not warranted by the information of the person making it, of that which is not true, though he believes it to be true;

3. The suppression of that which is true, by one having knowledge or belief of the fact;

4. A promise made without any intention of performing it; or,

5. Any other act fitted to deceive.

§ 1573. Constructive fraud consists:

1. In any breach of duty which, without an actually fraudulent intent, gains an advantage to the person in fault, or any one claiming under him, by misleading another to his prejudice, or to the prejudice of any one claiming under him; or,

2. In any such act or omission as the law specially declares to be fraudulent, without respect to actual fraud.

§ 1574. Actual fraud is always a question of fact.

§ 1575. Undue influence consists:

1. In the use, by one in whom a confidence is reposed by another, or who holds a real or apparent authority over him, of such confidence or authority for the purpose of obtaining an unfair advantage over him;

2. In taking an unfair advantage of another's weakness of mind; or,

3. In taking a grossly oppressive and unfair advantage of another's necessities or distress.

§ 1576. Mistake may be either of fact or law.

§ 1577. Mistake of fact is a mistake, not caused by the neglect of a legal duty on the part of the person making the mistake, and consisting in:

1. An unconscious ignorance or forgetfulness of a fact past or present, material to the contract; or,

2. Belief in the present existence of a thing material to the contract, which does not exist, or in the past existence of such a thing, which has not existed.

§ 1578. Mistake of law constitutes a mistake, within the meaning of this Article, only when it arises from:

1. A misapprehension of the law by all parties, all supposing that they knew and understood it, and all making substantially the same mistake as to the law; or,

2. A misapprehension of the law by one party, of which the others are aware at the time of contracting, but which they do not rectify.

§ 1579. Mistake of foreign laws is a mistake of fact.

§ 1580. Consent is not mutual, unless the parties all agree upon the same thing in the same sense. But in certain cases defined by the Chapter on Interpretation, they are to be deemed so to agree without regard to the fact.

§ 1581. Consent can be communicated with effect, only by some act or omission of the party contracting, by which he intends to communicate it, or which necessarily tends to such communication.

§ 1582. If a proposal prescribes any conditions concerning the communication of its acceptance, the proposer is not bound unless they are conformed to; but in other cases any reasonable and usual mode may be adopted.

§ 1583. Consent is deemed to be fully communicated between the parties as soon as the party accepting a proposal has put his acceptance in the course of transmission to the proposer, in conformity to the last section.

§ 1584. Performance of the conditions of a proposal, or the acceptance of the consideration offered with a proposal, is an acceptance of the proposal.

§ 1584.5. No person, firm, partnership, association, or corporation, or agent or employee thereof, shall, in any manner, or by any means, offer for sale goods, wares, merchandise, or services, where the offer includes the voluntary and unsolicited sending or providing of goods, wares, merchandise, or services not actually ordered or requested by the recipient, either orally or in writing. The receipt of any goods, wares, merchandise, or services shall for all purposes be deemed an unconditional gift to the recipient who may use or dispose of the goods, wares, merchandise, or services in any manner he or she sees fit without any obligation on his or her part to the sender or provider.

If, after any receipt deemed to be an unconditional gift under this section, the sender or provider continues to send bill statements or requests for payment with respect to the gift, an action may be brought by the recipient to enjoin the conduct, in which action there may also be awarded reasonable attorney's fees and costs to the prevailing party.

For the purposes of this section and limited to merchandise or services offered for sale through the mails, the "voluntary and unsolicited sending or providing of goods, wares, merchandise, or services not actually ordered or requested by the recipient, either orally or in writing," includes any merchandise or services selected by the company and offered to the consumer which will be mailed to him or her for sale or on approval or provided to him or her unless he or she exercises an option to reject the offer of sale or receipt on approval. Merchandise or services selected by the seller and offered for sale on a periodic basis must be affirmatively ordered by a statement or card signed by the consumer as to each periodic offer of merchandise or services. This paragraph shall not apply to any of the following:

(a) Contractual plans or arrangements complying with this subdivision under which the seller periodically provides the consumer with a form or announcement card which the consumer may use to instruct the seller not to ship the offered merchandise. Any instructions not to ship merchandise included on the form or card shall be printed in type as large as all other instructions and terms stated on the form or card. The form or card shall specify a date by which it shall be mailed by the consumer (the "mailing date") or received by the seller (the "return date") to prevent shipment of the offered merchandise. The seller shall mail the form or card either at least 25 days prior to the return date or at least 20 days prior to the mailing date, or provide a mailing date of at least 10 days after receipt by the consumer, except that whichever system the seller chooses for mailing the form or card, the system must be calculated to afford the consumer at least 10 days in which to mail his or her form or card. The form or card shall be preaddressed to the seller so that it may serve as a postal reply card or, alternatively, the form or card shall be accompanied by a return envelope addressed to seller. Upon the membership contract or application form or on the same page and immediately adjacent to the contract or form, and in clear and conspicuous language, there shall be disclosed the material terms of the plan or arrangement including all of the following:

(1) That aspect of the plan under which the subscriber must notify the seller, in the manner provided for by the seller, if he or she does not wish to purchase or receive the selection.

(2) Any obligation assumed by the subscriber to purchase a minimum quantity of merchandise.

(3) The right of a contract-complete subscriber to cancel his or her membership at any time.

(4) Whether billing charges will include an amount for postage and handling.

(b) Other contractual plans or arrangements not covered under subdivision (a), such as continuity plans, subscription arrangements, standing order arrangements, supplements and series arrangements under which the seller periodically ships merchandise to a consumer who has consented in advance to receive the merchandise on a periodic basis.

§ 1584.6. If a person is a member of an organization which makes retail sales of any goods, wares, or merchandise to its members, and the person notifies the organization of his termination of membership by certified mail, return receipt requested, any unordered goods, wares, or merchandise which are sent to the person after 30 days following execution of the return receipt for the certified letter by the organization, shall for all purposes be deemed unconditional gifts to the person, who may use or dispose of the goods, wares, or merchandise in any manner he sees fit without any obligation on his part to the organization.

If the termination of a person's membership in such organization breaches any agreement with the organization, nothing in this section shall relieve the person from liability for damages to which he might be otherwise subjected to pursuant to law, but he shall not be subject to any damages with respect to any goods, wares, or merchandise which are deemed unconditional gifts to him under this section.

If after any receipt deemed to be an unconditional gift under this section, the sender continues to send bill statements or requests for payment with respect thereto, an action may be brought by the recipient to enjoin such conduct, in which action there may also be awarded reasonable attorneys' fees and costs to the prevailing party.

§ 1585. An acceptance must be absolute and unqualified, or must include in itself an acceptance of that character which the proposer can separate from the rest, and which will conclude the person accepting. A qualified acceptance is a new proposal.

§ 1586. A proposal may be revoked at any time before its acceptance is communicated to the proposer, but not afterwards.

§ 1587. A proposal is revoked:

1. By the communication of notice of revocation by the proposer to the other party, in the manner prescribed by Sections 1581 and 1583, before his acceptance has been communicated to the former;

2. By the lapse of the time prescribed in such proposal for its acceptance, or if no time is so prescribed, the lapse of a reasonable time without communication of the acceptance;

3. By the failure of the acceptor to fulfill a condition precedent to acceptance; or,

4. By the death or insanity of the proposer.

§ 1588. A contract which is voidable solely for want of due consent, may be ratified by a subsequent consent.

§ 1589. A voluntary acceptance of the benefit of a transaction is equivalent to a consent to all the obligations arising from it, so far as the facts are known, or ought to be known, to the person accepting.

§ 1590. Where either party to a contemplated marriage in this State makes a gift of money or property to the other on the basis or assumption that the marriage will take place, in the event that the donee refuses to enter into the marriage as contemplated or that it is given up by mutual consent, the donor may recover such gift or such part of its value as may, under all of the circumstances of the case, be found by a court or jury to be just.

OBJECT OF A CONTRACT

§ 1595. The object of a contract is the thing which it is agreed, on the part of the party receiving the consideration, to do or not to do.

§ 1596. The object of a contract must be lawful when the contract is made, and possible and ascertainable by the time the contract is to be performed.

§ 1597. Everything is deemed possible except that which is impossible in the nature of things.

§ 1598. Where a contract has but a single object, and such object is unlawful, whether in whole or in part, or wholly impossible of performance, or so vaguely expressed as to be wholly unascertainable, the entire contract is void.

§ 1599. Where a contract has several distinct objects, of which one at least is lawful, and one at least is unlawful, in whole or in part, the contract is void as to the latter and valid as to the rest.

CONSIDERATION

§ 1605. Any benefit conferred, or agreed to be conferred, upon the promisor, by any other person, to which the promisor is not lawfully entitled, or any prejudice suffered, or agreed to be suffered, by such person, other than such as he is at the time of consent lawfully bound to suffer, as an inducement to the promisor, is a good consideration for a promise.

§ 1606. An existing legal obligation resting upon the promisor, or a moral obligation originating in some benefit conferred upon the promisor, or prejudice suffered by the promisee, is also a good consideration for a promise, to an extent corresponding with the extent of the obligation, but no further or otherwise.

§ 1607. The consideration of a contract must be lawful within the meaning of Section 1667.

§ 1608. If any part of a single consideration for one or more objects, or of several considerations for a single object, is unlawful, the entire contract is void.

§ 1609. A consideration may be executed or executory, in whole or in part. In so far as it is executory it is subject to the provisions of Chapter IV of this Title.

§ 1610. When a consideration is executory, it is not indispensable that the contract should specify its amount or the means of ascertaining it. It may be left to the decision of a third person, or regulated by any specified standard.

§ 1611. When a contract does not determine the amount of the consideration, nor the method by which it is to be ascertained, or when it leaves the amount thereof to the discretion of an interested party, the consideration must be so much money as the object of the contract is reasonably worth.

§ 1612. Where a contract provides an exclusive method by which its consideration is to be ascertained, which method is on its face impossible of execution, the entire contract is void; but this section shall not apply to the cases provided for in sections 1729 and 1730 of this code.

§ 1613. Where a contract provides an exclusive method by which its consideration is to be ascertained, which method appears possible on its face, but in fact is, or becomes, impossible of execution, such provision only is void; but this section shall not apply to the cases provided for in sections 1729 and 1730 of this code.

§ 1614. A written instrument is presumptive evidence of a consideration.

§ 1615. The burden of showing a want of consideration sufficient to support an instrument lies with the party seeking to invalidate or avoid it.

MANNER OF CREATING CONTRACTS

§ 1619. A contract is either express or implied.

§ 1620. An express contract is one, the terms of which are stated in words.

§ 1621. An implied contract is one, the existence and terms of which are manifested by conduct.

§ 1622. All contracts may be oral, except such as are specially required by statute to be in writing.

§ 1623. Where a contract, which is required by law to be in writing, is prevented from being put into writing by the fraud of a party thereto, any other party who is by such fraud led to believe that it is in writing, and acts upon such belief to his prejudice, may enforce it against the fraudulent party.

§ 1624. (a) The following contracts are invalid, unless they, or some note or memorandum thereof, are in writing and subscribed by the party to be charged or by the party's agent:

(1) An agreement that by its terms is not to be performed within a year from the making thereof.

(2) A special promise to answer for the debt, default, or miscarriage of another, except in the cases provided for in Section 2794.

(3) An agreement for the leasing for a longer period than one year, or for the sale of real property, or of an interest therein; such an agreement, if made by an agent of the party sought to be charged, is invalid, unless the authority of the agent is in writing, subscribed by the party sought to be charged.

(4) An agreement authorizing or employing an agent, broker, or any other person to purchase or sell real estate, or to lease real estate for a longer period than one year, or to procure, introduce, or find a purchaser or seller of real estate or a lessee or lessor of real estate where the lease is for a longer period than one year, for compensation or a commission.

(5) An agreement that by its terms is not to be performed during the lifetime of the promisor.

(6) An agreement by a purchaser of real property to pay an indebtedness secured by a mortgage or deed of trust upon the property purchased, unless assumption of the indebtedness by the purchaser is specifically provided for in the conveyance of the property.

(7) A contract, promise, undertaking, or commitment to loan money or to grant or extend credit, in an amount greater than one hundred thousand dollars ($100,000), not primarily for personal, family, or household purposes, made by a person engaged in the business of lending or arranging for the lending of money or extending credit. For purposes of this section, a contract, promise, undertaking or commitment to loan money secured solely by residential property consisting of one to four dwelling units shall be deemed to be for personal, family, or household purposes.

(b) Notwithstanding paragraph (1) of subdivision (a):

(1) An agreement or contract that is valid in other respects and is otherwise enforceable is not invalid for lack of a note, memorandum, or other writing and is enforceable by way of action or defense, provided that the agreement or contract is a qualified financial contract as defined in paragraph (2) and (A) there is, as provided in paragraph (3), sufficient evidence to indicate that a contract has been made or (B) the parties thereto by means of a prior or subsequent written contract, have agreed to be bound by the terms of the qualified financial contract from the time they reached agreement (by telephone, by exchange of electronic messages, or otherwise) on those terms.

(2) For purposes of this subdivision, a "qualified financial contract" means an agreement as to which each party thereto is other than a natural person and that is any of the following:

(A) For the purchase and sale of foreign exchange, foreign currency, bullion, coin or precious metals on a forward, spot, next-day value or other basis.

(B) A contract (other than a contract for the purchase of a commodity for future delivery on, or subject to the rules of, a contract market or board of trade) for the purchase, sale, or transfer of any commodity or any similar good, article, service, right, or interest that is presently or in the future becomes the subject of a dealing in the forward contract trade, or any product or byproduct thereof, with a maturity date more than two days after the date the contract is entered into. (C) For the purchase and sale of currency, or interbank deposits denominated in United States dollars.

(D) For a currency option, currency swap, or cross-currency rate swap.

(E) For a commodity swap or a commodity option (other than an option contract traded on, or subject to the rules of a contract market or board of trade).

(F) For a rate swap, basis swap, forward rate transaction, or an interest rate option.

(G) For a security-index swap or option, or a security or securities price swap or option.

(H) An agreement that involves any other similar transaction relating to a price or index (including, without limitation, any transaction or agreement involving any combination of the foregoing, any cap, floor, collar, or similar transaction with respect to a rate, commodity price, commodity index, security or securities price, security index, other price index, or loan price).

(I) An option with respect to any of the foregoing.

(3) There is sufficient evidence that a contract has been made in any of the following circumstances:

(A) There is evidence of an electronic communication (including, without limitation, the recording of a telephone call or the tangible written text produced by computer retrieval), admissible in evidence under the laws of this state, sufficient to indicate that in the communication a contract was made between the parties.

(B) A confirmation in writing sufficient to indicate that a contract has been made between the parties and sufficient against the sender is received by the party against whom enforcement is sought no later than the fifth business day after the contract is made (or any other period of time that the parties may agree in writing) and the sender does not receive, on or before the third business day after receipt (or the other period of time that the parties may agree in writing), written objection to a material term of the confirmation. For purposes of this subparagraph, a confirmation or an objection thereto is received at the time there has been an actual receipt by an individual responsible for the transaction or, if earlier, at the time there has been constructive receipt, which is the time actual receipt by that individual would have occurred if the receiving party, as an organization, had exercised reasonable diligence. For the purposes of this subparagraph, a "business day" is a day on which both parties are open and transacting business of the kind involved in that qualified financial contract that is the subject of confirmation.

(C) The party against whom enforcement is sought admits in its pleading, testimony, or otherwise in court that a contract was made.

(D) There is a note, memorandum, or other writing sufficient to indicate that a contract has been made, signed by the party against whom enforcement is sought or by its authorized agent or broker. For purposes of this paragraph, evidence of an electronic communication indicating the making in that communication of a contract, or a confirmation, admission, note, memorandum, or writing is not insufficient because it omits or incorrectly states one or more material terms agreed upon, as long as the evidence provides a reasonable basis for concluding that a contract was made.

(4) For purposes of this subdivision, the tangible written text produced by telex, telefacsimile, computer retrieval, or other process by which electronic signals are transmitted by telephone or otherwise shall constitute a writing, and any symbol executed or adopted by a party with the present intention to authenticate a writing shall constitute a signing. The confirmation and notice of objection referred to in subparagraph (B) of paragraph (3) may be communicated by means of telex, telefacsimile, computer, or other similar process by which electronic signals are transmitted by telephone or otherwise, provided that a party claiming to have communicated in that manner shall, unless the parties have otherwise agreed in writing, have the burden of establishing actual or constructive receipt by the other party as set forth in subparagraph (B) of paragraph (3).

(c) This section does not apply to leases subject to Division 10 (commencing with Section 10101) of the Commercial Code.

§ 1625. The execution of a contract in writing, whether the law requires it to be written or not, supersedes all the negotiations or stipulations concerning its matter which preceded or accompanied the execution of the instrument.

§ 1626. A contract in writing takes effect upon its delivery to the party in whose favor it is made, or to his agent.

§ 1627. The provisions of the Chapter on Transfers in General, concerning the delivery of grants, absolute and conditional, apply to all written contracts.

§ 1628. A corporate or official seal may be affixed to an instrument by a mere impression upon the paper or other material on which such instrument is written.

§ 1629. All distinctions between sealed and unsealed instruments are abolished.

§ 1630. Except as provided in Section 1630.5, a printed contract of bailment providing for the parking or storage of a motor vehicle shall not be binding, either in whole or in part, on the vehicle owner or on the person who leaves the vehicle with another, unless the contract conforms to the following:

(a) "This contract limits our liability—read it" is printed at the top in capital letters of 10-point type or larger.

(b) All the provisions of the contract are printed legibly in eight-point type or larger.

(c) Acceptance of benefits under a contract included within the provisions of this section shall not be construed a waiver of this section, and it shall be unlawful to issue such a contract on condition that provisions of this section are waived. A copy of the contract printed in large type, in an area at least 17 by 22 inches, shall be posted in a conspicuous place at each entrance of the parking lot. Nothing in this section shall be construed to prohibit the enactment of city ordinances on this subject that are not less restrictive, and such enactments are expressly authorized.

§ 1630.5. The provisions of any contract of bailment for the parking or storage of a motor vehicle shall not exempt the bailee from liability, either in whole or in part, for the theft of any motor vehicle, when such motor vehicle is parked or stored with such bailee, and the keys are required by such bailee to be left in the parked or stored vehicle.

§ 1631. Every person in this State who sells machinery used or to be used for mining purposes shall, at the time of sale, give to the buyer a bill of sale for the machinery. The seller shall keep a written record of the sale, giving the date thereof, describing the machinery, and showing the name and address of the buyer, and the buyer, if in this State, shall keep a record of his purchase, giving the name and address of the seller, describing the machinery, and showing the date of the purchase.

INTERPRETATION OF CONTRACTS

§ 1635. All contracts, whether public or private, are to be interpreted by the same rules, except as otherwise provided by this Code.

§ 1636. A contract must be so interpreted as to give effect to the mutual intention of the parties as it existed at the time of contracting, so far as the same is ascertainable and lawful.

§ 1637. For the purpose of ascertaining the intention of the parties to a contract, if otherwise doubtful, the rules given in this Chapter are to be applied.

§ 1638. The language of a contract is to govern its interpretation, if the language is clear and explicit, and does not involve an absurdity.

§ 1639. When a contract is reduced to writing, the intention of the parties is to be ascertained from the writing alone, if possible; subject, however, to the other provisions of this Title.

§ 1640. When, through fraud, mistake, or accident, a written contract fails to express the real intention of the parties, such intention is to be regarded, and the erroneous parts of the writing disregarded.

§ 1641. The whole of a contract is to be taken together, so as to give effect to every part, if reasonably practicable, each clause helping to interpret the other.

§ 1642. Several contracts relating to the same matters, between the same parties, and made as parts of substantially one transaction, are to be taken together.

§ 1643. A contract must receive such an interpretation as will make it lawful, operative, definite, reasonable, and capable of being carried into effect, if it can be done without violating the intention of the parties.

§ 1644. The words of a contract are to be understood in their ordinary and popular sense, rather than according to their strict legal meaning; unless used by the parties in a technical sense, or unless a special meaning is given to them by usage, in which case the latter must be followed.

§ 1645. Technical words are to be interpreted as usually understood by persons in the profession or business to which they relate, unless clearly used in a different sense.

§ 1646. A contract is to be interpreted according to the law and usage of the place where it is to be performed; or, if it does not indicate a place of performance, according to the law and usage of the place where it is made.

§ 1646.5. Notwithstanding Section 1646, the parties to any contract, agreement, or undertaking, contingent or otherwise, relating to a transaction involving in the aggregate not less than two hundred fifty thousand dollars ($250,000), including a transaction otherwise covered by subdivision (1) of Section 1105 of the Commercial Code, may agree that the law of this state shall govern their rights and duties in whole or in part, whether or not the contract, agreement, or undertaking or transaction bears a reasonable relation to this state. This section does not apply to any contract, agreement, or undertaking (a) for labor or personal services, (b) relating to any transaction primarily for personal, family, or household purposes, or (c) to the extent provided to the contrary in subdivision (2) of Section 1105 of the Commercial Code. This section applies to contracts, agreements, and undertakings entered into before, on, or after its effective date; it shall be fully retroactive. Contracts, agreements, and undertakings selecting California law entered into before the effective date of this section shall be valid, enforceable, and effective as if this section had been in effect on the date they were entered into; and actions and proceedings commencing in a court of this state before the effective date of this section may be maintained as if this section were in effect on the date they were commenced.

§ 1647. A contract may be explained by reference to the circumstances under which it was made, and the matter to which it relates.

§ 1648. However broad may be the terms of a contract, it extends only to those things concerning which it appears that the parties intended to contract.

§ 1649. If the terms of a promise are in any respect ambiguous or uncertain, it must be interpreted in the sense in which the promisor believed, at the time of making it, that the promisee understood it.

§ 1650. Particular clauses of a contract are subordinate to its general intent.

§ 1651. Where a contract is partly written and partly printed, or where part of it is written or printed under the special directions of the parties, and with a special view to their intention, and the remainder is copied from a form originally prepared without special reference to the particular parties and the particular contract in question, the written parts control the printed parts, and the parts which are purely original control those which are copied from a form. And if the two are absolutely repugnant, the latter must be so far disregarded.

§ 1652. Repugnancy in a contract must be reconciled, if possible, by such an interpretation as will give some effect to the repugnant clauses, subordinate to the general intent and purpose of the whole contract.

§ 1653. Words in a contract which are wholly inconsistent with its nature, or with the main intention of the parties, are to be rejected.

§ 1654. In cases of uncertainty not removed by the preceding rules, the language of a contract should be interpreted most strongly against the party who caused the uncertainty to exist.

§ 1655. Stipulations which are necessary to make a contract reasonable, or conformable to usage, are implied, in respect to matters concerning which the contract manifests no contrary intention.

§ 1656. All things that in law or usage are considered as incidental to a contract, or as necessary to carry it into effect, are implied therefrom, unless some of them are expressly mentioned therein, when all other things of the same class are deemed to be excluded.

§ 1657. If no time is specified for the performance of an act required to be performed, a reasonable time is allowed. If the act is in its nature capable of being done instantly—as, for example, if it consists in the payment of money only—it must be performed immediately upon the thing to be done being exactly ascertained.

§ 1659. Where all the parties who unite in a promise receive some benefit from the consideration, whether past or present, their promise is presumed to be joint and several.

§ 1660. A promise, made in the singular number, but executed by several persons, is presumed to be joint and several.

§ 1661. An executed contract is one, the object of which is fully performed. All others are executory.

§ 1662. Any contract hereafter made in this State for the purchase and sale of real property shall be interpreted as including an agreement that the parties shall have the following rights and duties, unless the contract expressly provides otherwise:

(a) If, when neither the legal title nor the possession of the subject matter of the contract has been transferred, all or a material part thereof is destroyed without fault of the purchaser or is taken by eminent domain, the vendor cannot enforce the contract, and the purchaser is entitled to recover any portion of the price that he has paid;

(b) If, when either the legal title or the possession of the subject matter of the contract has been transferred, all or any part thereof is destroyed without fault of the vendor or is taken by eminent domain, the purchaser is not thereby relieved from a duty to pay the price, nor is he entitled to recover any portion thereof that he has paid.

This section shall be so interpreted and construed as to effectuate its general purpose to make uniform the law of those states which enact it.

This section may be cited as the Uniform Vendor and Purchaser Risk Act.

UNLAWFUL CONTRACTS

§ 1667. That is not lawful which is:

1. Contrary to an express provision of law;

2. Contrary to the policy of express law, though not expressly prohibited; or,

3. Otherwise contrary to good morals.

§ 1668. All contracts which have for their object, directly or indirectly, to exempt any one from responsibility for his own fraud, or willful injury to the person or property of another, or violation of law, whether willful or negligent, are against the policy of the law.

§ 1669. Every contract in restraint of the marriage of any person, other than a minor, is void.

§ 1669.5. (a) Any contract for the payment of money or other consideration to a minor who has been alleged to be the victim of an unlawful sex act, or to his or her legal representative, by the alleged perpetrator of that unlawful sex act, or his or her legal representative, entered into on or after the time of the alleged unlawful sex act, and providing for any payments to be made more than one year after the date of the execution of the contract, is void as contrary to public policy. A district attorney may bring an action or intervene in any action to enjoin enforcement of any contract which is in violation of this section.

(b) This section does not apply after the date of the final judgment in a criminal case against the alleged perpetrator for the unlawful sex act described in subdivision (a).

(c) This section does not apply to a contract for the payment of money or other consideration made from a nonrevocable trust established for the benefit of the minor if the alleged perpetrator has no direct or indirect access to, or control over, the trust.

(d) This section does not apply to an alleged perpetrator of an unlawful sex act against a minor to the extent he or she agrees to pay, or is required by court order to pay, child support for that minor upon a dissolution or legal separation.

(e) For purposes of this section, "unlawful sex act," means a felony sex offense committed against a minor.

(f) Notwithstanding subdivision (a), any contract declared void as contrary to public policy under this section may still be enforced by a district attorney against the payor, and the proceeds thereof shall be deposited in the State Children's Trust Fund pursuant to Section 18969 of the Welfare and Institutions Code.

§1669.7. A contract for the payment of money or other consideration in violation of Section 132.5 of the Penal Code is void as contrary to public policy. The Attorney General or the district attorney of the county in which a violation of Section 132.5 of the Penal Code occurs may bring a civil action, or intervene in any civil action, to enjoin the enforcement of a contract that violates that section.

§ 1670. Any dispute arising from a construction contract with a public agency, which contract contains a provision that one party to the contract or one party's agent or employee shall decide any disputes arising under that contract, shall be resolved by submitting the dispute to independent arbitration, if mutually agreeable, otherwise by litigation in a court of competent jurisdiction.

§ 1670.5. (a) If the court as a matter of law finds the contract or any clause of the contract to have been unconscionable at the time it was made the court may refuse to enforce the contract, or it may enforce the remainder of the contract without the unconscionable clause, or it may so limit the application of any unconscionable clause as to avoid any unconscionable result.

(b) When it is claimed or appears to the court that the contract or any clause thereof may be unconscionable the parties shall be afforded a reasonable opportunity to present evidence as to its commercial setting, purpose, and effect to aid the court in making the determination.

§ 1670.6. A contract with a consumer located in California for the purchase of a good or service that is made in connection with a telephone solicitation made in or from outside of California and is primarily for personal, family, or household use, is unlawful if, with respect to that telephone solicitation, the telemarketer is in violation of Section 310.4(a)(6)(i) of, or has not complied with Section 310.5(a)(5) of, the Federal Trade Commission's Telemarketing Sales Rule (16 C.F.R. Part 310), as published in the Federal Register, Volume 68, Number 19, on January 29, 2003. This section shall apply only to those entities subject to, and does not apply to any transaction exempted under Section 310.6 of, the Telemarketing Sales Rule (16 C.F.R. Part 310), as published in the Federal Register, Volume 68, Number 19, on January 29, 2003.

LIQUIDATED DAMAGES
GENERAL PROVISIONS

§ 1671. (a) This section does not apply in any case where another statute expressly applicable to the contract prescribes the rules or standard for determining the validity of a provision in the contract liquidating the damages for the breach of the contract.

(b) Except as provided in subdivision (c), a provision in a contract liquidating the damages for the breach of the contract is valid unless the party seeking to invalidate the provision establishes that the provision was unreasonable under the circumstances existing at the time the contract was made.

(c) The validity of a liquidated damages provision shall be determined under subdivision (d) and not under subdivision (b) where the liquidated damages are sought to be recovered from either:

(1) A party to a contract for the retail purchase, or rental, by such party of personal property or services, primarily for the party's personal, family, or household purposes; or

(2) A party to a lease of real property for use as a dwelling by the party or those dependent upon the party for support.

(d) In the cases described in subdivision (c), a provision in a contract liquidating damages for the breach of the contract is void except that the parties to such a contract may agree therein upon an amount which shall be presumed to be the amount of damage sustained by a breach thereof, when, from the nature of the case, it would be impracticable or extremely difficult to fix the actual damage.

DEFAULT ON REAL PROPERTY PURCHASE CONTRACT

§ 1675. (a) As used in this section, "residential property" means real property primarily consisting of a dwelling that meets both of the following requirements:

(1) The dwelling contains not more than four residential units.

(2) At the time the contract to purchase and sell the property is made, the buyer intends to occupy the dwelling or one of its units as his or her residence.

(b) A provision in a contract to purchase and sell residential property that provides that all or any part of a payment made by the buyer shall constitute liquidated damages to the seller upon the buyer's failure to complete the purchase of the property is valid to the extent that payment in the form of cash or check, including a postdated check, is actually made if the provision satisfies the requirements of Sections 1677 and 1678 and either subdivision (c) or (d) of this section.

(c) If the amount actually paid pursuant to the liquidated damages provision does not exceed 3 percent of the purchase price, the provision is valid to the extent that payment is actually made unless the buyer establishes that the amount is unreasonable as liquidated damages.

(d) If the amount actually paid pursuant to the liquidated damages provision exceeds 3 percent of the purchase price, the provision is invalid unless the party seeking to uphold the provision establishes that the amount actually paid is reasonable as liquidated damages.

(e) For the purposes of subdivisions (c) and (d), the reasonableness of an amount actually paid as liquidated damages shall be determined by taking into account both of the following:

(1) The circumstances existing at the time the contract was made.

(2) The price and other terms and circumstances of any subsequent sale or contract to sell and purchase the same property if the sale or contract is made within six months of the buyer's default.

(f) (1) Notwithstanding either subdivision (c) or (d), for the initial sale of newly constructed attached condominium units, as defined pursuant to Section 783 of the Civil Code, that involves the sale of an attached residential condominium unit located within a structure of 10 or more residential condominium units and the amount actually paid to the seller pursuant to the liquidated damages provision exceeds 3 percent of the purchase price of the residential unit in the transaction both of the following shall occur in the event of a buyer's default:

(A) The seller shall perform an accounting of its costs and revenues related to and fairly allocable to the construction and sale of the residential unit within 60 calendar days after the final close of escrow of the sale of the unit within the structure.

(B) The accounting shall include any and all costs and revenues related to the construction and sale of the residential property and any delay caused by buyer's default. The seller shall make reasonable efforts to mitigate any damages arising from the default.

The seller shall refund to the buyer any amounts previously retained as liquidated damages in excess of the greater of either 3 percent of the originally agreed-upon purchase price of the residential property or the amount of the seller's losses resulting from the buyer's default, as calculated by the accounting.

(2) The refund shall be sent to the buyer's last known address within 90 days after the final close of escrow of the sale or lease of all the residential condominium units within the structure.

(3) If the amount retained by the seller after the accounting does not exceed 3 percent of the purchase price, the amount is valid unless the buyer establishes that the amount is unreasonable as liquidated damages pursuant to subdivision (e).

(4) Subdivision (d) shall not apply to any dispute regarding the reasonableness of any amount retained as liquidated damages pursuant to this subdivision.

(5) Notwithstanding the time periods regarding the performance of the accounting set forth in paragraph (1), if a "new qualified buyer" has entered into a contract to purchase the residential property in question, the seller shall perform the accounting within 60 calendar days after a new qualified buyer has entered into a contract to purchase.

(6) As used in this subdivision, the term "structure" shall mean either of the following:

(A) Improvements constructed on a common foundation.

(B) Improvements constructed by the same owner that must be constructed concurrently due to the design characteristics of the improvements or physical characteristics of the property on which the improvements are located.

(7) As used in this subdivision, the term "new qualified buyer" shall mean a buyer that:

(A) Has been issued a loan commitment, which satisfies the purchase agreement loan contingency requirement, by an institutional lender to obtain a loan for an amount equal to the purchase price less any downpayment possessed by the buyer.

(B) Has contracted to pay a purchase price that is greater than or equal to the purchase price to be paid by the original buyer.

§ 1676. Except as provided in Section 1675, a provision in a contract to purchase and sell real property liquidating the damages to the seller if the buyer fails to complete the purchase of the property is valid if it satisfies the requirements of Section 1677 and the requirements of subdivision (b) of Section 1671.

§ 1677. A provision in a contract to purchase and sell real property liquidating the damages to the seller if the buyer fails to complete the purchase of the property is invalid unless:

(a) The provision is separately signed or initialed by each party to the contract; and

(b) If the provision is included in a printed contract, it is set out either in at least 10-point bold type or in contrasting red print in at least eight-point bold type.

§ 1678. If more than one payment made by the buyer is to constitute liquidated damages under Section 1675, the amount of any payment after the first payment is valid as liquidated damages only if (1) the total of all such payments satisfies the requirements of Section 1675 and (2) a separate liquidated damages provision satisfying the requirements of Section 1677 is separately signed or initialed by each party to the contract for each such subsequent payment.

§ 1679. This chapter applies only to a provision for liquidated damages to the seller if the buyer fails to complete the purchase of real property. The validity of any other provision for liquidated damages in a contract to purchase and sell real property shall be determined under Section 1671.

§ 1680. Nothing in this chapter affects any right a party to a contract for the purchase and sale of real property may have to obtain specific performance.

§ 1681. This chapter does not apply to real property sales contracts as defined in Section 2985.

EXTINCTION OF CONTRACTS
CONTRACTS, HOW EXTINGUISHED

§ 1682. A contract may be extinguished in like manner with any other obligation, and also in the manner prescribed by this Title.

RESCISSION

§ 1688. A contract is extinguished by its rescission.

§ 1689. (a) A contract may be rescinded if all the parties thereto consent.

(b) A party to a contract may rescind the contract in the following cases:

(1) If the consent of the party rescinding, or of any party jointly contracting with him, was given by mistake, or obtained through duress, menace, fraud, or undue influence, exercised by or with the connivance of the party as to whom he rescinds, or of any other party to the contract jointly interested with such party.

(2) If the consideration for the obligation of the rescinding party fails, in whole or in part, through the fault of the party as to whom he rescinds.

(3) If the consideration for the obligation of the rescinding party becomes entirely void from any cause.

(4) If the consideration for the obligation of the rescinding party, before it is rendered to him, fails in a material respect from any cause.

(5) If the contract is unlawful for causes which do not appear in its terms or conditions, and the parties are not equally at fault.

(6) If the public interest will be prejudiced by permitting the contract to stand.

(7) Under the circumstances provided for in Sections 39, 1533, 1566, 1785, 1789, 1930 and 2314 of this code, Section 2470 of the Corporations Code, Sections 331, 338, 359, 447, 1904 and 2030 of the Insurance Code or any other statute providing for rescission.

§ 1689.2. A participant in an endless chain scheme, as defined in Section 327 of the Penal Code, may rescind the contract upon which the scheme is based, and may recover all consideration paid pursuant to the scheme, less any amounts paid or consideration provided to the participant pursuant to the scheme. In addition, the court may, upon motion, award reasonable attorney's fees to a prevailing plaintiff.

§ 1689.3. Any patient who contracts directly with a dental office or plan for services may rescind the contract or plan until midnight of the third business day after the day on which the patient signs the contract or plan. If services have been provided to the patient, the dental office shall be entitled to compensation for those services.

§ 1690. A stipulation that errors of description shall not avoid a contract, or shall be the subject of compensation, or both, does not take away the right of rescission for fraud, nor for mistake, where such mistake is in a matter essential to the inducement of the contract, and is not capable of exact and entire compensation.

§ 1691. Subject to Section 1693, to effect a rescission a party to the contract must, promptly upon discovering the facts which entitle him to rescind if he is free from duress, menace, undue influence or disability and is aware of his right to rescind:

(a) Give notice of rescission to the party as to whom he rescinds; and

(b) Restore to the other party everything of value which he has received from him under the contract or offer to restore the same upon condition that the other party do likewise, unless the latter is unable or positively refuses to do so.

When notice of rescission has not otherwise been given or an offer to restore the benefits received under the contract has not otherwise been made, the service of a pleading in an action or proceeding that seeks relief based on rescission shall be deemed to be such notice or offer or both.

§ 1692. When a contract has been rescinded in whole or in part, any party to the contract may seek relief based upon such rescission by

(a) bringing an action to recover any money or thing owing to him by any other party to the contract as a consequence of such rescission or for any other relief to which he may be entitled under the circumstances or

(b) asserting such rescission by way of defense or cross-complaint.

If in an action or proceeding a party seeks relief based upon rescission and the court determines that the contract has not been rescinded, the court may grant any party to the action any other relief to which he may be entitled under the circumstances.

A claim for damages is not inconsistent with a claim for relief based upon rescission. The aggrieved party shall be awarded complete relief, including restitution of benefits, if any, conferred by him as a result of the transaction and any consequential damages to which he is entitled; but such relief shall not include duplicate or inconsistent items of recovery.

If in an action or proceeding a party seeks relief based upon rescission, the court may require the party to whom such relief is granted to make any compensation to the other which justice may require and may otherwise in its judgment adjust the equities between the parties.

§ 1693. When relief based upon rescission is claimed in an action or proceeding, such relief shall not be denied because of delay in giving notice of rescission unless such delay has been substantially prejudicial to the other party.

A party who has received benefits by reason of a contract that is subject to rescission and who in an action or proceeding seeks relief based upon rescission shall not be denied relief because of a delay in restoring or in tendering restoration of such benefits before judgment unless such delay has been substantially prejudicial to the other party; but the court may make a tender of restoration a condition of its judgment.

MODIFICATION AND CANCELLATION

§ 1697. A contract not in writing may be modified in any respect by consent of the parties, in writing, without a new consideration, and is extinguished thereby to the extent of the modification.

§ 1698. (a) A contract in writing may be modified by a contract in writing.

(b) A contract in writing may be modified by an oral agreement to the extent that the oral agreement is executed by the parties.

(c) Unless the contract otherwise expressly provides, a contract in writing may be modified by an oral agreement supported by new consideration. The statute of frauds (Section 1624) is required to be satisfied if the contract as modified is within its provisions.

(d) Nothing in this section precludes in an appropriate case the application of rules of law concerning estoppel, oral novation and substitution of a new agreement, rescission of a written contract by an oral agreement, waiver of a provision of a written contract, or oral independent collateral contracts.

§ 1699. The destruction or cancellation of a written contract, or of the signature of the parties liable thereon, with intent to extinguish the obligation thereof, extinguishes it as to all the parties consenting to the act.

§ 1700. The intentional destruction, cancellation, or material alteration of a written contract, by a party entitled to any benefit under it, or with his consent, extinguishes all the executory obligations of the contract in his favor, against parties who do not consent to the act.

§ 1701. Where a contract is executed in duplicate, an alteration or destruction of one copy, while the other exists, is not within the provisions of the last section.

AUTHORITY OF AGENTS

§ 2309. An oral authorization is sufficient for any purpose, except that an authority to enter into a contract required by law to be in writing can only be given by an instrument in writing.

INTEREST AS DAMAGES

§ 3289. (a) Any legal rate of interest stipulated by a contract remains chargeable after a breach thereof, as before, until the contract is superseded by a verdict or other new obligation.

(b) If a contract entered into after January 1, 1986, does not stipulate a legal rate of interest, the obligation shall bear interest at a rate of 10 percent per annum after a breach.

For the purposes of this subdivision, the term contract shall not include a note secured by a deed of trust on real property.

DAMAGES FOR BREACH OF CONTRACT

(§ 3300.) Section Thirty-three Hundred. For the breach of an obligation arising from contract, the measure of damages, except where otherwise expressly provided by this Code, is the amount which will compensate the party aggrieved for all the detriment proximately caused thereby, or which, in the ordinary course of things, would be likely to result therefrom.

§ 3301. No damages can be recovered for a breach of contract which are not clearly ascertainable in both their nature and origin.

§ 3302. The detriment caused by the breach of an obligation to pay money only, is deemed to be the amount due by the terms of the obligation, with interest thereon.

§ 3304. The detriment caused by the breach of a covenant of "seizin," of "right to convey," of "warranty," or of "quiet enjoyment," in a grant of an estate in real property, is deemed to be:

1. The price paid to the grantor; or, if the breach is partial only, such proportion of the price as the value of the property affected by the breach bore at the time of the grant to the value of the whole property;

2. Interest thereon for the time during which the grantee derived no benefit from the property, not exceeding five years;

3. Any expenses properly incurred by the covenantee in defending his possession.

§ 3305. The detriment caused by the breach of a covenant against incumbrances in a grant of an estate in real property is deemed to be the amount which has been actually expended by the covenantee in extinguishing either the principal or interest thereof, not exceeding in the former case a proportion of the price paid to the grantor equivalent to the relative value at the time of the grant of the property affected by the breach, as compared with the whole, or, in the latter case, interest on a like amount.

§ 3306. The detriment caused by the breach of an agreement to convey an estate in real property, is deemed to be the price paid, and the expenses properly incurred in examining the title and preparing the necessary papers, the difference between the price agreed to be paid and the value of the estate agreed to be conveyed at the time of the breach, the expenses properly incurred in preparing to enter upon the land, consequential damages according to proof, and interest.

§ 3306a. The minimum detriment caused by the breach of an agreement to execute and deliver a quitclaim deed to real property is deemed to be the expenses incurred by the promisee in quieting title to such property, and the expenses incidental to the entry upon such property. Such expenses which shall include reasonable attorneys' fees shall be fixed by the court in the quiet title action.

§ 3307. The detriment caused by the breach of an agreement to purchase an estate in real property is deemed to be the excess, if any, of the amount which would have been due to the seller under the contract over the value of the property to him or her, consequential damages according to proof, and interest.

SPECIFIC PERFORMANCE OF OBLIGATIONS

(§ 3384.) Section Thirty-three Hundred and Eighty-four. Except as otherwise provided in this Article, the specific performance of an obligation may be compelled.

§ 3386. Notwithstanding that the agreed counterperformance is not orwould not have been specifically enforceable, specific performance may be compelled if:

(a) Specific performance would otherwise be an appropriate remedy; and

(b) The agreed counterperformance has been substantially performed or its concurrent or future performance is assured or, if the court deems necessary, can be secured to the satisfaction of the court.

§ 3387. It is to be presumed that the breach of an agreement to transfer real property cannot be adequately relieved by pecuniary compensation. In the case of a single-family dwelling which the party seeking performance intends to occupy, this presumption is conclusive. In all other cases, this presumption is a presumption affecting the burden of proof.

§ 3388. A party who has signed a written contract may be compelled specifically to perform it, though the other party has not signed it, if the latter has performed, or offers to perform it on his part, and the case is otherwise proper for enforcing specific performance.

§ 3389. A contract otherwise proper to be specifically enforced, may be thus enforced, though a penalty is imposed, or the damages are liquidated for its breach, and the party in default is willing to pay the same.

§ 3390. The following obligations cannot be specifically enforced:

1. An obligation to render personal service;

2. An obligation to employ another in personal service;

3. An agreement to perform an act which the party has not power lawfully to perform when required to do so;

4. An agreement to procure the act or consent of the wife of the contracting party, or of any other third person; or,

5. An agreement, the terms of which are not sufficiently certain to make the precise act which is to be done clearly ascertainable.

§ 3391. Specific performance cannot be enforced against a party to a contract in any of the following cases:

1. If he has not received an adequate consideration for the contract;

2. If it is not, as to him, just and reasonable;

3. If his assent was obtained by the misrepresentation, concealment, circumvention, or unfair practices of any party to whom performance would become due under the contract, or by any promise of such party which has not been substantially fulfilled; or;

4. If his assent was given under the influence of mistake, misapprehension, or surprise, except that where the contract provides for compensation in case of mistake, a mistake within the scope of such provision may be compensated for, and the contract specifically enforced in other respects, if proper to be so enforced.

§ 3392. Specific performance cannot be enforced in favor of a party who has not fully and fairly performed all the conditions precedent on his part to the obligation of the other party, except where his failure to perform is only partial, and either entirely immaterial, or capable of being fully compensated, in which case specific performance may be compelled, upon full compensation being made for the default.

§ 3394. An agreement for the sale of property cannot be specifically enforced in favor of a seller who cannot give to the buyer a title free from reasonable doubt.

§ 3395. Whenever an obligation in respect to real property would be specifically enforced against a particular person, it may be in like manner enforced against any other person claiming under him by a title created subsequently to the obligation, except a purchaser or incumbrancer in good faith and for value, and except, also, that any such person may exonerate himself by conveying all his estate to the person entitled to enforce the obligation.

REVISION OF CONTRACTS

§ 3399. When, through fraud or a mutual mistake of the parties, or a mistake of one party, which the other at the time knew or suspected, a written contract does not truly express the intention of the parties, it may be revised on the application of a party aggrieved, so as to express that intention, so far as it can be done without prejudice to rights acquired by third persons, in good faith and for value.

§ 3400. For the purpose of revising a contract, it must be presumed that all the parties thereto intended to make an equitable and conscientious agreement.

§ 3401. In revising a written instrument, the Court may inquire what the instrument was intended to mean, and what were intended to be its legal consequences, and is not confined to the inquiry what the language of the instrument was intended to be.

§ 3402. A contract may be first revised and then specifically enforced.

Selected Provisions of the California Code of Civil Procedure

Table of Contents

THE TIME OF COMMENCING ACTIONS OTHER THAN FOR THE RECOVERY OF REAL PROPERTY

§ 335. The periods prescribed for the commencement of actions other than for the recovery of real property, are as follows:

§ 337. Within four years: 1. An action upon any contract, obligation or liability founded upon an instrument in writing, except as provided in Section 336a of this code; provided, that the time within which any action for a money judgment for the balance due upon an obligation for the payment of which a deed of trust or mortgage with power of sale upon real property or any interest therein was given as security, following the exercise of the power of sale in such deed of trust or mortgage, may be brought shall not extend beyond three months after the time of sale under such deed of trust or mortgage.

2. An action to recover (1) upon a book account whether consisting of one or more entries; (2) upon an account stated based upon an account in writing, but the acknowl-

edgment of the account stated need not be in writing; (3) a balance due upon a mutual, open and current account, the items of which are in writing; provided, however, that where an account stated is based upon an account of one item, the time shall begin to run from the date of said item, and where an account stated is based upon an account of more than one item, the time shall begin to run from the date of the last item.

3. An action based upon the rescission of a contract in writing. The time begins to run from the date upon which the facts that entitle the aggrieved party to rescind occurred. Where the ground for rescission is fraud or mistake, the time does not begin to run until the discovery by the aggrieved party of the facts constituting the fraud or mistake. Where the ground for rescission is misrepresentation under Section 359 of the Insurance Code, the time does not begin to run until the representation becomes false.

§ 337a. The term "book account" means a detailed statement which constitutes the principal record of one or more transactions between a debtor and a creditor arising out of a contract or some fiduciary relation, and shows the debits and credits in connection therewith, and against whom and in favor of whom entries are made, is entered in the regular course of business as conducted by such creditor or fiduciary, and is kept in a reasonably permanent form and manner and is (1) in a bound book, or (2) on a sheet or sheets fastened in a book or to backing but detachable therefrom, or (3) on a card or cards of a permanent character, or is kept in any other reasonably permanent form and manner.

§ 339. Within two years: 1. An action upon a contract, obligation or liability not founded upon an instrument of writing, except as provided in Section 2725 of the Commercial Code or subdivision 2 of Section 337 of this code; or an action founded upon a contract, obligation or liability, evidenced by a certificate, or abstract or guaranty of title of real property, or by a policy of title insurance; provided, that the cause of action upon a contract, obligation or liability evidenced by a certificate, or abstract or guaranty of title of real property or policy of title insurance shall not be deemed to have accrued until the discovery of the loss or damage suffered by the aggrieved party thereunder.

2. An action against a sheriff or coroner upon a liability incurred by the doing of an act in an official capacity and in virtue of office, or by the omission of an official duty including the nonpayment of money collected in the enforcement of a judgment.

3. An action based upon the rescission of a contract not in writing. The time begins to run from the date upon which the facts that entitle the aggrieved party to rescind occurred. Where the ground for rescission is fraud or mistake, the time does not begin to run until the discovery by the aggrieved party of the facts constituting the fraud or mistake.

§ 339.5. Where a lease of real property is not in writing, no action shall be brought under Section 1951.2 of the Civil Code more than two years after the breach of the lease and abandonment of the property, or more than two years after the termination of the right of the lessee to possession of the property, whichever is the earlier time.

OF THE GENERAL PRINCIPLES OF EVIDENCE

§ 1856. (a) Terms set forth in a writing intended by the parties as a final expression of their agreement with respect to such terms as are included therein may not be contradicted by evidence of any prior agreement or of a contemporaneous oral agreement.

(b) The terms set forth in a writing described in subdivision (a) may be explained or supplemented by evidence of consistent additional terms unless the writing is intended also as a complete and exclusive statement of the terms of the agreement.

(c) The terms set forth in a writing described in subdivision (a) may be explained or supplemented by course of dealing or usage of trade or by course of performance.

(d) The court shall determine whether the writing is intended by the parties as a final expression of their agreement with respect to such terms as are included therein and whether the writing is intended also as a complete and exclusive statement of the terms of the agreement.

(e) Where a mistake or imperfection of the writing is put in issue by the pleadings, this section does not exclude evidence relevant to that issue.

(f) Where the validity of the agreement is the fact in dispute, this section does not exclude evidence relevant to that issue.

(g) This section does not exclude other evidence of the circumstances under which the agreement was made or to which it relates, as defined in Section 1860, or to explain an extrinsic ambiguity or otherwise interpret the terms of the agreement, or to establish illegality or fraud.

(h) As used in this section, the term agreement includes deeds and wills, as well as contracts between parties.

§ 1857. The language of a writing is to be interpreted according to the meaning it bears in the place of its execution, unless the parties have reference to a different place.

§ 1858. In the construction of a statute or instrument, the office of the Judge is simply to ascertain and declare what is in terms or in substance contained therein, not to insert what has been omitted, or to omit what has been inserted; and where there are several provisions or particulars, such a construction is, if possible, to be adopted as will give effect to all.

§ 1859. In the construction of a statute the intention of the Legislature, and in the construction of the instrument the intention of the parties, is to be pursued, if possible; and when a general and particular provision are inconsistent, the latter is paramount to the former. So a particular intent will control a general one that is inconsistent with it.

§ 1860. For the proper construction of an instrument, the circumstances under which it was made, including the situation of the subject of the instrument, and of the parties to it, may also be shown, so that the Judge be placed in the position of those whose language he is to interpret.

§ 1861. The terms of a writing are presumed to have been used in their primary and general acceptation, but evidence is nevertheless admissible that they have a local, technical, or otherwise peculiar signification, and were so used and understood in the particular instance, in which case the agreement must be construed accordingly.

§ 1862. When an instrument consists partly of written words and partly of a printed form, and the two are inconsistent, the former controls the latter.

§ 1864. When the terms of an agreement have been intended in a different sense by the different parties to it, that sense is to prevail against either party in which he supposed the other understood it, and when different constructions of a provision are otherwise equally proper, that is to be taken which is most favorable to the party in whose favor the provision was made.

§ 1865. A written notice, as well as every other writing, is to be construed according to the ordinary acceptation of its terms. Thus a notice to the drawers or indorsers of a bill of exchange or promissory note, that it has been protested for want of acceptance or payment, must be held to import that the same has been duly presented for acceptance or payment and the same refused, and that the holder looks for payment to the person to whom the notice is given.

§1866. When a statute or instrument is equally susceptible of two interpretations, one in favor of natural right, and the other against it, the former is to be adopted.

Selected Provisions of the California Commercial Code

(Uniform Commercial Code)

Table of Contents

SHORT TITLE, CONSTRUCTION, APPLICATION AND SUBJECTMATTER OF THE CODE

§1101. This code shall be known and may be cited as Uniform Commercial Code.

§1102. (1) This code shall be liberally construed and applied to promote its underlying purposes and policies.

(2) Underlying purposes and policies of this code are

(a) To simplify, clarify and modernize the law governing commercial transactions;

(b) To permit the continued expansion of commercial practices through custom, usage and agreement of the parties;

(c) To make uniform the law among the various jurisdictions.

(3) The effect of provisions of this code may be varied by agreement, except as otherwise provided in this code and except that the obligations of good faith, diligence, reasonableness and care prescribed by this code may not be disclaimed by agreement but the parties may by agreement determine the standards by which the performance of such obligations is to be measured if such standards are not manifestly unreasonable.

(4) The presence in certain provisions of this code of the words "unless otherwise agreed" or words of similar import does not imply that the effect of other provisions may not be varied by agreement under subdivision (3).

(5) In this code unless the context otherwise requires

(a) Words in the singular number include the plural, and in the plural include the singular;

(b) Words of the masculine or feminine gender include the masculine, the feminine, and the neuter, and when the sense so indicates words of the neuter gender may refer to any gender.

§1103. Unless displaced by the particular provisions of this code, the principles of law and equity, including the law merchant and the law relative to capacity to contract, principal and agent, estoppel, fraud, misrepresentation, duress, coercion, mistake, bankruptcy, or other validating or invalidating cause shall supplement its provisions.

§1104. This code being a general act intended as a unified coverage of its subject matter, no part of it shall be deemed to be impliedly repealed by subsequent legislation if such construction can reasonably be avoided.

§1105. (1) Except as provided hereafter in this section, when a transaction bears a reasonable relation to this state and also to another state or nation the parties may agree that the law either of this state or of such other state or nation shall govern their rights and duties. Failing such agreement this code applies to transactions bearing an appropriate relation to this state. (2) Where one of the following provisions of this code specifies the applicable law, that provision governs and a contrary agreement is effective only to the extent permitted by the law (including the conflict of laws rules) so specified:

Rights of creditors against sold goods. Section 2402.

Applicability of the division on leases. Sections 10105 and 10106.

Applicability of the division on bank deposits and collections. Section 4102.

Letters of credit. Section 5116.

Bulk sales subject to the division on bulk sales. Section 6103.

Applicability of the division on investment securities. Section8110.

Law governing perfection, the effect of perfection ornonperfection, and the priority of security interests andagricultural liens. Sections 9301 to 9307, inclusive.

§1106. (1) The remedies provided by this code shall be liberally administered to the end that the aggrieved party may be put in as good a position as if the other party has fully performed but neither consequential or special nor penal damages may be had except as specifically provided in this code or by other rule of law.

(2) Any right or obligation declared by this code is enforceable by action unless the provision declaring it specifies a different and limited effect.

§ 1107. Any claim or right arising out of an alleged breach can be discharged in whole or in part without consideration by a written waiver or renunciation signed and delivered by the aggrieved party.

§ 1108. If any provision or clause of this code or application thereof to any person or circumstances is held invalid, such invalidity shall not affect other provisions or applications of the code which can be given effect without the invalid provision or application, and to this end the provisions of this code are declared to be severable.

GENERAL DEFINITIONS AND PRINCIPLES OF INTERPRETATION

§ 1201. The following definitions apply for purposes of this code, subject to additional definitions contained in the subsequent divisions of this code that apply to specific divisions or chapters thereof, and unless the context otherwise requires:

(1) "Action," in the sense of a judicial proceeding, includes recoupment, counterclaim, setoff, suit in equity, and any other proceedings in which rights are determined.

(2) "Aggrieved party" means a party entitled to resort to a remedy.

(3) "Agreement" means the bargain of the parties in fact as found in their language or by implication from other circumstances, including course of dealing, usage of trade, and course of performance as provided in this code (Sections 1205, 2208, and 10207). Whether an agreement has legal consequences is determined by the provisions of this code, if applicable, and otherwise by the law of contracts (Section 1103). (Compare "contract.")

(4) "Bank" means any person engaged in the business of banking.

(5) "Bearer" means the person in possession of an instrument, document of title, or certificated security payable to bearer or endorsed in blank.

(6) "Bill of lading" means a document evidencing the receipt of goods for shipment issued by a person engaged in the business of transporting or forwarding goods, and that, by its terms, evidences the intention of the issuer that the person entitled under the document (Section 7403(4)) has the right to receive, hold, and dispose of the document and the goods it covers. Designation of a document by the issuer as a "bill of lading" is conclusive evidence of that intention. "Bill of lading" includes an airbill. "Airbill" means a document serving for air transportation as a bill of lading does for marine or rail transportation, and includes an air consignment note or air waybill.

(7) "Branch" includes a separately incorporated foreign branch of a bank.

(8) "Burden of establishing" a fact means the burden of persuading the triers of fact that the existence of the fact is more probable than its nonexistence.

(9) "Buyer in ordinary course of business" means a person that buys goods in good faith, without knowledge that the sale violates the rights of another person in the goods, and in the ordinary course from a person, other than a pawnbroker, in the business of selling goods of that kind. A person buys goods in the ordinary course if the sale to the person comports with the usual or customary practices in the kind of business in which the seller is engaged or with the seller's own usual or customary practices. A person that sells oil, gas, or other minerals at the wellhead or minehead is a person in the business of selling goods of that kind. A buyer in the ordinary course of business may buy for cash, by exchange of other property, or on secured or unsecured credit, and may acquire goods or documents of title under a preexisting contract for sale. Only a buyer that takes possession of the goods or has a right to recover the goods from the seller under Division

2 (commencing with Section 2101) may be a buyer in ordinary course of business. A person that acquires goods in a transfer in bulk or as security for or in total or partial satisfaction of a money debt is not a buyer in ordinary course of business.

(10) "Conspicuous." A term or clause is conspicuous when it is so written that a reasonable person against whom it is to operate ought to have noticed it. A printed heading in capitals (as: NONNEGOTIABLE BILL OF LADING) is conspicuous. Language in the body of a form is "conspicuous" if it is in larger or other contrasting type or color, except that in a telegram any stated term is "conspicuous." Whether a term or clause is "conspicuous" or not is for decision by the court.

(11) "Contract" means the total legal obligation that results from the parties' agreement as affected by this code and any other applicable rules of law. (Compare "agreement.")

(12) "Creditor" includes a general creditor, a secured creditor, a lien creditor, and any representative of creditors, including an assignee for the benefit of creditors, a trustee in bankruptcy, a receiver in equity, and an executor or administrator of an insolvent debtor's or assignor's estate.

(13) "Defendant" includes a person in the position of defendant in a cross-action or counterclaim.

(14) "Delivery," with respect to instruments, documents of title, chattel paper, or certificated securities, means the voluntary transfer of possession.

(15) "Document of title" includes a bill of lading, dock warrant, dock receipt, warehouse receipt, gin ticket, or compress receipt, and any other document that, in the regular course of business or financing, is treated as adequately evidencing that the person entitled under the document (Section 7403(4)) has the right to receive, hold, and dispose of the document and the goods it covers. To be a document of title, a document shall purport to be issued by a bailee and purport to cover goods in the bailee's possession that either are identified as or are fungible portions of an identified mass.

(16) "Fault" means wrongful act, omission, or breach.

(17) "Fungible," with respect to goods or securities, means goods or securities of which any unit is, by nature or usage of trade, the equivalent of any other like unit. Goods that are not fungible shall be deemed fungible for the purposes of this code to the extent that, under a particular agreement or document, unlike units are treated as equivalents.

(18) "Genuine" means free of forgery or counterfeiting.

(19) "Good faith" means honesty in fact in the conduct or transaction concerned.

(20) "Holder," with respect to a negotiable instrument, means the person in possession if the instrument is payable to bearer or, in the case of an instrument payable to an identified person, if the identified person is in possession. "Holder," with respect to a document of title, means the person in possession if the goods are deliverable to bearer or to the order of the person in possession.

(21) To "honor" is to pay or to accept and pay or, where a credit so engages, to purchase or discount a draft complying with the terms of the credit.

(22) "Insolvency proceedings" includes any assignment for the benefit of creditors or other proceedings intended to liquidate or rehabilitate the estate of the person involved.

(23) A person is "insolvent" who either has ceased to pay his or her debts in the ordinary course of business, cannot pay his or her debts as they become due, or is insolvent within the meaning of the federal bankruptcy law.

(24) "Money" means a medium of exchange authorized or adopted by a domestic or foreign government and includes a monetary unit of account established by an intergovernmental organization or by agreement between two or more nations.

(25) A person has "notice" of a fact when any of the following occurs:

(a) He or she has actual knowledge of it.

(b) He or she has received a notice or notification of it.

(c) From all the facts and circumstances known to him or her at the time in question, he or she has reason to know that it exists. A person "knows" or has "knowledge" of a fact when he or she has actual knowledge of it. "Discover" or "learn," or a word or phrase of similar import, refers to knowledge rather than to reason to know. The time and circumstances under which a notice or notification may cease to be effective are not determined by this code.

(26) A person "notifies" or "gives" a notice or notification to another by taking those steps that may be reasonably required to inform the other in ordinary course whether or not the other actually comes to know of it. A person "receives" a notice or notification when any of the following occurs:

(a) It comes to his or her attention.

(b) It is duly delivered at the place of business through which the contract was made or at any other place held out by him or her as the place for receipt of these communications.

(27) Notice, knowledge, or a notice or notification received by an organization is effective for a particular transaction from the time it is brought to the attention of the individual conducting that transaction and, in any event, from the time it would have been brought to his or her attention if the organization had exercised due diligence. An organization exercises due diligence if it maintains reasonable routines for communicating significant information to the person conducting the transaction and there is reasonable compliance with the routines. Due diligence does not require an individual acting for the organization to communicate information unless the communication is part of his or her regular duties, or unless he or she has reason to know of the transaction and that the transaction would be materially affected by the information.

(28) "Organization" includes a corporation, government or governmental subdivision or agency, business trust, estate, trust, partnership or association, two or more persons having a joint or common interest, or any other legal or commercial entity.

(29) "Party," as distinct from "third party," means a person who has engaged in a transaction or made an agreement within this division.

(30) "Person" includes an individual or an organization. (See Section 1102.)

(31) "Purchase" includes taking by sale, discount, negotiation, mortgage, pledge, lien, security interest, issue or reissue, gift, or any other voluntary transaction creating an interest in property.

(32) "Purchaser" means a person who takes by purchase.

(33) "Remedy" means any remedial right to which an aggrieved party is entitled with or without resort to a tribunal.

(34) "Representative" includes an agent, an officer of a corporation or association, a trustee, executor, or administrator of an estate, or any other person empowered to act for another.

(35) "Rights" includes remedies.

(36) (a) "Security interest" means an interest in personal property or fixtures that secures payment or performance of an obligation. The term also includes any interest of a cosignor and a buyer of accounts, chattel paper, a payment intangible, or a promissory note in a transaction that is subject to Division 9 (commencing with Section 9101). The special property interest of a buyer of goods on identification of those goods to a contract for sale under Section 2401 is not a "security interest," but a buyer may also acquire a "security interest" by complying with Division 9 (commencing with Section 9101). Except as otherwise provided in Section 2505, the right of a seller or lessor of goods under Division 2 (commencing with Section 2101) or Division 10 (commencing with Section 10101) to retain or acquire possession of the goods is not a "security interest," but a seller or lessor may also acquire a "security interest" by complying with Division 9 (commencing with Section 9101). The retention or reservation of title by a seller of goods notwithstanding shipment or delivery to the buyer (Section 2401) is limited in effect to a reservation of a "security interest."

(b) Whether a transaction creates a lease or security interest is determined by the facts of each case. However, a transaction creates a security interest if the consideration the lessee is to pay the lessor for the right to possession and use of the goods is an obligation for the term of the lease not subject to termination by the lessee, and any of the following conditions applies:

(i) The original term of the lease is equal to or greater than the remaining economic life of the goods. (ii) The lessee is bound to renew the lease for the remaining economic life of the goods or is bound to become the owner of the goods.

(iii) The lessee has an option to renew the lease for the remaining economic life of the goods for no additional consideration or nominal additional consideration upon compliance with the lease agreement.

(iv) The lessee has an option to become the owner of the goods for no additional consideration or nominal additional consideration upon compliance with the lease agreement.

(c) A transaction does not create a security interest merely because it provides one or more of the following:

(i) That the present value of the consideration the lessee is obligated to pay the lessor for the right to possession and use of the goods is substantially equal to or greater than the fair market value of the goods at the time the lease is entered into.

(ii) That the lessee assumes the risk of loss of the goods, or agrees to pay the taxes, insurance, filing, recording, or registration fees, or service or maintenance costs with respect to the goods.

(iii) That the lessee has an option to renew the lease or to become the owner of the goods.

(iv) That the lessee has an option to renew the lease for a fixed rent that is equal to or greater than the reasonably predictable fair market rent for the use of the goods for the term of the renewal at the time the option is to be performed.

(v) That the lessee has an option to become the owner of the goods for a fixed price that is equal to or greater than the reasonably predictable fair market value of the goods at the time the option is to be performed.

(vi) In the case of a motor vehicle, as defined in Section 415 of the Vehicle Code, or a trailer, as defined in Section 630 of that code, that is not to be used primarily for personal, family, or household purposes, that the amount of rental payments may be increased or decreased by reference to the amount realized by the lessor upon sale or disposition of the vehicle or trailer. Nothing in this subparagraph affects the application or administration of the Sales and Use Tax Law (Part 1 (commencing with Section 6001), Division 2, Revenue and Taxation Code).

(d) For purposes of this subdivision (36), all of the following apply:

(i) Additional consideration is not nominal if (A) when the option to renew the lease is granted to the lessee, the rent is stated to be the fair market rent for the use of the goods for the term of the renewal determined at the time the option is to be performed, or (B) when the option to become the owner of the goods is granted to the lessee, the price is stated to be the fair market value of the goods determined at the time the option is to be performed. Additional consideration is nominal if it is less than the lessee's reasonably predictable cost of performing under the lease agreement if the option is not exercised.

(ii) "Reasonably predictable" and "remaining economic life of the goods" are to be determined with reference to the facts and circumstances at the time the transaction is entered into.

(iii) "Present value" means the amount as of a date certain of one or more sums payable in the future, discounted to the date certain. The discount is determined by the interest rate specified by the parties if the rate is not manifestly unreasonable at the time the transaction is entered into; otherwise, the discount is determined by a commercially reasonable rate that takes into account the facts and circumstances of each case at the time the transaction was entered into.

(37) "Send," in connection with any writing or notice, means to deposit in the mail or deliver for transmission by any other usual means of communication with postage or cost of transmission provided for and properly addressed and, in the case of an instrument, to an address specified thereon or otherwise agreed or, if there is none, to any address reasonable under the circumstances. The receipt of any writing or notice within the time in which it would have arrived if properly sent has the effect of a proper sending. When a writing or notice is required to be sent by registered or certified mail, proof of mailing is sufficient, and proof of receipt by the addressee is not required unless the words "with return receipt requested" are also used.

(38) "Signed" includes any symbol executed or adopted by a party with present intention to authenticate a writing.

(39) "Surety" includes guarantor.

(40) "Telegram" includes a message transmitted by radio, teletype, cable, any mechanical method of transmission, or the like.

(41) "Term" means that portion of an agreement that relates to a particular matter.

(42) "Unauthorized" signature means one made without actual, implied, or apparent authority, and includes a forgery.

(43) "Value." Except as otherwise provided with respect to negotiable instruments and bank collections (Sections 3303, 4210, and 4211), a person gives "value" for rights if he or she acquires them in any of the following ways:

(a) In return for a binding commitment to extend credit or for the extension of immediately available credit whether or not drawn upon and whether or not a chargeback is provided for in the event of difficulties in collection.

(b) As security for, or in total or partial satisfaction of, a preexisting claim.

(c) By accepting delivery pursuant to a preexisting contract for purchase.

(d) Generally, in return for any consideration sufficient to support a simple contract.

(44) "Warehouse receipt" means a document evidencing the receipt of goods for storage issued by a warehouseman (Section 7102), and that, by its terms, evidences the intention of the issuer that the person entitled under the document (Section 7403(4)) has the right to receive, hold, and dispose of the document and the goods it covers. Designation of a document by the issuer as a "warehouse receipt" is conclusive evidence of that intention.

(45) "Written" or "writing" includes printing, typewriting, or any other intentional reduction to tangible form.

§ 1202. (1) A bill of lading, policy or certificate of insurance, official weigher's or inspector's certificate, consular invoice, or any other document authorized or required by the contract to be issued by a third party is admissible as evidence of the facts stated in the document by the third party in any action arising out of the contract which authorized or required the document.

(2) In any action arising out of the contract which authorized or required the document referred to in subdivision (1):

(a) A document in due form purporting to be the document referred to in subdivision (1) is presumed to be authentic and genuine. This presumption is a presumption affecting the burden of producing evidence.

(b) If the document is found to be authentic and genuine, the facts stated in the document by the third party are presumed to be true. This presumption is a presumption affecting the burden of proof.

§ 1203. Every contract or duty within this code imposes an obligation of good faith in its performance or enforcement.

§ 1204. (1) Whenever this code requires any action to be taken within a reasonable time, any time which is not manifestly unreasonable may be fixed by agreement.

(2) What is a reasonable time for taking any action depends on the nature, purpose and circumstances of such action.

(3) An action is taken "seasonably" when it is taken at or within the time agreed or if no time is agreed at or within a reasonable time.

§ 1205. (1) A course of dealing is a sequence of previous conduct between the parties to a particular transaction which is fairly to be regarded as establishing a common basis of understanding for interpreting their expressions and other conduct.

(2) A usage of trade is any practice or method of dealing having such regularity of observance in a place, vocation or trade as to justify an expectation that it will be observed with respect to the transaction in question. The existence and scope of such a usage are to be proved as facts. If it is established that such a usage is embodied in a written trade code or similar writing the interpretation of the writing is for the court.

(3) A course of dealing between parties and any usage of trade in the vocation or trade in which they are engaged or of which they are or should be aware give particular meaning to and supplement or qualify terms of an agreement.

(4) The express terms of an agreement and an applicable course of dealing or usage of trade shall be construed wherever reasonable as consistent with each other; but when

such construction is unreasonable express terms control both course of dealing and usage of trade and course of dealing controls usage of trade.

(5) An applicable usage of trade in the place where any part of performance is to occur shall be used in interpreting the agreement as to that part of the performance.

(6) Evidence of a relevant usage of trade offered by one party is not admissible unless and until he has given the other party such notice as the court finds sufficient to prevent unfair surprise to the latter.

§ 1206. (1) Except in the cases described in subdivision (2) of this section a contract for the sale of personal property is not enforceable by way of action or defense beyond five thousand dollars ($5,000) in amount or value of remedy unless there is some writing which indicates that a contract for sale has been made between the parties at a defined or stated price, reasonably identifies the subject matter, and is signed by the party against whom enforcement is sought or by his or her authorized agent.

(2) Subdivision (1) of this section does not apply to contracts for the sale of goods (Section 2201) nor of securities (Section 8113) nor to security agreements (Sections 9201 and 9203).

(3) Subdivision (1) of this section does not apply to a qualified financial contract as that term is defined in paragraph (2) of subdivision (b) of Section 1624 of the Civil Code if either (a) there is, as provided in paragraph (3) of subdivision (b) of Section 1624 of the Civil Code, sufficient evidence to indicate that a contract has been made or (b) the parties thereto, by means of a prior or subsequent written contract, have agreed to be bound by the terms of the qualified financial contract from the time they reach agreement (by telephone, by exchange of electronic messages, or otherwise) on those terms.

§ 1207. (a) A party who, with explicit reservation of rights, performs or promises performance or assents to performance in a manner demanded or offered by the other party does not thereby prejudice the rights reserved. Such words as "without prejudice," "under protest" or the like are sufficient.

(b) Subdivision (a) does not apply to an accord and satisfaction.

§ 1208. A term providing that one party or his successor in interest may accelerate payment or performance or require collateral or additional collateral "at will" or "when he deems himself insecure" or in words of similar import shall be construed to mean that he shall have power to do so only if he in good faith believes that the prospect of payment or performance is impaired. The burden of establishing lack of good faith is on the party against whom the power has been exercised.

§ 1209. An obligation may be issued as subordinated to payment of another obligation of the person obligated, or a creditor may subordinate his right to payment of an obligation by agreement with either the person obligated or another creditor of the person obligated. Such a subordination does not create a security interest as against either the common debtor or a subordinated creditor. This section shall be construed as declaring the law as it existed prior to the enactment of this section and not as modifying it.

§ 1210. Except as otherwise provided in Section 1202, the presumptions established by this code are presumptions affecting the burden of producing evidence.

SHORT TITLE, GENERAL CONSTRUCTION AND SUBJECT MATTER

§ 2101. This division shall be known and may be cited as Uniform Commercial Code—Sales.

§ 2102. Unless the context otherwise requires, this division applies to transactions in goods; it does not apply to any transaction which although in the form of an unconditional contract to sell or present sale is intended to operate only as a security transaction nor does this division impair or repeal any statute regulating sales to consumers, farmers or other specified classes of buyers.

§ 2103. (1) In this division unless the context otherwise requires:

(a) "Buyer" means a person who buys or contracts to buy goods.

(b) "Good faith" in the case of a merchant means honesty in fact and the observance of reasonable commercial standards of fair dealing in the trade.

(c) "Receipt" of goods means taking physical possession of them.

(d) "Seller" means a person who sells or contracts to sell goods.

(2) Other definitions applying to this division or to specified chapters thereof, and the sections in which they appear are:

"Acceptance." Section 2606.

"Banker's credit." Section 2325.

"Between merchants." Section 2104.

"Cancellation." Section 2106(4).

"Commercial unit." Section 2105.

"Confirmed credit." Section 2325.

"Conforming to contract." Section 2106.

"Contract for sale." Section 2106.

"Cover." Section 2712.

"Entrusting." Section 2403.

"Financing agency." Section 2104.

"Future goods." Section 2105.

"Goods." Section 2105.

"Identification." Section 2501.

"Installment contract." Section 2612.

"Letter of Credit." Section 2325.

"Lot." Section 2105.

"Merchant." Section 2104.

"Overseas." Section 2323.

"Person in position of seller." Section 2707.

"Present sale." Section 2106.

"Sale." Section 2106.

"Sale on approval." Section 2326.

"Sale or return." Section 2326.

"Termination." Section 2106.

(3) The following definitions in other divisions apply to this division:

"Check." Section 3104.

"Consignee." Section 7102.

"Consignor." Section 7102.

"Consumer goods." Section 9102.

"Dishonor." Section 3502.

"Draft." Section 3104.

(4) In addition Division 1 contains general definitions and principles of construction and interpretation applicable throughout this division.

§ 2104. (1) "Merchant" means a person who deals in goods of the kind or otherwise by his occupation holds himself out as having knowledge or skill peculiar to the practices or goods involved in the transaction or to whom such knowledge or skill may be attributed by his employment of an agent or broker or other intermediary who by his occupation holds himself out as having such knowledge or skill.

(2) "Financing agency" means a bank, finance company or other person who in the ordinary course of business makes advances against goods or documents of title or who by arrangement with either the seller or the buyer intervenes in ordinary course to make or collect payment due or claimed under the contract for sale, as by purchasing or paying the seller's draft or making advances against it or by merely taking it for collection whether or not documents of title accompany the draft. "Financing agency" includes also a bank or other person who similarly intervenes between persons who are in the position of seller and buyer in respect to the goods (Section 2707).

(3) "Between merchants" means in any transaction with respect to which both parties are chargeable with the knowledge or skill of merchants.

§ 2105. (1) "Goods" means all things (including specially manufactured goods) which are movable at the time of identification to the contract for sale other than the money in which the price is to be paid, investment securities (Division 8) and things in action. "Goods" also includes the unborn young of animals and growing crops and other identified things attached to realty as described in the section on goods to be severed from realty (Section 2107).

(2) Goods must be both existing and identified before any interest in them can pass. Goods which are not both existing and identified are "future" goods. A purported present sale of future goods or of any interest therein operates as a contract to sell.

(3) There may be a sale of a part interest in existing identified goods.

(4) An undivided share in an identified bulk of fungible goods is sufficiently identified to be sold although the quantity of the bulk is not determined. Any agreed proportion of such a bulk or any quantity thereof agreed upon by number, weight or other measure may to the extent of the seller's interest in the bulk be sold to the buyer who then becomes an owner in common.

(5) "Lot" means a parcel or a single article which is the subject matter of a separate sale or delivery, whether or not it is sufficient to perform the contract.

(6) "Commercial unit" means such a unit of goods as by commercial usage is a single whole for purposes of sale and division of which materially impairs its character or value on the market or in use. A commercial unit may be a single article (as a machine) or a set of articles (as a suite of furniture or an assortment of sizes) or a quantity (as a bale, gross, or carload) or any other unit treated in use or in the relevant market as a single whole.

§ 2106. (1) In this division unless the context otherwise requires "contract" and "agreement" are limited to those relating to the present or future sale of goods. "Contract for sale" includes both a present sale of goods and a contract to sell goods at a future time.

A "sale" consists in the passing of title from the seller to the buyer for a price (Section 2401). A "present sale" means a sale which is accomplished by the making of the contract.

(2) Goods or conduct including any part of a performance are "conforming" or conform to the contract when they are in accordance with the obligations under the contract.

(3) "Termination" occurs when either party pursuant to a power created by agreement or law puts an end to the contract otherwise than for its breach. On "termination" all obligations which are still executory on both sides are discharged but any right based on prior breach or performance survives.

(4) "Cancellation" occurs when either party puts an end to the contract for breach by the other and its effect is the same as that of "termination" except that the cancelling party also retains any remedy for breach of the whole contract or any unperformed balance.

§ 2107. (1) A contract for the sale of minerals or the like (including oil and gas) or a structure or its materials to be removed from realty is a contract for the sale of goods within this division if they are to be severed by the seller but until severance a purported present sale thereof which is not effective as a transfer of an interest in land is effective only as a contract to sell.

(2) A contract for the sale apart from the land of growing crops or other things attached to realty and capable of severance without material harm thereto but not described in subdivision (1) or of timber to be cut is a contract for the sale of goods within this division whether the subject matter is to be severed by the buyer or by the seller even though it forms part of the realty at the time of contracting, and the parties can by identification effect a present sale before severance.

(3) The provisions of this section are subject to any third party rights provided by the law relating to realty records, and the contract for sale may be executed and recorded in the same manner as a document transferring an interest in land and shall then constitute notice to third parties of the buyer's rights under the contract for sale.

FORM, FORMATION AND READJUSTMENT OF CONTRACT

§ 2201. (1) Except as otherwise provided in this section a contract for the sale of goods for the price of five hundred dollars ($500) or more is not enforceable by way of action or defense unless there is some writing sufficient to indicate that a contract for sale has been made between the parties and signed by the party against whom enforcement is sought or by his or her authorized agent or broker. A writing is not insufficient because it omits or incorrectly states a term agreed upon but the contract is not enforceable under this paragraph beyond the quantity of goods shown in the writing.

(2) Between merchants if within a reasonable time a writing in confirmation of the contract and sufficient against the sender is received and the party receiving it has reason to know its contents, it satisfies the requirements of subdivision (1) against the party unless written notice of objection to its contents is given within 10 days after it is received.

(3) A contract which does not satisfy the requirements of subdivision (1) but which is valid in other respects is enforceable:

(a) If the goods are to be specially manufactured for the buyer and are not suitable for sale to others in the ordinary course of the seller's business and the seller, before notice of repudiation is received and under circumstances which reasonably indicate that the goods are for the buyer, has made either a substantial beginning of their manufacture or commitments for their procurement;

(b) If the party against whom enforcement is sought admits in his or her pleading, testimony, or otherwise in court that a contract for sale was made, but the contract is not enforceable under this provision beyond the quantity of goods admitted; or

(c) With respect to goods for which payment has been made and accepted or which have been received and accepted (Section 2606).

(4) Subdivision (1) of this section does not apply to a qualified financial contract as that term is defined in paragraph (2) of subdivision (b) of Section 1624 of the Civil Code if either (a) there is, as provided in paragraph (3) of subdivision (b) of 1624 of the Civil Code, sufficient evidence to indicate that a contract has been made or (b) the parties thereto, by means of a prior or subsequent written contract, have agreed to be bound by the terms of the qualified financial contract from the time they reach agreement (by telephone, by exchange of electronic messages, or otherwise) on those terms.

§ 2202. Terms with respect to which the confirmatory memoranda of the parties agree or which are otherwise set forth in a writing intended by the parties as a final expression of their agreement with respect to such terms as are included therein may not be contradicted by evidence of any prior agreement or of a contemporaneous oral agreement but may be explained or supplemented

(a) By course of dealing or usage of trade (Section 1205) or by course of performance (Section 2208); and

(b) By evidence of consistent additional terms unless the court finds the writing to have been intended also as a complete and exclusive statement of the terms of the agreement.

§ 2204. (1) A contract for sale of goods may be made in any manner sufficient to show agreement, including conduct by both parties which recognizes the existence of such a contract.

(2) An agreement sufficient to constitute a contract for sale may be found even though the moment of its making is undetermined.

(3) Even though one or more terms are left open a contract for sale does not fail for indefiniteness if the parties have intended to make a contract and there is a reasonably certain basis for giving an appropriate remedy.

§ 2205. (a) An offer by a merchant to buy or sell goods in a signed writing which by its terms gives assurance that it will be held open is not revocable, for lack of consideration, during the time stated or if no time is stated for a reasonable time, but in no event may such period of irrevocability exceed three months; but any such term of assurance on a form supplied by the offeree must be separately signed by the offeror.

(b) Notwithstanding subdivision (a), when a merchant renders an offer, oral or written, to supply goods to a contractor licensed pursuant to the provisions of Chapter 9 (commencing with Section 7000) of Division 3 of the Business and Professions Code or a similar contractor's licensing law of another state, and the merchant has actual or imputed knowledge that the contractor is so licensed, and that the offer will be relied upon by the contractor in the submission of its bid for a construction contract with a third party, the offer relied upon shall be irrevocable, notwithstanding lack of consideration, for 10 days after the awarding of the contract to the prime contractor, but in no event for more than 90 days after the date the bid or offer was rendered by the merchant; except that an oral bid or offer, when for a price of two thousand five hundred dollars ($2,500) or more, shall be confirmed in writing by the contractor or his or her agent within 48 hours after it is rendered. Failure by the contractor to confirm such offer in writing shall release the merchant from his or her offer. Nothing in this subdivision shall prevent a merchant from providing that the bid or offer will be held open for less than the time provided for herein.

§ 2206. (1) Unless otherwise unambiguously indicated by the language or circumstances

(a) An offer to make a contract shall be construed as inviting acceptance in any manner and by any medium reasonable in the circumstances;

(b) An order or other offer to buy goods for prompt or current shipment shall be construed as inviting acceptance either by a prompt promise to ship or by the prompt or current shipment of conforming or nonconforming goods, but such a shipment of nonconforming goods does not constitute an acceptance if the seller seasonably notifies the buyer that the shipment is offered only as an accommodation to the buyer.

(2) Where the beginning of a requested performance is a reasonable mode of acceptance an offeror who is not notified of acceptance within a reasonable time may treat the offer as having lapsed before acceptance.

§ 2207. (1) A definite and seasonable expression of acceptance or a written confirmation which is sent within a reasonable time operates as an acceptance even though it states terms additional to or different from those offered or agreed upon, unless acceptance is expressly made conditional on assent to the additional or different terms.

(2) The additional terms are to be construed as proposals for addition to the contract. Between merchants such terms become part of the contract unless:

(a) The offer expressly limits acceptance to the terms of the offer;

(b) They materially alter it; or

(c) Notification of objection to them has already been given or is given within a reasonable time after notice of them is received.

(3) Conduct by both parties which recognizes the existence of a contract is sufficient to establish a contract for sale although the writings of the parties do not otherwise establish a contract. In such case the terms of the particular contract consist of those terms on which the writings of the parties agree, together with any supplementary terms incorporated under any other provisions of this code.

§ 2208. (1) Where the contract for sale involves repeated occasions for performance by either party with knowledge of the nature of the performance and opportunity for objection to it by the other, any course of performance accepted or acquiesced in without objection shall be relevant to determine the meaning of the agreement.

(2) The express terms of the agreement and any such course of performance, as well as any course of dealing and usage of trade, shall be construed whenever reasonable as consistent with each other; but when such construction is unreasonable, express terms shall control course of performance and course of performance shall control both course of dealing and usage of trade (Section 1205).

(3) Subject to the provisions of the next section on modification and waiver, such course of performance shall be relevant to show a waiver or modification of any term inconsistent with such course of performance.

§ 2209. (1) An agreement modifying a contract within this division needs no consideration to be binding.

(2) A signed agreement which excludes modification or rescission except by a signed writing cannot be otherwise modified or rescinded, but except as between merchants such a requirement on a form supplied by the merchant must be separately signed by the other party.

(3) The requirements of the statute of frauds section of this division (Section 2201) must be satisfied if the contract as modified is within its provisions.

(4) Although an attempt at modification or rescission does not satisfy the requirements of subdivision (2) or (3) it can operate as a waiver.

(5) A party who has made a waiver affecting an executory portion of the contract may retract the waiver by reasonable notification received by the other party that strict performance will be required of any term waived, unless the retraction would be unjust in view of a material change of position in reliance on the waiver.

§ 2210. (1) A party may perform his or her duty through a delegate unless otherwise agreed or unless the other party has a substantial interest in having his or her original promisor perform or control the acts required by the contract. No delegation of performance relieves the party delegating of any duty to perform or any liability for breach.

(2) Except as otherwise provided in Section 9406, unless otherwise agreed, all rights of either seller or buyer can be assigned except where the assignment would materially change the duty of the other party, or increase materially the burden or risk imposed on him or her by his or her contract, or impair materially his or her chance of obtaining return performance. A right to damages for breach of the whole contract or a right arising out of the assignor's due performance of his or her entire obligation can be assigned despite agreement otherwise.

(3) The creation, attachment, perfection, or enforcement of a security interest in the seller's interest under a contract is not a transfer that materially changes the duty of, or increases materially the burden or risk imposed on, the buyer or impairs materially the buyer's chance of obtaining return performance within the purview of subdivision (2) unless, and then only to the extent that, enforcement actually results in a delegation of material performance of the seller. Even in that event, the creation, attachment, perfection, and enforcement of the security interest remain effective, but (A) the seller is liable to the buyer for damages caused by the delegation to the extent that the damages could not reasonably be prevented by the buyer, and (B) a court having jurisdiction may grant other appropriate relief, including cancellation of the contract for sale or an injunction against enforcement of the security interest or consummation of the enforcement.

(4) Unless the circumstances indicate the contrary, a prohibition of assignment of "the contract" is to be construed as barring only the delegation to the assignee of the assignor's performance.

(5) An assignment of "the contract" or of "all my rights under the contract" or an assignment in similar general terms is an assignment of rights and, unless the language or the circumstances (as in an assignment for security) indicate the contrary, it is a delegation of performance of the duties of the assignor, and its acceptance by the assignee

constitutes a promise by him or her to perform those duties. This promise is enforceable by either the assignor or the other party to the original contract.

(6) The other party may treat any assignment which delegates performance as creating reasonable grounds for insecurity and may, without prejudice to his or her rights against the assignor, demand assurances from the assignee (Section 2609).

GENERAL OBLIGATION AND CONSTRUCTION OF CONTRACT

§ 2301. The obligation of the seller is to transfer and deliver and that of the buyer is to accept and pay in accordance with the contract.

§ 2303. Where this division allocates a risk or a burden as between the parties "unless otherwise agreed," the agreement may not only shift the allocation but may also divide the risk or burden.

§ 2304. (1) The price can be made payable in money or otherwise. If it is payable in whole or in part in goods each party is a seller of the goods which he is to transfer.

(2) Even though all or part of the price is payable in an interest in realty the transfer of the goods and the seller's obligations with reference to them are subject to this division, but not the transfer of the interest in realty or the transferor's obligations in connection therewith.

§ 2305. (1) The parties if they so intend can conclude a contract for sale even though the price is not settled. In such a case the price is a reasonable price at the time for delivery if

(a) Nothing is said as to price; or

(b) The price is left to be agreed by the parties and they fail to agree; or

(c) The price is to be fixed in terms of some agreed market or other standard as set or recorded by a third person or agency and it is not so set or recorded.

(2) A price to be fixed by the seller or by the buyer means a price for him to fix in good faith.

(3) When a price left to be fixed otherwise than by agreement of the parties fails to be fixed through fault of one party the other may at his option treat the contract as canceled or himself fix a reasonable price.

(4) Where, however, the parties intend not to be bound unless the price be fixed or agreed and it is not fixed or agreed there is no contract. In such a case the buyer must return any goods already received or if unable so to do must pay their reasonable value at the time of delivery and the seller must return any portion of the price paid on account.

§ 2306. (1) A term which measures the quantity by the output of the seller or the requirements of the buyer means such actual output or requirements as may occur in good faith, except that no quantity unreasonably disproportionate to any stated estimate or in the absence of a stated estimate to any normal or otherwise comparable prior output or requirements may be tendered or demanded.

(2) A lawful agreement by either the seller or the buyer for exclusive dealing in the kind of goods concerned imposes unless otherwise agreed an obligation by the seller to use best efforts to supply the goods and by the buyer to use best efforts to promote their sale.

§ 2307. Unless otherwise agreed all goods called for by a contract for sale must be tendered in a single delivery and payment is due only on such tender but where the circumstances give either party the right to make or demand delivery in lots the price if it can be apportioned may be demanded for each lot.

§ 2308. Unless otherwise agreed

(a) The place for delivery of goods is the seller's place of business or if he has none his residence; but

(b) In a contract for sale of identified goods which to the knowledge of the parties at the time of contracting are in some other place, that place is the place for their delivery; and

(c) Documents of title may be delivered through customary banking channels.

§ 2309. (1) The time for shipment or delivery or any other action under a contract if not provided in this division or agreed upon shall be a reasonable time.

(2) Where the contract provides for successive performances but is indefinite in duration it is valid for a reasonable time but unless otherwise agreed may be terminated at any time by either party.

(3) Termination of a contract by one party except on the happening of an agreed event requires that reasonable notification be received by the other party and an agreement dispensing with notification is invalid if its operation would be unconscionable.

§ 2310. Unless otherwise agreed

(a) Payment is due at the time and place at which the buyer is to receive the goods even though the place of shipment is the place of delivery; and

(b) If the seller is authorized to send the goods he may ship them under reservation, and may tender the documents of title, but the buyer may inspect the goods after their arrival before payment is due unless such inspection is inconsistent with the terms of the contract (Section 2513); and

(c) If delivery is authorized and made by way of documents of title otherwise than by subdivision (b) then payment is due at the time and place at which the buyer is to receive the documents regardless of where the goods are to be received; and

(d) Where the seller is required or authorized to ship the goods on credit the credit period runs from the time of shipment but postdating the invoice or delaying its dispatch will correspondingly delay the starting of the credit period.

§ 2311. (1) An agreement for sale which is otherwise sufficiently definite (subdivision (3) of Section 2204) to be a contract is not made invalid by the fact that it leaves particulars of performance to be specified by one of the parties. Any such specification must be made in good faith and within limits set by commercial reasonableness.

(2) Unless otherwise agreed specifications relating to assortment of the goods are at the buyer's option and except as otherwise provided in subdivisions (1)(c) and (3) of Section 2319 specifications or arrangements relating to shipment are at the seller's option.

(3) Where such specification would materially affect the other party's performance but is not seasonably made or where one party's co-operation is necessary to the agreed performance of the other but is not seasonably forthcoming, the other party in addition to all other remedies

(a) Is excused for any resulting delay in his own performance; and

(b) May also either proceed to perform in any reasonable manner or after the time for a material part of his own performance treat the failure to specify or to co-operate as a breach by failure to deliver or accept the goods.

§ 2312. (1) Subject to subdivision (2) there is in a contract for sale a warranty by the seller that

(a) The title conveyed shall be good, and its transfer rightful; and

(b) The goods shall be delivered free from any security interest or other lien or encumbrance of which the buyer at the time of contracting has no knowledge.

(2) A warranty under subdivision (1) will be excluded or modified only by specific language or by circumstances which give the buyer reason to know that the person selling does not claim title in himself or that he is purporting to sell only such right or title as he or a third person may have.

(3) Unless otherwise agreed a seller who is a merchant regularly dealing in goods of the kind warrants that the goods shall be delivered free of the rightful claim of any third person by way of infringement or the like but a buyer who furnishes specifications to the seller must hold the seller harmless against any such claim which arises out of compliance with the specifications.

§ 2313. (1) Express warranties by the seller are created as follows:

(a) Any affirmation of fact or promise made by the seller to the buyer which relates to the goods and becomes part of the basis of the bargain creates an express warranty that the goods shall conform to the affirmation or promise.

(b) Any description of the goods which is made part of the basis of the bargain creates an express warranty that the goods shall conform to the description.

(c) Any sample or model which is made part of the basis of the bargain creates an express warranty that the whole of the goods shall conform to the sample or model.

(2) It is not necessary to the creation of an express warranty that the seller use formal words such as "warrant" or "guarantee" or that he have a specific intention to make a warranty, but an affirmation merely of the value of the goods or a statement purporting to be merely the seller's opinion or commendation of the goods does not create a warranty.

§ 2314. (1) Unless excluded or modified (Section 2316), a warranty that the goods shall be merchantable is implied in a contract for their sale if the seller is a merchant with respect to goods of that kind. Under this section the serving for value of food or drink to be consumed either on the premises or elsewhere is a sale.

(2) Goods to be merchantable must be at least such as

(a) Pass without objection in the trade under the contract description; and

(b) In the case of fungible goods, are of fair average quality within the description; and

(c) Are fit for the ordinary purposes for which such goods are used; and

(d) Run, within the variations permitted by the agreement, of even kind, quality and quantity within each unit and among all units involved; and

(e) Are adequately contained, packaged, and labeled as the agreement may require; and

(f) Conform to the promises or affirmations of fact made on the container or label if any.

(3) Unless excluded or modified (Section 2316) other implied warranties may arise from course of dealing or usage of trade.

§ 2315. Where the seller at the time of contracting has reason to know any particular purpose for which the goods are required and that the buyer is relying on the seller's skill or judgment to select or furnish suitable goods, there is unless excluded or modified under the next section an implied warranty that the goods shall be fit for such purpose.

§ 2316. (1) Words or conduct relevant to the creation of an express warranty and words or conduct tending to negate or limit warranty shall be construed wherever reasonable as consistent with each other; but subject to the provisions of this division on parol or extrinsic evidence (Section 2202) negation or limitation is inoperative to the extent that such construction is unreasonable.

(2) Subject to subdivision (3), to exclude or modify the implied warranty of merchantability or any part of it the language must mention merchantability and in case of a writing must be conspicuous, and to exclude or modify any implied warranty of fitness the exclusion must be by a writing and conspicuous. Language to exclude all implied warranties of fitness is sufficient if it states, for example, that "There are no warranties which extend beyond the description on the face hereof."

(3) Notwithstanding subdivision (2)

(a) Unless the circumstances indicate otherwise, all implied warranties are excluded by expressions like "as is," "with all faults" or other language which in common understanding calls the buyer's attention to the exclusion of warranties and makes plain that there is no implied warranty; and

(b) When the buyer before entering into the contract has examined the goods or the sample or model as fully as he desired or has refused to examine the goods there is no implied warranty with regard to defects which an examination ought in the circumstances to have revealed to him; and

(c) An implied warranty can also be excluded or modified by course of dealing or course of performance or usage of trade.

(4) Remedies for breach of warranty can be limited in accordance with the provisions of this division on liquidation or limitation of damages and on contractual modification of remedy (Sections 2718 and 2719).

§ 2317. Warranties whether express or implied shall be construed as consistent with each other and as cumulative, but if such construction is unreasonable the intention of the parties shall determine which warranty is dominant. In ascertaining that intention the following rules apply:

(a) Exact or technical specifications displace an inconsistent sample or model or general language of description.

(b) A sample from an existing bulk displaces inconsistent general language of description.

(c) Express warranties displaced inconsistent implied warranties other than an implied warranty of fitness for a particular purpose.

§ 2319. (1) Unless otherwise agreed the term F.O.B. (which means "free on board") at a named place, even though used only in connection with the stated price, is a delivery term under which

(a) When the term is F.O.B. the place of shipment, the seller must at that place ship the goods in the manner provided in this division (Section 2504) and bear the expense and risk of putting them into the possession of the carrier; or

(b) When the term is F.O.B. the place of destination, the seller must at his own expense and risk transport the goods to that place and there tender delivery of them in the manner provided in this division (Section 2503);

(c) When under either (a) or (b) the term is also F.O.B. vessel, car or other vehicle, the seller must in addition at his own expense and risk load the goods on board. If the term is F.O.B. vessel the buyer must name the vessel and in an appropriate case the seller must comply with the provisions of this division on the form of bill of lading (Section 2323).

(2) Unless otherwise agreed the term F.A.S. vessel (which means "free alongside") at a named port, even though used only in connection with the stated price, is a delivery term under which the seller must

(a) At his own expense and risk deliver the goods alongside the vessel in the manner usual in that port or on a dock designated and provided by the buyer; and

(b) Obtain and tender a receipt for the goods in exchange for which the carrier is under a duty to issue a bill of lading.

(3) Unless otherwise agreed in any case falling within subdivision (1)(a) or (c) or subdivision (2) the buyer must seasonably give any needed instructions for making delivery, including when the term is F.A.S. or F.O.B. the loading berth of the vessel and in an appropriate case its name and sailing date. The seller may treat the failure of needed instructions as a failure of co-operation under this division (Section 2311). He may also at his option move the goods in any reasonable manner preparatory to delivery or shipment.

(4) Under the term F.O.B. vessel or F.A.S. unless otherwise agreed the buyer must make payment against tender of the required documents and the seller may not tender nor the buyer demand delivery of the goods in substitution for the documents.

§ 2320. (1) The term C.I.F. means that the price includes in a lump sum the cost of the goods and the insurance and freight to the named destination. The term C. & F. or C.F. means that the price so includes cost and freight to the named destination.

(2) Unless otherwise agreed and even though used only in connection with the stated price and destination, the term C.I.F. destination or its equivalent requires the seller at his own expense and risk to

(a) Put the goods into the possession of a carrier at the port for shipment and obtain a negotiable bill or bills of lading covering the entire transportation to the named destination; and

(b) Load the goods and obtain a receipt from the carrier (which may be contained in the bill of lading) showing that the freight has been paid or provided for; and

(c) Obtain a policy or certificate of insurance, including any war risk insurance, of a kind and on terms then current at the port of shipment in the usual amount, in the currency of the contract, shown to cover the same goods covered by the bill of lading and providing for payment of loss to the order of the buyer or for the account of whom it may concern; but the seller may add to the price the amount of the premium for any such war risk insurance; and

(d) Prepare an invoice of the goods and procure any other documents required to effect shipment or to comply with the contract; and

(e) Forward and tender with commercial promptness all the documents in due form and with any indorsement necessary to perfect the buyer's rights.

(3) Unless otherwise agreed the term C. & F. or its equivalent has the same effect and imposes upon the seller the same obligations and risks as a C.I.F. term except the obligation as to insurance.

(4) Under the term C.I.F. or C. & F. unless otherwise agreed the buyer must make payment against tender of the required documents and the seller may not tender nor the buyer demand delivery of the goods in substitution for the documents.

§ 2321. Under a contract containing a term C.I.F. or C. & F.

(1) Where the price is based on or is to be adjusted according to "net landed weights," "delivered weights," "out turn" quantity or quality or the like, unless otherwise agreed the seller must reasonably estimate the price. The payment due on tender of the documents called for by the contract is the amount so estimated, but after final adjustment of the price a settlement must be made with commercial promptness.

(2) An agreement described in subdivision (1) or any warranty of quality or condition of the goods on arrival places upon the seller the risk of ordinary deterioration, shrinkage and the like in transportation but has no effect on the place or time of identification to the contract for sale or delivery or on the passing of the risk of loss.

(3) Unless otherwise agreed where the contract provides for payment on or after arrival of the goods the seller must before payment allow such preliminary inspection as is feasible; but if the goods are lost delivery of the documents and payment are due when the goods should have arrived.

§ 2322. (1) Unless otherwise agreed a term for delivery of goods "ex-ship" (which means from the carrying vessel) or in equivalent language is not restricted to a particular ship and requires delivery from a ship which has reached a place at the named port of destination where goods of the kind are usually discharged.

(2) Under such a term unless otherwise agreed

(a) The seller must discharge all liens arising out of the carriage and furnish the buyer with a direction which puts the carrier under a duty to deliver the goods; and

(b) The risk of loss does not pass to the buyer until the goods leave the ship's tackle or are otherwise properly unloaded.

§ 2323. (1) Where the contract contemplates overseas shipment and contains a term C.I.F. or C. & F. or F.O.B. vessel, the seller unless otherwise agreed must obtain a negotiable bill of lading stating that the goods have been loaded on board or, in the case of a term C.I.F. or C. & F., received for shipment.

(2) Where in a case within subdivision (1) a bill of lading has been issued in a set of parts, unless otherwise agreed if the documents are not to be sent from abroad the buyer may demand tender of the full set; otherwise only one part of the bill of lading need be tendered. Even if the agreement expressly requires a full set

(a) Due tender of a single part is acceptable within the provisions of this division on cure of improper delivery (subdivision (1) of Section 2508); and

(b) Even though the full set is demanded, if the documents are sent from abroad the person tendering an incomplete set may nevertheless require payment upon furnishing an indemnity which the buyer in good faith deems adequate.

(3) A shipment by water or by air or a contract contemplating such shipment is "overseas" insofar as by usage of trade or agreement it is subject to the commercial, financing or shipping practices characteristic of international deepwater commerce.

§ 2324. Under a term "no arrival, no sale" or terms of like meaning, unless otherwise agreed,

(a) The seller must properly ship conforming goods and if they arrive by any means he must tender them on arrival but he assumes no obligation that the goods will arrive unless he has caused the nonarrival; and

(b) Where without fault of the seller the goods are in part lost or have so deteriorated as no longer to conform to the contract or arrive after the contract time, the buyer may proceed as if there had been casualty to identified goods (Section 2613).

§ 2325. (1) Failure of the buyer seasonably to furnish an agreed letter of credit is a breach of the contract for sale.

(2) The delivery to seller of a proper letter of credit suspends the buyer's obligation to pay. If the letter of credit is dishonored, the seller may on seasonable notification to the buyer require payment directly from him.

(3) Unless otherwise agreed the term "letter of credit" or "banker's credit" in a contract for sale means an irrevocable credit issued by a financing agency of good repute and, where the shipment is overseas, of good international repute. The term "confirmed credit"means that the credit must also carry the direct obligation of such an agency which does business in the seller's financial market.

§ 2326. (1) Unless otherwise agreed, if delivered goods may be returned by the buyer even though they conform to the contract, the transaction is

(a) A "sale on approval" if the goods are delivered primarily for use, and

(b) A "sale or return" if the goods are delivered primarily for resale.

(2) Goods held on approval are not subject to the claims of the buyer's creditors until acceptance; goods held on sale or return are subject to such claims while in the buyer's possession.

(3) Any "or return" term of a contract for sale is to be treated as a separate contract for sale within the statute of frauds section of this division (Section 2201) and as contradicting the sale aspect of the contract within the provisions of this division on parol or extrinsic evidence (Section 2202).

(4) If a person delivers or consigns for sale goods which the person used or bought for use for personal, family, or household purposes, these goods do not become the property of the deliveree or consignee unless the deliveree or consignee purchases and fully pays for the goods. Nothing in this subdivision shall prevent the deliveree or consignee from acting as the deliverer's agent to transfer title to these goods to a buyer who pays the full purchase price. Any payment received by the deliveree or consignee from a buyer of these goods, less any amount which the deliverer expressly agreed could be deducted from the payment for commissions, fees, or expenses, is the property of the deliverer and shall not be subject to the claims of the deliveree's or consignee's creditors.

§ 2327. (1) Under sale on approval unless otherwise agreed

(a) Although the goods are identified to the contract the risk of loss and the title do not pass to the buyer until acceptance; and

(b) Use of the goods consistent with the purpose of trial is not acceptance but failure seasonably to notify the seller of election to return the goods is acceptance, and if the goods conform to the contract acceptance of any part is acceptance of the whole; and

(c) After due notification of election to return, the return is at the seller's risk and expense but a merchant buyer must follow any reasonable instructions.

(2) Under a sale or return unless otherwise agreed

(a) The option to return extends to the whole or any commercial unit of the goods while in substantially their original condition, but must be exercised seasonably; and

(b) The return is at the buyer's risk and expense.

§ 2328. (1) In a sale by auction if goods are put up in lots each lot is the subject of a separate sale.

(2) A sale by auction is complete when the auctioneer so announces by the fall of the hammer or in other customary manner. Where a bid is made while the hammer is falling in acceptance of a prior bid the auctioneer may in his discretion reopen the bidding or declare the goods sold under the bid on which the hammer was falling.

(3) Such a sale is with reserve unless the goods are in explicit terms put up without reserve. In an auction with reserve the auctioneer may withdraw the goods at any time until he announces completion of the sale. In an auction without reserve, after the auctioneer calls for bids on an article or lot, that article or lot cannot be withdrawn unless no bid is made within a reasonable time. In either case a bidder may retract his bid until the auctioneer's announcement of completion of the sale, but a bidder's retraction does not revive any previous bid.

(4) If the auctioneer knowingly receives a bid on the seller's behalf or the seller makes or procures such a bid, and notice has not been given that liberty for such bidding is reserved, the buyer may at his option avoid the sale or take the goods at the price of the last good faith bid prior to the completion of the sale. This subdivision shall not apply to any bid at a forced sale.

TITLE, CREDITORS AND GOOD FAITH PURCHASERS

§ 2401. Each provision of this division with regard to the rights, obligations and remedies of the seller, the buyer, purchasers or other third parties applies irrespective of title to the goods except where the provision refers to such title. Insofar as situations are not covered by the other provisions of this division and matters concerning title become material the following rules apply:

(1) Title to goods cannot pass under a contract for sale prior to their identification to the contract (Section 2501), and unless otherwise explicitly agreed the buyer acquires by their identification a special property as limited by this code. Any retention or reservation by the seller of the title (property) in goods shipped or delivered to the buyer is limited in effect to a reservation of a security interest. Subject to these provisions and to the provisions of the division on secured transactions (Division 9), title to goods passes from the seller to the buyer in any manner and on any conditions explicitly agreed on by the parties.

(2) Unless otherwise explicitly agreed title passes to the buyer at the time and place at which the seller completes his performance with reference to the physical delivery of the goods, despite any reservation of a security interest and even though a document of title is to be delivered at a different time or place; and in particular and despite any reservation of a security interest by the bill of lading

(a) If the contract requires or authorizes the seller to send the goods to the buyer but does not require him to deliver them at destination, title passes to the buyer at the time and place of shipment; but

(b) If the contract requires delivery at destination, title passes on tender there.

(3) Unless otherwise explicitly agreed where delivery is to be made without moving the goods,

(a) If the seller is to deliver a document of title, title passes at the time when and the place where he delivers such documents; or

(b) If the goods are at the time of contracting already identified and no documents are to be delivered, title passes at the time and place of contracting.

(4) A rejection or other refusal by the buyer to receive or retain the goods, whether or not justified, or a justified revocation of acceptance revests title to the goods in the seller. Such revesting occurs by operation of law and is not a "sale."

§ 2402. (1) Except as provided in subdivisions (2) and (3), rights of unsecured creditors of the seller with respect to goods which have been identified to a contract for sale are subject to the buyer's rights to recover the goods under this division (Sections 2502 and 2716).

(2) A creditor of the seller may treat a sale or an identification of goods to a contract for sale as void if as against him or her a retention of possession by the seller is fraudulent or void under any rule of law of the state where the goods are situated, except that retention of possession in good faith and current course of trade by a merchant-seller for a commercially reasonable time after a sale or identification is not fraudulent or void.

(3) Nothing in this division shall be deemed to impair the rights of creditors of the seller:

(a) Under the provisions of the division on secured transactions (Division 9); or

(b) Where identification to the contract or delivery is made not in current course of trade but in satisfaction of or as security for a pre-existing claim for money, security or the like and is made under circumstances which under any rule of law of the state where the goods are situated would apart from this division constitute the transaction a fraudulent transfer or voidable preference.

§ 2403. (1) A purchaser of goods acquires all title which his transferor had or had power to transfer except that a purchaser of a limited interest acquires rights only to the extent of the interest purchased. A person with voidable title has power to transfer a good title to a good faith purchaser for value. When goods have been delivered under a transaction of purchase the purchaser has such power even though

(a) The transferor was deceived as to the identity of the purchaser, or

(b) The delivery was in exchange for a check which is later dishonored, or

(c) It was agreed that the transaction was to be a "cash sale," or

(d) The delivery was procured through fraud punishable as larcenous under the criminal law.

(2) Any entrusting of possession of goods to a merchant who deals in goods of that kind gives him power to transfer all rights of the entruster to a buyer in ordinary course of business.

(3) "Entrusting" includes any delivery and any acquiescence in retention of possession for the purpose of sale, obtaining offers to purchase, locating a buyer, or the like; regardless of any condition expressed between the parties to the delivery or acquiescence and regardless of whether the procurement of the entrusting or the possessor's disposition of the goods have been such as to be larcenous under the criminal law.

(4) The rights of other purchasers of goods and of lien creditors are governed by the divisions on secured transactions (Division 9), bulk transfers (Division 6) and documents of title (Division 7).

PERFORMANCE

§ 2501. (1) The buyer obtains a special property and an insurable interest in goods by identification of existing goods as goods to which the contract refers even though the goods so identified are nonconforming and he has an option to return or reject them. Such identification can be made at any time and in any manner explicitly agreed to by the parties. In the absence of explicit agreement identification occurs

(a) When the contract is made if it is for the sale of goods already existing and identified;

(b) If the contract is for the sale of future goods other than those described in paragraph (c), when goods are shipped, marked or otherwise designated by the seller as goods to which the contract refers;

(c) If the contract is for the sale of unborn young or future crops, when the crops are planted or otherwise become growing crops or the young are conceived.

(2) The seller retains an insurable interest in goods so long as title to or any security interest in the goods remains in him and where the identification is by the seller alone he may until default or insolvency or notification to the buyer that the identification is final substitute other goods for those identified.

(3) Nothing in this section impairs any insurable interest recognized under any other statute or rule of law.

§ 2502. (1) Subject to subdivisions (2) and (3), and even though the goods have not been shipped, a buyer who has paid a part or all of the price of goods in which he or she has a special property under the provisions of the immediately preceding section may on making and keeping good a tender of any unpaid portion of their price recover them from the seller if either:

(a) In the case of goods bought for personal, family, or household purposes, the seller repudiates or fails to deliver as required by the contract.

(b) In all cases, the seller becomes insolvent within 10 days after receipt of the first installment on their price.

(2) The buyer's right to recover the goods under paragraph (a) of subdivision (1) vests upon acquisition of a special property, even if the seller had not then repudiated or failed to deliver.

(3) If the identification creating his or her special property has been made by the buyer, he or she acquires the right to recover the goods only if they conform to the contract for sale.

§ 2503. (1) Tender of delivery requires that the seller put and hold conforming goods at the buyer's disposition and give the buyer any notification reasonably necessary to enable him to take delivery. The manner, time and place for tender are determined by the agreement and this division, and in particular

(a) Tender must be at a reasonable hour, and if it is of goods they must be kept available for the period reasonably necessary to enable the buyer to take possession; but

(b) Unless otherwise agreed the buyer must furnish facilities reasonably suited to the receipt of the goods.

(2) Where the case is within the next section respecting shipment tender requires that the seller comply with its provisions.

(3) Where the seller is required to deliver at a particular destination tender requires that he comply with subdivision (1) and also in any appropriate case tender documents as described in subdivisions (4) and (5) of this section.

(4) Where goods are in the possession of a bailee and are to be delivered without being moved

(a) Tender requires that the seller either tender a negotiable document of title covering such goods or procure acknowledgment by the bailee of the buyer's right to possession of the goods; but

(b) Tender to the buyer of a nonnegotiable document of title or of a written direction to the bailee to deliver is sufficient tender unless the buyer seasonably objects, and receipt by the bailee of notification of the buyer's rights fixes those rights as against the bailee and all third persons; but risk of loss of the goods and of any failure by the bailee to honor the nonnegotiable document of title or to obey the direction remains on the seller until the buyer has had a reasonable time to present the document or direction, and a refusal by the bailee to honor the document or to obey the direction defeats the tender.

(5) Where the contract requires the seller to deliver documents

(a) He must tender all such documents in correct form, except as provided in this division with respect to bills of lading in a set (subdivision (2) of Section 2323); and

(b) Tender through customary banking channels is sufficient and dishonor of a draft accompanying the documents constitutes nonacceptance or rejection.

§ 2504. Where the seller is required or authorized to send the goods to the buyer and the contract does not require him to deliver them at a particular destination, then unless otherwise agreed he must (a) Put the goods in the possession of such a carrier and make such a contract for their transportation as may be reasonable having regard to the nature of the goods and other circumstances of the case; and (b) Obtain and promptly deliver or tender in due form any document necessary to enable the buyer to obtain possession of the goods or otherwise required by the agreement or by usage of trade; and (c) Promptly notify the buyer of the shipment. Failure to notify the buyer under paragraph (c) or to make a proper contract under paragraph (a) is a ground for rejection only if material delay or loss ensues.

§ 2505. (1) Where the seller has identified goods to the contract by or before shipment:

(a) His procurement of a negotiable bill of lading to his own order or otherwise reserves in him a security interest in the goods. His procurement of the bill to the order of a financing agency or of the buyer indicates in addition only the seller's expectation of transferring that interest to the person named.

(b) A nonnegotiable bill of lading to himself or his nominee reserves possession of the goods as security but except in a case of conditional delivery (subdivision (2) of Section 2507) a nonnegotiable bill of lading naming the buyer as consignee reserves no security interest even though the seller retains possession of the bill of lading.

(2) When shipment by the seller with reservation of a security interest is in violation of the contract for sale it constitutes an improper contract for transportation within the preceding section but impairs neither the rights given to the buyer by shipment and identification of the goods to the contract nor the seller's powers as a holder of a negotiable document.

§ 2506. (1) A financing agency by paying or purchasing for value a draft which relates to a shipment of goods acquires to the extent of the payment or purchase and in addition to its own rights under the draft and any document of title securing it any rights of the shipper in the goods including the right to stop delivery and the shipper's right to have the draft honored by the buyer.

(2) The right to reimbursement of a financing agency which has in good faith honored or purchased the draft under commitment to or authority from the buyer is not impaired by subsequent discovery of defects with reference to any relevant document which was apparently regular on its face.

§ 2507. (1) Tender of delivery is a condition to the buyer's duty to accept the goods and, unless otherwise agreed, to his duty to pay for them. Tender entitles the seller to acceptance of the goods and to payment according to the contract.

(2) Where payment is due and demanded on the delivery to the buyer of goods or documents of title, his right as against the seller to retain or dispose of them is conditional upon his making the payment due.

§ 2508. (1) Where any tender or delivery by the seller is rejected because nonconforming and the time for performance has not yet expired, the seller may seasonably notify the buyer of his intention to cure and may then within the contract time make a conforming delivery.

(2) Where the buyer rejects a nonconforming tender which the seller had reasonable grounds to believe would be acceptable with or without money allowance the seller may if he seasonably notifies the buyer have a further reasonable time to substitute a conforming tender.

§ 2509. (1) Where the contract requires or authorizes the seller to ship the goods by carrier

(a) If it does not require him to deliver them at a particular destination, the risk of loss passes to the buyer when the goods are duly delivered to the carrier even though the shipment is under reservation (Section 2505); but

(b) If it does require him to deliver them at a particular destination and the goods are there duly tendered while in the possession of the carrier, the risk of loss passes to the buyer when the goods are there duly so tendered as to enable the buyer to take delivery.

(2) Where the goods are held by a bailee to be delivered without being moved, the risk of loss passes to the buyer

(a) On his receipt of a negotiable document of title covering the goods; or

(b) On acknowledgment by the bailee of the buyer's right to possession of the goods; or

(c) After his receipt of a nonnegotiable document of title or other written direction to deliver, as provided in subdivision (4)(b)of Section 2503.

(3) In any case not within subdivision (1) or (2), the risk of loss passes to the buyer on his receipt of the goods if the seller is a merchant; otherwise the risk passes to the buyer on tender of delivery.

(4) The provisions of this section are subject to contrary agreement of the parties and to the provisions of this division on sale on approval (Section 2327) and on effect of breach on risk of loss (Section 2510).

§ 2510. (1) Where a tender or delivery of goods so fails to conform to the contract as to give a right of rejection the risk of their loss remains on the seller until cure or acceptance.

(2) Where the buyer rightfully revokes acceptance he may to the extent of any deficiency in his effective insurance coverage treat the risk of loss as having rested on the seller from the beginning.

(3) Where the buyer as to conforming goods already identified to the contract for sale repudiates or is otherwise in breach before risk of their loss has passed to him, the

seller may to the extent of any deficiency in his effective insurance coverage treat the risk of loss as resting on the buyer for a commercially reasonable time.

§ 2511. (1) Unless otherwise agreed, tender of payment is a condition to the seller's duty to tender and complete any delivery.

(2) Tender of payment is sufficient when made by any means or in any manner current in the ordinary course of business unless the seller demands payment in legal tender and gives any extension of time reasonably necessary to procure it.

(3) Subject to the provisions of this code on the effect of an instrument on an obligation (Section 3310), payment by check is conditional and is defeated as between the parties by dishonor of the check on due presentment.

§ 2512. (1) Where the contract requires payment before inspection nonconformity of the goods does not excuse the buyer from so making payment unless (a) the nonconformity appears without inspection or (b) despite tender of the required documents the circumstances would justify injunction against honor under this code (subdivision (b) of Section 5109).

(2) Payment pursuant to subdivision (1) does not constitute an acceptance of goods or impair the buyer's right to inspect or any of his remedies.

§ 2513. (1) Unless otherwise agreed and subject to subdivision (3), where goods are tendered or delivered or identified to the contract for sale, the buyer has a right before payment or acceptance to inspect them at any reasonable place and time and in any reasonable manner. When the seller is required or authorized to send the goods to the buyer, the inspection may be after their arrival.

(2) Expenses of inspection must be borne by the buyer but may be recovered from the seller if the goods do not conform and are rejected.

(3) Unless otherwise agreed and subject to the provisions of this division on C.I.F. contracts (subdivision (3) of Section 2321), the buyer is not entitled to inspect the goods before payment of the price when the contract provides

(a) For delivery "C.O.D." or on other like terms; or

(b) For payment against documents of title, except where such payment is due only after the goods are to become available for inspection.

(4) A place or method of inspection fixed by the parties is presumed to be exclusive but unless otherwise expressly agreed it does not postpone identification or shift the place for delivery or for passing the risk of loss. If compliance becomes impossible, inspection shall be as provided in this section unless the place or method fixed was clearly intended as an indispensable condition failure of which avoids the contract.

§ 2514. Unless otherwise agreed documents against which a draft is drawn are to be delivered to the drawee on acceptance of the draft if it is payable more than three days after presentment; otherwise, only on payment.

§ 2515. In furtherance of the adjustment of any claim or dispute

(a) Either party on reasonable notification to the other and for the purpose of ascertaining the facts and preserving evidence has the right to inspect, test and sample the goods including such of them as may be in the possession or control of the other; and

(b) The parties may agree to a third party inspection or survey to determine the conformity or condition of the goods and may agree that the findings shall be binding upon them in any subsequent litigation or adjustment.

BREACH, REPUDIATION AND EXCUSE

§ 2601. Subject to the provisions of this division on breach in installment contracts (Section 2612) and unless otherwise agreed under the sections on contractual limitations of remedy (Sections 2718 and 2719), if the goods or the tender of delivery fail in any respect to conform to the contract, the buyer may

(a) Reject the whole; or

(b) Accept the whole; or

(c) Accept any commercial unit or units and reject the rest.

§ 2602. (1) Rejection of goods must be within a reasonable time after their delivery or tender. It is ineffective unless the buyer seasonably notifies the seller.

(2) Subject to the provisions of the two following sections on rejected goods (Sections 2603 and 2604),

(a) After rejection any exercise of ownership by the buyer with respect to any commercial unit is wrongful as against the seller; and

(b) If the buyer has before rejection taken physical possession of goods in which he does not have a security interest under the provisions of this division (subdivision (3) of Section 2711), he is under a duty after rejection to hold them with reasonable care at the seller's disposition for a time sufficient to permit the seller to remove them; but

(c) The buyer has no further obligations with regard to goods rightfully rejected.

(3) The seller's rights with respect to goods wrongfully rejected are governed by the provisions of this division on seller's remedies in general (Section 2703).

§ 2603. (1) Subject to any security interest in the buyer (subdivision (3) of Section 2711), when the seller has no agent or place of business at the market of rejection a merchant buyer is under a duty after rejection of goods in his possession or control to follow any reasonable instructions received from the seller with respect to the goods and in the absence of such instructions to make reasonable efforts to sell them for the seller's account if they are perishable or threaten to decline in value speedily. Instructions are not reasonable if on demand indemnity for expenses is not forthcoming.

(2) When the buyer sells goods under subdivision (1), he is entitled to reimbursement from the seller or out of the proceeds for reasonable expenses of caring for and selling them, and if the expenses include no selling commission then to such commission as is usual in the trade or if there is none to a reasonable sum not exceeding 10 percent on the gross proceeds.

(3) In complying with this section the buyer is held only to good faith and good faith conduct hereunder is neither acceptance nor conversion nor the basis of an action for damages.

§ 2604. Subject to the provisions of the immediately preceding section on perishables if the seller gives no instructions within a reasonable time after notification of rejection the buyer may store the rejected goods for the seller's account or reship them to him or resell them for the seller's account with reimbursement as provided in the preceding section. Such action is not acceptance or conversion.

§ 2605. (1) The buyer's failure to state in connection with rejection a particular defect which is ascertainable by reasonable inspection precludes him from relying on the unstated defect to justify rejection or to establish breach

(a) Where the seller could have cured it if stated seasonably; or

(b) Between merchants when the seller has after rejection made a request in writing for a full and final written statement of all defects on which the buyer proposes to rely.

(2) Payment against documents made without reservation of rights precludes recovery of the payment for defects apparent on the face of the documents.

§ 2606. (1) Acceptance of goods occurs when the buyer

(a) After a reasonable opportunity to inspect the goods signifies to the seller that the goods are conforming or that he will take or retain them in spite of their nonconformity; or

(b) Fails to make an effective rejection (subdivision (1) of Section 2602), but such acceptance does not occur until the buyer has had a reasonable opportunity to inspect them; or

(c) Does any act inconsistent with the seller's ownership; but if such act is wrongful as against the seller it is an acceptance only if ratified by him.

(2) Acceptance of a part of any commercial unit is acceptance of that entire unit.

§ 2607. (1) The buyer must pay at the contract rate for any goods accepted.

(2) Acceptance of goods by the buyer precludes rejection of the goods accepted and, if made with knowledge of a nonconformity, cannot be revoked because of it unless the acceptance was on the reasonable assumption that the nonconformity would be seasonably cured. Acceptance does not of itself impair any other remedy provided by this division for nonconformity.

(3) Where a tender has been accepted:

(A) The buyer must, within a reasonable time after he or she discovers or should have discovered any breach, notify the seller of breach or be barred from any remedy; and

(B) If the claim is one for infringement or the like (subdivision (3) of Section 2312) and the buyer is sued as a result of such a breach, the buyer must so notify the seller within a reasonable time after he or she receives notice of the litigation or be barred from any remedy over for liability established by the litigation.

(4) The burden is on the buyer to establish any breach with respect to the goods accepted.

(5) Where the buyer is sued for breach of a warranty or other obligation for which his or her seller is answerable over:

(A) He or she may give the seller written notice of the litigation. If the notice states that the seller may defend and that if the seller does not do so he or she will be bound in any action against the seller by the buyer by any determination of fact common to the two litigation actions, then unless the seller after seasonable receipt of the notice does defend he or she is so bound.

(B) If the claim is one for infringement or the like (subdivision (3) of Section 2312) the original seller may demand in writing that the buyer turn over to the seller control of the litigation, including settlement, or else be barred from any remedy over and if the seller also agrees to bear all expense and to satisfy any adverse judgment, then unless the buyer after seasonable receipt of the demand does turn over control the buyer is so barred.

(6) The provisions of subdivisions (3), (4) and (5) apply to any obligation of a buyer to hold the seller harmless against infringement or the like (subdivision (3) of Section 2312).

§ 2608. (1) The buyer may revoke his acceptance of a lot or commercial unit whose nonconformity substantially impairs its value to him if he has accepted it

(a) On the reasonable assumption that its nonconformity would be cured and it has not been seasonably cured; or

(b) Without discovery of such nonconformity if his acceptance was reasonably in duced either by the difficulty of discovery before acceptance or by the seller's assurances.

(2) Revocation of acceptance must occur within a reasonable time after the buyer discovers or should have discovered the ground for it and before any substantial change in condition of the goods which is not caused by their own defects. It is not effective until the buyer notifies the seller of it.

(3) A buyer who so revokes has the same rights and duties with regard to the goods involved as if he had rejected them.

§ 2609. (1) A contract for sale imposes an obligation on each party that the other's expectation of receiving due performance will not be impaired. When reasonable grounds for insecurity arise with respect to the performance of either party the other may in writing demand adequate assurance of due performance and until he receives such assurance may if commercially reasonable suspend any performance for which he has not already received the agreed return.

(2) Between merchants the reasonableness of grounds for insecurity and the adequacy of any assurance offered shall be determined according to commercial standards.

(3) Acceptance of any improper delivery or payment does not prejudice the aggrieved party's right to demand adequate assurance of future performance.

(4) After receipt of a justified demand failure to provide within a reasonable time not exceeding 30 days such assurance of due performance as is adequate under the circumstances of the particular case is a repudiation of the contract.

§ 2610. When either party repudiates the contract with respect to a performance not yet due the loss of which will substantially impair the value of the contract to the other, the aggrieved party may

(a) For a commercially reasonable time await performance by the repudiating party; or

(b) Resort to any remedy for breach (Section 2703 or Section 2711), even though he has notified the repudiating party that he would await the latter's performance and has urged retraction; and

(c) In either case suspend his own performance or proceed in accordance with the provisions of this division on the seller's right to identify goods to the contract notwithstanding breach or to salvage unfinished goods (Section 2704).

§ 2611. (1) Until the repudiating party's next performance is due he can retract his repudiation unless the aggrieved party has since the repudiation canceled or materially changed his position or otherwise indicated that he considers the repudiation final.

(2) Retraction may be by any method which clearly indicates to the aggrieved party that the repudiating party intends to perform, but must include any assurance justifiably demanded under the provisions of this division (Section 2609).

(3) Retraction reinstates the repudiating party's rights under the contract with due excuse and allowance to the aggrieved party for any delay occasioned by the repudiation.

§ 2612. (1) An "installment contract" is one which requires or authorizes the delivery of goods in separate lots to be separately accepted, even though the contract contains a clause "each delivery is a separate contract" or its equivalent.

(2) The buyer may reject any installment which is nonconforming if the nonconformity substantially impairs the value of that installment and cannot be cured or if the nonconformity is a defect in the required documents; but if the nonconformity does not fall within subdivision (3) and the seller gives adequate assurance of its cure the buyer must accept that installment.

(3) Whenever nonconformity or default with respect to one or more installments substantially impairs the value of the whole contract there is a breach of the whole. But the aggrieved party reinstates the contract if he accepts a nonconforming installment without seasonably notifying of cancellation or if he brings an action with respect only to past installments or demands performance as to future installments.

§ 2613. Where the contract requires for its performance goods identified when the contract is made, and the goods suffer casualty without fault of either party before the risk of loss passes to the buyer, or in a proper case under a "no arrival, no sale" term (Section 2324) then

(a) If the loss is total the contract is avoided; and

(b) If the loss is partial or the goods have so deteriorated as no longer to conform to the contract the buyer may nevertheless demand inspection and at his option either treat the contract as avoided or accept the goods with due allowance from the contract price for the deterioration or the deficiency in quantity but without further right against the seller.

§ 2614. (1) Where without fault of either party the agreed berthing, loading, or unloading facilities fail or an agreed type of carrier becomes unavailable or the agreed manner of delivery otherwise becomes commercially impracticable but a commercially reasonable substitute is available, such substitute performance must be tendered and accepted.

(2) If the agreed means or manner of payment fails because of domestic or foreign governmental regulation, the seller may withhold or stop delivery unless the buyer provides a means or manner of payment which is commercially a substantial equivalent. If delivery has already been taken, payment by the means or in the manner provided by the regulation discharges the buyer's obligation unless the regulation is discriminatory, oppressive or predatory.

§ 2615. Except so far as a seller may have assumed a greater obligation and subject to the preceding section on substituted performance:

(a) Delay in delivery or nondelivery in whole or in part by a seller who complies with paragraphs (b) and (c) is not a breach of his duty under a contract for sale if performance as agreed has been made impracticable by the occurrence of a contingency the nonoccurrence of which was a basic assumption on which the contract was made or by compliance in good faith with any applicable foreign or domestic governmental regulation or order whether or not it later proves to be invalid.

(b) Where the causes mentioned in paragraph (a) affect only a part of the seller's capacity to perform, he must allocate production and deliveries among his customers but may at his option include regular customers not then under contract as well as his own requirements for further manufacture. He may so allocate in any manner which is fair and reasonable.

(c) The seller must notify the buyer seasonably that there will be delay or nondelivery and, when allocation is required under paragraph (b), of the estimated quota thus made available for the buyer.

§ 2616. (1) Where the buyer receives notification of a material or indefinite delay or an allocation justified under the preceding section he may by written notification to the seller as to any delivery concerned, and where the prospective deficiency substantially impairs the value of the whole contract under the provisions of this division relating to breach of installment contracts (Section 2612), then also as to the whole, (a) Terminate and thereby discharge any unexecuted portion of the contract; or

(b) Modify the contract by agreeing to take his available quota in substitution.

(2) If after receipt of such notification from the seller the buyer fails so to modify the contract within a reasonable time not exceeding 30 days the contract lapses with respect to any deliveries affected.

(3) The provisions of this section may not be negated by agreement except insofar as the seller has assumed a greater obligation under the preceding section.

REMEDIES

§ 2701. Remedies for breach of any obligation or promise collateral or ancillary to a contract for sale are not impaired by the provisions of this division.

§ 2702. (1) Where the seller discovers the buyer to be insolvent he may refuse delivery except for cash including payment for all goods theretofore delivered under the contract, and stop delivery under this division (Section 2705).

(2) Where the seller discovers that the buyer has received goods on credit while insolvent he may reclaim the goods upon demand made within 10 days after the receipt, but if misrepresentation of solvency has been made to the particular seller in writing within three months before delivery the 10-day limitation does not apply. Except as provided in this subdivision the seller may not base a right to reclaim goods on the buyer's fraudulent or innocent misrepresentation of solvency or of intent to pay.

(3) The seller's right to reclaim under subdivision (2) is subject to the rights of a buyer in ordinary course or other good faith purchaser under this division (Section 2403). Successful reclamation of goods excludes all other remedies with respect to them.

§ 2703. Where the buyer wrongfully rejects or revokes acceptance of goods or fails to make a payment due on or before delivery or repudiates with respect to a part or the whole, then with respect to any goods directly affected and, if the breach is of the whole contract (Section 2612), then also with respect to the whole undelivered balance, the aggrieved seller may

(a) Withhold delivery of such goods;

(b) Stop delivery by any bailee as hereafter provided (Section 2705);

(c) Proceed under the next section respecting goods still unidentified to the contract;

(d) Resell and recover damages as hereafter provided (Section 2706);

(e) Recover damages for nonacceptance (Section 2708) or in a proper case the price (Section 2709);

(f) Cancel.

§ 2704. (1) An aggrieved seller under the preceding section may

(a) Identify to the contract conforming goods not already identified if at the time he learned of the breach they are in his possession or control;

(b) Treat as the subject of resale goods which have demonstrably been intended for the particular contract even though those goods are unfinished.

(2) Where the goods are unfinished an aggrieved seller may in the exercise of reasonable commercial judgment for the purposes of avoiding loss and of effective realization either complete the manufacture and wholly identify the goods to the contract or cease manufacture and resell for scrap or salvage value or proceed in any other reasonable manner.

§ 2705. (1) The seller may stop delivery of goods in the possession of a carrier or other bailee when he discovers the buyer to be insolvent (Section 2702) and may stop delivery of carload, truckload, planeload or larger shipments of express or freight when the buyer repudiates or fails to make a payment due before delivery or if for any other reason the seller has a right to withhold or reclaim the goods.

(2) As against such buyer the seller may stop delivery until

(a) Receipt of the goods by the buyer; or

(b) Acknowledgment to the buyer by any bailee of the goods except a carrier that the bailee holds the goods for the buyer; or

(c) Such acknowledgment to the buyer by a carrier by reshipment or as warehouseman; or

(d) Negotiation to the buyer of any negotiable document of title covering the goods.

(3) (a) To stop delivery the seller must so notify as to enable the bailee by reasonable diligence to prevent delivery of the goods.

(b) After such notification the bailee must hold and deliver the goods according to the directions of the seller but the seller is liable to the bailee for any ensuing charges or damages.

(c) If a negotiable document of title has been issued for goods the bailee is not obliged to obey a notification to stop until surrender of the document.

(d) A carrier who has issued a nonnegotiable bill of lading is not obliged to obey a notification to stop received from a person other than the consignor.

§ 2706. (1) Under the conditions stated in Section 2703 on seller's remedies, the seller may resell the goods concerned or the undelivered balance thereof. Where the resale is made in good faith and in a commercially reasonable manner the seller may recover the difference between the resale price and the contract price together with any incidental damages allowed under the provisions of this division (Section 2710), but less expenses saved in consequence of the buyer's breach.

(2) Except as otherwise provided in subdivision (3) or unless otherwise agreed resale may be at public or private sale including sale by way of one or more contracts to sell or of identification to an existing contract of the seller. Sale may be as a unit or in parcels and at any time and place and on any terms but every aspect of the sale including the method, manner, time, place and terms must be commercially reasonable. The resale must be reasonably identified as referring to the broken contract, but it is not necessary that the goods be in existence or that any or all of them have been identified to the contract before the breach.

(3) Where the resale is at private sale the seller must give the buyer reasonable notification of his intention to resell.

(4) Where the resale is at public sale

(a) Only identified goods can be sold except where there is a recognized market for a public sale of futures in goods of the kind; and

(b) It must be made at a usual place or market for public sale if one is reasonably available and except in the case of goods which are perishable or threaten to decline in value speedily the seller must give the buyer reasonable notice of the time and place of the resale; and

(c) If the goods are not to be within the view of those attending the sale the notification of sale must state the place where the goods are located and provide for their reasonable inspection by prospective bidders; and

(d) The seller may buy.

(5) A purchaser who buys in good faith at a resale takes the goods free of any rights of the original buyer even though the seller fails to comply with one or more of the requirements of this section.

(6) The seller is not accountable to the buyer for any profit made on any resale. A person in the position of a seller (Section 2707) or a buyer who has rightfully rejected or justifiably revoked acceptance must account for any excess over the amount of his security interest, as hereinafter defined (subdivision (3) of Section 2711).

§ 2707. (1) A "person in the position of a seller" includes as against a principal an agent who has paid or become responsible for the price of goods on behalf of his principal or anyone who otherwise holds a security interest or other right in goods similar to that of a seller.

(2) A person in the position of a seller may as provided in this division withhold or stop delivery (Section 2705) and resell (Section 2706) and recover incidental damages (Section 2710).

§ 2708. (1) Subject to subdivision (2) and to the provisions of this division with respect to proof of market price (Section 2723), the measure of damages for nonacceptance or repudiation by the buyer is the difference between the market price at the time and place for tender and the unpaid contract price together with any incidental damages provided in this division (Section 2710), but less expenses saved in consequence of the buyer's breach.

(2) If the measure of damages provided in subdivision (1) is inadequate to put the seller in as good a position as performance would have done then the measure of damages is the profit (including reasonable overhead) which the seller would have made from full performance by the buyer, together with any incidental damages provided in this division (Section 2710), due allowance for costs reasonably incurred and due credit for payments or proceeds of resale.

§ 2709. (1) When the buyer fails to pay the price as it becomes due the seller may recover, together with any incidental damages under the next section, the price

(a) Of goods accepted or of conforming goods lost or damaged within a commercially reasonable time after risk of their loss has passed to the buyer; and

(b) Of goods identified to the contract if the seller is unable after reasonable effort to resell them at a reasonable price or the circumstances reasonably indicate that such effort will be unavailing.

(2) Where the seller sues for the price he must hold for the buyer any goods which have been identified to the contract and are still in his control except that if resale be-

comes possible he may resell them at any time prior to the collection of the judgment. The net proceeds of any such resale must be credited to the buyer and payment of the judgment entitles him to any goods not resold.

(3) After the buyer has wrongfully rejected or revoked acceptance of the goods or has failed to make a payment due or has repudiated (Section 2610), a seller who is held not entitled to the price under this section shall nevertheless be awarded damages for nonacceptance under the preceding section.

§ 2710. Incidental damages to an aggrieved seller include any commercially reasonable charges, expenses or commissions incurred in stopping delivery, in the transportation, care and custody of goods after the buyers' breach, in connection with return or resale of the goods or otherwise resulting from the breach.

§ 2711. (1) Where the seller fails to make delivery or repudiates or the buyer rightfully rejects or justifiably revokes acceptance then with respect to any goods involved, and with respect to the whole if the breach goes to the whole contract (Section 2612), the buyer may cancel and whether or not he has done so may in addition to recovering so much of the price as has been paid

(a) "Cover" and have damages under the next section as to all the goods affected whether or not they have been identified to the contract; or

(b) Recover damages for nondelivery as provided in this division (Section 2713).

(2) Where the seller fails to deliver or repudiates the buyer may also

(a) If the goods have been identified recover them as provided in the division (Section 2502); or

(b) In a proper case obtain specific performance or replevy the goods as provided in this division (Section 2716).

(3) On rightful rejection or justifiable revocation of acceptance a buyer has a security interest in goods in his possession or control for any payments made on their price and any expenses reasonably incurred in their inspection, receipt, transportation, care and custody and may hold such goods and resell them in like manner as an aggrieved seller (Section 2706).

§ 2712. (1) After a breach within the preceding section the buyer may "cover" by making in good faith and without unreasonable delay any reasonable purchase of or contract to purchase goods in substitution for those due from the seller.

(2) The buyer may recover from the seller as damages the difference between the cost of cover and the contract price together with any incidental or consequential damages as hereinafter defined (Section 2715), but less expenses saved in consequence of the seller's breach.

(3) Failure of the buyer to effect cover within this section does not bar him from any other remedy.

§ 2713. (1) Subject to the provisions of this division with respect to proof of market price (Section 2723), the measure of damages for nondelivery or repudiation by the seller is the difference between the market price at the time when the buyer learned of the breach and the contract price together with any incidental and consequential damages provided in this division (Section 2715), but less expenses saved in consequence of the seller's breach.

(2) Market price is to be determined as of the place for tender or, in cases of rejection after arrival or revocation of acceptance, as of the place of arrival.

§ 2714. (1) Where the buyer has accepted goods and given notification (subdivision (3) of Section 2607) he or she may recover, as damages for any nonconformity of tender, the loss resulting in the ordinary course of events from the seller's breach as determined in any manner that is reasonable.

(2) The measure of damages for breach of warranty is the difference at the time and place of acceptance between the value of the goods accepted and the value they would have had if they had been as warranted, unless special circumstances show proximate damages of a different amount.

(3) In a proper case any incidental and consequential damages under Section 2715 also may be recovered.

§ 2715. (1) Incidental damages resulting from the seller's breach include expenses reasonably incurred in inspection, receipt, transportation and care and custody of goods rightfully rejected, any commercially reasonable charges, expenses or commissions in connection with effecting cover and any other reasonable expense incident to the delay or other breach.

(2) Consequential damages resulting from the seller's breach include

(a) Any loss resulting from general or particular requirements and needs of which the seller at the time of contracting had reason to know and which could not reasonably be prevented by cover or otherwise; and

(b) Injury to person or property proximately resulting from any breach of warranty.

§ 2716. (1) Specific performance may be decreed where the goods are unique or in other proper circumstances.

(2) The decree for specific performance may include such terms and conditions as to payment of the price, damages, or other relief as the court may deem just.

(3) The buyer has a right of replevin for goods identified to the contract if after reasonable effort he or she is unable to effect cover for such goods or the circumstances reasonably indicate that such effort will be unavailing or if the goods have been shipped under reservation and satisfaction of the security interest in them has been made or tendered. In the case of goods bought for personal, family, or household purposes, the buyer's right of replevin vests upon acquisition of a special property, even if the seller had not then repudiated or failed to deliver.

§ 2717. The buyer on notifying the seller of his intention to do so may deduct all or any part of the damages resulting from any breach of the contract from any part of the price still due under the same contract.

§ 2718. (1) Damages for breach by either party may be liquidated in the agreement subject to and in compliance with Section 1671 of the Civil Code. If the agreement provides for liquidation of damages, and such provision does not comply with Section 1671 of the Civil Code, remedy may be had as provided in this division.

(2) Where the seller justifiably withholds delivery of goods because of the buyer's breach, the buyer is entitled to restitution of any amount by which the sum of his or her payments exceeds:

(a) The amount to which the seller is entitled by virtue of terms liquidating the seller's damages in accordance with subdivision (1), or

(b) In the absence of such terms, 20 percent of the value of the total performance for which the buyer is obligated under the contract or five hundred dollars ($500), whichever is smaller.

(3) The buyer's right to restitution under subdivision (2) is subject to offset to the extent that the seller establishes:

(a) A right to recover damages under the provisions of this chapter other than subdivision (1), and

(b) The amount or value of any benefits received by the buyer directly or indirectly by reason of the contract.

(4) Where a seller has received payment in goods their reasonable value or the proceeds of their resale shall be treated as payments for the purposes of subdivision (2); but if the seller has notice of the buyer's breach before reselling goods received in part performance, his or her resale is subject to the conditions laid down in this division on resale by an aggrieved seller (Section 2706).

§2719. (1) Subject to the provisions of subdivisions (2) and (3) of this section and of the preceding section on liquidation and limitation of damages,

(a) The agreement may provide for remedies in addition to or in substitution for those provided in this division and may limit or alter the measure of damages recoverable under this division, as by limiting the buyer's remedies to return of the goods and repayment of the price or to repair and replacement of nonconforming goods or parts; and

(b) Resort to a remedy as provided is optional unless the remedy is expressly agreed to be exclusive, in which case it is the sole remedy.

(2) Where circumstances cause an exclusive or limited remedy to fail of its essential purpose, remedy may be had as provided in this code.

(3) Consequential damages may be limited or excluded unless the limitation or exclusion is unconscionable. Limitation of consequential damages for injury to the person in the case of consumer goods is invalid unless it is proved that the limitation is not unconscionable. Limitation of consequential damages where the loss is commercial is valid unless it is proved that the limitation is unconscionable.

§2720. Unless the contrary intention clearly appears, expressions of "cancellation" or "rescission" of the contract or the like shall not be construed as a renunciation or discharge of any claim in damages for an antecedent breach.

§2721. Remedies for material misrepresentation or fraud include all remedies available under this division for nonfraudulent breach. Neither rescission or a claim for rescission of the contract for sale nor rejection or return of the goods shall bar or be deemed inconsistent with a claim for damages or other remedy.

§2722. Where a third party so deals with goods which have been identified to a contract for sale as to cause actionable injury to a party to that contract

(a) A right of action against the third party is in either party to the contract for sale who has title to or a security interest or a special property or an insurable interest in the goods; and if the goods have been destroyed or converted a right of action is also in the party who either bore the risk of loss under the contract for sale or has since the injury assumed that risk as against the other;

(b) If at the time of the injury the party plaintiff did not bear the risk of loss as against the other party to the contract for sale and there is no arrangement between them for disposition of the recovery, his suit or settlement is, subject to his own interest, as a fiduciary for the other party to the contract;

(c) Either party may with the consent of the other sue for the benefit of whom it may concern.

§ 2723. (1) If an action based on anticipatory repudiation comes to trial before the time for performance with respect to some or all of the goods, any damages based on market price (Section 2708 or Section 2713) shall be determined according to the price of such goods prevailing at the time when the aggrieved party learned of the repudiation.

(2) If evidence of a price prevailing at the times or places described in this division is not readily available the price prevailing within any reasonable time before or after the time described or at any other place which in commercial judgment or under usage of trade would serve as a reasonable substitute for the one described may be used, making any proper allowance for the cost of transporting the goods to or from such other place.

(3) Evidence of a relevant price prevailing at a time or place other than the one described in this division offered by one party is not admissible unless and until he has given the other party such notice as the court finds sufficient to prevent unfair surprise.

§ 2724. Whenever the prevailing price or value of any goods regularly bought and sold in any established commodity market is in issue, reports in official publications or trade journals or in newspapers or periodicals of general circulation published as the reports of such market shall be admissible in evidence. The circumstances of the preparation of such a report may be shown to affect its weight but not its admissibility.

§ 2725. (1) An action for breach of any contract for sale must be commenced within four years after the cause of action has accrued. By the original agreement the parties may reduce the period of limitation to not less than one year but may not extend it. (2) A cause of action accrues when the breach occurs, regardless of the aggrieved party's lack of knowledge of the breach. A breach of warranty occurs when tender of delivery is made, except that where a warranty explicitly extends to future performance of the goods and discovery of the breach must await the time of such performance the cause of action accrues when the breach is or should have been discovered.

(3) Where an action commenced within the time limited by subdivision (1) is so terminated as to leave available a remedy by another action for the same breach such other action may be commenced after the expiration of the time limited and within six months after the termination of the first action unless the termination resulted from voluntary discontinuance or from dismissal for failure or neglect to prosecute.

(4) This section does not alter the law on tolling of the statute of limitations nor does it apply to causes of action which have accrued before this code becomes effective.

RETAIL SALES

§ 2800. As used in this chapter "goods" means goods used or bought for use primarily for personal, family or household purposes.

§ 2801. In any retail sale of goods, if the manufacturer or seller of the goods issues a written warranty or guarantee as to the condition or quality of all or part of the goods which requires the buyer to complete and return any form to the manufacturer or seller as proof of the purchase of the goods, such warranty or guarantee shall not be unenforceable solely because the buyer fails to complete or return the form. This section does not relieve the buyer from proving the fact of purchase and the date thereof in any case in which such a fact is in issue.

The buyer must agree in writing to any waiver of this section for the waiver to be valid. Any waiver by the buyer of the provisions of this section which is not in writing is contrary to public policy and shall be unenforceable and void.

Selected Provisions of the California Family Code

Table of Contents

CAPACITY TO CONTRACT

§ 6700. Except as provided in Section 6701, a minor may make a contract in the same manner as an adult, subject to the power of disaffirmance under Chapter 2 (commencing with Section 6710), and subject to Part 1 (commencing with Section 300) of Division 3 (validity of marriage).

§ 6701. A minor cannot do any of the following:

   (a) Give a delegation of power.

   (b) Make a contract relating to real property or any interest therein.

   (c) Make a contract relating to any personal property not in the immediate possession or control of the minor.

DISAFFIRMANCE OF CONTRACTS

§ 6710. Except as otherwise provided by statute, a contract of a minor may be disaffirmed by the minor before majority or within a reasonable time afterwards or, in case of the minor's death within that period, by the minor's heirs or personal representative.

§ 6711. A minor cannot disaffirm an obligation, otherwise valid, entered into by the minor under the express authority or direction of a statute.

§ 6712. A contract, otherwise valid, entered into during minority, may not be disaffirmed on that ground either during the actual minority of the person entering into the contract, or at any time thereafter, if all of the following requirements are satisfied:

   (a) The contract is to pay the reasonable value of things necessary for the support of the minor or the minor's family.

   (b) These things have been actually furnished to the minor or to the minor's family.

   (c) The contract is entered into by the minor when not under the care of a parent or guardian able to provide for the minor or the minor's family.

§ 6713. If, before the contract of a minor is disaffirmed, goods the minor has sold are transferred to another purchaser who bought them in good faith for value and without notice of the transferor's defect of title, the minor cannot recover the goods from an innocent purchaser.

Appendix B

Sample Contracts

BILL OF SALE FOR MOTOR VEHICLE OR VESSEL

IN CONSIDERATION of the sum of _____ ($_____)

USD, paid by check, the receipt of which consideration is acknowledged,

_____ (The Seller) of _____, _____, California,

SELLS AND DELIVERS to _____ (The Purchaser) of _____

_____, _____, _____ _____, on or before _____,

20_____. The following Motor Vehicle (The Motor Vehicle):

MAKE:	BODY TYPE:
YEAR:	VEHICLE INDENTIFICATION
COLOR:	NUMBER:

The Seller expressly disclaims all warranties, whether expressed or implied. Vehicle is being sold "AS IS."

The purchaser has been given the opportunity to inspect the Motor Vehicle or to have it inspected and the purchaser has accepted the Motor Vehicle in its existing condition.

Executed on the _____ day of _____ 2005.

_____   _____

(Seller)   (Purchaser)

CONTRACT FOR SALE OF GOODS

Agreement made and entered into this [date] , by and between [name of seller], of [address] [city] , [state] , herein referred to as "Seller", and [name of buyer] , of [address] [city] , [state] , herein referred to as "Buyer".

Seller hereby agrees to transfer and deliver to buyer, on or before [date] , the following goods:

_____

_____

Buyer agrees to accept the goods and pay for them in accordance with the terms of the contract.

Buyer and Seller agree that identification shall not be deemed to have been made until both parties have agreed that the goods in question are to be appropriated and fulfill the requirements of performance of said contract with the buyer.

Buyer agrees to pay for the goods at the time they are delivered and at the place where he receives said goods.

Goods shall be deemed received by buyer when delivered to address of buyer as herein described.

Until such time as said goods have been received by buyer, all risk of loss from any causualty to said goods shall be on seller.

Seller warrants that the goods are now free from any security interest or other lien or encumbrance, that they shall be free from same at the time of delivery, and that he neither knows nor has reason to know of any outstanding title or claim of title hostile to his rights in the goods.

Buyer has the right to examine the goods on arrival and has [number] of days to notify seller of any claim for damages on account of the condition, grade or quality of the goods. That said notice must specifically set forth the basis of his claim, and that his failure to either notice seller within the stipulated period of time or to set forth specifically the basis of his claim will constitute irrevocable acceptance of the goods.

This agreement has been executed in duplicate, whereby both buyer and seller have retained one copy each, on [date].

_____

_____

[Signatures]

ASSIGNMENT OF CONTRACT

FOR VALUE RECEIVED, the undersigned does hereby sell, transfer, assign and set over to _____ all his right, title and interest in and to a certain contract dated _____, 20__ by and between the undersigned and _____, a copy of which is annexed hereto.

This assignment is made without warranty, representation and recourse.

Dated: _____

Accepted: _____

Approved: _____

ASSIGNMENT OF MONEY DUE

For good and valuable consideration, the undersigned hereby assigns, transfers and delivers to _____, all sums due or which shall become due and owing to the undersigned from _____ by reason of a certain agreement dated _____, 20__ by and between the undersigned and _____.

Signed under seal this _____day of _____, 20__.

_____   _____
Witness   Assignor

Notice of the above assignment is hereby acknowledged on

_____, 20__.

_____
Obligor

GENERAL RELEASE.

BE IT KNOWN, that _____, (hereinafter referred to as "Releasor"), for and in consideration of the sum of _____ ($ _____) Dollars, and other valuable consideration received from or on behalf of _____, (hereinafter referred to as "Releasee"), the receipt of which is hereby acknowledged, does hereby remise, release, acquit, satisfy, and forever discharge the said Releasee, of and from all manner of actions, causes of action, suits, debts, covenants, contracts, controversies, agreements, promises, claims and demands whatsoever, which said Releasor ever had, now has, or which any personal representative, successor, heir or assign of said Releasor, hereafter can, shall or may have, against said Releasee, by reason of any matter, cause or thing whatsoever, from the beginning of time to the date of this instrument.

Releasor understands that California Civil Code section 1542 provides:

"A general release does not extend to claims which the creditor does not know or suspect to exist in his favor at the time of executing the release, which if known by him must have materially affected his settlement with the debtor."

In connection with the general release set forth above, Releasor hereby expressly waives and relinquishes every past, present or future right or benefit she had, has or may have, under Calif. Civil Code § 1542 and/or any similar law, statute, provision or policy to the fullest extent permitted by law.

IN WITNESS WHEREOF, the said Releasor has hereunto set hand and seal this _____day of _____, 20___

Signed, sealed and delivered in the presence of: "RELEASOR" STATE OF CALIFORNIA COUNTY OF _____.

Index